THE MEN WE LEFT BEHIND

The Men We Left Behind

Henry Kissinger, the Politics of Deceit and the Tragic Fate of POWs After the Vietnam War

Mark Sauter and Jim Sanders

National
Press
Books

Washington, D.C.

Library of Congress Cataloging-in-Publication Data

Sauter, Mark.
The Men We Left Behind: Henry Kissinger, the politics of deceit and the tragic fate of POWS after the Vietnam War
by Mark Sauter and Jim Sanders
400 pp., 15.25 cm x 22.85 cm
$23.95
Includes biographical references and index.
1. Vietnamese Conflict, 1961-1975—Prisons and prisoners, North Vietnamese.
2. Prisoners of war—Vietnam.
3. Prisoners of war—United States.
I. Sanders, Jim.
II. Title
DS559.4.S28 1993
959.704'37—dc20
93-20612
CIP

1 2 3 4 5 6 7 8 9 10

Acknowledgments and Authors' Note

The authors would like to acknowledge the following:

Former POWs and friends Mike Benge and Eugene "Red" McDaniel, who came home but never forgot those who didn't.

Mike Maharry and *The Morning News Tribune*, for crusading. *Inside Edition* and *American Journal* for picking up the battle.

Tracy Usry, who followed the leads wherever they took him.

Our friends among the staff of the Select Committee who continued the investigation.

Offley, Schanberg, Denton, Liu, Landreth and other reporters who pushed the story forward. Also Nigel Cawthorne, Monika Jensen-Stevenson, William Stevenson, and Rod Colvin who somehow managed to write important POW books when the cover-up was even tighter than it is now.

Dolores Alfond and Ted Sampley. They and their families have walked point for many years and taken the hits for so many others.

The other leaders of the American POW movement, Ben Alford, Charles Bates, William T. Bennett, Larry Bise, Denny Clark, Marsha Cummings, Norman A. Doney, Mary Howard, Richard Keeton, LuAnne LaBonne, John LeBoutillier, Jack Laeufer, Wilma Laeufer, Kay Ogle, Bill Opferman, Lynn O'Shea, Daniel Perrin, Chuck Schantag, Bonny S. Stilwell, Barbara L. Sworski, and the American Legion and its Dick Christian. And the POW activist bikers, who wear their wallets on chains and their hearts on their sleeves.

Mel Berger, our agent at the William Morris Agency, who assisted in placing the book with the publisher.

Joel Joseph, Alan Sultan, Shawn Ortiz, Talia Greenberg and Cathleen Connolly of National Press Books who had the courage to publish *The Men We Left Behind*.

Bobby Egan and Khai, whose friendship and devotion to human rights is a model for the American and Vietnamese people as a whole.

The Korean and Cold War POW/MIA families, who may not have suffered more, but certainly suffered longer.

The Pentagon POW team, which worked hard to hinder our research on this book and even refused to answer questions for our final fact checking. They will take pleasure in our mistakes. We find only sadness in theirs.

The vast majority of men and women in the U.S. military, including those in Task Force Russia and even some in the Pentagon's POW offices, who would never abandon their fellow troops.

Stacey Sauter and Liz Sanders, who stood by us with little complaint and much loyalty after being "volunteered" for yet another hardship tour.

A Note on Spelling

The names and places in Southeast Asia have always been subject to change, at least from the perspective of their spelling in English. Different styles of transliteration from Asian tongues to English render dramatically different spellings. And changing governments have often altered the names of cities and provinces.

In the following text, the traditional U.S. spelling of certain place names is used to avoid confusing those readers who have long followed the issue or served in Southeast Asia. For instance, the famous 1981 CIA reconnaissance mission in Laos was to Nhom Marrot—not Gnommarat as the area is now called on some maps.

Similar problems also exist with the spelling and/or order of Asian names. In this book we use the individual's preferred spelling of his or her name, and if that is not available, the spelling most familiar to American readers.

In the issue of spelling as well as all other areas of this book, any errors are ours. And any credit must go to the tireless POW relatives, Senate investigators and concerned activists who made this work possible.

Contents

Introduction

Evidence of a Crime

"We have nothing that would indicate that an American prisoner—confirmed information or evidence, firm evidence, or convincing evidence—that an American prisoner was being held against his will."
—Charles "Chuck" Trowbridge, long-time Defense Intelligence Agency (DIA) POW/MIA Official, at hearings before the United States Senate Select Committee on POW/MIA Affairs, 1992

"Let me ask you then, in conclusion of this point, what is evidence? . . . I want a specific example of what this panel [of Pentagon officials] would accept as evidence that there is an American POW in Southeast Asia today. What would you accept? Does the President of the United States have to see some of these people?"
—Senator Robert Smith (R-N.H.) at hearings before the United States Senate Select Committee on POW/MIA Affairs, 1992

Imagine that FBI agents are investigating the suspicious disappearance of a child. Investigators quickly learn the missing boy was last seen in the company of a man with a previous conviction for kidnapping. Further research shows the suspect is poverty stricken and has angrily declared that the missing child's family had cheated him out of a large sum of money. Following the disappearance, the suspect even hinted to the family that their child might be found if they would just pay up on the old debt.

Then the G-men get a major break. A witness comes forward, claiming that during a visit to the suspect's home he saw and even spoke with a little boy tied up in the closet.

Being thorough investigators, the FBI agents don't just take the witness on his word. They question him for days, trying to expose discrepancies in his story; they even imply that he is a liar. They check every detail that can be verified with other sources. They search his background for any character flaw, trying to determine whether he has an ulterior motive.

Passing Polygraphs and Snapping Pictures

But the story holds up. The agents learn that the witness is a solid citizen. Every detail of his story that can be tested checks out. So they bring in a polygraph machine. Experts put the witness through another round of gruelling questions. The polygraph test reveals not a single hint of deception. Just to be sure, the agents give the man a second lie-detector test, which he also passes.

The agents become excited. They ask the witness to draw detailed sketches of the suspected kidnapper's hideout, dispatch undercover agents to take pictures of the hideout. The agents can't see into the house because it's surrounded by a large fence and the shades are drawn, but they do find a neighbor who reports the suspect has bragged about kidnapping the missing child. Back at the Bureau, that neighbor passes her polygraph examination. And once developed, the pictures taken during the mission match the eyewitness's sketch exactly, down to the bars on the windows. FBI photo-analysts even spot what appears to be a crayon drawing on one of the windows. The experts are divided, but at least one concludes that the drawing is the missing boy's initials.

Yet the agents want an airtight case, so they obtain a warrant to tap the suspect's phone. Before long, they intercept a call from the suspect to his brother. The suspect says that he thinks the FBI is onto him and tells his brother to come by and pick up the kidnap victim.

But before the FBI can get a search warrant, a local newspaper prints an article about the expedition to photograph the suspect's home. Agents rush to the suspect's house, where he meets them at the door. He's smug and full of false politeness, happy to show there's no kidnapped boy in his home. Despite the suspect's denials, there's little doubt the FBI would arrest the man on the spot; he would almost certainly be convicted of kidnapping.

But suppose the Pentagon were in charge of the same kidnapping investigation. In that case, there would be no trial, because the Pentagon would declare there was absolutely "no evidence" the suspect had kidnapped the boy.

No Evidence?

Based on history, we can predict the Pentagon's response because every detail of the scenario just described corresponds to actual information on U.S. POWs in Southeast Asia. The Pentagon, despite having testimony from eyewitnesses who have passed polygraphs, and despite having intercepted communist radio messages reporting POWs alive in Vietnam and Laos years after the war, says there is "no evidence" that any Americans were kept by the communists.

The bureaucrats admit there's "information" but deny there's any "evidence." Yet the authors—a former policeman and a veteran investigative reporter—have seen men convicted for serious crimes on far less "information" than exists for the existence of U.S. POWs in Southeast Asia after 1973.

Let's look at such standard elements of criminal investigation as consideration of motive, opportunity and evidence. Even before U.S. involvement there, Vietnam had a history of holding back foreign POWs. The rulers of Hanoi had several strong motives to keep Americans. The confusion of the Vietnam War and eventual victory of the communists offered them the opportunity to retain many Americans.

Then there's the evidence. Many Americans last known to be under Vietnamese control never returned home. As we will see, numerous sources say other U.S. POWs were shipped to the Soviet Union, North Korea and China.

Hundreds of fleeing Indochinese refugees report seeing Americans under Vietnamese or Laotian control years after the war. Many of those refugees passed polygraph tests about their sightings. The Pentagon has photographed prisons where the refugees reported Americans, and intercepted communist radio messages concerning the care of U.S. POWs. Meantime, Hanoi has offered to sell back American prisoners.

Criminal Histories

We consider that "evidence." But given that kind of data, why would the American government fail to make the recovery of its lost fighting men a true national priority? The answer to that side of the equation is found in history, which shows the U.S. failed to press its case against previous communist enemies who held back

American POWs in the wake of World War II, the Korean conflict and the Cold War.

The United States government, history has now shown, refused to admit to the American people that U.S. POWs were kept behind in Siberia, China and North Korea after those earlier conflicts.* The reason was simple: U.S. policy-makers were not willing to risk costly wars, or even major diplomatic battles, to recover a relatively small number of lost soldiers.

And, as one long-time observer of the federal government has noted, Washington bureaucrats will never voluntarily acknowledge a problem they don't know how to solve.

So barring a miraculous breakthrough—say, the release of clear videotapes showing specific American prisoners—the Pentagon will never admit there is "evidence" of U.S. POWs in Southeast Asia. Yes, there's information. But there can never be evidence. Because the existence of evidence would require the bureaucrats to take action. If the government officially and publicly conceded that live American captives exist in Southeast Asia, there would be a new hostage crisis involving the U.S., Vietnam, Laos and possibly other nations. And no U.S. President has been willing to accept that situation.

Policy Dictates Intelligence

The unwillingness of U.S. authorities to face a hostage crisis of epic proportions has led to the unstated requirement that "evidence" cannot exist, which in turn leads to a fascinating molding of the huge amount of intelligence that does reach American hands. Say a refugee reports seeing American POWs. No amount of questioning can shake his story and no amount of background checking can locate any discrepancies. The refugee passes polygraph tests. The testimony stands.

There is no way that report can be accepted as "proof." Remarkably, the Pentagon's filing system for POW reports, which includes categories for "fabrications" and reports of Soviets mistaken for American prisoners, has no category for U.S. POWs actually held after the war.

Therefore any report of a real POW is categorized as "unresolved." For many years, there were scores of unresolved cases.

---

*See James D. Sanders, Mark A. Sauter and R. Cort Kirkwood, *Soldiers of Misfortune* (Bethesda, MD, 1992).

As of this writing, the government has launched a major campaign to "resolve" as many of the reports as possible. For example, when the Pentagon, after years of effort, could not break the polygraphed testimony of a refugee who reported having seen U.S. POWs in Laos, the Pentagon "resolved" the case as a sighting of Soviet advisors—even though the POWs were under guard and the guards *told* the refugee they were American POWs.

Imagine a case where there were 100, ten or even two independent first-hand witnesses to a crime whose testimony could not be broken by even the toughest cross-examination. Then add corroborating evidence from other witnesses, photographs and communications intercepts. That is the kind of information showing that U.S. POW-MIAs remained in communist hands after the war. But the Pentagon says it does not constitute "evidence."

Of course, the U.S. government's best evidence on POW/MIAs remains classified. The DIA, CIA, State Department and NSA simply refuse to release much of their POW information. Although in theory the federal Freedom of Information Act (FOIA) requires release of most such data, American intelligence agencies have cynically escaped from their legal requirements to share the truth with the American people. On several occasions, the DIA has flatly denied possessing any documents on certain POW issues, only to release portions of those very documents later on. The CIA, required by law to respond to FOIA requests within ten working days, has still not released or even officially denied POW files requested by the authors three years ago. The Pentagon also refuses to release the bulk of files on many individual POW/MIAs. Even though the government declared them dead twenty years ago, the Pentagon says it would be a violation of the men's "privacy" to release their files to the public. Finally, the Pentagon hides behind the cloak of "national security." The military has refused to give the authors POW documents dating back to 1946, saying the release of those records could cause "serious damage" to America's security.

Of course, it has always been the Pentagon's practice to hide data on many issues behind the cloak of "national security." And the Pentagon investigators—many of them fine and dedicated professionals—are in fact the detectives in this case, gathering information for decision-makers in the Pentagon, State Department and White House. It's up to those top officials to make the final conclusions that drive policy. But for political reasons, those decision-makers refuse to declare, one way or the other, whether Americans are being held in Southeast Asia.

Useful Ambiguity

By keeping open the possibility that some American POWs remain alive, the U.S. government bows to domestic political pressure for a full accounting *and* covers itself if a POW ever does come home. It also has an additional bargaining chip to use in hard-ball negotiations with Vietnam and Laos on such issues as drug control, oil rights and international diplomacy. And, some American apologists for Hanoi claim the entire POW issue has been fabricated by the U.S. to punish Vietnam and provoke racism and militarism in America.

On the other hand, by denying there is any "proof" of the existence of American POWs, the White House can avoid a hostage crisis and the ensuing need to pay for and/or rescue all the POWs.

Neither the American public nor the Congress has ever been granted full access to the intelligence available at the Pentagon and White House. Therefore, no truly independent and informed panel, or "jury," has been able to determine whether there is "proof" that Americans were kept in Indochina and whether any remain alive.

A criminal jury can convict someone for kidnapping or murder even if the victim is never found; an impartial panel with access to all the information could declare that American POWs were kept after 1973 even without absolute evidence such as the hypothetical videotape. On the other hand, an impartial panel could also declare that available evidence indicates that no Americans were held in Southeast Asia after the war.

An Impartial Jury?

That's why POW family members and activists lauded the 1991 creation of the Senate Select Committee on POW/MIA Affairs, which was given $1.9 million and subpoena powers to find the truth. Armed with those resources, the Senate was in a position to act as a sort of grand jury inquest into the POW issue. POW/MIA relatives and activists asked just two things of the committee: that it pursue *all* the evidence without fear or favor, and that it analyze the evidence and come to clear conclusions— in understandable English—about America's POW/MIAs.

The Senate Committee did neither. As will be seen later, the Committee made deliberate decisions to leave many key POW/MIA issues unresolved. It was considered more important to avoid irritating the Bush Administration and to keep to a pre-arranged, politically motivated schedule than to get to the bottom of the POW scandal.

Ironically, the Senate's staff of professional intelligence investigators did come to some tough and clear conclusions. They employed the same techniques used to track Soviet SS-25 missiles during the Cold War and SCUD missiles during the Gulf War, carefully sorting through a huge amount of data. Their 1992 internal report stated: "The intelligence indicates that American prisoners of war have been held continuously after [1973's] Operation Homecoming."

Murky "Bipartisanship"

Faced with such a crystal clear—and explosive—finding, the Senate committee's chairman, Sen. John Kerry (D-Mass.), with plenty of help from other key Senators, suppressed the investigators' report. And at the end of their investigation in 1993, instead of making clear findings one way or the other, the Senate succumbed to mealy-mouthed "bipartisanship."

Were Americans still in communist prisons after early 1973? Concluded the Senate: "We acknowledge that there is no proof that U.S. POWs survived, but neither is there proof that all those who did not return had died. There is evidence that indicates . . . the possibility of survival, at least for a small number, after Operation Homecoming." In other words: it's possible, but after more than a year of work and almost 1.9 million in the taxpayers' money, we can't or won't even say whether it's likely or unlikely. That way, according to the logic of Congress, if by the grace of God a POW does come home, no one can say we had written him off. Meantime, we haven't created serious problems for the Pentagon or White House.

On the other critical question—are Americans alive today in Southeast Asia?—the Senate again abdicated responsibility. "[T]he Senate cannot provide compelling evidence to support that possibility today," their report concluded, again avoiding any firm judgment.

However, the Senate committee did take a strong stand on one important issue, the question of whether some U.S. POW/MIAs secretly returned to America after 1973: The Senate declared that such allegations are "fantasies."

We'll let you decide on that, along with the overall POW issue. While the Pentagon still keeps the most compelling POW "information" classified, we present some of the rest of the evidence in this book. We believe that after seeing it you'll conclude, "beyond a reasonable doubt," the following:

1) The North Vietnamese demand that ransom be paid for American POWs;

2) Nixon and Kissinger deceived Congress and the American people, never revealing that a hostage/ransom crisis existed;

3) The U.S. government knew that Americans remained in communist hands after Homecoming in 1973;

4) Some may yet be alive;

5) The U.S. government has not done nearly enough to bring them home.

And that is more than a shame. It's a crime.

—*James D. Sanders and Mark A. Sauter,*
Spring 1993

PART I

A Criminal History

Chapter 1

The Victims

"No more lies!" —*POW/MIA Families*

"Would you please shut up and sit down!"
—*President George Bush, Arlington, Virginia, July 24, 1992*

A searing anger was building inside Jane Duke Gaylor that warm July Friday as she waited to see the President. For more than twenty years she had kept the feelings in check—enduring the grief, mixed with anger and uncertainty, over losing her son Charles as an MIA during the Vietnam War. The explosive psychological brew still didn't show in the pleasant face of this patriotic senior citizen, a trim and bespectacled Republican Party activist whose soft voice was smoothed by a Texas drawl. But just the day before, the government had lit her fuse.

After keeping her waiting for hours that day, a State Department bureaucrat finally handed the 71-year-old woman a sketch, the kind done by police artists. The official told Gaylor the sketch was of an American reported alive in Hanoi years after the end of the Vietnam War.

The American had been seen by a Vietnamese defector who had gotten to know the faces of three U.S. "servicemen" held in Vietnam as late as 1979. Everything in the former Vietnamese government official's story had checked out; he had passed a polygraph examination, and the Pentagon was convinced he was telling the truth. And, the State Department official told Mrs. Gaylor, based on the description and other evidence, the Pentagon's top expert on Vietnam POWs believed the sketch could well portray her son, Charles Duke Jr., an Air Force veteran and civilian aircraft technician who mysteriously disappeared in Vietnam in 1970.

Duke, 26, had been working in Pleiku fixing airplane engines for the private Dynalectron Corp., hoping to earn enough money to return to the States and go to veterinary school. A little after 9 a.m. on Saturday, May 30, 1970, Duke and his friend Kit Mark, another civilian technician, were seen preparing to take their Honda motorcycles for a weekend joy-ride to Bald Mountain, about seven miles south of their base.

Duke had been scheduled to go home on June 1, and when he failed to show up for his trip, U.S. military units launched an unsuccessful search. "Both men were considered to be highly dependable and reliable employees of stable character," the State Department reported, and U.S. officials feared the worst.

Aside from rumors that communist forces had captured and perhaps killed Duke and Mark, Gaylor received almost no other information on the fate of her son until late 1991. It was then that Garnett "Bill" Bell, Vietnam POW expert and then chief of the Pentagon's POW/MIA office in Hanoi, gave testimony to the U.S. Senate Select Committee on POW/MIA Affairs.

Bell, a fluent speaker of Vietnamese who had worked on the prisoner of war issue since the 1960s in Army intelligence and then civilian Pentagon posts, testified that despite years of Pentagon denials, there was indeed hard evidence that some Americans remained alive in Vietnam after all U.S. POWs were supposed to have been returned in early 1973. One of those men, Bell testified, could have been Charles Duke.

In the months after Bell's testimony, Gaylor fought to find out more. But the government had avoided giving her the sketch until July 23, 1992. And it wasn't just the delay in getting the picture that infuriated Gaylor. It was also the information that came with it. She learned the Vietnamese defector, the source of possible evidence on Charles Duke, had not given his information to the U.S. in 1991. Or the year before. Or even the year before that.

He had reported his evidence in 1979. For more than ten years, the U.S. government had had information indicating that her only child—the beloved son she called "Bubba"—could be alive in Hanoi.

But no one ever told her.

The President Gets An Earful

It was more than a mother could bear, staring again and again at that sketch, comparing it with faded snapshots and memories of long ago. And knowing that while her Charles may have been in Vietnam—for years during which she could have been looking for him, years during which he could have suffered or even died—the government had hidden this evidence from her and the other POW/MIA families. These dark thoughts plagued Jane Gaylor as she waited at the Arlington, Virginia hotel where the President of the United States was about to appear. "I was angry, angry," she said afterwards. "It was just building up all these years."

Gaylor was not the only angry person in that hotel conference room. Many other POW/MIA relatives gathered for the annual convention of the National League of Families, the Pentagon-sponsored POW family group, had lost their patience and even their faith in the U.S. government by the summer of 1992. As Jane Gaylor sat in a middle seat three rows back from the front, other POW/MIA family members from the vocal Texas delegation settled around her. And soon the President, in the middle of his campaign for re-election, was before them. No doubt confident that he commanded the loyalties of these conservative military families, Bush launched into yet another boiler-plate POW speech, full of vague promises and lofty generalities, with the usual pledge that accounting for U.S. POW/MIAs was a top administration priority.

It was more than many of the families could take.

Mothers and wives and brothers and sisters rose to confront the commander-in-chief. They demanded that the President open the Pentagon's huge secret POW files and negotiate seriously with Vietnam and Laos to free their captives. Gaylor thrust forward a picture of "Bubba" and cried out to the President: "No more lies! No more lies! Tell us the truth!" She doesn't regret her shouted pleas. "I don't think we were being rude. We were just trying to get his attention. We couldn't get it any other way."

The POW relatives certainly got the attention of President Bush, who snapped at the family members to "shut up and sit down."

"I know there's doubt and I know people are saying . . . right from the heart, Go over there and bring them back. Do you think if I knew of one single person and where he is and how it was that I wouldn't do that? Of course I'd do that," the President declared.

But Jane Gaylor and the families knew better. They knew the U.S. government had failed to pursue even those measures its own experts said were needed to learn the truth about America's POW/MIAs. And now, after more than 10 years of cover-up, they had learned about the secret testimony of Bill Bell, which was full of examples of what made them shouting mad.

Bill Bell Tells The Truth

As Bell noted in a Pentagon cable following his November 6, 1991, testimony to the Senate: "I realize my opinion . . . will not be a popular one, but after having considered the information carefully and being under oath, I felt compelled to answer affirmatively to the question posed to me." The question posed by the Senate was simple: Was there hard evidence that any of the approximately 2,200 U.S. POW/MIAs in Southeast Asia had been kept behind by the communists? Bell's answer was equally simple. "Yes," he said, becoming the first serving Pentagon official in memory—perhaps the first ever—to give that response.

His honesty would cost Bell dearly. As one Senate staffer put it: "He got screwed because of his testimony." Yet Bell's answers, especially the revealing follow-up information he gave the Senate, should have caused equal problems for the government. Indeed, Bell's testimony should have cause an explosion around the POW issue. But it didn't.

It took the combined efforts of Hanoi, the Senate committee's leaders and the Pentagon to keep Bell's testimony contained. First, Hanoi refused to allow Bell to return to his job in Vietnam. Once that flap was smoothed over, the Pentagon simply reassigned Bell to Thailand, giving his job in Vietnam to an officer who couldn't speak Vietnamese and had only limited experience with the POW issue. Finally, the staff director of the Senate POW committee classified Bell's detailed debriefing at so high a level that many Senate investigators couldn't even read it, thereby insuring it received almost no follow-up attention. As one Senate staffer put it: "It was not pushed [by the Senate] . . . because no one had access to the deposition."

But Bell's information couldn't be kept under wraps forever. Bell said it was clear at least 10 Americans had been kept by the Vietnamese. If that was true, then it was possible—indeed probable—that other reports of Americans kept in Vietnam and Laos after 1973 were true.

Along with other cases described in following chapters of this book, Bell's testimony emphasized evidence provided by a U.S. intelligence source dubbed "The Mortician"—the man whose information so upset Jane Gaylor.

The Mortician had provided compelling first-hand information on two Americans seen in Hanoi until at least 1979. Based upon sketches produced by the Mortician, along with other intelligence, Bell testified that one of the Americans might be Charles Duke. The second could be either Kit Mark, Duke's buddy, or Jimmy Malone, an Army radioman captured by the communists in 1966.

While those identifications were not certain, Bell said, there was no doubt about one thing: the Mortician had seen two Americans who never returned from the Vietnam War.

The Mortician's Secrets

The "Mortician" is really a chubby Vietnamese man of Chinese descent named Tran Vien Loc. He fled Vietnam in April 1979 after a wave of political persecution against Chinese ethnics. On his way out, Vietnamese officials told Loc he'd be killed if he told his secrets to any agents of the U.S., so he did not talk to American officials when he arrived at a Hong Kong refugee camp. But another refugee let U.S. intelligence in on the Mortician's background, and he was soon flown from Hong Kong to the United States for debriefing.[1]*

Soon after interrogating Loc, the Pentagon determined his information was absolutely valid. It was considered so important that Rear Admiral A.L. Kelln, the acting director of the Defense Intelligence Agency (DIA), which handles POW/MIA intelligence, secretly urged top officials to review the U.S. policy of denying there was proof of American POWs in Southeast Asia. However, the DIA director cautioned that: "Any review should keep in mind the protection of those U.S. personnel [POWs] still in Vietnam."[2]

The Pentagon decided instead to play down the Mortician's story and to continue to deny there was any "evidence" of U.S. POW/MIAs in Southeast Asia. But the facts in Loc's secret DIA file, released to the Senate, spoke for themselves. From 1956 to 1979, he worked in the Directorate of Cemeteries for Hanoi City.

---

*In a gross error similar to the Pentagon's repeated failure to protect refugee witnesses from communist retaliation, the Senate POW committee revealed Loc's full name and current U.S. hometown in a public document. Since Hanoi knows the Mortician's name, the authors use it here. Unlike the Senate, we chose not to disclose his current hometown, where he now lives under the witness protection program.

Among Loc's duties was the collection of French and U.S. remains for use as political bargaining chips.

In 1974 Loc was asked to travel several blocks from his office to the department in charge of POW records and remains. It was there—at Office 22, Group 875, Department of Military Justice, General Political Directorate, Headquarters Ministry of Defense at No. 3 Duong Thanh Street, Hanoi—that Loc saw for the first time U.S. servicemen kept in Vietnam after the war. He would later see the same three men on numerous occasions. Other officials told Loc the three Caucasians were "progressive American servicemen" who had asked for asylum in Vietnam after the war.

The Americans might have been "progressive," but they were not free. The men "were closely supervised," Loc later told the Pentagon. And they were not alone. The assistant chief of Vietnam's POW office, Major Pham Dinh Huan, told the Mortician there were more Americans still in Southeast Asia, and some—the major implied there might be as many as six—worked as technicians at Da Phuc Airfield, north of Hanoi.

According to a Pentagon report on the Mortician: "He [Loc] was told that if an American had cooperated during initial interrogation, he would be segregated, held in solitary confinement in a U.S. PW camp in the northwest sector of the City of Hanoi and exploited for technical information." Indeed, a wartime intelligence report indicated that a POW camp in the northern part of Hanoi housed five to 15 U.S. prisoners who were sent to work everyday at 6:30 a.m. for duties at the Da Phuc airfield.

Perhaps those were the same Americans described by the Major, still working at the airfield ten years later.

A Secret Camp System?

Loc's information provided new fuel for one of the most bitter disputes in the POW issue: whether the Vietnamese maintained a separate camp system from which no Americans returned alive. As of this writing, the DIA publicly claims there is "no evidence" of such a system. The Pentagon claims that all U.S. POWs in North Vietnam were held in a single camp system and eventually consolidated in the Hanoi area. The DIA insists that the several hundred Americans in this system kept good track of one another, and that all of them alive in 1973 were released. But the Mortician's information supported many other indications that some Americans were held separately from those who returned during Operation Homecoming in early 1973.

Reports of a separate POW camp system make sense both historically and logically. The Soviets established a separate camp system during the Korean War, when many Americans selected for permanent communist slavery were initially held in secret Chinese prison camps from which no POWs ever returned. The many Soviet, Chinese and North Korean advisors supporting the Vietnamese military during the war would certainly have recommended a system that worked so well in the previous communist fight against U.S. troops in Asia.

The separate camp system also explained why few if any Americans returned at the end of the Vietnam War reported being interrogated about such issues as their knowledge of U.S. nuclear weapons systems. And why no returned U.S. serviceman said he'd been questioned by Soviets or seen other POWs under Russian interrogation—despite overwhelming evidence, discussed later, that dozens of Americans were shipped from Vietnam to Russia. Clearly, the men subjected to technical interrogations and those shipped to Russia had been held in camps apart from the regular POWs.

The secret camp near Hanoi whose presence was reported by the Mortician was only one tentacle of the separate POW system. After marine Robert "Bobby" Garwood, who was captured in South Vietnam in 1965 and later identified as one of the three Americans seen by the Mortician, began cooperating with his guards, he was removed from the normal POW camps and other U.S. prisoners (he returned to the U.S. in 1979). Pentagon specialist Bill Bell later concluded from evidence from sources other than the Mortician that at least two secret camps existed in Vietnam. As we will see later in this book, other sources demonstrate the existence of yet more secret Vietnamese and Laotian camps holding Americans never returned at the end of the war.

"Criminals of War"

In addition to borrowing the strategy of establishing separate POW camp systems, the Vietnamese took another trick from the Soviets—categorizing POWs as war criminals in order to strip them of their citizenship and rights under the Geneva Convention. After World War II, Moscow used false war crime convictions to retain large numbers of German POWs needed to rebuild the Soviet economy. This legal fiction was also used by China to keep Americans in Asia after the Korean War.

From the earliest days of the Vietnam War, Hanoi refused to comply with the Geneva Convention, declaring that U.S. captives were criminals, not POWs. When Bobby Garwood learned that other Americans were being released in early 1973, he asked his camp's political officer why he too wasn't going home. The officer explained that Vietnam could do whatever it wanted with its American captives, because they weren't POWs. "Nobody declared war on anybody, so prisoners of war are nonexistent.' He said: 'The only thing that we have and have held are criminals of war.' "

Garwood has sworn under oath and during a successful polygraph examination that he saw many other U.S. prisoners in Vietnam—some under limited control, others held in strict prisons. But Garwood claims the guards never called any of them "POWs." "Through my entire existence in Vietnam, I never heard them referred to as prisoners of war. [They were called] criminals of war, criminals, pirates, rapists, murderers, et cetera," the former POW remembered.[3]

As had the Chinese and Soviets before them, the Vietnamese could therefore declare they held no American POWs. Instead, their prisons housed former Americans now holding the status of Vietnamese or stateless "progressives," "students" and "criminals."

A Vietnamese official told other Third World officials during a 1977 Tunisian conference that U.S. "criminals" guilty of "crimes against the Vietnamese people" still existed in his country. According to a Pentagon report on the meeting:

> These Americans reportedly renounced their citizenship and were placed in reeducation camps for a period of three years. At the end of this three-year period they will be expected to admit their crimes and make a "self-criticism" at which time they will be judged and either set free in Vietnam as free citizens, or, in the case of a lack of admission of guilt and refusal of self-criticism, they will be "sentenced."[4]

Those Americans who accepted their "crimes" were on the way to becoming categorized as "progressives"; such prisoners were allowed a much more normal life. The communists apparently placed Garwood in this category, describing him to Vietnamese inmates in his camp as "a progressive American prisoner who had confessed my crimes against the Vietnamese people, and [that] due to the humanitarian policy of the SRV [Hanoi] had decided to give me lenience and let me become part of the work force."

The more "progressive" the prisoner, the more freedom and privileges he had. According to the Vietnamese official visiting Tunisia in 1977: "Americans remaining in Vietnam are those who married Vietnamese women and have given up their U.S. citizenship and have become naturalized Vietnamese."[5] The men seen by the Mortician probably fall into this category, as Loc "observed a wedding band of Asian design on at least one of the Americans." On July 24, 1974, a refugee who later passed a U.S. polygraph test saw three Caucasian prisoners at a party for reeducation camp inmates in Laos. They were known to local residents as American POWs, but their Vietnamese-controlled Laotian guards insisted they be called "students," presumably of communist indoctrination.[6]

A Thin Line

In the world of the communist prison system, there is often no clear distinction between a prisoner and collaborator. Only a few Americans willingly defected to the enemy side during the Vietnam War. All other known "collaborators," including several POWs returned to heroes' welcomes in 1973, only began cooperating with the enemy after being captured and subjected to varying degrees of abuse. For instance, Garwood was captured as a bonafide POW and served time under extremely harsh conditions before giving in to his captors, who still kept him under close guard. (He was later convicted in the U.S. of collaborating with, but not deserting to, the enemy.)

Following the first Indochina War of 1946-1954, hundreds of French troops, both Frenchmen and soldiers from French colonies and the Foreign Legion, stayed behind and married Vietnamese women. They were called "ralliers," for having rallied to the communist side. Many were deserters and collaborators. But the French ultimately learned that not everyone who "rallied" was a true convert to communism. Vietnam kept many French intelligence officials and technicians, who were given little if any chance to return home.

As the U.S. military now concedes, any man can be broken by the sort of torture and psychological manipulation skillfully employed by the military of Vietnam and other communist nations. In the main POW system, at such famous camps as the "Hanoi Hilton," U.S. POWs helped one another "bounce back" from the guilt of breaking under pressure. POWs knew that just about everyone had been forced to give information beyond the proverbial "name, rank and serial number," and they realized they were not alone in their forced cooperation with the enemy.

Eugene "Red" McDaniel, a highly decorated naval aviator often described as one of the most brutally tortured POWs in Vietnam, said the support of other prisoners was critical in getting past the pain and guilt of Vietnamese interrogation. "If you thought you were the only guy who weakened, it would demoralize you. And you would punish yourself," McDaniel says. "That could destroy you very quickly."

Secure in the knowledge that they were not alone in cooperating with the enemy, POWs in the known prison system had no fear of returning home. They had learned via communist propaganda that even men who went beyond accepted boundaries—who violated the orders of senior POWs by accepting early release, informing on other inmates and repeatedly assisting the enemy through propaganda statements and broadcasts—were welcomed back to the U.S.

Perhaps most importantly, men in the main Vietnamese prison system also realized their existence was known to many other prisoners, and that it would be difficult for the Vietnamese guards to carry out the oft-repeated threat: "We can keep you forever."

But American captives isolated from their countrymen had no such solace. An isolated prisoner might have believed he was the only POW to talk. He could have been convinced he'd be court-martialled if he returned home.

Thus, those who requested asylum may have "chosen" to stay in Vietnam because of misinformation and unfounded fear instilled in separate, isolated camps. No doubt some of the "collaborators" were men of weak character, limited intellect or even leftist sympathies. Others may have actually been criminals who committed offenses against the Vietnamese people or other

Americans. Yet it is certain that some of America's finest were also kept by the communists.

Abandoned Heroes

As during the Korean War, the communists did not just retain "progressives" after the war. They also kept "reactionaries," the communist term for POWs who refused to be broken. Aleksandr Solzhenitsyn, famed Russian witness to the communist prison system, put it this way:

> If the government of North Vietnam has difficulty explaining to you what happened to your brothers, your American POWs who have not yet returned, I can explain this quite clearly on the basis of my own experience in the Gulag Archipelago [the Soviet prison system]. There is a law in the Archipelago that those who have been treated the most harshly and who have withstood the most bravely—who are the most honest, the most courageous, the most unbending—never again come out into the world. They are never again shown to the world because they will tell tales that the human mind can barely accept. Some of your returned POWs told you that they were tortured. This means that those who have remained were tortured even more, but did not yield an inch. These are your best people. These are your foremost heroes who, in a solitary combat, have stood the test.[7]

Solzhenitsyn spoke those words in 1975, more than two years after all U.S. prisoners were supposed to have come home. Yet even the "best people" have limits, both physical and psychological. As the lonely years wore on and the U.S. government denied their very existence, some of the toughest and most honorable POWs must have died or made some sort of separate peace with their communist captors.

Garwood, who is fluent in Vietnamese, says that months and even years after the war his Vietnamese guards compared him favorably to other, tougher U.S. POWs still in captivity, whom the jailers considered "very stubborn and belligerent."

But Garwood says that over the long run there was no choice but to cooperate. "If you want to commit suicide in Vietnam, it's not a complicated problem," he testified. "They didn't just come up and put a gun to your head and blow you away. There were rations taken way from you, you were deprived into basically isolation, deprivation, humiliation. They had their ways, most of it psychological. After all was done and said, you prayed for [death]."

As Jane Duke Gaylor puts it: "I know that if my son is a collaborator, [first] they had him [as a] POW. He had to do what he had to do to survive."

That is why the Geneva Convention on Prisoners of War does not permit changes in the status of prisoners after they're captured; a POW cannot be assumed to have made a free choice while still under the total control of a hostile power. In Korea, POWs who wanted to stay with the side that had captured them had to reaffirm their choice to neutral parties, in theory preventing either side from intimidating prisoners into not going home. At the end of the Korean War, 21 Americans publicly chose to remain with the communists (although most later changed their minds and returned to the U.S.), while tens of thousands of communist Chinese and Korean troops refused to go home, electing instead to stay in South Korea or to go to Taiwan.

The Pentagon knew such issues would arise during Vietnam. A 1969 Pentagon study on Hanoi's POW policies, still partially classified, emphasized that under international law "A combatant who wanted to be treated as a deserter would have to declare himself such at the time he joined the enemy, but would not be able to do so after months or years of captivity."[8]

So the two men seen by the Mortician, even if they eventually "rallied" to the Vietnamese side, were probably still legally "POWs," and had likely endured remarkable hardships for America. But despite knowledge of the Geneva Convention, Korean War history and Hanoi's retention of French "ralliers" who were really POWs, the U.S. government has apparently decided to write off the men seen by the Mortician as "collaborators," leaving them to the mercy of Vietnam.

Instead of publicly recognizing the reality of the communist prison experience, the U.S. government perpetuates the notion that any American not still locked up in a cell block or bamboo cage must be some sort of dirty communist collaborator. The DIA admits it has dozens of reports of alleged Americans "living freely" in Southeast Asia, but separates these men from others seen in a "captive environment." The clear implication is that those "living freely" have chosen to stay in Indochina and can be written off.

This ignores the fact that even an American under the loosest constraints would find it difficult, if not impossible, to escape. Garwood said his jailers often complained about the boring job of guarding him and other U.S. prisoners. "They said: 'Where are they [the Americans] going to escape to? There is no way these people can escape. Even if you turn them loose in a field they stand out like a sore thumb.' "

Afraid to Come Home

Some of the most potent restraints are invisible. When Garwood revealed his presence to a Finnish diplomat and got word of his existence back to the U.S., several of his Vietnamese friends were punished and even shot. U.S. POWs with Asian friends and families are no doubt frightened at the consequences of leaving them behind in the totalitarian nations of Southeast Asia.

Americans "living freely" probably also fear the U.S. government, in part because of the treatment accorded Garwood, who was not only court-martialled but also stripped of his back pay and denounced upon his return to the U.S. Indeed, in secret communications with the U.S. before Garwood's return, the Vietnamese government insisted the marine be treated as a traitor and not a returning prisoner of war.

The fear American POWs may have of returning to U.S. control no doubt once helped Hanoi retain and control them. But that fear has apparently now become a problem for Vietnam, which continues to face intense pressure from the American people, if not the Pentagon, to account for all U.S. POW/MIAs, no matter their current politics or living conditions.

Since 1987, a DIA report concludes, a naturalized American of Vietnamese background working for Hanoi has been spreading the word to U.S. officials that some Americans do want to go home, and that Vietnam will let them. But the Vietnamese agent says Hanoi won't publicly announce the existence of the Americans until "a face-saving explanation can be formulated." "He repeatedly hints that SRV [Vietnamese] officials want the U.S. Government to announce a policy of amnesty for these men," according to a Pentagon record.

In private, the DIA concedes that any American now in Vietnam "is unlikely to come home unless he is assured he will not be prosecuted, leaving his reputation intact and his financial security insured." Yet the Pentagon refuses to offer such assurances. Instead, the U.S. government's failure to make the POW issue a true "highest priority" sends Vietnam the unmistakable message that it's not serious about recovering all Americans held in Vietnam. Despite certain knowledge that Vietnam knows the names of American POW/MIAs kept in Southeast Asia after 1973, the U.S. government has failed to force the issue with Hanoi.

In the Pentagon's own words, written in a previously classified 1990 memo: "Major Pham Teo, who is the senior SRV [Vietnamese] Ministry of Defense representative seconded to the Vietnamese Office for Missing Persons, and other officials of the SRV Ministries of Defense and Interior, know the identities and current status and locations of these two Americans [reported by the "Mortician."][9]

Yet Vietnam apparently refuses to give America that information and still publicly claims that no U.S. servicemen other than Garwood remained in their country after the war.

A Dirty Little Secret

Rather than denouncing Hanoi for its blatant lies, top U.S. military officials and Senators publicly praise Vietnam for its "cooperation" on the POW issue. Lieutenant Colonel Jack Donovan, who replaced Bill Bell, told *The New York Times* in March 1993: "They [the Vietnamese] are bending over backward to help us."[10]

In effect, the U.S. and Vietnam have tacitly agreed to keep parts of the POW issue unresolved. When Garwood left Vietnam in 1979, Colonel Thai of the Cuc Quan Phap, Vietnam's Department of Military Justice, warned him not to expose the dirty little secret between Vietnam and the United States.

> He said: "I strongly suggest that you let us deal with the United States about those people. There is nothing you can do about their situation. If you try to speak or tell anything about what you saw, what you have heard, where you have been, then the blood of these people will be on your hands and not ours."
>
> ". . . whether they go home as you are now, or they go home in a box, it makes no difference to us. The blood of foreigners has enriched Vietnam for thousands of years."

Since 1979, when Garwood and the Mortician left Vietnam with information on Americans still alive in communist hands, eyewitnesses and intercepts of communist radio transmissions have continued to show the presence of U.S. POWs in Vietnam and Laos, both in conventional prisons and in more relaxed situations.

Some of the Americans appear to the same men at the Da Phuc airfield reported by the Mortician. As late as October 1988, the Pentagon received a report that six American POWs were working at "a large airbase north of Hanoi." The airmen, one black and the rest white, helped the Vietnamese repair fixed and rotary wing aircraft. They lived in a special underground room at the base. "The PW's are confined underground during the daytime to prevent them from being seen," the report said.[11]

Jane Gaylor knows one of those men could be her son. And she knows the U.S. government hid evidence about his fate and failed to take actions needed to bring home the men reported by the Mortician. "They have lied to us," she says.

"I have been distraught. I don't know: is this my son [in the sketch]?" Gaylor says. "[But] whether it's my son or not, it's someone's son.

"I think they ought to let the men come home. And I don't think there should be any talk of collaborating. After all," Gaylor says, "look what our government's done. It's abandoned them."

Chapter 2

The POW History of Vietnam

"They [the Vietnamese guards] threatened me: 'We're still hold-
ing French POWs and we're going to do the same thing to you
if you don't cooperate.' "
—*Mike Benge, U.S. POW returned in 1973*

In late 1973, months after all Americans were supposed to have
returned home, Bobby Garwood was searching a canal for frogs
to supplement his meager diet at the Bat Bat POW camp near Son
Tay, North Vietnam. Suddenly, a man in traditional Vietnamese
garb who'd been working with a water buffalo in a nearby rice
paddy sloshed up to Garwood. As he approached, Garwood saw
that the man's face, under the weathered skin of an Asian peasant,
appeared to be Caucasian.

"He came up to me and rattled off this French. . . . And then he
saw that I couldn't speak French, [so] he spoke Vietnamese. He
said: 'Do you speak Vietnamese? And I said 'Yes.' And he just
started talking."

The man explained that he lived in the nearby Ba Vi prison
camp. He was a Moroccan captured while serving with the
French Foreign Legion at the battle of Dien Bien Phu nearly 20
years before. He'd given up his Moroccan citizenship when he
joined the Legion, but had not served long enough to gain French
citizenship. In effect, he had been a man without a country when
captured by the communists.

Explained the grizzled Legionnaire: "There is no diplomat to
go to. There is no one to argue your case for you . . . a lot of us
ended up getting stuck here and we tried to make the best of the
situation."

To improve morale and help make the camp self-supporting,
Hanoi had imprisoned prostitutes with the prisoners from the
French Indochina War. Now many of the foreigners were married
with families, resigned to living out their existences in a hostile
land, the Moroccan said.

"And he looked to be late 60s, early 60s, and I just found it totally amazing. I kind of visualized myself looking like him after the same time period," Garwood recalled under oath during his Senate deposition.

While Garwood's chance encounter was startling, the fact that Hanoi retained POWs from both its First (French) and Second (American) Indochina Wars comes as no surprise to students of POW history. By the mid-1950s, long before the official beginning of America's Vietnam War, Hanoi had refined the strategy of retaining foreign prisoners and remains to serve political and economic objectives.

At the same time, the U.S. government, heading towards war in Southeast Asia, had concluded it would probably have to write off U.S. prisoners in future Cold War brushfires, but would have to adopt a "rather cynical attitude" on the subject. (See Chapter 3, *The POW History of America*.) Given this convergence of Vietnamese and U.S. history, there could be little doubt American POWs would remain behind after the U.S. pulled out of Indochina in 1973.

The Lessons of The First Vietnam War

Meantime, the Pentagon was learning that its next opponent also had a "cynical attitude" about POWs. By 1955, all members of the French military captured by the Vietnamese should have been home. But according to French records, of 4,995 French POWs that Paris claimed were once in communist hands, 2,350 were never repatriated. Of 5,349 Foreign Legionnaires captured by Vietnamese forces, 2,867 remained under communist control.[1]

Most of the unaccounted for French troops had died in captivity. But the Vietnamese also balked at returning enemy remains, even those killed in action and buried in official French cemeteries. For decades after the French withdrawal, Hanoi used the French dead to extort huge amounts of money from Paris, charging up to 20 times the actual cost for returning the bodies (a practice Hanoi would later repeat with the Americans).[2]

Many French troops left alive in Vietnam probably wished they were among those expensive war dead. Hanoi forcibly repatriated hundreds of Foreign Legionnaires to their countries of birth in communist Eastern Europe, where many of them were tried by "people's courts" and then jailed or executed. According to one Russian account, the Vietnamese also forcibly repatriated a U.S. POW of Hungarian background to a similar fate during America's Vietnam War.

Hanoi kept hundreds of other foreign POWs in Vietnam. Among them were many African, Spanish and Moroccan members of the French military, who were indoctrinated for future revolutionary work in their homelands. The Vietnamese also retained hundreds of French natives, claiming the men were "ralliers" who rallied to the communist side and volunteered to stay in Vietnam.

During the mid-1950s, Hanoi released 380 ralliers. Another 60 enlisted Frenchman, along with their Vietnamese families, returned in 1962 to France, where they faced court-martials for desertion.[3]

Against Their Will

But it became clear that not all Frenchmen who remained in Vietnam after the war had freely chosen their fate. Some were held against their will, and even many who "rallied" may have been denied a real choice by communist intimidation and indoctrination.

For example, French radioman Yves Le Bray returned to France more than ten years after his capture in December 1953, *Newsweek* reported in 1964. The communists had "packed off" Le Bray "to become a slave laborer" near the Chinese border at Lang Son, the report said.

Just like the Americans who would later be seen by the Mortician, the Frenchman had been isolated from friendly foreigners and kept under constant supervision by communist officials. When French diplomats learned about Le Bray they immediately pressed for his freedom. The 32-year-old soon returned home to his Breton village of Pleudihen, where town officials were forced to remove his name from the war monument to those villagers "mort pour la France [died for France]."[4]

By 1968, Paris still carried 40 of its men as POWs, 36 as deserters and 358 as "disparus"—French for disappeared.[5]

Prisoners from the French colonies also remained in Vietnam during the 1960s. U.S. intelligence reported blacks from the French forces cutting grass at North Vietnam's Cuu Long Agricultural Center. The men had taken Vietnamese prostitutes as wives, but according to one source "were still prisoners since they were not allowed to leave North Vietnam."[6]

The fate of other POW/MIAs emerged in May 1971, when North Vietnamese defector Dr. Dang Tan revealed Hanoi's strategy of detaining foreign POWs against their will after the French Indochina War. According to a State Department telegram describing Tan's information, Hanoi divided the men into three categories separate from voluntary ralliers. The first group of prisoners kept by Hanoi was composed of men from the French colonies. These men were pressured to stay in Vietnam, and, along with other more willing compatriots, were given communist indoctrination in preparation for insurgencies in their nations.[7]

The second group held in Vietnam was composed of French intelligence officers and Vietnamese experts "whose release would not be in the interests of NVN [North Vietnam]," the State Department reported.

"Technicians," mostly Frenchmen, made up the third group. The men had been "pressured or induced" to remain in NVN because their skills were needed to rebuild Vietnam's economy. The technicians were allowed to marry Vietnamese women, but the wives would not be permitted to leave Vietnam even if their French husbands were eventually allowed to go home.

Dr. Tan said he had met many of these men at Vietnam's General Railroad Department, where an estimated 300 French POWs worked. Vietnamese Foreign Ministry defector Le Quang Khai later corroborated the 1971 report. According to Khai: "They (French POWs) were not allowed to return to their country because some of them were useful for the war against America, and some were just kept because Vietnam feared that these men might release information which is considered harmful for Vietnam."

Declared Dead But Still Alive

Hanoi's retention of French POWs caused remarkably little harm to relations with France, which wrote off all its POWs in 1971 and restored diplomatic links with Vietnam in 1973. Even then, Frenchmen remained alive in communist prison areas, as Vietnamese guards often reminded U.S. POWs. "They threatened me: 'We're still holding French POWs and we're going to do the same thing to you if you don't cooperate,' " said Mike Benge, a civilian U.S. POW returned in 1973.

According to the CIA, Moroccans were still returning home in the early 1970s, almost twenty years after they were originally captured.[8] During the mid-1970s, Bobby Garwood saw prisoners from the First Indochina War and was told 200 Caucasians from the French Army were still alive in one camp complex alone, information supported by U.S. intelligence files. 1983 State Department telegrams, their full texts still classified, even allude to the secret return of French POWs during the 1980s.[9]

Dishonesty is the Official Policy

But France and America were not the only foreign nations forced to contend with Vietnamese hostage politics—or Hanoi's policy of flat-out lying on the POW issue. When Saigon fell to the communists on April 30, 1975, a number of South Koreans were captured. Two of the men, military officer Dai Yong Rhee and policeman Byung Ho Sun, were tossed into Saigon's Chi Hoa prison.

South Korea, which had supported South Vietnam with combat troops, opened a dialogue with Hanoi to win the men's release. But the Vietnamese absolutely denied imprisoning the Koreans (at the same time, they were making similar denials about holding U.S. prisoners).

Eventually, the Koreans bribed a prison guard and got a picture of one of the prisoners. But even photographic evidence could not prompt Hanoi to drop its denials. Finally, South Korea got down to real negotiations with the Vietnamese. Korea reportedly ended up paying for its prisoners with money and/or medical supplies, and Vietnam released the two men in 1980.

Senate Foreign Relations committee investigator Tracy Usry later interviewed the former prisoners in Korea. They said Americans were also held in their Saigon prison, but were apparently shipped north to Hanoi at some point during their captivity.[10]

Long after the Koreans returned home, Americans and Frenchmen remained in Vietnam. Ironically, in April 1982 the State Department reported that a French Foreign Legionnaire "deserter" who had been in Southeast Asia for thirty-years had recently seen eight American POWs in Vietnam. In the best tradition of the "cynical attitude," the State Department has kept details of the incident hidden.[11]

Chapter 3

The POW History of America

*"The [POW] problem becomes almost a philosophical one. . . . If
we are in for fifty years of peripheral 'fire fights' we may be forced
to adopt a rather cynical attitude on this for political reasons."*
*—June 1955 Pentagon policy on POWs in future wars, classified
until obtained by the authors during the 1990s*

Officially, U.S. intervention in Vietnam began with the Tonkin
Gulf Resolution in August 1964. But President Eisenhower had
first dispatched U.S. military advisers to Vietnam, and U.S. per-
sonnel fought, flew and sometimes died in battles across
Southeast Asia during the 1950s. In 1954, U.S. troops first fell into
Vietnamese hands.

On June 14, 1954, a group of young American servicemen
assigned to the French air base at Danang decided to go for a
swim. The Americans, three airmen and two soldiers, were part
of a U.S. detachment providing support to French troops then
battling the communist-controlled Viet Minh independence
movement. Two of the airmen were mechanics for the C-119
cargo planes supporting the French. The other airman was a cook,
and the two soldiers loaded cargo for parachute drops. All were
enlisted men with limited military experience.

During the drive to the beach, one of the men expressed
concern about going to an area reputed to be infested with
communist guerillas. His buddies responded by teasing their
nervous comrade for being a "worry-wart." The razzing inten-
sified when the worried American noticed a group of fishermen
approaching while his buddies swam in the warm South China
Sea. The teasing suddenly stopped when one of the "fishermen"
pulled out a grenade and ordered the Americans back onto their
truck. They were now prisoners of war.

The Viet Minh treated their U.S. captives well, releasing them
on August 31, 1954, as part of POW exchanges under the Geneva
Convention settling the First Indochina War. But the U.S. govern-

ment soon learned that despite their relatively easy captivity, the Americans had cooperated with their captors. A classified Air Force study reported the "high degree to which the five learned from—if not accepted—Viet Minh indoctrination."[1]

The two Army men had even given English lessons to their interrogator. As Army intelligence noted with dismay: "This is another post-Korean incident of captured United States personnel failing to restrict themselves to name, rank, service number, and date of birth during enemy interrogations."[2]

POWs Are a Familiar Problem

The behavior of the American captives was bitterly familiar to the Eisenhower Administration, still struggling with POW problems from the previous conflict in Asia. During the Korean War, which ended in 1953, many Americans cooperated with their captors, while large numbers of others died of abuse, starvation and disease in communist POW camps. Even worse, hundreds more Americans, some known by name to U.S. intelligence, had been kept by the communists after the war (see *Soldiers of Misfortune*). The CIA and military intelligence reported the men were being retained as diplomatic bargaining chips, hostages for aid, intelligence assets and slave labor.

Even as the first American prisoners were being captured on a sandy beach in Vietnam, Korean War POWs still languished in the far chillier climes of China, Siberia and North Korea. And the existence of the Korean War POWs was proving a political liability for the Eisenhower Administration, which was fighting political pressure to take a tougher stand against the Soviet-bloc. The wives and mothers of the POW/MIAs demonstrated in front the of the White House, even returning their loved ones' decorations, ranging from Purple Hearts to the Congressional Medal of Honor. "Our sons want your loyalty, not your medals," the mothers wrote to President Eisenhower.

Perhaps more important to the White House, hawkish members of Congress and the media were also clamoring for Eisenhower to recover the American prisoners. But U.S. diplomatic protests to Beijing and Moscow failed utterly. And Eisenhower refused to approve plans by the Joint Chiefs of Staff for an air and sea blockade of China to force the return of U.S. prisoners. Such drastic military measures, one expert noted, had not even been employed during the height of the Korean War, when Soviet advisors and huge Chinese armies engaged in direct combat with U.S. troops.[3]

In early 1955, White House intelligence officer Philip Corso briefed Eisenhower on the POW situation. Ike already knew some Americans had been kept in North Korean and Chinese camps at the end of the war, and Corso told him that at least 800 more had been packed like animals onto trains and shipped to Siberia. Corso, an experienced Army intelligence officer who specialized in the POW issue, predicted the Soviets would never acknowledge or release the men. And, despite Corso's personal view that Eisenhower was not tough enough on Moscow, the officer concluded that under current policy constraints there was no way to win the return of the prisoners.

"I recommended that the report not be made public because the POWs should be given up for being dead since we knew the Soviets would never relinquish them. Out of concern for the POWs' families, the President agreed," Corso recalled.

According to Corso, his report of the POWs in Siberia "could never be made public and it never was."*

The U.S. Government Adopts a "Cynical Attitude"

The frustrated U.S. government soon commissioned a special study to draw wider conclusions about the POW issue and its role in the Cold War. The June 1955 report by the Pentagon's Defense Advisory Committee on Prisoners of War, entitled "Recovery of Unrepatriated Prisoners of War," summed up the U.S. dilemma.[4] Analyst James J. Kelleher implicitly acknowledged that diplomacy was ineffective, and the U.S. was not prepared to employ force against the communists. Such an operation would probably kill more Americans than it saved, along with risking the ignition of World War III. The bottom line: "We have been unable, under existing national policy considerations, to bring about an accounting by the Commies [for the Korean War POWs]."

---

*As of this writing, that 1955 report is still classified on orders of the Bush Administration. However, Corso's account of the POWs in Siberia and the White House briefing have been confirmed by other records and Senate investigators.

The Pentagon analyst then looked ahead, well aware that during the previous year, Sino-Soviet advisors and arms, including Chinese troops and captured U.S. equipment shipped south from the former battlefields of Korea, had helped defeat France in Vietnam. America had funded most of the failed French effort against the Viet Minh, and pressure was growing for the U.S. military to pick up the battle against Vietnamese communism.

The Pentagon saw itself heading toward a new war against old enemies in Asia. And there was no doubt coming Cold War battles in Vietnam and elsewhere would feature the same bitter POW controversies encountered during Korea. So Kelleher suggested a new strategy for the future. "The [POW] problem becomes almost a philosophical one," Kelleher wrote, explaining: "If we are 'at war,' cold, hot or otherwise, casualties and losses must be expected and perhaps we must learn to live with this type of thing. If we are in for fifty years of peripheral 'fire fights' we may be forced to adopt a rather cynical attitude on this for political reasons."

The U.S. government quickly accepted Kelleher's "cynical attitude." Since there was no acceptable way of solving the Korean War POW problem, the U.S. government decided to make it go away. Despite secret evidence to the contrary, top executive branch officials began denying that any Americans were still in communist hands. And intelligence reports proving the continued survival of the men were classified and hidden even from Congress. (The Korean War POW cover-up continued in full force until 1992, when the Pentagon and State Department were forced to begin admitting at least some of the truth.) Gradually, the issue slipped from the newspapers and political debate, remaining alive only in the hearts of POW relatives and activists. The "cynical attitude" had worked.

"On Limited War"

Air Force officer Laird Gutterson says the equivalent of the "cynical attitude" soon made it into the Pentagon's basic plan for the future. Colonel (then Captain) Gutterson says he was one of five young Air Force officers assigned to review a "top secret" paper which, in 1957, had just been adopted by the Department of Defense as its "bible," for the future. Allegedly written by a young academic named Dr. Henry Kissinger,[5] the paper outlined the "human chess game" of limited wars of the future.

Gutterson was then a faculty member of the Air Warfare College at Maxwell Air Force Base, attached to the Squadron Officers School as a lecturer. But all these years later, he still remembers the Kissinger study. It was now impractical to fight a nuclear war, Gutterson recalls the document saying, because the world economy could not survive such a battle. There was now a need for nations to joust with each other in order to determine which world power would dominate given regions of the world. But the jousting could not turn into direct conflict between the super powers, because that could mean nuclear conflict.

Instead, limited wars would pit "minor champions" of the competing powers against each other. There would have to be "a gentleman's agreement" among the major powers that certain rules of conflict would be followed, "because no one wanted nuclear war." The rules included prohibitions against strategic bombing within 150 miles of a major power's border and mining of international harbors. (Both issues later came up during Vietnam, when the U.S. maintained a no-bombing "buffer" along the Chinese border and caused an international flap when it attacked and mined North Vietnamese harbors.)

A major power could step in if its surrogate was losing, but it was not acceptable for the opposing power to likewise respond because of the likelihood of nuclear confrontation. The major powers would recognize the potential for confrontation and force the surrogates to accept a political solution. The major power's troops would then be withdrawn and the crisis averted.

The major powers could actually benefit from their limited interventions, which would allow them battlefield tests of new strategies, equipment and weapons systems. A significant drawback for the U.S. in such an approach, the document maintained, was that the United States would not know whether all American POWs had been released after a limited war, since it would not control the enemy's territory at the end of the conflict. "We would have to accept the former enemy's statements concerning the fate of our POWs," Gutterson recalls the paper concluding.

The document's reasoning, Gutterson believed from his reading of classified Korean War records, was based on the United States' experience during the Korean War when the Soviet Union shipped American POWs by the trainload to Siberia and never returned them. Other Americans had been left in China and North Korea.

But retired General Orval A. Anderson, Commandant of the first Air War College, told Gutterson that Kissinger's reasoning on POWs came not just from America's Korean War experiences, but also from U.S. experience in World War II, when thousands of American Army Air Corp personnel—POWs held in German camps in Poland—were liberated by the Red Army and disappeared.

Anderson, who was an operations officer with the 8th Air Force in Europe during World War II, told Gutterson it was "common knowledge" that American POWs were kept by Stalin after World War II. The Allied command "pleaded with [General George C.] Marshall to [allow them to] fly in, take over the prisons and take the people out." But Marshall said no.

Many officers who created waves over the issue were transferred out of Europe in order to break up the trouble-makers "because we were close to open revolt over the situation," Anderson told Gutterson.

Now Gutterson and four other officers were being told to write a review on a paper which essentially committed to official policy the loss of American POWs from the anticipated low-intensity wars of the future. Each of the five officers wrote a "stinging denouncement" of the Kissinger paper, Gutterson says.

They were soon called in one by one and given direct orders to write a good review, so that the Kissinger text could bear the Air University's stamp of approval as well as that of the Department of Defense.

Gutterson says all five men submitted their resignations as officers rather than sign on to what they considered a fatally flawed concept. General Anderson then called Gutterson, and, after a multi-hour conversation, convinced him not to resign. Anderson arranged for Gutterson's resignation to be withdrawn. He would also "not be required to give an official review" of Kissinger's document. The other four officers, said Gutterson, let their resignations stand.

While Kissinger's theory was not confined to any single conflict, Gutterson remembers that the paper "outlined in detail the Vietnam War." The United States had clearly not learned the lessons of Korea, Gutterson believed. And now the Department of Defense had adopted a limited war strategy based on what at least five young officers were convinced was a fatally flawed document.

While Dr. Kissinger vehemently denies writing the "top-secret" manuscript, Colonel Gutterson remembers that in 1957 Dr. Kissinger authored a book entitled *Nuclear Weapons and Foreign Policy.* Chapter Five of that book, "What Price Deterrence? The Problems of Limited War," closely parallels the classified manuscript outined by Gutterson.[6]

Kissinger made the following points in that chapter:

- "There may occur limited wars between the major powers which are kept from spreading by tacit agreement between the contestants. . . . "
- "A limited war . . . is fought for specific political objectives. . . . It reflects an attempt to affect the opponent's will, not to crush it, to make the conditions to be imposed seem more attractive than continued resistance, to strive for specific goals and not for complete annihilation."
- "The characteristics of a limited war . . . [include] the existence of ground rules which define the relationship of military to political objectives."
- "Limited war is essentially a political act. . . . Its distinguishing feature is that it has no purely 'military' solution."
- "It is no longer possible to impose unconditional surrender at an acceptable cost."
- "An attempt to reduce the enemy to impotence would remove the psychological balance which makes it profitable for both sides to keep the war limited."
- "If we could develop the forces capable of conducting limited war and of getting into position rapidly, we should be able to defeat the Soviet Union or China in local engagements despite their interior position . . . This is the case despite the seemingly contrary lessons of the war in Korea."
- "Limited war has become the form of conflict which enables us to derive the strategic advantage from our industrial potential. . . . Thus the argument that limited war may turn into a contest of attrition is an argument in favor of a strategy of limited war. A war of attrition is the one war the Soviet bloc could not win."
- "In a limited war the problem is to apply graduated amounts of destruction for limited objectives and also

to permit the necessary breathing spaces for political
contacts."

Kissinger even predicted the challenges that would bedevil
policy-makers during the Vietnam War. But as Kissinger would
learn, Hanoi would win the psychological battle in Vietnam.

Gutterson himself would become a victim of that strategy, later
spending five years as a guest of the North Vietnamese at the
Hanoi Hilton. He considers himself lucky to have come home at
all.

PART II

Motive and Opportunity

Chapter 4

Motives

"Fundamentally, I would have to say I can find no rational reason for them to hold prisoners."
—Henry Kissinger, 1992 Senate testimony

"Americans were being held in Hanoi pending the settlement of an agreement with the U.S. on American reconstruction aid to Vietnam. The instructor said the Vietnamese were 'not stupid' and would hold these Americans until the the three billion dollars in promised aid was paid."
—Vietnamese communist official, quoted in post-1973 U.S. intelligence report[1]

For years, U.S. officials have declared that Hanoi had no motive to retain U.S. POWs after the Vietnam War. That official line made it difficult, if not impossible, for American negotiators to make progress in the sporadic POW/MIA talks the U.S. conducted with Vietnam in the years immediately following the war. In the meantime, intelligence analysts remained in step with the policy-makers, dismissing reports of POWs in communist control on the grounds that Vietnam had no reason to keep Americans imprisoned. In reality, the communist leaders of Indochina not only had strong reasons to retain U.S. prisoners, but also declared their motives on many occasions. Following, in their own words, are some of the reasons the Vietnamese retained American POWs.

The Vietnam War Wasn't Over for Vietnam

Strategically speaking, it would have made no sense for North Vietnam to release all U.S. POWs in early 1973 when America was still attacking Hanoi's troops and arming South Vietnam. At least one highly credible DIA official has testified that some Americans were kept to trade later for communists held back by Saigon. Other U.S. POWs had seen key North Vietnamese facilities and if released could have given valuable military intelligence to Saigon and the U.S., which was still bombing North Vietnamese targets and troops. U.S. captives were also valuable as an insurance policy in case America resumed large-scale hostilities.

> You don't think the United States or anyone else would think that Vietnam would be so foolish as to return everyone, and [then] Vietnam would have nothing. [A] mere signature on a piece of paper. There's no way that we can convince the populace or our allies that would prevent the United States from coming—just after they got what we gave them and they were satisfied—from returning and bombing Vietnam.
>
> The war's not over. The U.S. is not out of Vietnam. They left people behind in Saigon in plain clothes . . . . It just went from uniforms to plain clothes. They still have the B-52 bases in Guam.

So said Vietnamese security official Lieutenant Colonel Xuan in 1973.[1]

Vietnam expected America would return to the bargaining table for the rest of its POWs when the war was really over.

> For now, we have officially published a list of 368 POWs, the rest are not acknowledged. The government of the United States is aware of this . . . . —North Vietnamese General Lieutenant Tran Van Quang, September 15, 1972[2]

> After the war, they [Vietnam's leaders] expected America to come back and talk about normalization. And the only card they had was POW/MIAs. But the Americans never came back. This is the official analysis of the Vietnamese Foreign Ministry." —Le Quang Khai, defector from the Vietnamese Foreign Ministry

Hanoi Wanted the Aid Money Promised by the U.S.

At the Paris Peace Talks, America promised in writing to give billions of dollars in U.S. aid to Vietnam. The aid, linked to the POW issue during negotiations, was never delivered.

> If we take a path of concession toward Americans and liberate POWs we would be at a great loss . . . . Nixon must compensate North Vietnam for the great damage inflicted on it by the destructive war. —General Lieutenant Tran Van Quang, as quoted in 1972[3]

POWs Are Just Another Weapon In the Ongoing Struggle

Hanoi believed the POWs could be used as diplomatic bargaining chips and would force America to remain diplomatically and economically engaged with North Vietnam.

> Vietnam thought the U.S. would have to approach Vietnam to discuss normalization even though the U.S. would have to do it at the expense of relations with the People's Republic of China. They [Vietnamese leaders] believed the U.S. government, under the pressure of American [popular] opinion, must talk with Vietnam to negotiate unsolved problems, and the POW/MIA issue, of course, is the most important one [for the U.S.]. —Le Quang Khai

> . . . There are indications that the leadership of the DRV considers that the issue of the liberation of American POWs is a part of the whole Vietnamese problem and can be regularized only after the resolution of the political and military issues. —Top Secret 1972 Soviet report on Hanoi's POW policies[4]

> NVN [North Vietnam] had not released all U.S. and ARVN [South Vietnamese] PW because the complete release of all PW was . . . a long range polit[ical] strategy of NVN and could not be accomplished before all the problems of Vietnam were solved. —Viet Cong Cadre, Speaking in 1974[5]

> Military cadre mentioned in informal sessions that the Democratic Republic of Vietnam [North Vietnam] Government had not released all of the U.S. prisoners of war it held in spring 1973. These cadre added that the SRV [Socialist Republic of Vietnam], the successor of the DRV, would continue to hold these POW's and use them occasionally as bargaining counters as necessary. —North Vietnamese officials talking during 1976-7[6]

Chapter 5

Opportunity

In February 1968, a combat patrol from Bravo Company, 1st Battalion, 26th Marines was beset by the enemy outside the barbed wire of America's fortress at Khe Sanh, South Vietnam.

When the fighting was over, the Marines—renowned for refusing to leave their dead behind—brought back 18 of their fallen comrades. The men were later buried at the National Cemetery in St. Louis, Missouri. Almost five years later, on Jan. 28, 1973, Sergeant Ronald Ridgeway—one of the 18 "dead and buried" marines—returned alive from a communist POW camp.

The story of Ronald Ridgeway is a cautionary tale for those seeking to write off the last U.S. POW/MIAs of the Vietnam War. As of this writing, the Pentagon lists 2,260 Americans as unaccounted for in Southeast Asia. 1,094 of those men and women are categorized as KIA/BNR, meaning "killed in action/body not recovered." The other 1,166 are POW/MIAs, the category for those known to have been captured or lost under conditions in which they might have survived.

And then there is the most important list: the "last known alive" or "Vessey" list. Named for special POW/MIA emissary to Hanoi General John Vessey Jr. (U.S. Army, Ret.), the list is for Americans who were captured or whose fate should be known to Hanoi. These names are selected from the over all POW/MIA list of 2,260 and represent, in theory, the most compelling cases of Americans whose fate should be known to the communists. This list, which for some time contained 133 U.S. names, has become the yardstick used in measuring Vietnamese cooperation on the POW issue.

Rather than requiring Hanoi to reveal all it knows about every U.S. POW/MIA, the U.S. has set this much lower and more objective standard. As discussed in a later chapter, the chairman of the Senate's POW Committee, Senator John Kerry, even had his chief aide give Vietnam suggestions on how to "account" for Americans on the Vessey list with the minimum amount of information. But Kerry even took a step further in easing Hanoi's load. During his committee's investigation, he declared "that valid questions remain about 43" U.S. POW/MIAs. It was all part of the momentum to "resolve" the POW issue. Of course, Hanoi has stonewalled, stalled, lied and otherwise refused to account for even the men on Kerry's short list. Despite that, the Vessey and Kerry lists reflect a remarkably cynical and/or ignorant view of the casualty accounting process and communist POW history. But even if Hanoi miraculously decided to account for every person on the Vessey list, that would leave many other American POWs abandoned in Southeast Asia.

Back From the Dead

For all the arguing that goes on about them, one fact is clear: America's KIA/BNR and POW/MIA lists are simply not accurate. Some men called POW/MIAs were killed in their incidents and could never have been POWs. More importantly, men listed as MIA and even KIA were really captured. The truth about the lists first became apparent during the war, when the KIA category proved inaccurate. During the war, the Navy learned that five of its aviators listed as KIA were really POWs. Pentagon POW expert Roger Shields described the experience of a seasoned Navy pilot, a veteran of many combat missions and duty with the elite Blue Angels demonstration team.

During one mission, the aviator watched an anti-aircraft missile slam into a nearby F-4, demolishing it in a huge fireball. The Navy pilot *knew* his buddies were dead. "He said he watched the aircraft all the way, there was nothing, there were no chutes, nothing was ever heard, no beepers, no indication that anyone ever ejected safely. And yet both of those men showed up very quickly as having been captured. Without any injuries I might add," Shields remembered.[1]

A marine named Nelson escaped from the enemy, only to find he was officially dead. "On 22 JAN 68, LCPL Steven Devon Nelson, previously reported KIA on 7 JAN 68, and [another American] were returned to USMC control at Danang. The men allegedly escaped when their NVA guard fell asleep."[2]

Army Private 1st Class Donald Sparks was declared dead after he was left with severe wounds on a South Vietnamese battlefield in July 1967. Imagine the Pentagon's embarrassment almost a year later when a letter from Sparks was found on the corpse of a Viet Cong soldier. The letter, dated April 11, 1970, was addressed to the young soldier's parents in Iowa.

"I have not heard [or] seen another American in nearly 10 months now. . . . All this time I have continually been treated very well by the Vietnamese people," Sparks wrote, adding "I can't thank them enough for their care." At some point, the young Iowa farm boy may have changed his mind about the Viet Cong, because they never released him, nor did they return his remains at the end of the war. One returned POW claimed to have seen Sparks alive in a North Vietnamese prison as late as March 1973.

In one case, a Vietnamese source identified the picture of a missing marine as the man he'd seen in communist captivity. U.S. intelligence dismissed the source's report because the marine had already been declared KIA/BNR.[3] When the Vietnam War finally ended in January 1973, the communists revealed they had captured at least 20 men whom the Pentagon had believed died. Some of those men came home alive in the 1973 prisoner exchanges. Others, in effect, had to be declared dead a second time.[4] That happened in the case of Army Sergeant Billy Knight, whose helicopter went down in 1965. The Army claimed to have recovered his body from the burned chopper and returned it to the U.S. for burial in February 1966. But in January 1973, the Viet Cong announced that they had captured Knight in November 1965 and that he had died in their captivity the next month.[5]

Of course, in cases where no remains were returned, the U.S. couldn't really tell which POWs had died and which had actually been retained by the communists. The Viet Cong said marine Earl Weatherman died during an escape attempt during the 1960s, but he was seen alive years later by Bobby Garwood in North Vietnam.

At times, the communists' lies were almost comical. In January 1973, the Viet Cong announced that POW Carl Nicotera had died on December 5, 1966. There were two problems with that statement: Nicotera had never been a POW and he was still alive.

"Carl Nicotera is alive and resides in Connecticut, United States. His service in Vietnam and serial number were verified by U.S. Army officials on 28 January 1973," the DIA noted, adding with characteristic understatement: "The body identified by the PRG [Viet Cong] is an individual other than the subject."[6]

The Remains Game

Of course, the Viet Cong may simply have made an honest mistake in identifying a body. After all, that happened at a suspiciously high rate even to the supposedly high tech morticians of the U.S. military.

Sergeant First Class Frank C. Parish disappeared when his unit was ambushed by communists near My Tho, South Vietnam during 1968. Then, in 1973, the Pentagon said they had found and scientifically identified Parish's remains, returning them to the United States for burial in a Texas cemetery.

In early 1990, Parish's brother stopped by the cemetery for a visit. He was astonished to discover that the remains identified as Frank had been quietly exhumed. The family learned the Pentagon had recently discovered the real remains of Frank Parish. In the intervening years, another missing soldier had rested under Frank Parish's headstone. As of this writing, it is unclear who was resting under the headstone of Frank Parish.[7]

For years, the Army's Central Identification Laboratory in Hawaii (CIL-HI) was plagued by sometimes bizarre errors. Congressional studies in 1986 and 1987 noted serious problems in the lab's work, raising the possibility that more men who had been "accounted for" and buried in the U.S. were really still missing.

For many years after the war, CIL-HI employed Dr. Tadao Furue, an anthropologist who specialized in the "morphological approximation" method of identifying remains. Furue helped "resolve" the cases of many U.S. POW/MIAs.

But there was a problem, however, as congressional investigators later learned. Furue was not a "Doctor." He had no Ph.D.; his only major academic achievement was a bachelor's degree from the University of Tokyo, Senate investigator Tracy Usry reported during a POW probe previous to the Senate Select Committee's.

Worse, "morphological approximation" was not even an accepted, or effective, forensic practice. A top civilian anthropologist called in to review CIL-HI concluded: "It is clear from their bones that the problem in the CIL-HI reports results either from extreme carelessness, incompetence, fabrication of data, or some combination of these things."[8]

Not surprisingly, the lab's sloppiness allowed it to meet the political objective of "accounting" for as many Americans as possible. For instance, on October 5, 1990, the Pentagon buried four U.S. POW/MIAs from Indochina with full military honors. The men's names were taken off the lists for which an accounting was still sought. But at least two of the four could still be alive. Their coffins were empty. The Pentagon had declared the entire crew of a downed helicopter was dead on the basis that identifiable remains from two of the men had been found.

The cruel irony of the identification is that one of the men on the flight, a man later "buried" in the U.S., may not have died in the incident at all. He was reportedly captured after the incident, and a Laotian prisoner later identified him from a picture as an American in a communist POW camp. The DIA branded the Laotian a liar and closed the case. If in the future, another Asian refugee ever reports seeing the man, the report will be dismissed, because the American has now been " accounted for."[9]

The Pentagon is now willing to identify a set of remains based on one tooth. Apparently, the U.S. government believes the Vietnamese, who are notified of all U.S. searches in advance, are too stupid to "salt" crash sites with teeth easily removed from a living POW. After all, the Pentagon publicly concedes that Hanoi warehoused hundreds of U.S. remains to trade back for concessions. And Vietnamese official Nguyen Can reportedly admitted that some U.S. corpses were refrigerated and then planted back at their crash site. So why wouldn't Hanoi yank the tooth of a prisoner and place it at his crash site?

Of course, the Vietnamese aren't always that devious; the U.S. has also caught them trying to pass off pig and cow bones as the remains of U.S. POW/MIAs.

Life Sentence for Going AWOL

When the communists announced their (partial) list of American POWs in 1973, at least one and perhaps two of the captured Americans were not on any U.S. list; the men were deserters whose names had been dropped from the rolls.[10] According to official policy, the Pentagon isn't looking for Americans who disappeared in Vietnam after deserting or going AWOL (absent without leave).

The military doesn't even know exactly how many Americans deserted in Southeast Asia. A February 1971 memo from the Joint Chiefs of Staff reports "approximately 1,500 military personnel have deserted in Vietnam since 1964. Military services cannot estimate accurately how many of these personnel remain in Vietnam."[11]

The vast majority of Americans listed as Vietnam deserters apparently left the military while on the way to Indochina or on leave outside Southeast Asia, but were listed as Vietnam deserters because their units were stationed there. However, "before the final exodus of American troops in 1973, a muster revealed 350 could not be found (a few turned up on the final American departure in 1975)," according to one DIA record.[12]

Even the Joint Casualty Resolution Center, whose mandate was to keep looking for Americans in Southeast Asia after the war, failed to keep up with the deserters. "[T]his office does not maintain an active interest in, nor dossiers on, deserters/collaborators," the Center wrote in 1974.[13]

In 1992 the DIA claimed it had records on just 21 troops believed to have gone AWOL or deserted in Vietnam—a mere fraction of those whose fates remain a mystery. It doesn't take an intelligence expert to wonder how the Pentagon can locate and identify real POWs if it doesn't have complete records on other Caucasians and blacks roaming the streets and jungles of Indochina. But the failure to keep records on the deserters reflects a more horrible reality: some of those men were probably regular POWs rather than disciplinary cases. After all, a number of G.I.s were snatched from their hootches and recreational areas. If a soldier failed to show up for head count in a war zone, how was his commander to know he hadn't been kidnapped? Even the Pentagon admitted: "U.S. authorities were often not able to determine if an individual had fallen into enemy hands, had left the country, or had gone 'native'. . . ."[14]

And what if a soldier had been AWOL when captured? Being absent without leave was certainly a crime. But did it merit being abandoned to a lifetime in communist hands? One incident illustrates the point. In mid-November 1969, two uniformed American servicemen and their Vietnamese girlfriends were driving a jeep down South Vietnam's Highway 4, according to a U.S. intelligence record. The group stopped by the side of the road for a rest break, unknowingly parking right next to a reconnaissance team from the communist 308th Infantry Battalion.

A Viet Cong platoon immediately captured the travellers, who were armed only with one M-16 rifle. The women were summarily executed, according to a Vietnamese soldier who later fell into

U.S. hands. The Americans were marched off to communist captivity, forced to remove their shoes and stagger along in their socks to prevent them from running away. The men were hidden during the day and forced to march at night. Finally, after two days of travel, including one leg by sampan, they reached the Viet Cong's SR-2 Headquarters.[15]

There the men were photographed and questioned by interrogator Sau Quang and interpreter Dao Tan Lang. "The two POWs told Quang that they were on leave . . . when they were captured," reported a Vietnamese source who had seen the men in captivity.

Finally, after two days at headquarters, the men were carried off by two squads from the 308th Infantry. "The PWs were being carried in hammocks because their feet were too badly cut and bruised from walking to SR-2 HQ in their socks to allow them to walk any further," the source said.

U.S. intelligence took the report quite seriously, especially since the "source answered all control questions accurately and without hesitation." But as British author Nigel Cawthorne first noted, no pair of Americans went missing in those circumstances during November 1969, according to official Pentagon lists. However, Americans Daniel T. Bailey and Rudolpho Andres Adventio are both listed as going AWOL on the same day early that month. Perhaps they were the two Americans captured. If so, no one's looking for them. Because they were considered AWOL, they're not on the DIA's POW list or the Vietnam Memorial. Instead, they have been written off by the U.S. government.

Mysterious Battles

"Operation Buffalo" was a series of hellish engagements during July 1967 between outmanned U.S. marines and the North Vietnamese Army (NVA) troops in Quang Tri Province, just below the demilitarized zone (DMZ) separating South and North Vietnam. On July 2nd, along Route 561, in a battle long forgotten by just about everybody except those who fought it so bravely, North Vietnamese troops overran Bravo Company of the 1st Battalion, 9th Marines, 3rd Marine Division.

A wounded marine named Henderson watched the Vietnamese roar across American lines.

Suddenly there were shouted commands in Vietnamese, and just as abruptly, NVA came swarming out of the brush . . . . They were just a wild mob, some of them with insane faces as they ran firing into trees, bushes, and men so indiscriminately that Henderson was convinced that NVA were accidentally killing other NVA. Others stumbled along vacant-eyed, rushing right past him without pause.... The NVA shouted to each other as they ran past, little guys in green with grass sticking up from their helmets and gear, so that in moments the brush had swallowed them back up as they streaked on for the main road. . . .

wrote Keith William Nolan in his vivid book about the battle, *Operation Buffalo: USMC Fight for the DMZ.*[16]

Later, the marines went back to claim their dead and missing, some mutilated by the enemy and/or swollen beyond recognition by the heat. The book accurately notes the DIA's official claim that despite all the chaos and confusion of the battle, only one marine, Lance Corporal Wayne Wilson, could not be accounted for.

However, the DIA explanation fails to square with that of an official marine history that reportedly claims nine men disappeared in the battle. Yet another official military record says that five men were missing from the engagement.

But nowhere, except in one intelligence report, and perhaps Hanoi's secret POW files, is there the claim that 23 American marines were captured in the battle. But that is just what one survivor of the battle reported.[17] The survivor was a North Vietnamese soldier from the 8th Battalion of the 90th NVA Regiment, captured the day after the main battle, when U.S. bombs knocked him unconscious. When he awoke, he was a prisoner of the United States marines.

The Vietnamese soldier had received good training before the battle. An officer who spoke English taught the troops useful American phrases for combat, and the soldier paid close attention to his lessons. According to U.S. intelligence, when questioned after his capture, "Source actually said the following words in very good English: Hands Up!; Hands Down!; Surrender, not die; After me!"

The Vietnamese troops also got lessons in how to handle U.S. prisoners. "The lieutenant stated that the prisoner should be well fed and well treated. No one was to take anything such as rings or watches from the prisoners. If this order was disobeyed the violator would be punished by the lieutenant himself," the U.S. intelligence report stated. Wounded Americans were to be sent straight to the 90th Regiment's hospital.

After the battle, the Vietnamese soldier did not see any wounded. But he did report seeing many U.S. POWs. "The prisoners were being marched, in pairs, away from the battlefield. Each pair was guarded by one NVA soldier, who walked approximately two meters behind them. . . . Behind the last prisoners marched a squad of Vietnamese soldiers. The prisoners were not tied or blindfolded," the Vietnamese soldier said.

"One of the members of the squad following the prisoners stated that the U.S. prisoners were being taken to the 90th Regt HQ. . . . He also told source that they had captured a total of 23 prisoners from the battle," U.S. intelligence said.

But how could that be? Although the Vietnamese soldier appeared to be telling the truth about everything else, only one marine officially disappeared from the battle. Was the soldier lying? Or were the marines captured and then slaughtered? That's possible, but in comments on the interrogation of the Vietnamese soldier, written more than a month after the battle, the marines admit five men from the battle were still missing. Perhaps those men were eventually found, and Wayne Wilson really is the only POW/MIA from the battle. But it could also be true that the marines mistakenly accounted for men who were actually still missing, just as they "buried" Ronald Ridgeway, only to have him return home alive in 1973. If so, then those five MIAs, along with Wilson, may well have been captured. But unless Hanoi suddenly admits it, their fate may never be known, because the U.S. government has declared them dead.

The mystery of "Operation Buffalo" bears an eerie similarity to another case involving marines in combat near the DMZ, this time men from the 4th Marine Division engaged in "Operation Kingfisher." On September 21, 1967, Lance Corporal Kenneth Plumadore and 14 other leathernecks were left behind during a fierce battle in Quang Tri Province. The Pentagon ultimately declared that Plumadore had died in the battle.

Then, in June 1992, Plumadore's sister received a staggering letter from the Pentagon. "American forces learned that PAVN (People's Army of Vietnam) forces captured the 15th individual and took him away in the direction of Vinh Linh," the letter said. Later, Vietnamese records confirmed that a marine, almost certainly Plumadore, had been taken from the battlefield.[18]

Now the Pentagon and Vietnamese claim Plumadore died days after the battle, perhaps in Vinh Linh, North Vietnam. But the marine's family is still fighting for the whole truth—which is probably a good idea, especially since Vinh Linh allegedly had a secret POW camp that retained Americans after the war.

The Mystery Man of Hoa Lao

On August 27, 1972, the Vietnamese brought a new prisoner into Hoa Lao prison, nicknamed the "Hanoi Hilton." Although at least one U.S. POW saw the man, he has never been identified—the new prisoner was covered in bandages. "The man had black hair, average weight, about five feet nine inches tall, and was in full body cast," according to an Air Force intelligence report.

The Pentagon guessed that the man might have been shot down shortly before his appearance at the prison. One report suggested the mystery POW might be naval aviator Roderick Lester, downed on August 20th. Another Pentagon report, for unknown reasons, suggested the man might have been soldier Larry Kier, who disappeared after an ammunition dump exploded near him in 1970. But these are all guesses. The identity of the Hanoi Hilton's mysterious guest is still not known, but no POW with injuries of his type was returned by the Vietnamese. In this case as in so many others, Hanoi may have taken the opportunity to keep the American POW forever.

Chapter 6

Left for Dead

Don't expect the U.S. government to demand an accounting for Army officer Donald "Butch" Carr, even though he was known to be a POW. The Green Beret's aircraft went down over Laos on July 6, 1971. Soon after, a communist soldier who later fell into U.S. hands got a good look at an American POW captured by an anti-aircraft company in Laos before he was taken away "to the North."

The source was less than 10 feet away from the American and watched him for 15 minutes. U.S. intelligence officials later showed the source pictures of POW/MIAs. "Photographs selected are of Donald G. Carr, listed MIA," U.S. military intelligence reported.

In addition, information supplied by the source on Carr's capture matched the details of his loss down to the type of airplane, an OV-10 spotter, he was in. It wasn't tough for Army intelligence to conclude: "Time frame, a/c [aircraft] type, and physical description support the CARR correlation."[1]

Sadly for Butch Carr, the U.S. government isn't holding Vietnam or Laos accountable for him, because officially he was never captured. The DIA lists Carr as a "category 4" POW/MIA, meaning the U.S. has no reason to believe the communists know his fate. This is true for other Americans. In many cases the Pentagon publicly claims their fate is a complete mystery, implying that the Vietnamese and the DIA really can't be expected to account for them. But in reality, there is previously classified information on these POW/MIAs indicating that both Hanoi and the Pentagon should be held responsible for the men.

Categories

All Americans missing in Southeast Asia fall into one of five categories:

- *"Category 1"* is for cases in which the communists have "confirmed knowledge" of the POW/MIA. This includes men identified by name in communist radio broadcasts or reported to be prisoners by "highly reliable intelligence sources."
- *"Category 2"* is for cases in which the communists have "suspect knowledge." They are often people from the same incident as a "Category 1" American—i.e., the copilot of a plane from which the pilot was known to have been captured.
- *"Category 3"* describes cases where the enemy had "doubtful knowledge"—Americans lost over water or in desolate areas where they may never have been found by the enemy
- *"Category 4"* is for Americans whose fate is a mystery.
- And *"Category 5"* is used in incidents where the Pentagon claims the POW/MIA was certainly killed but his remains are "non-recoverable."

Those categories, which started out only as general guidelines, have now become an important tool in deciding which POW/MIA cases get attention. Sadly, in the Pentagon's public relations battle to minimize the POW tragedy, only the relatively small number of Americans, those in categories 1 and 2, mostly those on the "Vessey List," receive most attention from the military. And the standard for Vietnam to "resolve" the POW issue has now been fixed on explaining the fate of just several dozen Americans. But as discussed in the previous chapter, the names of actual U.S. POWs are likely sprinkled across all the categories. Many of them are not on the "Vessey List." And sadly for those men not on the Pentagon's priority list, their cases will likely never receive thorough attention from U.S. and Vietnamese officials. According to the U.S., Hanoi will be get credit for "resolving" the POW issue simply by accounting for the "Vessey List," and those POW/MIAs left off it are just out of luck.

Bumming a Cigarette

In June 1970, a communist soldier saw 10 American POWs being prepared for movement across the Tchepone River in Laos.

The soldier got a good look at two of the men, who were wearing fatigues and appeared malnourished and badly sunburned. One of the Americans used sign language to ask the soldier for a cigarette. The soldier, whose testimony "revealed no attempt at deception," later identified that American as Marshall Kipina, and said the other prisoner he got a good look at was Edward Guillory, Army intelligence reported (an entirely different report confirmed Guillory's capture).

"Source believed the US PW were being sent to NVN [North Vietnam] to provide the NVN Government with more US personnel to use as a bargaining lever in the event of a cease-fire agreement between the U.S. and NVN."[2]

But Kipina and Guillory did not turn out to be very good bargaining chips. Guillory is listed in Category 2 and Kipina in Category 4. In other words, the Pentagon claims there's no evidence either man was captured.

An Easy Hop

The situation was similar for the men aboard Huey chopper serial number 69-15619. It was supposed to be a "milk run flight." On January 8, 1973, six American soldiers took to the skies of Vietnam aboard the UH-1H helicopter from the Army's 62nd Aviation Company. The crew of the chopper normally shuttled the U.S. advisor for a Vietnamese airborne division from one assignment to the next. On this day, they were flying what the Army would later describe as a "support mission" in the area of Quang Tri City, North Vietnam.

That aircraft was last seen flying across the Thach Han River into enemy territory. Suddenly the aircraft began to circle, hosing down a target with its door guns. Then, with devastating accuracy, an enemy SA-7 anti-aircraft missile rocketed into the chopper's tail boom. One "Mayday" came over U.S. radio frequencies before the crew of the American chopper disappeared into history, less than a month before the end of the Vietnam War.

When U.S. POWs began returning over the next several months, the military asked them whether they had seen the men on that helicopter: Richard Knutson, Mickey Wilson, William Stinson, Manuel Lauterio, Elbert Bush, and William Deane.

One returning POW said he had talked with Richard Knutson, according to research by the office of Senator Bob Smith. But the DIA later concluded the returnee mistook Knutson for another man with a similar name. Yet according to a member of the chopper's unit, the Knutson in communist captivity may well have been aboard the ill-fated Huey; U.S. rescuers from the 62nd Aviation Company saw four crash survivors alive on the ground, which was under total North Vietnamese control.

And, just weeks after the crash, a CIA agent reported information on the incident. At a long meeting that began at 8 p.m. on January 12, 1973, members of the Viet Cong's Quang Tri Province Communist Party Committee told their subordinates about the downing of an American helicopter. According to the communist officials, troops of the 35th Quang Tri Provincial Regular Company had shot down the helicopter on January 8th. And the officials gave the location of the shootdown, which also matched exactly the place where the Huey had gone down. Most importantly, the Viet Cong leaders announced they had captured four Americans, sending two of them on to North Vietnam.

The DIA also received another report concerning the wreckage of the chopper. According to the report, there were two bodies in the wreckage—exactly matching the two earlier reports that said four Americans had survived the crash.

While they are listed as Category 1, for some reason the men lost on the chopper that January day are not on the U.S. government's priority POW lists. In other words, the Vietnamese do not have to account for them in order to get credit for "resolving" the POW issue.

A Curious "Escape"

According to the DIA, Army officer Richard Lee Bowers "died in escape on capture day" on March 24, 1969. But the DIA has yet to explain how a man who died the day he was captured was seen alive two days later. According to a Vietnamese eyewitness, a motorized sampan stopped along the bank of the Rach Ngan Dua River two days after the battle in which Bowers was captured. The four Viet Cong guards, all armed with AK-47s, asked whether it was safe to go ahead.

"Source provided the escorting party with the necessary information and was able to observe the captured Americans during this time. During this time source learned the circumstances of capture of the U.S. POWs," Army intelligence reported.

Since it was about 3 a.m., the source had a hard time seeing the Americans, who were lying in the bottom of the boat, partially camouflaged by branches. The source could see that the patches had been ripped from their uniforms, making it harder for any witnesses to report their identities to U.S. officials. Despite those limitations, the source was able to provide descriptions of the U.S. POWs, one of whom resembled Bowers. Combined with the details of his capture, the Department of the Army concluded the man was probably Bowers, on his way to the U-Minh Forest.[3] That forest, known in Vietnamese as the "forest of darkness," was a communist stronghold. According to later U.S. intelligence records, a number of American POWs were kept in the U-Minh and never returned at the end of the war. But Bowers, listed as Category 1, was killed on the day of his escape, the Pentagon says, so no one's looking for him there.

Teach Or Die

At the end of the Vietnam War, the communists were forcing an American captain, "under threat of death," to teach them how to use a 105 mm howitzer, Army intelligence reported in July 1973. At the same Vietnamese POW camp near Ba-To were U.S. sergeants, who were forced to grow their own food. While the Army believed it knew the identity of the American captain, it refuses to this day to release his name.[4] There is no way to tell into what category this hapless captain was placed or whether the U.S. government is doing enough to resolve his case—and the Pentagon is keeping it that way.

The Likable Harry Brown

Harry Willis Brown, an Army enlisted man, was captured in February 1968. That October, a communist soldier saw a black POW in tattered fatigues being held at Commo-Liaison Station T-13, a way station on the Ho Chi Minh trail to North Vietnam. "The PW had a very jovial personality, and source felt it would be easy for him to win sympathy. Source almost positively identified him as Harry W. Brown."

The source learned that Brown had been at the station for about a day and was being treated well. "Because of his friendly personality, the PW was able to win the friendship of the guards.... He was allowed to go fishing and swimming in a nearby stream with source. The PW had an Air Vietnam handbag in which he carried cigarettes, cigarette lighter, safety razor and hammock," the Pentagon reported.

In August 1970, a second communist soldier and his unit were given a 20-minute tour of a North Vietnamese POW camp in the Nam Dan District of North Vietnam's Nghe An Province. A camp guard told the source that about 40 American POWs were in the camp. The Americans were well fed and could play ping pong with each other. The source actually saw four of the men, two of whom he identified as marine Doyle Sprick and the friendly Harry Brown, who had apparently made it all the way to a POW camp in North Vietnam.[5]

But neither Brown nor Sprick ever made it back to the U.S. According to the DIA, Brown is category 4, meaning that there's no indication that he was captured.

The Separate System

One of the reasons Harry Brown was probably not declared a POW by the Pentagon is that he was not seen in an "accepted" POW camp. As noted earlier, the DIA declares there is "no evidence" that Hanoi established a separate system of POW camps from which no U.S. prisoners returned.

U.S. POWs were reported in camps, both "accepted" and "suspected," across Indochina. The camps were closely watched by American intelligence, which obtained detailed reports on many of the facilities. But at the end of the war, Hanoi only returned POWs from a handful of those prisons. And those POWs didn't know anything about POWs in the other camps.

That meant Vietnam had organized a "separate" POW system from which no Americans returned, the DIA's former director, Eugene Tighe, and former deputy director, Jerry Tuttle, have now concluded. After all, during Korea the communists established just such a system in order to retain U.S. POWs, and intelligence received during Vietnam indicated that Hanoi employed the same strategy.

But at the end of the Vietnam War, that conclusion was unacceptable to the Pentagon, which had been told by President Nixon that "all" U.S. POWs had come home. So the DIA officially declared that there really must not have been U.S. POWs in those other prisons after all. The Pentagon's "evidence" for denying the existence of a separate system: no U.S. POWs returned from Vietnam brought back evidence of the other camps. The DIA has stuck with that claim ever since.

But the Pentagon denials are not just inaccurate (as discussed later, returning U.S. POWs *did* have evidence of a separate system); they are also indicative of grossly circular reasoning. If Vietnam had created a separate and secret system, its very purpose would have been to hide some POWs from U.S. intelligence and other Americans who were to be returned at the end of the war. If the system worked, returning POWs would be expected to know little or nothing about the separate system.

Indeed, at least three former Vietnamese officials (the Mortician and two others whose identities must be safeguarded), along with a top Warsaw Pact defector (former Czech General Major Jan Sejna, whose evidence is discussed later), say the entire Vietnamese POW system was designed from the very beginning with stringent counter-intelligence safeguards to ensure that returning U.S. POWs would be ignorant of the separate system and the other Americans it held.

Those communist experts say American prisoners were immediately evaluated—often during transit immediately after capture—to determine in which system they should be placed. As the DIA report on the Mortician noted: selected U.S. POWs were "segregated," "held in solitary confinement," and "exploited for technical information."

Consolidation or Disperal?

The Pentagon's main support for denying a separate system rests on the claim that all U.S. POWs were consolidated around Hanoi after 1970, following an unsuccessful U.S. effort to rescue prisoners at the outlying Son Tay POW camp.

Returned POW Admiral James Stockdale repeated the official line during testimony to the Senate POW committee. "It was the Son Tay Raid of November 1970 that prompted the North Vietnamese to bring them all—all of these chickens out in the satellite camps back, all back to the Hoala [sic] Prison [Hanoi Hilton]," testified Stockdale.

But even after November 1970, U.S. POWs were reported in camps far outside Hanoi. That's because Hanoi did not consolidate American POWs after Son Tay. Instead, Vietnam *dispersed* its prized captives.

That was confirmed during a 1977 Paris meeting between a U.S. POW activist and Vietnamese diplomat Do Thanh. The diplomat stated flat out: "At the time of the Son Tay Raid, prisoners were widely *dispersed* in small numbers. . . . "[6]

In 1979, Vietnamese defector Le Dinh confirmed that American POWs had been dispersed after the Son Tay Raid. He said U.S. POWs were ultimately held in 12 prisons, and 700 were never returned.[7]

Finally, in his now famous but then secret September 1972 speech to the Vietnamese Politburo (later found in the Soviet archives), Vietnamese General Lieutenant Tran Van Quang said: "American POWs are held in 11 prisons. . . . " The General noted that Hanoi had admitted holding only 368 POWs (authors' note: those in Stockdale's Hanoi system).

"[T]he rest [those in the separate system] are not acknowledged," the General added.

The 1972 speech, discussed in detail later, stated flatly that Hanoi was secretly holding hundreds of POWs who were never returned to the U.S. It clearly corroborated the existence of a separate POW system. But when the speech was publicly released in 1993, Hanoi and the U.S. attempted to debunk it with a newly "found" Vietnamese POW ledger that "accounted" for all U.S. POWs held in North Vietnam.

But an internal DIA report—leaked to the authors by a Pentagon POW expert disgusted with the DIA's incompetence—noted: "Log entries are generally chronological, but not in strict shootdown order. It appears the entries were made upon the individual's entry into *the Hanoi area prison system* and subsequent interrogation." [authors' emphasis][8]

In other words, some missing Americans were absent from the ledger, which only covered the Hanoi prison system, anyway. And this was the Pentagon's "evidence" that there was no separate prison system.

In reality, as the 1972 speech shows, Hanoi held American POWs in separate, secret POW camps from which no one ever returned. "The government of the United States is aware of this, but they don't know the exact number of POWs," the general noted.

One mysterious POW camp was at North Vietnam's Ba Vi Mountain, where French prisoners had earlier been held. The Pentagon refused to tell the authors whether any U.S. POWs returned from the camp, which is not on even one declassified list of "accepted" POW camps. But declassified POW records indicate a number of Americans were held there during and after the Vietnam War.

Indeed, the famous Son Tay Raid to liberate U.S. POWs in 1970 was started to rescue POWs from Ba Vi, according to recently declassified Pentagon documents. Air Force intelligence had "definitely" identified five U.S. prisoners working as woodcutters on the mountain. When the Air Force asked permission to rescue the men, the Pentagon decided to attempt a much larger operation targeted at the nearby Son Tay Camp.

"Why go after the 5 when we could go after and liberate those two camps? Let's go . . . after Son Tay," said Brigadier General Donald D. Blackburn USA (Ret.), then the Defense Secretary's Special Assistant for Counterinsurgency and Special Actions.[9]

But by the time the U.S. rescue force reached Son Tay, all the POWs were gone, shipped to Hanoi. But the Pentagon isn't saying what happened to the prisoners reported at Ba Vi, who may have included Air Force officers Donald Downing and Paul Raymond. "U.S. intelligence received a report from an ethnic Khmer in December 1971 of the sighting of a U.S. POW in November 1970 at a prison . . . near Ba Vi Mountain. He identified one of the POWs as similar to Captain Downing."[10]

Downing never came home. The name of his co-pilot, Paul Raymond, was passed by word of mouth or tap code in the prison system. But the DIA wrote off Raymond because—officially at least—there was no evidence he or Downing had survived their incident.

But perhaps both of them did survive—in Ba Vi. In August 1976, a North Vietnamese captain allegedly saw a truck carrying U.S. POWs still held at the Ba Vi prison.[11]

What About the Amputees?

Another topic that strains the credulity of the stories told by the Pentagon and the Vietnamese is that of amputees. In any war, there are amputees. But the Pentagon confirmed in 1993 that no full amputees returned from Vietnamese prison camps. Their absence shocked U.S. intelligence experts, who knew that many men lost limbs after ejecting from jet aircraft. The experts also knew that Hanoi had the medical equipment to perform necessary amputations and a policy of keeping U.S. POWs alive.

So what happened to the U.S. amputees? The answer lies in intelligence reports and long-time North Vietnamese policies.

Hanoi separated amputees from other wounded soldiers who managed to make it back from the battlefields of South Vietnam, according a senior U.S. POW expert. Multiple sources told U.S. intelligence during the war that many amputees were not returned to their home villages, but rather confined to special camps in order to prevent them from hurting the morale of the Vietnamese people.

Hanoi apparently decided that releasing U.S. amputees would reflect poorly on Vietnamese medical care. There is evidence, discussed later, that Vietnam sent at least one U.S. amputee to East Germany for treatment, but such a man could not be released without exposing both an East bloc-POW connection and the limitations of the Vietnamese medical system.

"It's policy not to provide any information that is embarrassing. So those who may have suffered injuries from unskilled [Vietnamese] medical treatment would be kept," the authors were told by Le Quang Khai, a defector from the Vietnamese Foreign Ministry.

A one-armed U.S. POW resembling Army Captain Lawrence Booth was reported in Cambodia during 1971, but Booth never came home and has since been declared dead. Some U.S. amputees were reportedly kept at a special POW camp in Dong Anh, about 20 kilometers north of Hanoi; in 1971, U.S. intelligence issued a report describing a heavily guarded POW camp, surrounded by brick walls and barbed wire fences, in the town.

"There are about 50 US PWs at the camp; most of them are pilots. Three of them have each lost a leg because of AA [anti-aircraft] fire," the report said. Other prisoners had been seriously injured when they were attacked by local villagers during and perhaps after their capture—also "embarrassing" for the Vietnamese, who claimed they treated their POWs well.[12]

After the war, there were additional sightings of American amputees imprisoned in Vietnam. For example, Bobby Garwood reported seeing an American POW with only one leg outside Yen Bai during 1976. Another source reported two U.S. amputee POWs outside Pleiku after the war.

"No Evidence"

In March 1973, a Laotian communist tried to buy supplies with traveller's checks signed by Air Force officer Richard Elzinga; Elzinga had been shot down over Laos three years before. Despite that evidence that communist forces had access to Elzinga or his body, the Pentagon lists him as "Category 3," meaning the enemy has "doubtful knowledge" of him. Pilot Wallace Hynds Jr. is in the same category, even though the Vietnamese had his I.D. card.

U.S. investigators learned the Vietnamese had aviator Robert Mack Brown's I.D. card, but kept him in "Category 4," indicating there was no indication whether the enemy knew what happened to him. The I.D. card of Air Force Officer John Robert Burns was displayed in a Laotian museum, but officially the U.S. only "suspected" the enemy knew his fate. The Vietnamese said they captured an American airman of E-6 rank on December 19, 1972. Charlie Poole was the only such E-6 lost on that day, but the Pentagon lists Hanoi's knowledge of his fate as "suspect."[13]

A heavily censored DIA document concerns information believed true about reported U.S. POWs fitting the description of soldiers Wayne Allen and Francis Graziosi. But officially, the Pentagon lists the men as "Category 4," meaning there's no evidence the men were captured.[14]

At last report, aviator Bruce Walker was about to be captured by North Vietnamese troops after evading them for 11 days. His I.D. card later appeared in Vietnamese hands, but the Pentagon only "suspects" Hanoi of knowing his fate. On and on it goes, with the U.S. constantly reducing expectations about the extent of Hanoi's knowledge and responsibility concerning missing Americans. In these cases and others, the Pentagon knows Vietnam had a POW or his body, but claims publicly it only "suspects" Hanoi of having information on his fate.

In some cases, the Pentagon has gone to great lengths to explain away the possibility that certain men were captured. Three different POWs reported seeing the name "Ross" on the wall of a Vietnamese POW camp. No known POW had the last name of "Ross." So some Air Force experts correlated the name to aviator Joseph Ross, who was presumed dead when his plane had gone down in North Vietnam during 1968. But the DIA claimed there was "no evidence" Ross had survived his incident. Other returnees said they had passed the name of a prisoner named "Major Thompson." When the experts said that might be downed aviator William J. Thompson, the DIA said there was no reason to think he survived his crash either. But the ironic thing is that *both Ross and Thompson were on the same plane.* What are the odds that these two names would both appear in the prison system? It's both tantalizing and horrifying to imagine they had both survived and tried to pass word of their existence, confident that at least one of them would succeed in getting word out, thinking that that would be enough to prompt the U.S. to demand their return.[15]

Green Beret Jerry "Mad Dog" Shriver was last seen surrounded by the enemy in the aftermath of a classified mission in Cambodia. An enemy leader shouted, "Don't kill the prisoner. Just grab him." Then U.S. soldiers saw an communist soldier holding up what appeared to be Shriver's weapon. When American forces later returned to the battlefield, they found the bodies of other men lost in the engagement, but Shriver was nowhere to be seen.

The next information on his fate came from returned POW Norris Charles, a "human memory bank" who memorized the names of Americans in the Vietnamese prison system. "Charles seems positive this man is a POW," the Air Force reported in 1973. But again, the DIA says there's "no evidence" Shriver was captured.

When his aircraft was hit by fire from an enemy MIG fighter, Air Force officer Burris Begley radioed that he was ejecting. Later, the name "Begley" was seen scratched on the floor of an interrogation room at the Hanoi Hilton. But the Pentagon says "there is no indication" Begley survived his incident.[16]

It seems likely that Begley had a fleeting chance to leave evidence of his survival. And it has been officially ignored.

PART III

Ransom Negotiations

1964-1973

Chapter 7

Hiding From History

*"What has happened to this country that a Congressional Com-
mittee would inquire whether any American official of whatever
administration would fail to move heaven and earth to fight for
the release of American POWs and for an accounting of the
missing? There is no excuse, two decades after the fact, for anyone
to imply that the last five Presidents from both parties, their
White House staffs, Secretaries of State and Defense, and career
diplomatic and military services either knowingly or negligently
failed to do everything they could to recover and identify all of
our prisoners and MIAs."*
—Henry A. Kissinger, 1992

Henry Kissinger and Richard Nixon want you to take them at
their word. They want you to believe they did everything possible
to recover all of America's POWs from Southeast Asia. But as of
this writing, more than 20 years after the Vietnam War officially
ended, both Kissinger and Nixon are ensuring that the whole
truth about their actions remain hidden.

When the Senate Select Committee on POW/MIAs asked for
full disclosure of the historical record, both men declined. Nixon
refused to release a Watergate tape, particularly one of a series
believed to contain important information on his
administration's POW/MIA policies. Kissinger, with the help of
former associates such as Brent Scowcroft, then in the Bush
Administration, saw to it that transcripts of his 1973 negotiations
remain censored.

Rather than fight for the whole truth, the Senate Committee
chose to roll over in what Capitol Hill insiders euphemistically
call "bipartisan support for executive privilege." Indeed, Kissinger received special access to the Senate's final POW report
before it was published, then ensured it contained only limited
criticism of the Nixon Administration actions.

The hard work by Kissinger and Nixon, along with their Senate supporters, guarantee that the full truth about POW negotiations during the Vietnam War will not be known for some time, if ever. But enough of the truth has slipped past the Washington Old Boys network to draw some conclusions.

The Price of Withdrawal

From the earliest years of U.S.-Vietnamese negotiations, the only real issue was how, not whether, the U.S. would pull out of Vietnam and leave Saigon to fend for itself. The other basic fact was that while the U.S. wanted to withdraw with as few entanglements as possible, Hanoi wanted reparations for the damage America had inflicted on Vietnam. As Vernon Walters, a senior soldier-diplomat in the Nixon Administration, later put it: "Reparations were *sine qua non* for peace, [for the] return [of] the prisoners, for everything."

The main bargaining leverage Hanoi had was U.S. POWs, and from almost the beginning North Vietnam made it clear that the U.S. would have to pay for its prisoners. Hanoi also hoped to use its American captives for a second purpose—to win concessions for its allies in Laos and Cambodia.

Accurate Predictions

During the war, Vietnam occupied much of Laos and essentially directed that nation's Pathet Lao communists. Hanoi also controlled large areas of Cambodia and retained significant influence over certain factions of Cambodia's communist movement. In later years, Hanoi would use its allies to play a sort of shell game with U.S. prisoners. While Vietnamese troops held U.S. POWs in Cambodia and Laos, Hanoi could tell the U.S. that there were no American prisoners "in Vietnam." In turn, Lao and Cambodian officials could say there were no Americans under their "control." Indeed, at the Paris Peace Talks that settled the war, the Laotian and Cambodian communist movements—which both had U.S. POWs on their territory—were not even represented.

The intermingled issues of POWs, aid and diplomacy were hellishly complicated. But in a war that clouded the judgment of some of the finest minds in the American foreign policy establishment, one strategic projection on the issue has stood the test of time. It is an obscure 1969 study by a former State Department official named Anita Lauve, then working for the Rand Corporation. The U.S. government had commissioned the quasi-official think-tank to write a paper outlining the likely role of the POW issue in negotiations to end the Vietnam War. Lauve, an old Indochina hand, was given the job.

As of this writing, her study is still kept partially classified by the Pentagon. An outraged member of the U.S. government leaked the full report to the authors, who soon realized why members of the executive branch from both parties have for the last twenty-five years wanted to hide its contents from the American people. It revealed an explosive truth.

In 1968 (and again in 1969 in a revised report), Lauve predicted, with remarkable prescience, how Hanoi would attempt to use American POWs to win financial aid and diplomatic concessions from the U.S. She foresaw that America would have to pay for its prisoners and recommended the best way to go about this. Perhaps more importantly, she stressed that the Indochinese communists would not settle for mere promises of financial aid in return for POWs. If the U.S. really wanted to recover its fighting men, then Washington would have to follow through on any pledges made to Hanoi.

The problem was, when the Vietnam War ended in 1973, the United States executive branch was unable, and perhaps unwilling, to back up its promises. Certainly the U.S. Treasury held enough cash to purchase the POWs, for whom Hanoi wanted several billion dollars. But it was political capital that the Nixon Administration lacked. Heading into the Watergate crisis, Nixon and his advisors believed it too expensive politically to tell the truth about the Paris negotiations and the secret wars in Laos and Cambodia. Nixon and Kissinger even concealed from Congress the fact that they had promised specific amounts of aid to Hanoi.

In the end, rather than pay for unrepatriated U.S. POWs, the Nixon Administration chose to deny their existence.

A Firm Linkage Between Money and POWs

To this day, U.S. officials refuse to admit firm linkage between the identification and release of POWs and U.S. aid to Vietnam. The historical record proves otherwise. As you read the pages in the following chapters of this book, bear in mind the following conclusions of the 1969 Rand study:

- In the actual release of prisoners, they [the Vietnamese] will be guided by political objectives rather than by the terms of agreements.

- With respect to American prisoners in Communist custody, the DRV [North Vietnam], the Viet Cong, and the Pathet Lao will, in all probability, insist on negotiating separately and directly with the United States for their release. The price will be high, and will very likely include political and military concessions and also the payment of reparations or ransom to the DRV.

- A quid pro quo that the DRV is likely to demand—and one that the United States may want to consider accepting—is the payment of 'reparations' to North Vietnam in exchange for U.S. prisoners.

- The United States could avoid giving the appearance of paying reparations or ransom money if it could reach its agreement with the DRV in private, and if all funds paid out to Hanoi were then publicly labeled part of the U.S. contribution to a postwar recovery program.

- No matter what terms are agreed upon, it would be unduly optimistic to believe that the DRV and the Viet Cong will release all U.S. prisoners immediately after conclusion of an agreement in the expectation that the United States will meet its military, political or monetary commitments. More likely, they will insist on awaiting concrete evidence of U.S. concessions before releasing the majority of American prisoners, and will retain some of them until all U.S. commitments have been fulfilled.

The U.S. never did fulfill its commitments under the Paris Peace Treaty. Of course, neither did the North Vietnamese. But Hanoi never lied about the implicit quid pro quo on the prisoners. For years after the war, Vietnamese officials openly linked a full accounting of U.S. POW/MIAs to payment of the U.S. aid money promised but never delivered by the Nixon Administration. In 1977, Vietnam even rejected a U.S. offer which would, in effect, have dropped the POW issue and given Hanoi unconditional diplomatic recognition. Vietnam said there could be no deal until it got its money from America. During the 1980s, when the U.S. began focusing on the recovery of POWs, Hanoi again began linking them to money.

For Money, Mainly

In contrast to Hanoi's honesty, U.S. officials actively attempted to rewrite the historical record, obscuring Vietnam's motive in keeping American prisoners. Some American POWs were kept by Vietnam for reasons unrelated to the Paris Peace talks—reasons including their technical skills, knowledge of communist secrets and perhaps even for their value as hostages to trade for communist POWs held by Saigon and for diplomatic concessions from the U.S.

But the fate of most U.S. servicemen was linked to ransom. The truth is, like so many other things in life, the POW issue really began with a fight over money.

Chapter 8

1965-1967: Hostages of War

In 1965, the United States Air Force began to rain steel and fire on North Vietnam during an operation dubbed "Rolling Thunder." Along with the bombs came U.S. airmen parachuting from their stricken aircraft. These were not the first U.S. POWs of the Vietnam War; other Americans had been captured during earlier airstrikes and in ground combat across Southeast Asia. But things had changed by 1965. "Rolling Thunder" was considered an "offensive" operation, as opposed to earlier "defensive" airstrikes launched in retaliation for communist attacks. Large numbers of U.S. ground troops were arriving in South Vietnam. And the Soviets had taken a new hard line in support of their communist allies in Hanoi. In 1965, the U.S. and North Vietnam had begun to settle down for a long war.

By December 1965, the North Vietnamese were floating the idea of holding "war crimes" trials for the Americans shot down while bombing North Vietnam. Since the U.S. had not declared war on North Vietnam, Hanoi declared, the men captured while bombing Vietnam were not POWs but criminals. Their trials were set to begin on or about December 20th, the fifth anniversary of the founding of the National Liberation Front of South Vietnam or Viet Cong.

A major U.S. diplomatic offensive, including dire threats of retaliation, apparently averted the first POW crisis of the war. December 20 came and went with no further overt posturing by the North Vietnamese. President Johnson temporarily stopped the bombing of Hanoi five days later, probably as a signal of conciliation.

From New York, CBS News sent a cable to Ho Chi Minh asking "whether you have decided as yet to place on trial the captive American airmen?" Ho's answer was brief: "No trial in view."

CBS pressed further: "Could you also advise us under what conditions in your opinion peace could return?" Ho's brevity disappeared: "The American government sent troops to wage barbarous war against the Vietnamese people, causing immense suffering, death, and destruction. Let the United States stop its aggression and withdraw its soldiers from Vietnam, then peace will return immediately. Greetings."

An Old Pro

The first crisis having been averted, the President tapped Ambassador at Large W. Averell Harriman to work on the POW issue. "They have pulled me into it. I've got to supervise it," Harriman told Robert F. Kennedy during a monitored telephone call on April 30, 1966.

Harriman had vast experience dealing with communists who were holding American POWs. As Ambassador to Moscow in 1944-45, he had become involved in the POW/hostage crisis at the end of World War II, when Stalin held thousands of American, British and Commonwealth POWs hostage to his political demands. Harriman had continually recommended stronger political and diplomatic measures as a counter to the growing crisis, but was overruled by President Franklin D. Roosevelt in March 1945.

Some of the World War II POWs were returned when the United States and Britain partially met Stalin's demands. But the West finally tired of Macchiavellian machinations, and the POWs were abandoned and false documents created to write off diplomatic and political failure. Harriman had also seen the bitter POW politics of the Korean War, which dragged out the conflict and left behind American prisoners in North Korea, China and Siberia.*

Now Harriman was again asked to supervise an impending POW crisis—and the prospects for success seemed even dimmer than in earlier conflicts. By 1966, Harriman had grown skeptical about America's prospects in Vietnam. Perhaps that influenced his thinking on the POW issue, leading him to recover prisoners whenever he could, fearing that at least some of those left in enemy hands at the end of the war would never return home.

---

*See James D. Sanders, Mark A. Sauter and R. Cork Kirkwood, *Soldiers of Misfortune* (Bethesda, MD 1992).

During his tenure, the United States would push hard to recover its POWs, even if it required trading them for communist prisoners or commodities. The strategy worked in the short-term, winning freedom for some Americans. But over the long-term, the U.S. was reinforcing Hanoi's belief that U.S. POWs were valuable bargaining chips.

At virtually the same moment Harriman became involved in POW matters in 1966, the Soviets quietly approached the United States about negotiating a swap of Soviet spies held in the West for American pilots shot down in Southeast Asia. Two West German lawyers with extensive experience in East-West spy trades were used by the East Germans and Soviets to make the approach.[1]

But the negotiations were cancelled when someone leaked the information to the *Sunday Observer* in London, which ran a story on July 10, 1966, under the banner of "Exchange Krogers for U.S. Airmen." Datelined Washington, D.C., the article revealed that:

> The Soviet Union, according to intelligence sources here, has offered to help to negotiate the release of American prisoners held by North Vietnam in return for the surrender of the spies Peter and Helen Kroger, now serving 20-year sentences in Britain.
>
> British and American security authorities are reported as being "vigorously opposed" to the offer and to be treating it as further proof of Soviet anxiety about information the Krogers could have revealed since they were convicted in the Portland Spy Ring case of 1961.
>
> Earlier this year Soviet authorities made persistent efforts to gain the repatriation of the Krogers in return for the release of Gerald Brooke, the British college lecturer, who was sentenced to five years for anti-Soviet activities in 1965. These efforts were officially rejected by the British government.
>
> In its second bid for the Krogers' release the Soviet Union has undoubtedly succeeded in touching a sensitive spot. The pictures issued this week of American pilots being paraded through the streets of Hanoi—and subsequent demands on Hanoi radio for their execution—have aroused a national anxiety as to the fate of American prisoners-of-war in North Vietnam.

But the fact that intelligence officials chose to reveal the latest Soviet offer makes it unlikely that it will be taken any further.

The United States has always had a special interest in the Krogers. Born US citizens under their real names of Morris Cohen and Lona Petka, both lived in America until 1950.

The FBI believes they were involved in the Rosenberg spy ring and that they worked directly for Colonel Abel, the Soviet master spy captured in 1957 and exchanged for Francis Gary Powers, the U-2 pilot, in 1962.

In response to the leaked story, the State Department instructed the London Embassy on how to respond to press inquiries about the proposed swap: "The Soviets have made no such proposal to us. Matter of disposition of the Krogers is British decision since they are in British custody."[2]

Either American or British intelligence had leaked the Soviet approach in order to deal a death blow any political deal in the works. It was only a temporary setback for the Soviets, however. They would return in a few years with a more attractive offer.

1966: Establishing a Market for POWs

In May 1966, Harriman moved to establish a mechanism for buying and swapping POWs. Although the U.S. had already unsuccessfully offered "cash payments" to the communists in return for at least one captured American (diplomat Gustav Hertz), Harriman decided to try again with the most accessible enemy force—the Viet Cong, whose forces roamed within easy driving distance of Saigon.

He dispatched a secret telegram to the London and Saigon embassies suggesting that Australian journalist Wilfred G. Burchett be approached as a possible intermediary.[3] Burchett was a boozy communist agent of influence who had helped wring confessions out of U.S. POWs in Korea and then turned to flogging the East-bloc line in Southeast Asia.

Burchett, the State Department noted, was "well known as [a] communist ideologue and propagandist currently residing in Pnomh Penh who has in the past visited Viet Cong areas, including camps where Americans [were] held captive. We have no reason to think Burchett [is] anything less than fully sympathetic with Viet Cong cause. However [we] believe it may be worth a discreet try to see if he would be willing to approach VC in attempt to obtain release of some or all Americans held by VC. We recognize VC might want something in return. It would be up to intermediary, such as Burchett, to find out what—for example, prisoners in exchange for material aid such as medicines."[4]

Robert Shaplen, a journalist for *New Yorker* magazine, agreed to approach Burchett for the United States government. He was briefed in Washington, D.C. and then flew to Phnom Penh, Cambodia, "carrying a personal letter from Harriman to [Cambodia's King Norodom] Sihanouk unrelated to prisoners."[5]

Shaplen contacted Burchett "with surprisingly good results. Burchett has agreed to take up the question of prisoners on humanitarian grounds. Shaplen has given him a brief note to be delivered to [Viet Cong official] Tran Buu Kiem outlining a possible deal. He is to let the Vietnamese communists know that the American Government is prepared to consider some suitable quid pro quo, e.g. the release of communist prisoners or the supply of drugs."[6]

Down to Negotiations

The note was delivered, and eventually Tran Bach Dang, communist Political Commissar of the Saigon Military Region, responded. The now-retired Major General admitted the ensuing POW negotiations in his memoirs, and details about them have been revealed by former CIA Vietnam expert Frank Snepp. Remarkably, as Pentagon POW expert Bill Bell has noted, both the DIA and Senate Committee failed to investigate the swaps. Pentagon POW officials even denied any knowledge or records of the swaps, perhaps because they are still supposed to be classified. Of course, the early prisoner negotiations provide critical background for understanding later developments in the POW scandal.*

By 1967, the Viet Cong and U.S. government were conducting informal POW negotiations. The communists wanted ten of their jailed operatives, which was unacceptable to the Thieu regime and the CIA.

---

* Many details of the prisoner swaps from the intercession of Tran Bach Dang on come from *Decent Interval* (Random House, New York, 1977) by Frank Snepp, a former CIA expert on Vietnam.

After considerable haggling, South Vietnam turned over two low-level communists, one of whom happened to be Tran Bach Dang's wife, according to Snepp. The Viet Cong reciprocated by releasing two junior U.S. POWs—marine José Agosto-Santos and soldier Luis Ortiz-Rivera. Saigon then let go two of the people on the Viet Cong's original list, plus two other communists not on the list. Along with the bonus prisoners, Washington sent a list of 10 U.S. POWs "for whom it wanted an accounting," Snepp has said.

The response was silence. Then the 1968 Tet offensive began, and both Americans and Viet Cong were too busy killing one another in cities across South Vietnam to conduct delicate POW negotiations. In early 1969, the Viet Cong again contacted the U.S. Embassy. For more than two years, communist operatives and CIA men sitting by a special phone in the embassy maintained sporadic contact. At one point, the embassy even ran ads in the *Saigon Post* newspaper to facilitate the talks.

A Rejected Offer

In October 1971, the communists suddenly released Army Sergeant John Sexton. "When the American trudged out of the jungle several miles south of the small town of Snoul, Cambodia, he carried with him a Communist request for reciprocity. In return for his [Sexton's] freedom, Dang was demanding the release of two of his senior operatives within the next three days. One of them was a Communist labor agitator named Le Van Hoai. The other was Nguyen Van Tai [a captured communist intelligence officer]," Snepp revealed.

Thieu, backed by the CIA, rejected the offer. Sexton was only a sergeant—the two Viet Cong were the senior enemy intelligence experts captured in the war. So the Viet Cong came back with a counteroffer. They would trade U.S. diplomat Douglas Ramsey, captured in 1966, for the two communist POWs. Amazingly, the U.S. turned down this offer, plus another one the next year to trade a newly captured Viet Cong official for Ramsey. The U.S. diplomat sat in his cage until Operation Homecoming, when he was released with other POWs.

"This story is not unique," Snepp has written. "On several occasions during the last years of the Vietnam war, the communists secretly offered to release various American prisoners, only to be held off by the U.S. government as it angled for 'better terms,' " Snepp said. The former CIA official noted that at least Ramsey survived to come home. Other POWs who could have been traded out, Snepp says, died in captivity. And, in a remarkable historical footnote, Bobby Garwood said under oath that he was informed by Snepp that the Viet Cong were once willing to trade him during the war—but the U.S. government didn't think he was important enough.

The important thing about all these negotiations is that they established a precedent for the bartering of POWs. In 1972 President Nixon even publicly offered to exchange ten communist prisoners for every American released. But neither side, however, got back all of its prisoners.

Although the Paris Peace Accord between the U.S. and North Vietnam was signed in 1973, no corresponding agreement was implemented between the North and South Vietnamese at the time, and both Vietnamese sides were dragging their feet about prisoner exhanges. Thus, at the same time America was demanding that the communists release all their U.S. captives, Saigon was refusing to liberate thousands of communist prisoners—including Nguyen Van Tai, the intelligence officer for whom the communists had desperately tried to engineer a swap in 1971.

The Viet Cong, increasingly dominated by their North Vietnam allies after suffering terrible losses during the 1968 Tet Offensive, needed their imprisoned cadre back in order to counterbalance Hanoi's power and fight on. Is it realistic to think the Viet Cong would release all its US POWs when they could be used later to swap for communist cadre?

Not according to Bill Bell, the Pentagon expert on Vietnamese POW policies. During secret testimony before the United States Senate, he testified that the Viet Cong probably kept U.S. POWs to swap after the war. "[A]ll of the Vietnamese prisoners were never released and I felt that the Vietnamese would always hold American prisoners if we did not release all of their prisoners," he said in a 1991 deposition.

Don't forget, according to the Pentagon, by the end of the war there was "documented information on some 40 US MIA's who were confirmed to have been captured by PRG [People's Revolutionary Government or Viet Cong] forces. These men were never repatriated as POWs, nor do their names appear on the PRG list of US DIC's [died in captivity] . . . . [there is] incontrovertible evidence of these men's capture and the PRG failure to acknowledge their existence."[7] A March 1, 1973 Pentagon report concluded that the "PW issue is the only significant leverage which they [the Viet Cong] have over the U.S. They also realize that it is a rapidly disappearing asset. They undoubtedly feel strong compulsion to use this leverage which they can."

On April 1, 1973, the Viet Cong revealed that they had not produced a full list of their POWs during the peace talks. Four days after the last American was officially released under Operation Homecoming—days after the White House declared that all American POWs were on their way home—a U.S. Army officer captured by the V.C. on November 15, 1969, walked out of the jungle. Robert Thomas White's name had not been on the PRG list of POWs handed over to the American side on January 27th when the Paris Agreement between the U.S. and North Vietnam was signed.

White's appearance may have indicated the communist belief that POW swapping could continue after Operation Homecoming. But the U.S. was apparently still not interested in trading lowly American POWs for important communist intelligence officials still in Saigon's hands. For example, the CIA reportedly believed Nguyen Van Tai, the V.C. intelligence official still being held by the South, was too valuable to release under any conditions. Snepp claims the CIA proposed a better plan to Saigon. Tai was ultimately tossed out of a plane two miles above the South China Sea.

Is it any wonder the Viet Cong kept U.S. POWs?

Trading Medicine for POWs

While sometimes successful, the actual direct physical exchange of prisoners was a complicated and potentially risky process. It was easier to arrange the release of POWs in exchange for commodities. Recently declassified U.S. records indicate that on at least one occasion medical supplies were given to the Viet Cong in connection with the release of U.S. civilian captives.[8]

The U.S. government considered—and may have employed—similar arrangements to free captured servicemen. A senior U.S. official recommended such a trade with the Laotian communists, against whom the U.S. was waging a secret war.

According to Frank Sieverts, Special Assistant to the Under Secretary of State for POW Affairs: "An approach to the PL [Pathet Lao communists] could take the form of implying that the

Americans fell into their hands by accident, not in connection with actions in or against Laos. . . . Our offer would suggest that we are willing to compensate generously for the 'mistake' by providing medical supplies or other form of 'kumshaw' [considerations] in exchange for release of our personnel. We are soliciting Ambassador [William] Sullivan's views on this subject."[9]

Sullivan, U.S. representative to Laos, was skeptical of the chances for success of a ransom effort in Laos, where many areas were occupied by the North Vietnamese Army, which also exercised control over the Pathet Lao. Sullivan cabled back to the State Department: "Doubt feasibility of ransom of prisoners. PL taking increasingly hard line."[10]

But Sieverts thought even Hanoi might be amenable to a medicine-for-POWs deal. He sent a secret telegram to Harriman suggesting that a non-government contact be established with the DRV [Democratic Republic of Vietnam or North Vietnam]: "It is not unlikely that the terms of release would involve a trade of medical supplies for men. We know that the DRV is spending difficult-to-obtain hard currencies to purchase medical supplies, and we have some intelligence reports that they are interested in a 'Castro-type deal.' The Administration could best handle such a deal in the same way the Cuban ransom [for U.S.-backed guerillas captured by Castro] was handled—i.e. without obvious Government involvement, but through hard-to-detect Government financing in the form of generous tax deductions for the companies 'donating' medical supplies."[11]

But Sieverts also noted the downside of bringing in private parties to negotiate with Hanoi: "[W]e might have a hard time controlling the amount of medical supplies to be traded. The DRV could name a figure, and public pressure could make haggling, or refusal, difficult. We have asked the Defense Department and CIA to give us their estimates of how much damage would be done to our war effort by giving the DRV various amounts of medical supplies. If we decide to proceed with some such approach, the question remains how it should be handled. In our view there should be as little governmental involvement as possible, both to maintain our freedom to respond negatively to the DRV terms and to avoid the risk of losing the advantages of a private approach by some form of disclosure of the U.S. involvement."[12]

As the U.S. considered and employed various trades to win freedom for its POWs, apparently no one inside the American government questioned or analyzed the obvious problem associated with such deals. Once a reward, especially a monetary reward, was placed on the table for the return of American POWs, ransom became a legitimate issue in any future negotiation. This was a point not missed by the North Vietnamese, Viet Cong, or the Pathet Lao.

It Pays to Advertise

On December 2, 1966, USAF Captain Robert R. Gregory and Lieutenant Leroy Stutz, flying an RF4C, were shot down near Hanoi. Both were captured and transported to Hanoi in the same vehicle. Gregory was unconscious during the entire trip and was separated from Stutz once they reached Hanoi.[13]

Gregory was never seen again, and even though his buddy could prove that Gregory was captured, the North Vietnamese did not admit holding him, dead or alive. This type of case, where the North Vietnamese clearly held an American and could easily account for him, was common as the war wore on. An American government official would later say, "If you don't advertise, you can't sell." The North Vietnamese were not shy about advertising that they were holding POWs not on the official lists.

The Soviets Test the Market

In early 1967, at the same time Harriman was initiating POW swaps in Southeast Asia, the Soviets quietly approached the United States about negotiating a trade of Soviet spies held in Britain for American pilots shot down in Southeast Asia.

A West Berlin lawyer, Herr Stange, "who has long been active in East-West exchanges [of spies], told a mission officer January 25 [1967] that the GDR [East Germany] was making a new offer to get back the Soviet spies Peter and Helen Kroger. The GDR is willing in exchange, to turn over to US two wounded US fliers captured in Vietnam and currently in an East German hospital," the State Department reported in classified telegrams.[14]

Stange had discussed the offer with "a representative of the GDR State Prosecutor's Office on January 21 and 22," before approaching the U.S. During these discussions he "had learned that several—perhaps five or six—wounded US fliers were now in the hospital just outside East Berlin.[15] The two offered in exchange for the Krogers were both severely wounded." One of the POWs had lost both legs. Stange speculated that the East Germans "would be willing in the end to exchange more than two for such valuable prizes as the Krogers."[16]

An unidentified American diplomat assured Stange that the United States "wished to explore any reasonable possibility that might get our captured servicemen released," but the Krogers were controlled by the British, who would have to be involved in, and approve of, any negotiations. The U.S. also asked for the names and serial numbers of the POWs held in East Germany, but Stange did not think it would be possible to obtain this information until there had been a "reaction in principle" from the Western side. Stange "added that there was no doubt in his mind that the East Germans did in fact have the wounded US fliers."

The next day, January 27, the State Department sent a "secret-EXDIS" telegram to the Berlin Mission:

> Department wishes follow-up Stange's offer concerning release of wounded US fliers reported in REFTEL. Mission Berlin should inform Stange that we are favorably disposed to discuss his offer and that as useful first step we would be interested in obtaining names and serial numbers of the US servicemen now in East Germany of whom he spoke.[17]

The American Embassy in London was instructed to "give us your assessment of probable British attitude towards release or exchange of Krogers. Do not discuss with UK authorities for time being."[18] On January 31, a U.S. Mission Officer met with Stange's boss, East German lawyer Wolfgang Vogel, telling him that the United States wished to pursue the matter. Vogel, in turn, passed the message to his contact in the East German government (GDR), Chief State Prosecutor Streit.

At this meeting Vogel revealed that the Soviet Union was actually behind the offer to swap POWs for spies. While in Moscow negotiating for the release of West German "newspaper-woman Kischke," he was approached "by Soviet security officers" who wanted him to open negotiations once again for the Krogers.[19]

Vogel met again with GDR Chief State Prosecutor Streit on February 3. Two unidentified Soviets were also in attendance at the meeting; Vogel did not ask who they were but assumed they were "security men." They demanded that the "West must commit itself in principle to returning the Krogers before progress can be made toward freeing the captured US fliers."[20]

The Soviets "also refused to provide names and serial numbers, maintaining that this information would represent a concession in advance to the US, which did not now know for sure which of its men missing in Vietnam were actually dead and which still alive."[21] In other words, once an agreement in principle was reached to place the Krogers on the negotiating table—with the blessing of the British government, the names and serial numbers of American POWs to be offered in exchange would become a legitimate bargaining point.

Stange again advised the American diplomats that "when it got down to hard bargaining, the East would be willing to give up more than two fliers for the Krogers."

Frank Sieverts briefed the Secretary of State by written memo:

> We have no substantial evidence other than this report that captured US pilots are held anywhere other than North Vietnam. The whole effort may be no more than a further ploy by the Soviets to get back the Krogers, whom the British are most reluctant to give up.... Since the offer came through a disavowable intermediary, we cannot take a stronger line without knowing more specifically whether US pilots are in fact in East Germany, and who they may be ... we intend to ask the British whether and under what conditions the Krogers might be available for trade, and what in addition to captured US pilots the British might want to exchange.[22]

The U.S. Embassy in London was then instructed to approach the British Foreign Office about the

> offer to swap Krogers for injured U.S. pilots, noting that offer, while unofficial, appears to have East German and Soviet approval.... Embassy should emphasize that matter is unofficial and in exploratory stage. If Krogers available under any conditions, or for purposes of further discussion, HMG [Her Majesty's Government] welcome to join us in developing joint response to offer....[23]

The London Embassy responded that the two key people competent to deal with this sensitive subject were both out of London, but that the embassy would bring up the matter with them when they returned the next week.[24] One week later contact was made with the British Foreign Office.[25] About three weeks later the British government advised the United States that the Krogers were not to be put on the negotiating table. At this stage of the negotiations, the United States government graphically demonstrated that there was a true diplomatic virgin lurking within the highest levels of the State Department. The Berlin Mission was instructed to relay the following messages to the Soviets and East Germans through Stange and Vogel:

> 1. You should express concern over the fate of captured pilots, and request information about their health and welfare. You should further ask Vogel to try to arrange visit to prisoners by representative of International Committee of the Red Cross (ICRC) or other neutral organization or country. We would hope this would be permitted as act of basic humanity; 2. If sick or wounded pilots are in East Germany their repatriation to U.S. is obligation under Geneva Convention on Prisoners of War (Articles 109 and 110).[26]

With the delivery of these two naive messages, the perception of the State Department as an effective conduit of sensitive negotiations was certainly damaged; the Americans had shown themselves unable to play the game. And, in spite of one last weak attempt by the U.S. Mission, Berlin, to revive the negotiations, by June 1967 they signaled defeat—messaging the Secretary of State that "We seem to have reached an impasse in the Stange-Vogel channel. Consideration might be given to whether other ways, outside this channel, should be explored."[27]

The five or six American pilots held in East Germany were apparently never returned; no American returned from captivity had been held in the Soviet Union or East Germany.

However, in 1992 the German government released a statement that said the United States had given Vogel a "mandate" to negotiate directly with North Vietnam for an exchange of American POWs for the Krogers.[28] The deal, he said, was concluded in 1969 and the cover story apparently created was that

British professor Gerald Brooke was exchanged for the Krogers. The ever vigilant Western press failed to notice that Brooke was in the last year of his prison sentence and would have soon been released anyway, thereby ignoring *prima facie* proof that there was more to the deal than either government was admitting. The U.S. government has yet to discuss the alleged swap.

Chapter 9

1968: Getting Down to Serious Business

"The paramount and overriding goal of any and all North Viet-namese negotiations is the reunification of Vietnam under the aegis of Hanoi and the maintenance of its indisputable sovereignty. Diplomatic initiatives which infringe upon, or pose a potential danger to, this goal, are simply non-negotiable."
—Colonel William W. Tombaugh, U.S. Army, 1975 Pentagon study on Paris peace talks

By spring 1968, the future of the Vietnam War appeared clear to many observers. The Tet Offensive, while a military disaster for the communists, turned into an unintended communist propaganda bonanza. More and more Americans were being turned against the war, and President Johnson had declared he would not run for reelection.

And the U.S. had gotten another reminder of how complicated the POW issue was going to be. The government received a report from Australian intelligence that "an ex-French soldier who remained in North Vietnam at the end of the French-Indo-China war" was finally on his way home—fourteen years after the North Vietnamese assured the French they had returned all of their POWs.[1]

On May 10, 1968, U.S. and Vietnamese negotiators gathered in Paris for talks on how to end the war. After two days of haggling over procedural matters, the "first session of official conversa-tions" began.[2] The North Vietnamese opened by demanding "the unconditional cessation of the bombing and other acts of war against the DRV and thereafter discussing other problems which interest both sides."[3]

Averell Harriman, chief U.S. negotiator, stated that the Americans' objective was "to preserve the right of the SVN [South

Vietnamese] people to determine their own future without out-side interference or coercion.[4]

"We are prepared to withdraw our forces as the other side withdraws its forces in the North, stops the infiltration, and the level of violence thus subsides," Harriman concluded.

The United States' position at the negotiating table was extraordinarily weak from the outset. The U.S. had asked the North Vietnamese to negotiate. The North Vietnamese had only reluctantly agreed, and then only after setting a non-negotiable demand—the cessation of bombing by the U.S.

Further, the North Vietnamese were motivated by what they saw as a mission—the reunification of Vietnam, as agreed to in the 1954 Geneva Accords. They had historically demonstrated they were prepared to fight for generations to accomplish this goal.

But the United States failed to address this basic motivation of the North Vietnamese, much less come up with a logical plan of action designed to first bring Hanoi to the negotiating table with a willingness to compromise with the United States.

The United States even failed to produce a coherent plan for using defined military action to help Harriman force the few concessions possible from North Vietnam.

Army officer William Tombaugh, who witnessed the peace talks and then analyzed them for the Pentagon, concluded that U.S. negotiators never fully understood Hanoi's mission to reunify Vietnam at all costs. One month into the negotiations Hanoi clearly stated its motive for staying in the war. "Vietnam is one, [the] Vietnamese people are one people and no one has [the] right to divide them, any Vietnamese has [the] right to fight for his country in any part of his country," Hanoi's team declared.[5]

U.S. Money on The Table

Johnson's negotiating team sensed the U.S. could not fight its way out of the war, so it proposed buying its way out. No later than July 10, 1968, the issue of money was placed on the table. Harriman stated that "After World War II, [the] US helped its former allies, and its former enemies to rebuild Europe. The same was true in Asia. The same can be true in VN and in SE Asia if the present conflict can be ended."[6]

Of course, the money was also linked to the POW issue. An early version of the Rand Corporation's study had already predicted the POW issue would assume center stage in the negotiations, and Hanoi would demand cash for its American prisoners.

Philip Habib, former Under Secretary of State for Political Affairs, and a member of Harriman's 1968 negotiating team, remembers that "one of the first lists of negotiating points put forward by the North Vietnamese . . . bracketed the release of prisoners with what they described as 'U.S. responsibility for war damage in Vietnam' in a single numbered point."[7]

1969: Nixon's Team Takes Over

In all its dealings with the Western powers, the DRV [North Vietnam] has felt tricked, deceived and betrayed. As a consequence, Western motives, intentions and objectives are viewed with near-paranoic suspicion. There is little—if any—conviction that the pledges and promises of the West possess any validity. The arbitrary scrapping of the "solemn agreements" concluded in Paris in 1946 and Geneva in 1954 is seared into the memory of the revolutionaries who continue to occupy the Politburo seats of power . . . . The paramount and overriding goal of any and all North Vietnamese negotiations is the reunification of Vietnam under the aegis of Hanoi and the maintenance of its indisputable sovereignty. Diplomatic initiatives which infringe upon, or pose a potential danger to this goal are simply non-negotiable. —Colonel William W. Tombaugh, USA, National War College[8]

As the Nixon Administration came into power in January 1969, Averell Harriman had two "farewell" conversations with North Vietnamese negotiators Le Duc Tho and Xuan Thuy. They took the opportunity to send a message to Nixon: Hanoi would rely on "US popular impatience to end the war rather than on its own military force"; the release of prisoners of war would be tied to a formal settlement, rather than to any separate arrangement; and, while Hanoi might be ready to establish relations with Washington after a settlement was reached, they also wanted economic assistance.[9]

Le Duc Tho said the policy of "Vietnamization," or replacing U.S. troops with Vietnamese, was doomed to failure.

Le Duc Tho "asserted that [Vietnamization] was just another form of 'neocolonialism' " which would fail "because the South Vietnamese Government would fall anyhow once American forces left." Tho warned "that President Nixon should 'draw a lesson' from past experience," which had allegedly shown "that US recalcitrance in accepting Hanoi's earlier proposals had only prolonged the war without materially changing the outcome."[10]

Based on the history of the war to that date, Tho's statements were highly accurate. The North did not have to defeat the Americans on the field of battle; all that was required was that they not lose the war. The South Vietnamese government had not been able to consolidate its hold politically, and the U.S. had not attempted to develop a South Vietnamese army capable of defending the country without a massive infusion of foreign troops.

U.S. military policy under President Johnson had consisted of little more than a war of attrition—which the U.S. could not win over the long term, because it did not have the staying power to make such a war viable. Johnson was run out of office because of a failure to win, or at least end, the war by 1968. Meanwhile, anti-war forces within the United States gathered strength. Time was clearly on Hanoi's side and Le Duc Tho was merely stating what appeared on their side to be obvious.

Still Trying For at Least a Tie

But what was so obvious to the North Vietnamese was at best obscure to the National Security Council (NSC), which developed "A General Strategy and Plan of Action for Vietnam Negotiations" for the incoming Nixon team.[11] Their "first priority objectives in timing and importance" were:

> Agreed or tacit mutual withdrawal. This is fundamental, and must in the end mean that all North Vietnamese military forces now in South Vietnam, as well as political cadre and others who came from the North from 1959 on, are withdrawn all the way to North Vietnam under conditions where we are satisfied that this has take place . . . . In addition, it is equally fundamental that we achieve the withdrawal of all North Vietnamese military forces from Cambodia and the sanctuary areas of Laos, all the way to

North Vietnam, whether or not rpt [sic] not such forces can be proved to have been in South Vietnam.[12]

These were terms to be inflicted upon a thoroughly beaten enemy. Yet, when they were written, the United States government had no new strategy to apply unbearable military force, no agreement or prospect of agreement with the Soviets to stop supplying the DRV (in fact the Soviets had said precisely the opposite), and no intelligence indicators that the North was losing its will to fight.

The NSC further advised the negotiators:

> As to the pace of private talks, our posture at all times should be ready but not rpt [sic] not eager, measured and steady but not rpt [sic] not hasty. We want to make all the headway we can, and as rapidly as we can. But our chances of doing this will in fact be greater if Hanoi never gets the misleading impression that we are bargaining from weakness, under time deadlines, or subject to serious opinion pressures.[13]

So, as long as the North Vietnamese didn't read *The Washington Post*, and learn of the lack of support for the war in the U.S., the U.S. negotiators were in pretty good shape.

By 1969 U.S. domestic support for the war was plummeting. But the Nixon team had a solution for the lagging public spirit, a plan to whip up America's support for the war in Southeast Asia. Early in the war, U.S. officials had downplayed evidence that Hanoi was brutalizing its American captives. The U.S. feared angering North Vietnam and hardening its bargaining position. But in May 1969 the American government reversed its strategy, launching the "Go Public" campaign to highlight Hanoi's mistreatment of American POWs. Over the next two years, carefully orchestrated public demonstrations and Congressional hearings pushed the POW issue to the forefront of the U.S. agenda in Vietnam. The wives and children of the missing provided new inspiration to the American people, additional and highly emotional reasons to punish the enemy.

The "Go Public" strategy did have a downside, however. By raising the profile of the POWs, by transforming their safe return into a central objective of the war effort, the Nixon Administration made the men much more valuable as bargaining chips for Hanoi. After a time, some POW relatives and peace activists began to see the POWs as more important than the original, and by now hazy, reasons for the war. Some families even demanded a unilateral U.S. withdrawal in exchange for the prisoners.

Of course, in reality the Nixon Administration perceived more important goals than the return of the POWs. There was no way, at least not yet, that America would abandon South Vietnam just for a few hundred U.S. prisoners.

But the Nixon team had thought ahead. Along with propaganda themes demonizing the Vietnamese for their brutal treatment of POWs, the public U.S. stance was that the return of prisoners was a "humanitarian issue."

POWs Cost Money

While the National Security Council seemed hopelessly and unrealistically optimistic in the list of objectives it provided negotiatiators, other attitudes abounded.

In private, U.S. planners knew full well that the POWs were and had always been linked to broader issues. The Rand Corporation's upgraded 1969 study *Prisoners of War In Indochina*[14] inserted some modest realism into the information base available to the American negotiators. Again, the key points were:

- The North Vietnamese and the Viet Cong will try to avoid submitting complete nominal lists of prisoners.
- In the actual release of prisoners, they will be guided by political objectives rather than by the terms of agreements.
- With respect to American prisoners in Communist custody, the DRV, the Viet Cong, and the Pathet Lao will, in all probability, insist on negotiating separately and directly with the United States for their release. The price will be high, and will very likely include political and military concessions and also the payment of reparations or ransom to the DRV.
- A quid pro quo that the DRV is likely to demand—and one that the United States may want to consider accepting—is the payment of "reparations" to North Vietnam in exchange for U.S. prisoners.
- The United States could avoid giving the appearance of paying reparations or ransom money if it could reach

its agreement with the DRV in private, and if all funds paid out to Hanoi were then publicly labeled part of the U.S. contribution to a postwar recovery program.[15]

- No matter what terms are agreed upon, it would be unduly optimistic to believe that the DRV and the VC will release all U.S. prisoners immediately after conclusion of an agreement in the expectation that the United States will meet its military, political or monetary commitments. More likely, they will insist on awaiting concrete evidence of U.S. concessions before releasing the majority of American prisoners, and *will retain some of them until all U.S. commitments have been fulfilled.* [authors' emphasis][16]

The 1969 report accurately predicted communist actions four years in the future.

Henry Cabot Lodge, head of the U.S. negotiating team in Paris under the Nixon Administration, soon recognized the accuracy of the Rand study. After several months of negotiations, he sent word to the State Department: "I surmise that they [DRV] may want a price for our men. We should, therefore, try to find out the price and to advance the timing as far as possible. We owe it to our men who are held by the enemy to do no less—to leave no stone unturned."[17]

Lodge requested permission to approach the DRV negotiators with the following: "Although the United States cannot consider the payment of reparations, which would be thoroughly inappropriate . . . the USG[overnment] would be willing to consider offering an appropriate amount of goods (e.g., a bulldozer or tractor, or other object of material value, per prisoner) in return for the early release of American prisoners."[18] The American Embassy in Saigon saw Lodge's request and responded:

> As for the idea of offering to ransom prisoners, we think it would be a serious mistake. We have intelligence that Hanoi intends to use our prisoners to try to extract concessions from us, whether in the form of ransom, reparations, or concessions on other negotiations issues . . . the other side can be expected to delay release of our prisoners until late in the negotiation/settlement process in order to extract the maximum concessions from us in return for such release. It seems to us, therefore, that the price demanded by them

for release of our prisoners will depend on their assessment of what the traffic will bear. To make a ransom offer at this time would therefore not make the other side more willing to release prisoners but would cause them to raise the price and would carry the grave risk of delaying rather than accelerating release of prisoners.[19]

The U.S. decided to put off the negotiation of specific POW ransoms with Vietnam and keep pushing for a better settlement on the issue of withdrawal from South Vietnam.

Chapter 10

1969: Arranging An Elegant Bug-Out

In August 1969, National Security Advisor Henry Kissinger arrived in Paris to begin three years of secret, top-level negotiations separate from the official publicly conducted peace talks, which thus far had consisted mostly of dueling propaganda statements. Kissinger immediately went to work on the top American priority, mutual withdrawal. The Johnson Administration's proposal had been for the North Vietnamese to begin withdrawing all of its forces back to North Vietnam; then, six months later, the United States would begin to withdraw. This proposal was changed by Kissinger to one of mutual withdrawal with the U.S. leaving no forces in the South.

This too was unacceptable to Hanoi. At an early secret session "Xuan Thuy launched into a forty-five minute monologue recounting the Vietnamese struggle against centuries of outside aggressors. Each had withdrawn. The United States would have to do the same, unconditionally and unilaterally."[1]

The DRV had made it clear from the beginning that as far as they were concerned there was only one Vietnam. The Geneva Accords of 1954 had provided for a two-year division of Vietnam, and a temporary DMZ at the 17th parallel. Therefore, according to DRV logic, the concept of a mutual withdrawal had no basis—only the United States should have to withdraw.

In August, Kissinger "issued an unveiled warning: if there was no progress by November, then the U.S. would have to 'consider steps of grave consequence.' " Nixon passed the same threat to the Soviet Union through President Nicolae Ceausescu of Romania.[2]

Now that the threat had been made, Kissinger met with a group of aides to come up with a recommendation. At the first meeting he mused: "I can't believe that a fourth-rate power like North Vietnam doesn't have a breaking point."[3]

The project to find that breaking point was codenamed "Duck Hook." But while Nixon continued to threaten Hanoi up to and past the November 1st deadline, Duck Hook was cancelled. There seemed to be no truly threatening action that would not bring China into the war as an ally of the North Vietnamese. Essentially, the threat had been an idle one, and U.S. warnings of military action would no longer carry significant weight at the negotiating table.

The Retreat Begins

In effect, the first critical issue between the U.S. and North Vietnam had been settled. In the end, the U.S. would not use massive military power to subdue North Vietnam. Instead, America would attempt to prop up South Vietnam, a country North Vietnam was convinced it could defeat over time. Now only two major issues remained: the conditions of America's eventual withdrawal from the South and the return of the U.S. POWs.

By 1970 the first American troop withdrawals from Vietnam were underway as the Vietnamization of the war began in earnest. The North Vietnamese had always believed that time was on their side, and now they watched as the Americans began their exodus without even requiring concessions at the bargaining table.

In a background discussion with reporters, Kissinger claimed that Vietnamization could lead to a negotiated settlement, but only if the South gained strength equal to the departing American forces. "If, however, we withdraw at a rate that gives Hanoi the feeling that we are really just looking for an excuse to get out, then it will thwart negotiations, because they will just sit there and wait." If that happened, Kissinger continued, Vietnamization would be nothing more than "an elegant bug-out" ("bug-out" was a U.S. military term describing what happened when troops broke and ran in the face of enemy attack).[4]

North Vietnam had no problem seeing the beginning of just such an American "bug-out." "If the U.S. could not prevail with a half million troops, Le Duc Tho asked, 'how can you succeed when you let your puppet troops do the fighting?' "[5]

With that simple and logical statement on the table, the DRV began a negotiating "sitzkrieg" (from the German term for the period during World War I when there was no action—a sitting war.") During talks in March and April 1970, Kissinger offered timetables for the mutual withdrawal of U.S. and North Vietnamese troops. Le Duc Tho rejected all offers and told Kissinger no further meetings were necessary until the United States changed its position. The talks broke down.

The POW Card

Hanoi now knew that America had not only decided to avoid an all-out war against the North, but also planned on substantial disengagement of troops in South Vietnam. That was certainly good for Hanoi, but it caused one problem. If the U.S. was prepared to pull ground troops out of Vietnam, what leverage did Hanoi have to force America to remain engaged in Southeast Asia and repair the damage it had already inflicted on the North?

The answer was obvious. America could not turn its back on Indochina until it recovered its POWs. Shortly after the latest negotiations broke down, Hanoi played its POW card. North Vietnam had been watching as the "Go Public" campaign turn U.S. POWs into national heroes and attempted to wed the POW/MIA issue to a hawkish view of the war. So the communists decided to bring their own U.S. supporters into the POW game. The DRV released a list of 335 (later increased to 339) U.S. prisoners held in North Vietnam, relaying the names through the "Committee of Liaison," an organization of anti-war activists.

"Committee and NVN have implied this may be all the prisoners in North Vietnam. USG[overnment] certain there are more," a U.S. official reported.[6] The Pentagon knew for sure that some POWs in Vietnamese hands were not on the list. One such American was Lieutenant Colonel George E. Day, who had been the cellmate of an American pilot released in 1968. When an issue was made of this particular case, the DRV quietly added Day's name to their official list of POWs. While this would never happen again, the lesson was absolutely clear to the U.S.—Hanoi was not about to expose its hole card by revealing all the POWs it held.

America got another reminder of Hanoi's real POW policies in May, 1971, when communist defector Dr. Dang Tan reported the continued retention of French POWs in North Vietnam.[7] After Senator J. William Fulbright of Arkansas heard of Dr. Tan's revelations, he asked the State Department for its analysis. The response was: " . . . we have no independent information to confirm his [Tan's] reported statement that French prisoners of war were detained against their will in North Vietnam years after the 1954 settlement."

As discussed earlier in this book, the State Department knew this was untrue, and that French Army POWs had been retained in North Vietnam. Yet this information was withheld even from senior United States legislators. The executive branch apparently wanted to keep the reality of Hanoi's POW policies from the Congress, perhaps fearful the legislators might learn the truth about the need to pay money to end the war.

Yet only shortly thereafter, Frank Sieverts, a State Department official who approved the letter to Senator Fulbright, wrote in a classified message: "The communist side implicitly linked prisoner release and reparations in the ninth point of their 'ten point' proposal of May 8, 1969. . . . If the other side [Hanoi] asks for reparations in connection with the release of US/FW [Free World] prisoners, we should state that we consider these subjects unrelated. (However, we should be prepared to listen to the other side's demands and to reconsider our position should it appear that our prisoners will not be released in the absence of reparations.)"[8]

Feeding Congress the lie that French POWs were not kept after the Indochina War, while at the same time preparing memos on paying ransom disguised as reparations, was not only wrong—it was also bad policy. The Nixon Administration was undercutting its future ability to rally Congressional support if the POWs did become hostage to the payment of ransom.

Trust Us On The Lists

But the defector Dr. Tan brought news of more immediate import. On May 10, 1971 CIA Director Richard Helms sent a message to Henry Kissinger to suppress the defector's information on U.S. prisoners, and it was not fully released until June 1993 when the CIA declassified some records on the case.

The CIA documents show that Helms informed Kissinger that Tan was "knowledgeable of North Vietnamese policies with respect to the handling of US prisoners of war." Tan had claimed the existence of about "500 or more [U.S. POWs] who were not named by NVN in Paris. These unnamed American POWs will continue to be exploited by NVN and will serve as the tool for NVN in blackmailing the USA."

While U.S. experts debated whether Hanoi could be hiding so many prisoners beyond those already admitted to be in North Vietnam, Tan insisted that "some [U.S. POWs] may never be released. . . . " He explained that Hanoi had carefully kept the names of many U.S. prisoners from escaping to the West or even other communist nations.

"By not revealing either the names or the [full] number of American POWs, the DRV will hold the upper hand in any future negotiations . . . " the CIA had noted in a 1970 report based partly on Tan's information.

By May 1971, the U.S. knew that Hanoi had a policy of secretly holding American POWs. World opinion would help force North Vietnam to release U.S. prisoners whose existence had been admitted. But the secretly held American captives were really hostages, whose release would require tough negotiations and concessions by the U.S. That is—if the U.S. was willing to pay the price.

During the Kissinger-Le Duc Tho negotiations in Paris on August 16, 1971, the DRV moved ahead on the POW front, proposing that "the two sides will produce the complete lists of military personnel and civilians captured during the war on the day an agreement is signed."[9] The North Vietnamese were asking the Americans to sign an agreement without the North Vietnamese having acknowledged all U.S. prisoners actually in its possession. The U.S. was supposed to trust Hanoi to turn over a complete and accurate list.

This was ridiculous on its face. But Kissinger accepted the proposal, and it appeared in the final agreement in substantially the same form. As Senate POW investigators later noted: "Despite the concerns expressed at the time by Secretary [of Defense] Laird and others about whether the DRV could be trusted on this issue, the U.S. side made no effort to re-open the matter in later negotiations or proposals."[10]

For almost four years the United States had mounted a publicity campaign, exploiting POW/MIA wives, pressuring the world press, posturing before Congress, all in an effort to force the North Vietnamese to account for American POWs under the rules of the Geneva Convention. In short, America had dramatically inflated the negotiating value of its POWs.

Then, in 1970, the DRV had produced a list of 339 live POWs held in North Vietnam—a list which was *prima facie* fraudulent.

And no list had been produced for POWs held in South Vietnam or Laos, despite that fact that Hanoi controlled POWs in both those countries.

This all hinted at exactly what the Rand Corporation had predicted: a hostage crisis at the end of the war. The entire situation screamed out to Kissinger that the U.S. needed POW lists far in advance of signing any agreement to ensure that Hanoi wasn't holding back U.S. prisoners for future bargaining.

By accepting the last-minute transfer of lists, Kissinger didn't just give Hanoi a chance to withhold POWs—his actions dared them to do so. In effect, Kissinger was sending the message that he would not be blackmailed by the POWs. This was Kissinger's version of "Dirty Harry," swaggering into Paris, letting Le Duc Tho know, in private of course, that those sniveling POW housewives were just a publicity front. The White House had bigger fish to fry. If the Commies wanted to withhold POWs, they could go right ahead because the White House Tough Guys would just walk away, leaving North Vietnam with no hostage bargaining leverage.[11]

Unfortunately the North Vietnamese didn't buy the Dirty Harry bluff, nor was it a credible strategy (unless, of course, Nixon and Kissinger had, by 1971, actually formulated a strategy which included abandoning POWs if necessary). Hanoi knew that public pressure in the U.S. would make it extraordinarily difficult to write off, or even bluff about writing off, American POWs.

Hanoi could demand concessions for a list of POWs held in North Vietnam, then continue negotiations related to the completeness of the list. After that, talks would have to begin on the lists of POWs held in Laos and Cambodia, whose communist movements were not even represented in Paris. This was a U.S. negotiator's nightmare, particularly when he was constantly losing bargaining leverage: American troops unilaterally withdrawn, Congressional support for the war eroding, and constant anti-war rallies in the streets of America.

Added to these problems was the lack of a coherent, credible, coordinated negotiating policy. American credibility had been destroyed when Nixon backed down after delivering several warnings to North Vietnam that they would be severely bombed if there was no progress at the Paris peace table by November 1969.

Publicly the U.S. government manipulated and maximized media coverage of the POW issue, at least as it related to the pain, suffering and efforts of the prisoners and their families. The importance of the POWs was increasing daily. But then, at the negotiating table, Kissinger suddenly downplayed their importance, walking away from full POW accountability by agreeing that POW lists could wait until a peace agreement was already signed.

The North Vietnamese would have been fools not to exploit such a contradiction between the strategy of an American negotiator and the feelings of his domestic audience.

1972: Reconstruction, Ransom or Both?

We were very careful throughout the course of the negotiation to ensure that there was never a linkage between actual release of our POWs and the actual delivery of reconstruction aid. —Henry A. Kissinger, November 2, 1992

To see what is in front of one's nose needs a constant struggle. —George Orwell, *In Front of Your Nose*

In a way, Kissinger's legalistic defense of his Paris negotiating record is accurate: No U.S. aid was actually given to the Vietnamese, and not all POWs in Hanoi's control were actually returned to the U.S. But no matter what Kissinger says today, it was clear in 1973 that Hanoi's cooperation in accounting for American POW/MIAs, including those in Laos and Cambodia, would be directly linked to the receipt of U.S. aid.

President Nixon publicly revealed the secret Kissinger-Le Duc Tho negotiations as well as the U.S. eight point peace plan on January 25, 1972. Point two declared that "The US is prepared to undertake a massive reconstruction program in Indochina of several billion dollars, in which North Vietnam could share."[12]

After more than three years of fruitless negotiations, the United States began to move toward the promise of ransom and reparations to extricate itself from the war. Just as the Rand Corporation had warned, ransom would probably have to be paid, albeit disguised as post-war reconstruction aid.

The North Vietnamese did demand payment, and they connected it to the return of the POWs. And once money was placed on the table by the weaker negotiator, in this case the United States, it could not be removed without serious consequences.

The negotiations seemed close to conclusion by the fall of 1972, but there was still one hitch. During the September 15th negotiation session Kissinger again emphasized that Hanoi was responsible for all American POWs in Southeast Asia, not just those imprisoned in North Vietnam.

This was yet another problem predicted by the Rand study. North Vietnamese negotiators had repeatedly rejected responsibility for POWs in Laos and Cambodia (even though all parties at the negotiating table knew the Vietnamese army controlled U.S. POWs in at least parts of both countries). Hanoi's leverage would certainly increase if the U.S. could be forced to negotiate separately with the Laotian and Cambodian communists, who were to varying degrees under Vietnam's control. In essence, Hanoi was trying to add two new partners on its side of the negotiating table.

State Department position papers had strongly warned against being placed in such a position. Because of this problem, it seems that Kissinger's highest priority was not the return of POWs held outside North Vietnam, but an agreement with the DRV, no matter how vague, that would satisfy those State Department position paper warnings and demonstrate to history that he had not been outmaneuvered in his negotiating.

During the September 26 secret negotiations, Kissinger addressed the problem of dealing with three communist governments separately over the issue of POWs:

> **Kissinger:** . . . There is one point about which I can leave no doubt in your mind. The President will under no circumstances sign an agreement that leaves any American prisoners anywhere in Indochina. There would be no support in America whatsoever for any arrangements that drew a distinction between American prisoners that are held in Vietnam and American prisoners that are held in Laos and Cambodia. Now the modalities by which this may be achieved or the language that is used to express it is of course subject to negotiation. . . .
> **Le Duc Tho:** So you mean by that there is a difference between reality and language?

Kissinger: If we have assurances that all American prisoners held in Indochina will be returned as a result of the agreement, then we can negotiate about the language that expresses that reality. . . .

Le Duc Tho: As I told you last time that the American prisoners in Cambodia, there are none. In Laos, there are very few. But if you *satisfactorily solve the political question and the question of reparations then we can find an understanding.* But it is a question under the competence of Laos and Cambodia, and we have to exchange views with them. *And moreover, this cannot be written down in a signed document.* [authors' emphasis][13]

In other words, Hanoi demanded payment of reparations before resolving the question of POWs outside Vietnam. The North Vietnamese had first linked the two issues in 1968 and now, in 1972, they firmly reiterated the position. Kissinger, thanks to the briefing in the study by the Rand Corporation, was not surprised by Hanoi's position, although he didn't like it and had tried to avoid it. But Hanoi had also just made a major face-saving concession: dropping its demand that South Vietnamese President Thieu must resign before an agreement could be signed.

The momentum was headed toward a peace treaty in time for the 1972 election, and Kissinger was not about to derail the process by insisting on real guarantees concerning the U.S. POWs in Laos and Cambodia. The U.S. and North Vietnam reached a tentative agreement on the treaty before them, which still linked reparations to the POW issue.

Trying For A Better Deal

To his credit, President Nixon made one last attempt to dump the POW linkage. He sent a "top secret sensitive" cable straight to North Vietnam's Prime Minister, Pham Van Dong. The cable began by declaring, "The text of the [peace] agreement can now be considered complete." But Nixon then switched focus and asked for the following "unilateral declaration":

With respect to U.S. military men and civilians held in Indochinese countries outside of Vietnam, the DRV undertakes to make arrangements for their identification and return to the United States authority in accordance with the same schedule established for the release of U.S. military men and civilians detained in Vietnam. The DRV will also assure that the provision in the overall agreement for the verification of those military men and civilians considered missing in action will be applied also in Laos and Cambodia.[14]

Throughout the secret negotiations this had been the number-one goal of Kissinger—to tie the return of all POWs in Southeast Asia to one agreement signed by the DRV. And it was the DRV's equally adamant goal *not* to be "unconditionally" tied to the return of POWs throughout Southeast Asia. On this point they never relented. Instead they firmly linked the issue of POWs in Laos to the payment of reparations.

For the United States negotiators to have completed "the text of an agreement" and then demanded *ex post facto* a significant unilateral concession repeatedly rejected throughout the negotiating process, was nothing short of incompetent. Not surprisingly, the DRV Prime Minister refused to make the suggested unilateral declaration. The Americans in Laos would be held hostage to DRV reparation demands, demands which the U.S. secretly agreed to meet.

Pham Van Dong's carefully worded response to Nixon reiterated Le Duc Tho's September 26 statement to Kissinger linking POWs to reparations:

> ... the DRV side will carry out, *without any change,* what it has declared to the U.S. side. But it should be made clear that the questions of Laos and Cambodia must be settled in accordance with the sovereignty of these two countries.... However, the Democratic Republic of Vietnam will do its utmost to come to an agreement with its allies, with a view of finding a satisfactory solution to the questions with which the United States is concerned. . . . [authors' emphasis][15]

What had the DRV declared it would carry out, "without any change"? If the U.S. paid reparations and "satisfactorily solve[d] the political question[s]," then and only then would the DRV help the United States come to an agreement on the POWs held in Laos. The Prime Minister also supported Le Duc Tho's September

26 statement that any agreement would be "in accordance with the sovereignty of" Laos and Cambodia.

The Prime Minister's message did, however, suggest that if North Vietnam's preconditions were met and if the United States negotiated with the Pathet Lao and reached an agreement, the Pathet Lao were prepared to release the American POWs under their control by December 30, 1972.

Nixon abandoned the conditions outlined in his October 20 cable to Pham Van Dong when, on October 22 he wrote:

> The President notes with appreciation the message from the Prime Minister of the DRV which satisfies all his points with respect to Laos and Cambodia as well as U.S. prisoners.[16]

In fact, however, none of Nixon's "points" had been accepted. Instead, the President had accepted a statement that continued to link reparations as a precondition for DRV cooperation in getting the Pathet Lao to release their POWs. And, by accepting Dong's language, Nixon abandoned the United States position that the North Vietnamese must be responsible for the return of all U.S. POWs in Southeast Asia.[17]

Signing the Contract

By late October 1972, the U.S. and North Vietnam had agreed on a peace treaty. Kissinger even declared that "peace is at hand." He should have waited.

The South Vietnamese had not been informed about details of the impending deal. Their first knowledge of the completed agreement was not from the U.S., but from captured Viet Cong documents. And the more South Vietnamese officials learned about the treaty, the angrier they became.

Just two months earlier, on August 17, Kissinger had met with South Vietnamese leader Nguyen Van Thieu in Saigon at the President's Palace and painted a far different picture than the one now emerging:

> **Thieu:** About the prisoners of war, you have nothing?
> **Kissinger:** I think they are keeping the prisoners as *black-mail* .... I thought at first it would be best to have a ceasefire as soon as possible because of our elections. But upon

reflection I have decided that it is easier if we keep up the bombing through the elections. . . . You see, our strategy is that we are prepared to step up the military pressure on the DRV immediately, drastically and brutally one or two weeks after our election. We want to be in a position that they have rejected our reasonable proposals. After that we will put everything on the prisoner of war question. They think they can use the prisoners of war to overthrow you. If we can move quickly after the elections, we can destroy so much that they will not come back and harm you for a long time to come. . . . [18]

But now in late October, as Kissinger arrived at the Presidential Palace in Saigon to explain the agreement, it seemed possible that America could conclude the peace treaty before the election. And that meant no bombing to protect South Vietnam.

After Thieu read the English and Vietnamese versions of the proposed agreement, he refused to accept it. Despite intense pressure by the United States, South Vietnam continued to hold out, finally persuading the U.S. to ask for a deal slightly more to Saigon's liking.

And following his re-election, Nixon was finally forced to deliver on at least some of Kissinger's promises to South Vietnam. After a new round of peace talks derailed in Paris, America launched Operation Linebacker II, the bombing of North Vietnam. On December 17, 129 B-52 bombers in three waves obliterated targets in the Hanoi area while F-111s attacked MiG air bases. Simultaneously, Thieu was unequivocally told by Nixon that once the bombing stopped, Thieu would agree to whatever terms the North Vietnamese were willing to accept, or the United States would conclude a separate agreement with Hanoi and cancel future aid to South Vietnam. [19]

After all the years of fighting and the thousands and thousands of dead on all sides, the U.S. was ready to accept essentially the same peace terms that were available in the 1960s. As John Negroponte, Kissinger's aide put it, "We bombed the North Vietnamese into accepting our concession." [20] While being pounded by B-52 bombers, the North Vietnamese signaled their readines to resume talks, so on January 8, 1973, Kissinger and the DRV negotiators were once again face-to-face in Paris.

Back At The Table

Although Kissinger had recently described them as "just a bunch of shits . . . tawdry, filthy shits,"[21] when he faced the Vietnamese again in early January, Kissinger immediately disclaimed responsibility for the Christmas bombing, blaming it on other Nixon officials. " 'It was not my responsibility,' he told Le Duc Tho in Paris. 'It was not my fault about the bombing.' "[22] The pleasantries out of the way, Kissinger got down to business.[23]

For the next four days the two sides agreed to essentially cosmetic changes to the October 1972 agreement, with Le Duc Tho verbally agreeing "that all U.S. military and civilian prisoners detained in Laos shall be released no later than 60 days following the signature of the Agreement."[24]

Although this was merely a verbal assurance on the part of the DRV, Kissinger sent a "top secret sensitive exclusively eyes only" cable to Washington, D.C. alleging that he had finally obtained "Ironclad guarantees on our prisoners in Laos and Cambodia."[25]

The Paris Peace Accords were anounced to the world on January 23 and signed on January 27. Two days later in Washington, D.C., the Joint Chiefs of Staff told Kissinger they hoped for "forty or forty-one" POWs from Laos.[26] Indeed, some military planners knew about up to 60 American POWs awaiting rescue in Laos.

Chapter 11

Alive and Waiting in Laos

"No prisoners were left behind by the deliberate act or negligent omission of American officials.

Anyone suggesting otherwise is playing a heartless game with the families of the MIAs, who are entitled to the consolation that their government kept faith with their suffering."
—Henry A. Kissinger, 1992 statement to the U.S. Senate

In the fall of 1972, Lieutenant Neil L. Simstein, U.S. Navy Medical Corp, was stationed in Yokosuka, Japan. Commander Donald Schuler, also Navy Medical Corp, "requested that I meet with him on a matter of importance." After dinner at Simstein's home, Schuler "requested that my wife not be present while he was discussing a situation with me.[1]

"He pledged me to secrecy and asked if I would volunteer for a special mission that involved the release of the prisoners of war. I said I would. He then went into a discussion of a team being formed known as Q.R.R.T. [Quick Reaction and Recovery Team] that could be utilized in any number of ways during the proposed forthcoming release of prisoners of war from Southeast Asia."

Simstein was instructed to "draw gear for any possible weather condition, including arctic weather gear. My instructions were to keep separate bags packed—i.e., one for tropical weather and one for arctic weather." Sweden and South Vietnam were mentioned as possible POW post-recovery destinations. Simstein was put on standby and told to wait for further instructions.

Weeks later, while playing tennis, the Military Police showed up and demanded identification. After establishing his identity the MPs escorted him home. He was told that a staff car would arrive in 30 minutes and he was to take tropical gear.

"I was whisked off to Yokota Air Force Base about 5 o'clock in the evening. I reported in as a top security traveler and then waited until about 6 o'clock in the morning before my flight took off." The C-130 flew to Kadina Air Force Base on Okinawa. He was told to remain aboard while other passengers deplaned.

> A number of Army, Navy and Marine Corp personnel got onto the plane at that point, and before we took off again my name was called out. I made my presence known and a Navy Lieutenant Commander by the name [of] Ernest Mares approached me and filled me in on what I apparently had been missing for some time. The Q.R.R.T. Team had been assembled in Okinawa and neither I nor the team members had any explanation as to why I had not been included up until that time. Nonetheless, we proceeded to Clark Air Force Base, where we were isolated in our own barracks and compound. The area appeared to have been rapidly put together, with trailer houses, emergency ground wiring, etc.
>
> Structurally the team was composed of a colonel as Commanding Officer. He was Army. The X.O. [executive officer] was a Marine Corp Lieutenant Colonel. He apparently was involved in the military Penal System and ran some of the military prisons, specifically the one in Portsmouth. There was another Marine Lieutenant Colonel, an Army Special Forces Captain, Mr. Mares, the Navy Lieutenant Commander who was to serve as our Air-OPs officer, a Special Forces Army physician and a number of Special Forces—senior enlistees, most of whom had a primary M.O.S. as medics.
>
> . . . I found out that our mission was to go into Laos. . . . I was told that a specific camp in Laos was known to be holding somewhere in the area of 60 POWs. The camp had apparently been identified by overflights. The identity of many, if not all of the POWs in the camp, were known. The factor that was not known was whether the Laotians were going to let us into the camp peaceable [sic] or whether this was going to be a forced extraction. We were supposed to fly from Clark to Long Binh. From there . . . we were supposed to take choppers to our destination. Any support combat troops that were coming with us, if necessary, were going to be coming from Long Binh.
>
> At approximately 1700 hours, on the evening prior to our scheduled take off for Long Binh, we were just beginning a briefing session when our C.O. was called out of the room. He came back in very briefly to say we were to sit and wait

for him and then he was whisked away to I have no idea where. It seems like he was gone for approximately an hour and when he came back he was very grim. He told us that our team was disbanded. Almost everyone would be going back to their base of origin and that was that. The mood, of course, was glum and immediately questions were fired, but all the C.O. would say was that he was not at liberty to discuss anything regarding the mission and would not entertain any questions. He was apparently assigned to go to Long Binh that night where he then was helicoptered to a pre-established site in South Vietnam where he met with a Viet Cong representative who turned over several Americans, both active duty and civilians.

Simstein was then assigned to the regular pool of Navy physicians who would be taking care of Navy and Marine Corp returning POWs.

The U.S. decision-makers apparently decided that shooting their way into the POW camp in Laos to rescue the 60 Americans was too risky politically. So a plan with less political and physical risk was planned and implemented.[2]

On February 1, Army Sergeant Joseph Futrell was the NCOIC (Non-commissioned officer in charge) on a mission to get to American POWs out of Cambodia and Laos. Operating out of Bien Hoa, South Vietnam, eight American helicopters flew Canadian officers from the International Control Commission (ICC) more than 20 kilometers inside Cambodia, and picked up a few emaciated Americans, who were flown directly to a hospital in Saigon.

Over a three-day period, four missions were flown into Cambodia and Americans brought out. The American POWs were clearly under Hanoi's control, with North Vietnamese officers through the rank of major general being observed.

On each mission, two American civilians from the Saigon Embassy, along with military intelligence officers, Canadian ICC and International Red Cross members accompanied the flights. It was their job to contact the NVA (North Viatnamese) and bring the POWs to the helicopters.

Futrell said that, on the third trip into Cambodia, four POWs, a warrant officer, two Army pilots and an Air Force pilot were brought to the helicopters in ox carts. They had been held in underground isolation so long they "had difficulty under-standing English," and were very sensitive to sunlight. On another trip, an Air Force colonel was brought out. Futrell described him as 6' 2" and 104-105 pounds, "a frail frame of a person."

Three unsuccessful trips were made into Laos, where they were turned back by heavy anti-aircraft fire. The Laos excursions were not an organized repatriation like the trips into Cambodia. Instead, when small groups of American POWs were seen under guard and on the move in Laos, Futrell's helicopters, with the Canadian ICC in tow, flew in with the idea of attempting to contact the guards and peacefully return the POWs.

One group of six Americans was spotted being moved by sampan inside Laos, but as the U.S. helicopters entered Laotian airspace, they were met with gunfire and had to turn back. The next day two more unsuccessful attempts were made; finally, the mission was scrubbed.

Futrell then went to Saigon, where he was debriefed by an Air Force major general. He was "sworn to secrecy" and shipped out of Vietnam.[3]

Some 21 American POWs who had been kept in long-term confinement in Cambodia were returned during this secret operation. Futrell heard from officers attached to the mission that DRV (North Vietnam) representatives at another unknown location in South Vietnam were coordinating this operation with the U.S.

Humanitarian concerns can be dismissed out of hand as the motivating factor behind this secret release. Because the North Vietnamese went to great lengths to improve the health and physical condition of POWs targeted for return, the uniformly emaciated condition of the secret returnees indicates this was a last-minute agreement. And, the North Vietnamese were certainly offered something of value as an inducement to return them secretly.

The timing of this secret mission, February 1-3, 1973 strongly suggests a connection to Nixon's February 1st letter to the DRV telling them that $3.25 billion in "reconstruction" aid was going to be given to them by the United States—"without condition." None of the POWs acknowledged by Hanoi, however, could be held hostage by the DRV to ensure the payment of the $3.25 billion. No government, not even Hanoi, is going to publicly admit to holding POWs for ransom—that is a delicate and secret dance performed only by diplomats and politicians at the highest levels of government.

Both Hanoi and Washington, D.C. had motives to establish a test case for the delivery of money in exchange for "hostage" POWs—i.e., POWs not on the DRV and PRG (Viet Cong) January 27, 1973, lists of acknowledged POWs. The secret return of 21 POWs, exchanged at a few million per head, was a reasonable test of both sides' willingness and ability to perform on their secret agreement.

North Vietnam would certainly want to see proof of the American ability to "sensitively and quietly" repatriate hostage POWs. Once the first exchange was successfully accomplished, Hanoi's exposure was diminished because the United States had become a willing partner—or accomplice. We can only speculate on the logic behind the action. Washington and Hanoi have the answer, and they're not talking.

None of the 60 Americans held in that mysterious Laotian POW camp returned.[4] Indeed, no American serviceman captured in Laos and held in long-term Laotian detention facilities by the Pathet Lao and Vietnamese ever returned home, at least not officially. And the American government soon began denying such U.S. POWs ever existed.

Seven days after Futrell's mission was canceled, the PRG released 19 American military personnel and eight civilians from POW camps in South Vietnam, as part of the Paris Accords.

Chapter 12

Kissinger's "Firm Guarantees"

"In the end, the U.S. side got what it wanted—firm guarantees regarding U.S. POWs and MIAs throughout Indochina."
—Henry A. Kissinger, November 2, 1992

Two days after the Paris Peace Accords were signed, Kissinger met in Washington, D.C. with 22 members of the National League of Families of American Prisoners and Missing in Southeast Asia, where he fielded questions:

> **Question:** Do you foresee any special problems on issues not mentioned specifically in the provisions of the protocols?
> **Kissinger:** No, I do not see any special problems. . . . But we have *absolute* assurance that all American prisoners of war held anywhere in Indochina will be released. [authors' emphasis]
> **Question:** What happens if they welsh on one or another of the provisions?
> **Kissinger:** They know that if there is any welshing on one issue, it is over for the rest too. They know that one condition on which we have not compromised is the issue of our men. We will brutally enforce the release of the men on the lists.
> **Question:** Are there any indications how many men they will release?
> **Kissinger:** No, absolutely none. They have not, for example, told us how many men may be in Laos. I have the impression that the men captured in Laos are being held in North Vietnam and that they will be released in North Vietnam.
> **Question:** Will we accept the POW lists as complete?
> **Kissinger:** No. We will not accept them as complete or as definite. However, we also do not believe they will hide any POWs.

Question: Laos is such a grey area. Do the North Vietnamese dictate there?

Kissinger: . . . Understandings on Laos are *absolutely* clear concerning POW releases in a time frame similar to that in Vietnam. [authors' emphasis]

Question: Is there any likelihood that Americans are being held in small villages in Laos and South Vietnam?

Kissinger: It is unlikely and really unfeasible. And we will go to extraordinary lengths to find out. . . . They have tended to collect their prisoners together. They can't use the men for *blackmail* if we don't know they hold them. And if we learn that they are holding some, but not releasing them, they must fear our reaction. [authors' emphasis]

Question: Are the U.S. reconstruction payments of $7 1/2 billion an incentive to the North Vietnamese?

Kissinger: They cannot hold our men in *ransom*. They must perform and fulfill their obligations. . . . There cannot be *blackmail* by them. After they perform, then there can be some . . . reconstruction assistance. [authors' emphasis]

Question: What if they deny that men whose photographs they have earlier released were ever captured by them?

Kissinger: They better have a damn good explanation of where the man was held or where he is buried . . . . they know it is not riskless for them to cross us.

At that very time, American intelligence was compiling dossiers on POWs whose post-capture photos left no doubt they had been in communist hands. When later pressed to return the men, Hanoi said it knew nothing about them. There was no U.S. retaliation.

It is hard to imagine playing a more heartless game with the POW families than the one played that day in the Roosevelt Room of the White House by Henry Kissinger. National security considerations would have precluded him from telling the truth:

> Of course the communists will keep some for bargaining leverage—we are absolutely certain of it. Ransom and reparations are now the name of the game. We know, for instance, that 60 Americans at this very moment are being held in Laos, but we can't figure out how to rescue them without causing even more problems with the release of other American POWs in North and South Vietnam. And

blackmail—let's talk about blackmail. The communists have used the POWs to blackmail us for the last four years. Actually, they've been using POWs to blackmail us since World War II. You should have seen what a lousy job FDR and Eisenhower did—they lost thousands of Americans to communist blackmail. We'll lose a lot less in Vietnam—a few lost to China, more to the U.S.S.R., and the rest are in Laos and North Vietnam. So, in reality, we have won a moral victory because we are going to lose far fewer POWs than some of the great leaders in American history.

Kissinger could not, at that point in history, reveal the truth—but he did not have to tell outright lies. Bureaucrats and diplomats are well versed at giving non-answers to real questions. But Kissinger chose the route of giving macho answers that made him appear to be the master negotiator to the POW families. It was a heartless performance.

Where Are the Real Lists?

On January 27, Hanoi released lists of American POWs held in North and South Vietnam. The lists were minus the names of many men known or suspected to be in enemy hands. Air Force General Eugene Tighe, later director of the DIA, remembers that intelligence experts felt "shock and sadness" about the incomplete prisoner lists. Not only were the lists from Vietnam incomplete, the lists did not include any POWs from Laos.

When the DRV's "firm guarantees" failed to produce a list of American POWs held by the Pathet Lao, a message went out from the White House situation room on January 31 to be delivered to Le Duc Tho:

> The U.S. side wishes to express the serious view it takes of the failure of the North Vietnamese side to produce a list of American prisoners held in Laos. Given the constant position of the U.S. with respect to its prisoners and the messages exchanged between the President and the Prime Minister of the DRV in October, the NVN side was bound to know that the U.S. side would insist on the same procedures for Laos as for Vietnam. *While it is true that procedures for dealing with prisoners in Laos were not explicitly part of the formal agreement,* it will be very difficult to believe that the North Vietnamese side is approaching implementation of

the agreement with good will if the list is not forthcoming immediately. It must also be clearly understood that failure to solve this issue must have the effect of impairing the utility of Dr. Kissinger's visit to Hanoi, because it will restrict his ability to discuss *positive programs* [i.e. aid]. . . . [authors' emphasis][1]

The White House message to Le Duc Tho tied the return of American POWs to "positive programs." There was only one positive program Kissinger was going to discuss in Hanoi, and that was money. Ransom. Reparations. Reconstruction. They all mean the same thing, but some words are less offensive to the honor of a country trying to buy its way out of a negotiating mess.

It was not relevant that North Vietnam "was bound to know that the U.S. side would insist on the same procedures for Laos as for Vietnam," because there was nothing in the Paris Accords, or any of the written side agreements, to make this a "firm guarantee." The DRV (North Vietnamese) had very deliberately placed themselves in a position whereby they could not be held accountable for POWs throughout Southeast Asia.

Kissinger, and presumably Nixon, knew this to be the case.[2] So the U.S. was reduced to suggesting that "positive programs" were endangered because of Hanoi's unwillingness to demonstrate "good will" by turning over the list of U.S. POWs held in Laos.

Hanoi attempted to use the POW problem in Laos to force the U.S. to put earnest money on the table—while the U.S. maneuvered to obtain the POWs by merely dangling the possibility of aid. Once again, Kissinger was outmaneuvered, precisely because there was no firm guarantee that American POWs held in Laos would become the responsibility of the DRV.

Ransom/Reparations/Reconstruction

Personally, I have no proof whether Americans were kept behind by Hanoi. The Vietnamese are certainly capable of such a cynical act and of lying about it, even though their motive would be obscure. —Henry A. Kissinger, September 22, 1992[3]

. . . we delayed delivery to [the DRV] of a confidential Presidential letter on recommending to Congress

reconstruction assistance after peace had been established.
. . . The Nixon letter of February 1973 noted the
Administration's intention to ask Congress for some $3.25
billion for reconstruction in Vietnam, provided other
provisions of the Agreements were implemented and were
in conformity with American constitutional procedures.
—Henry A. Kissinger, September 22, 1992[4]

On the first day of February 1973, the U.S. traded a promise of
aid for a list of POWs. A message from Nixon to the DRV Prime
Minister, outlining the United States position on post-war
reconstruction aid to Hanoi, was turned over to the North Vietnamese in Paris by American Colonel Georges Guay:

> I exchanged the President's memorandum for the list of US
> prisoners in Laos with customer at 1600 today, 1 Feb 1973.
> When I arrived he made a grab for the envelope containing
> the message and without breaking his fingers I told him
> that my instructions were to exchange the memorandum
> for his list. He then said I could read his list while he read
> the memorandum and if we didn't like what we read we
> could return each others papers. All this with a huge smile
> while he again reached for the envelope. I smiled in return
> and while picking up the envelope with both hands (tight
> grip) asked him if he had the list. He chuckled, said that he
> had and stood up. He went to a cabinet and produced an
> envelope from which he extracted what was obviously a
> very short list of names. I took the memorandum out of the
> envelope and passed it to him, while he passed the list to
> me.
> There are a total of 10 people on the list, eight military
> and two civilians [one was Canadian]. . . .
> Comment: I did not tell him that I felt like returning the
> list and taking back the memorandum until they displayed
> a more serious attitude. In all honesty, though, he did seem
> to be somewhat embarrassed when he said that was all
> "they" had given him.[5]

After four years of negotiations the United States had delivered
a letter from the President of the United States outlining the U.S.
position on providing the North Vietnamese with post-war
money. The U.S. attempted to make this top-secret, government-

to-government understanding strong enough for the DRV to believe they had an ironclad agreement to receive reparations in the guise of reconstruction aid, while allowing the U.S. to deny paying ransom for POWs.

Nixon's letter precisely followed the Rand Corporation's advice that "The United States could avoid giving the appearance of paying reparations or ransom money if it could reach its agreement with the DRV in private, and if all funds paid out to Hanoi were then publicly labeled part of the *U.S. contribution to a postwar recovery program. . . ."*[6] [authors' emphasis]:

> The President wishes to inform the Democratic Republic of Vietnam of the principles which will govern United States participation in the postwar reconstruction of North Vietnam. . . . the United States undertakes this participation in accordance with its traditional policies. These principles are as follows:
> 1) The Government of the United States of America will contribute to postwar reconstruction in North Vietnam without any political conditions. . . .[7]

In exchange for this seeming commitment to provide aid, a list of nine American POWs, eight military and one civilian, was turned over to the U.S. The list was a sham. All nine POWs had been captured in Laos by the North Vietnamese and shipped to North Vietnam. None of the Americans had been under long-term Pathet Lao/Vietnamese control in Laos.[8]

Hanoi's Surprise

The U.S. had been had. Just as the Rand study had predicted, Vietnam would not settle the POW issue just on the *promise* of aid. The next day Nixon fired off a letter of protest to the DRV:

> The list of American prisoners held in Laos which was presented in Paris on February 1, 1973, is unsatisfactory. U.S. records show that there are 317 American military men unaccounted for in Laos and it is inconceivable that only ten of these men would be held prisoner in Laos.
> The United States side has on innumerable occasions made clear its extreme concern with the prisoner issue. There can be no doubt therefore that the *implementation* of

any American undertaking is related to the satisfactory resolution of this problem.

It should also be pointed out that failure to provide a complete list of prisoners in Laos or a satisfactory explanation of the low number thus far presented would seriously impair the mission of Dr. Kissinger to Hanoi. [authors' emphasis][9]

The choice of words in this message leave no doubt that Nixon had again connected money to POWs. A written "understanding" delivered with his offer of $3.25 billion in aid said: "It is understood that the recommendations of the joint Economic Commission mentioned in the President's note to the Prime Minister will be *implemented* by each member in accordance with its own constitutional provisions."

The only "American undertaking" awaiting "implementation" was the "reconstruction " aid to North Vietnam—which, by Presidential decree, was now even more strongly tied to resolution of the POW problem in Laos. And, Kissinger's trip to Hanoi to discuss "positive programs"—i.e. ransom/reparations/reconstruction—was now "seriously impair[ed]" by Hanoi's "failure to provide a complete list of prisoners in Laos," which they, in any case, were not bound to do by any agreement with the United States.

For the second time in four days, Nixon had dangled the "positive programs" in front of the DRV and threatened its removal unless the Laotian POW problem was satisfactorily resolved. Whatever the wording, this was clearly a debate over ransom for the POWs.

A "Mexican Stand-off" in Southeast Asia

The failure of either the United States or Hanoi to make the first move to break the impasse can be explained by the Rand Corporation warning: "No matter what terms are agreed upon, it would be unduly optimistic to believe that the DRV and the VC will release all U.S. prisoners immediately after [the] conclusion of an agreement in the expectation that the United States will meet its military, political, or monetary commitments. More likely, they will insist on awaiting concrete evidence of U.S. concessions before releasing the majority of American prisoners, and will retain some of them until all U.S. commitments have been fulfilled."[10]

American POWs in Laos, Vietnam and Cambodia were being held hostage to Hanoi's demand of ransom. The United States had agreed in writing to pay a minimum of $3.25 billion, but not immediately—only after the two governments spent months negotiating the details. But the United States was demanding that Hanoi immediately produce a list of those still being held, merely on the assurances of a secret, and now obviously far from ironclad, $3.25 billion promise of aid from Nixon.

The problem was that delivery of a list of POWs held in Laos made it possible for the United States to blackmail Hanoi, in the court of world opinion, to deliver the acknowledged POWs forthwith—before the ransom was paid, leaving the North Vietnamese with no bargaining leverage, and ultimately, no ransom. So the two sides were stuck, with no apparent resolution possible that included the return of the hostage POWs.

Hanoi's response was to stall for time, proposing "that the list of prisoners [from Laos] which we passed to you not be made public before a solution to the Laos problem."[11] By this time, the American Quick Response and Reaction Team being held in readiness at Clark Air Base to rescue 60 American POWs at one location in Laos had been disbanded; and the $3.25 billion in bait had not produced live POWs, or even the promise of POWs held in Laos by the Pathet Lao.

Kissinger met with the DRV in Hanoi February 10-12, but there was no resolution to the Laotian problem, and the impasse continued.

Meanwhile, the Pathet Lao role in the unfolding drama was so miniscule they had not been told by Hanoi what it was they were supposed to be doing and saying. The United States received information through a "sensitive" source that the Pathet Lao had "provided no information thus far on U.S. prisoners, even disclaiming knowledge of the list of ten—which came from the DRV."[12]

Pathet Lao representative Soth Petrasy met with a U.S. embassy official in Laos, on February 21. Soth "stated that the LPF does hold foreign prisoners including Americans." He did not know how many or their names, but would ask Pathet Lao headquarters in Sam Neua to provide the information. "He also clearly stated that whatever the U.S. and North Vietnam had agreed to regarding prisoners captured in Laos was not his concern. He said that the question of prisoners taken in Laos is to be resolved by the Lao themselves and could not be negotiated by outside parties over the heads of the Lao."[13]

Two weeks later, the DRV plan for dragging out the POW hostage crisis in order to force the United States to actually put the pledged "reconstruction" money on the table, began to emerge: ". . . Soth said that as far as he knew, LPF hold[s] US prisoners. However, information on numbers held and procedure for repatriation would probably be made available as RLG [Royal Lao Govt] and LPF experts elaborate a written protocol.... As this protocol is elaborated, Soth opined he would be able to give us information from Sam Neua re number of US PWs held in Laos and where, when and how they will be released."[14] Soth "disclaimed any knowledge of USG-DRV understanding that all US PWs captured in Indochina—including those in Laos—would be released through Hanoi. He merely repeated that LPF detain[s] US PWs in Laos."[15]

If Hanoi could successfully tie the POW issue to the negotiations underway in Laos, the U.S. would be maneuvered into completing the reconstruction aid negotiations before the POW hostage crisis was resolved, because the Laotian negotiations could be dragged out for an indeterminate period of time.

Chapter 13

March 1973: What Do We Do Now?

Three days later the National Security Council (NSC) recommended to Kissinger that the withdrawal of the last American troops not begin until the U.S. had received the list of the last group of POWs, and the withdrawal not be completed until all of the POWs, including those in Laos, had been released.[1]

On the same day, March 13, Kissinger met with top officials in the White House:

> **State:** You won't complete the withdrawal until the Lao prisoners are released?
> **Kissinger:** Yes, that's right.
> **DoD:** How many are there in Laos?
> **NSC:** They've told us they hold more American prisoners than the eight on the list we received from North Vietnam.
> **Kissinger:** They have? They told us they hold more than eight?
> **NSC:** That's right.
> **State:** We've had contact with the Pathet Lao several times.
> **Kissinger:** And they have admitted they hold more?
> **State:** Yes.
> **Kissinger:** I didn't know that. How many more?
> **State:** They haven't said. They've been giving us the runaround on the details. This is something you may want to keep in mind. You may want to notify the DRV that the Pathet Lao have told us this and ask them to be more forthcoming on POWs in Laos.
> **DoD (to Kissinger):** Will you handle this through your channel?
> **Kissinger:** Yes.[2]

The next day a message was sent to the DRV asking for a clarification of Soth's statement about POWs in Laos, but no reply was received, nor was one actually necessary—the maneuvering for position by both sides was obvious.

So on March 15 the Secretary of State tried to get the American Ambassador to Laos to apply pressure:

> 1. . . . we suspect DRV has instructed Pathet Lao to move slowly at this stage in order to prolong its military presence, and exacerbate the issue of U.S. POWs in Laos.
> 2. You should show our displeasure at Pathet Lao foot-dragging in every quarter where it will register some effect. We especially wish you to single out Soviet ambassador for the full treatment, and give as your personal estimate the prospect that the cease-fire cannot, repeat not last much longer in the absence of progress on the political front. . . . You should also state that we continue to hold North Vietnam to its commitments on releasing all U.S. POWs in Laos by March 28 and will not tolerate any delays. Rogers.[3]

Even in secret cables, the Secretary of State continued to flog the Kissinger myth that the North Vietnamese had a "commitment" to release all U.S. POWs held in Laos. Regardless of such wishful thinking, no such commitment existed.

Two days later the Pathet Lao headquarters in Sam Neua passed a message to the American side saying the U.S. "already know[s] the names and total number of US POWs captured in Laos; and (B) the POWs will be released by the LPF [Pathet Lao] in Laos and not in Hanoi."[4]

What Commitment?

Two days after that, on March 19, the North Vietnamese gave a clear and unequivocal signal of their thoughts on their "commitment" when they told the U.S. "they had no authority to discuss the release of prisoners captured in Laos . . . . the Pathet Lao were responsible for negotiating the release of any U.S. prisoners detained by them."[5]

More Macho Kissinger

Kissinger, apparently working on the theory that if you repeat a lie often enough, someone will believe it, twenty-four hours later sent the following message to Le Duc Tho:

The U.S. side has become increasingly disturbed about the question of American prisoners held or missing in Laos. As the DRV knows, there is a *firm* and *unequivocal* understanding that all American prisoners in Laos will be released within 60 days of the signing of the Vietnam Agreement. The DRV side has on many occasions solemnly reaffirmed its responsibility to carry out this understanding which was one of the fundamental considerations underlying the US signature of the Vietnam Agreement. Despite this background there has been almost no progress on this issue and the deadline for release is now only weeks away.

In its message of March 14, the U.S. side once again registered its strong concern and asked for an explanation from the DRV side of the statements made by the LPF representative in Vientiane which were contradictory to the understanding with the DRV side. There has been no response to third message. Indeed in the past week there has been further evidence that the DRV and its allies are not taking their obligations seriously. Further conversations between US and LPF representatives in Vientiane have proved completely unsatisfactory. Furthermore, on March 19 the DRV representative to the POW sub-commission informed the American representative that the Pathet Lao were responsible for the release of American prisoners and gave no assurance that this would take place by the agreed date of March 28, 1973.

The U.S. side wishes to reiterate that such an approach is totally contrary to the understanding reached by the two sides and that it expects all American prisoners in Laos to be released no later than March 28, 1973. The U.S. side holds the DRV side fully responsible for ensuring that this release takes place on schedule. In addition, as the U.S. side has made clear on many occasions, the list of only nine American prisoners presented belatedly by the Pathet Lao is clearly incomplete. There continues to be no satisfactory explanation concerning the smallness of this list nor any assurance that further efforts will be forthcoming. In view of the very short time left before the deadline for the release of American prisoners in Laos, the U.S. side expects an immediate response to this message and the firm assurance of the DRV side that it will live up to its solemn responsibilities. Failure to do so would have the most serious consequences. Certainly the U.S. side cannot be expected to complete its withdrawals from South Vietnam until this closely linked question is satisfactorily resolved.[6]

Since none of the substantive portions of this message were based on reality, Kissinger was apparently posturing for the history books. There was no "firm and unequivocal understanding." The DRV had never "solemnly reaffirmed its responsibility" for the return of American POWs held in Laos. And, it was not "one of the fundamental considerations underlying the US signature of the Vietnam Agreement," because there was absolutely no written agreement or understanding with the DRV on the subject.

One cannot truthfully consider an oral statement, particularly one that the DRV adamantly refused to commit to writing, a "fundamental consideration" of competent statesmen who are deciding whether or not to sign an agreement. The only fundamental consideration here was to put more of the macho Kissinger on the record for posterity.

What Do We Do Now?

Acting DIA Director John R. Deane sent a secret memorandum to the Chairman of the Joint Chiefs on March 21, 1973 concerning the intelligence community's view of the POW situation in Laos. General Deane wrote that the DRV's purported "Laos list" of February 1, 1973 was limited exclusively to U.S. POWs captured in Laos by the North Vietnamese and did not represent U.S. POWs captured by the Pathet Lao. He also said it was the intelligence community's view that: "There is evidence that the Pathet Lao have information on captured/missing U.S. personnel and should be able to provide a list of alive PWs in addition to information on the fate of many others." As the intelligence community knew, the Pathet Lao should have been able to at least identify the 60 American POWs it had concentrated in one location just prior to the Paris Accords being signed. And, by now, the Pentagon had reason to believe that an additional twenty Americans, captured in South Vietnam and Laos, were in Hanoi, but not on any list provided by the DRV, PRG or Pathet Lao.[7]

The next day the President authorized Admiral Moorer to send the following cable[8] to the Commander-in-Chief, Pacific:

1. ... The United States position is as follows: "The U.S. will complete the withdrawal of its military forces from South Vietnam in accordance with the release of all, repeat all, American prisoners held throughout Indochina."
2. Do not commence withdrawal of the fourth increment until the following two conditions are met: (1) U.S. has been provided with a complete list of all U.S. PW's including those held by the Pathet Lao, as well as the time and place of release. (2) The first group of PW's have been physically transferred to U.S. custody.[9]

The message was clear and unequivocal—the United States government knew that American POWs continued to be held in Laos. Kissinger's latest message to Le Duc Tho had suggested the United States would not complete its withdrawal of American forces from Southeast Asia unless these POWs were identified and released.[10] Now the U.S. seemed to be moving toward a rare moment in which it actually backed up Kissinger's threats with action.

Nine hours later, the American Ambassador to Laos, Mac-Murtrie Godley, sent a cable to the Secretary of State advocating a two-step approach to obtaining the release of American prisoners captured in Laos:

We believe the LPF holds, throughout Laos, more prisoners than found on the DRV list ... we should concentrate our efforts on getting these nine listed men repatriated as soon as possible. The release of the nine PW's already acknowledged seems possible within the time frame of the Vietnam agreement. However, we do not believe it is reasonable to expect the LPF to be able to produce an accurate total PW list by March 28. The LPF just has not focused on the PW repatriation and accounting problem until very recently and probably cannot collect, in the next few days, the information we require .... We should continue to press for the release of the nine acknowledged U.S. PW's within the time limit of the Vietnam agreement, but deal with the questions of accounting for our MIAs, and determining whether there are additional PW's to be repatriated, within the framework and time limits of the Laos cease-fire and military protocol.[11]

At long last the United States government was at least partially awakening to the realities of the recently negotiated Paris Accords—there was no requirement for the Pathet Lao to turn over American POWs under that agreement, nor an obligation for the DRV to make it happen. According to the technical wording of the peace agreement, Hanoi could *not* be held accountable for the POWs held in Laos. There was no justification, at least in narrow legal terms, for the U.S. to renege on its promise to pull out American troops. The next day Moorer rescinded his March 22 cable not to complete the withdrawal of American troops unless all US POWs throughout Southeast Asia were returned.

The DRV/Pathet Lao goal of attaching the POW question to the negotiations underway in Laos prevailed. The DRV now had time to determine whether the reparations the United States had agreed to pay, under the guise of reconstruction, would actually be delivered in exchange for the U.S. POWs who were held in Laos.

The next day, March 23, a Swedish film crew returned from Sam Neua where they had been told by an unidentified official that the LPF did hold some American POWs.[12] Three days later, Pathet Lao representative Soth Petrasy said that the Pathet Lao had decided to accede to the U.S. request for the release and return of the nine U.S. POWs held in Laos.[13]

But the Pathet Lao were going to release only the nine POWs the United States had asked for—not all POWs under their control. Soth said he was not aware of other POWs being held, but if there were any, he was willing "to discuss these matters within the framework of [the] Vientiane agreement at a later stage."[14]

Once again, the United States had clearly been told that Kissinger's attempts to revise the Paris agreement unilaterally would not be tolerated. The POW question had been permanently removed from the Paris March 28 deadline and transferred to the Laotian negotiations—over which the United States had no effective control.

March 27, the NSC "summarized the situation in a memorandum to Dr. Kissinger."[15]

The next day, Assistant Secretary of Defense Eagleburger sent the following memo to Secretary of Defense Richardson:

> DIA concludes that the LPF may hold a number of unidentified U.S. POWs although we cannot accurately judge how

many. The American Embassy, Vientiane, agrees with this judgment. . . . The U.S. is prepared to accept release of the ten men on the 1 February list along with the other U.S. personnel being held in NVN as the final condition for complete U.S. troop withdrawal. However, there has been no accounting of U.S. personnel in Laos. . . . Hence, assuming all the prisoners currently being held in NVN are released by 28 March, we still have the Laos MIA question remaining unresolved.[16]

Clearly, Nixon and Kissinger had now officially dropped the charade that all POWs must be released by March 28 because it was the "ironclad" duty of the DRV to make it happen. The next question was whether they would allow themselves to be dragged into the Laotian negotiations in a continuing attempt to gain the release of the POWs held in Laos by the Pathet Lao.

If they did so, earnest money would have to be placed on Hanoi's table under the guise of "reconstruction," to meet the DRV's demand for ransom. Otherwise, there was absolutely no reason to continue to be strung along by the communists.

Secretary of Defense Elliot Richardson was not willing to walk away from the Americans still held in Laos just yet, nor to pay ransom for them. So on March 28 he sent a memo to Kissinger recommending "the following diplomatic track in order to gain an accounting of our men held/missing in Laos":

A. After the recovery of the last prisoners from NVN [North Vietnam], Hanoi should be advised unequivocally that we still hold them responsible for the return of all POWs being held in Indochina. And in this regard, any further mine sweeping activity as well as all future US reconstruction assistance should be described as wholly dependent upon the accounting for and/or release of US prisoners being held in Laos. . . .

B. In the meantime [about 28 March], a strong demarche should be made to the ranking LPF representative in Vientiane. . . . This initiative should plainly and forcefully assert that the U.S. will no longer play games with the POW issue in Laos. The LPF should be told that we know they hold US prisoners, and we demand their immediate release as well as an accounting and information on all those who may have died. . . .

D. Shortly after 28 March, assuming the LPF have not responded favorably, intensive and obvious tactical air reconnaissance of North and South Laos should commence. Additionally, the movement of a new carrier task force into the waters off Vietnam should be publicly announced.

E. Concommitant with the foregoing, the LPF and NVN should be privately advised that the Thai Volunteer Forces now in Laos will not be removed until there is a satisfactory resolution of the POW issue.[17]

The policy recommended by Richardson to gain the release of the POWs still held in Laos, it should be remembered, was to work within the framework and time frame of the Laotian negotiations, then underway. This policy was rejected no later than March 29, and the Nixon Administration indisputably began to abandon the POWs as a necessary part of a broader effort to rewrite history in a more favorable light.

The Cover-Up Begins in Earnest

American prisoners may have been kept in Vietnam by a treacherous enemy in violation of agreements and human decency. But no one was left by the deliberate act or negligent omission of any American official.
—Henry A. Kissinger, September 22, 1992[18]

A key element of legislative or diplomatic statesmanship is to win the other side's approval of language which comes closer to the draftsman's intention than to the other side's, and that will stand up in . . . the court of world public opinion. —Henry A. Kissinger, November 2, 1992[19]

On March 27, 1973, Richard Nixon and his closest advisers were recorded on the White House tapes discussing how to get out from underneath the horrific combination of the ongoing Vietnam nightmare and the looming Watergate crisis. "My view would be to get the Vietnam [issue] out of the way. . . . " the President said.

Two days later Nixon began to publicly disengage from the Laotian quagmire, telling the American people: "For the first time in 12 years, no American military forces are in Vietnam. All of our American POWs are on their way home."[20] It was a clear signal that the Nixon Administration was not going to allow itself to be drawn into the Laotian negotiations and thereby be forced to put what little political capital the Administration had left on the line for Congressional approval of a ransom payment of at least $3.25 billion.

To do so would cause other, greater problems. The linkage between POWs and "reconstruction" would have to be admitted in order to give Congress a reason to approve of something that had absolutely no support on the Hill in the spring of 1973. Such an admission would inevitably lead to an unraveling of the Administration, as a Democratically controlled House and Senate probed into what actually transpired over the course of Kissinger's secret negotiations. It would also inevitably raise questions about the secret war in Laos, which later became an issue in the debate over impeaching Nixon. It was easier to write off the POWs, cover it up and then rewrite history. And the Nixon Administration did, after all, have significant historical precedent from World War II, the Korean conflict and the Cold War to guide them.

One week after Nixon's speech, the Senate—which still didn't understand the link between aid and POWs—voted 88-3 to bar the use of any previously appropriated funds to provide economic aid to the DRV. And the next day the Pathet Lao declared publicly that they held no POWs. The linkage continued: as the money was withdrawn from the bargaining table, so too were the POWs.

During the same time frame, Deputy Secretary of Defense William Clements summoned Dr. Roger Shields, head of the Defense Department's POW/MIA Task Force, to his office to discuss DoD's need for a new public formulation of its POW/MIA policy. According to Dr. Shields' deposition, taken by the Senate Select Committee:

> [Clements] indicated to me that he believed that there were no Americans alive in Indochina. And I said: I don't believe that you could say that . . . I told him that he could not say that. And he said: you didn't hear what I said. And I said: you can't say that. And I thought he was probably going to fire me. . . . [21]

But Dr. Shields did as he was told, and at an April 12 press conference said: "We have no indications at this time that there are any Americans alive in Indochina."[22] While Shields later claimed his statements were misreported, the bureaucracy in the departments of State and Defense took them to be a signal, and the message quickly became the Administration line on POWs.

Veteran diplomat and Kissinger protegé Winston Lord was part of the Nixon team. But even he has conceded that the Nixon Administration's public denials destroyed America's negotiating position with Hanoi. "If you're publicly saying we have no indication [of live POWs], how can you press them privately or any other way to release [the prisoners]? . . . . Leaving aside the human and other political dimensions, it's terrible [negotiating strategy]. You lose all your leverage with the other side," he told the Senate in 1992.[23]

Six days after Shields' statement, the United States used B-52s to bomb the Ho Chi Minh trail one last time, and then walked out on the economic aid talks because of North Vietnamese cease-fire violations. The Joint Casualty Resolution Center, whose mission was to account for missing soldiers, jumped on the band wagon on April 21 with the statement that "there is no indication that any Americans listed as missing in action in Southeast Asia are still alive."

In less than three weeks the United States had transformed its POW policy from agreeing that only nine American POWs shot down in Laos would be returned under the Paris Accords—and that the remainder would have to be negotiated for (read ransomed) under the Laotian negotiations—to an abandonment of the POWs held by the Pathet Lao.

Kissinger Negotiates for the History Books

Between mid-May and June 1973, I conducted twelve days of talks with the North Vietnamese. I reviewed in detail the North's violations including the failure to account for all the MIAs and US personnel missing in Laos.
—Henry A. Kissinger, September 22, 1992[24]

On May 23 Kissinger met with Le Duc Tho to "review in detail the North's . . . failure to account for all the MIAs and US personnel missing in Laos." The transcripts of that meeting, heavily censored at Dr. Kissinger's lawyers' insistence, give an

extraordinary glimpse at Kissinger's behind-the-scenes fight for
America's POWs:

> **Kissinger:** Our understanding is that we can apply Article
> 8(b) [on POWs]. We can claim that it applies to all of
> Indochina, because there is no geographic limit stated. You
> will not accept this publicly, but you will not contradict this
> publicly either. And you will be most helpful to us in this
> respect.
>
> **Le Duc Tho:** We will do this say to help you in Laos.
>
> **Kissinger:** Yes. Is this a correct understanding of what
> Ambassador Sullivan and Minister Thach have discussed?
>
> **Le Duc Tho:** But in Laos. Minister Thach has told Ambas-
> sador Sullivan that we will help you to coordinate with our
> ally in Laos in getting information about the missing in
> action in Laos. As to those in Cambodia, we will wait until
> after the solution and we will deal with this question.
>
> **Kissinger:** You don't understand the point I am making.
>
> **Le Duc Tho:** Have I well understood you, that when you
> make a statement about this question for the whole of
> Indochina, we will not state it?
>
> **Kissinger:** You will not contradict it.
>
> **Le Duc Tho:** We will say nothing about it.
>
> **Kissinger:** But without saying so, you will help us. We have
> an understanding on your honor that you will help us.
>
> **Le Duc Tho:** We have to cooperate with our Lao friends.
> As to the statement you will make *for the purpose of public
> opinion,* we will say nothing. [authors' emphasis]
>
> **Kissinger:** Yes, but also for the purpose of reality. If you
> will help us. It will be helpful if you give us your assistance
> without making a public statement about it. You have often
> told me you could do things that are not written down.
>
> **Le Duc Tho:** I agree. But I have to add that we have to
> cooperate with our Lao friends because it is their
> sovereignty.
>
> **Kissinger:** I understand. Now we would still like a sentence
> from you which I don't understand why you can't give
> us—which says that "the DRV has been informed that there
> are no U.S. prisoners being held in Laos—that all the
> prisoners held in Laos have been released." It would be
> very important for us.
>
> **Le Duc Tho:** I have acknowledged to you that all of them
> have been released.

Kissinger: Then why can't you write it down?[25]

The answer to that question is so damaging that the next two pages of transcript have been blacked out—hidden from the American people to this writing on orders from the White House, the Senate Select Committee on POW/MIAs and Henry Kissinger himself.

The only thing that escaped the censors' black pen was the final sentence, two pages later, of a proposed statement: "[(d) The DRV side has been informed that there are no U.S. prisoners being held in Laos]."

So Kissinger wasn't attempting to get back POWs, or even obtain an accounting for the MIAs—he was soliciting Le Duc Tho's assistance in writing them off. Months later, when the Laotian agreement was finalized, the State Department was able to trot out this lie negotiated by Kissinger and present it as proof there was no further reason to ask the Pathet Lao to return America's POWs.

Villains

> The United States government kept faith with those who served their country. If servicemen were kept by our enemies, there is only one villain and one villain only: the cold-hearted rulers in Hanoi. —Henry A. Kissinger, September 22, 1992

We disagree. While the cold-hearted rulers in Hanoi are certainly villians, they were not the only parties to the American "bug-out" that left U.S. POWs in Southeast Asia.

Kissinger and his apologists in the U.S. Senate make two basic claims: first, there was no clear link between POWs and aid; and second, the Vietnamese are totally to blame if any U.S. POWs remained in Indochina after the war. The first claim is a proveable falsehood, the second a matter of opinion. The link between U.S. POWs and ransom/reparations/reconstruction aid is clear in the historical record. As for Hanoi, it is true that North Vietnam was in 1973 and remains as of this writing a totalitarian communist nation, governed by essentially ammoral and duplicitous tryants. Those men would almost certainly have kept some U.S. POWs even if the U.S. had paid up at the end of the war.

However, a bargain was struck in Paris during January 1973. In effect, the U.S. agreed to pay for its POWs. But it never did. How then can America place all the blame on Hanoi for refusing to return the prisoners?

Kissinger correctly points out that during the immediate post-war period, the U.S. Congress refused to allow the Nixon Administration to reinforce Saigon and pay or punish Hanoi. "The Congress took all three levers away, denying us both the carrot and the stick," Dr. Kissinger has said. "When the Congress eliminated our leverage, we were trapped in the classic nightmare of every statesman. We had nothing to back up our tough words, but more tough words."[26]

But the Doctor fails to note that Congress was not informed of all the issues at stake. U.S. legislators did not know the full connection between U.S. aid and the POWs, and the Nixon Administration certainly didn't rush to tell them.

Some observers say Henry Kissinger made the best deal possible at the time. Perhaps. But all that can be said for sure is that in 1973, the United States made a deal with the devil. And the deal fell through. You don't have to sympathize with the devil to realize that his bargaining partner must accept part of the blame.

PART IV

Hiding the Crime

Chapter 14

1973-76: Creating a Myth

" 'Did they try to brainwash you?' asked one of the wire-service reporters.

The young man frowned thoughtfully, and darted a quick glance toward the gold-braid group. The ranking admiral returned a stern look, and the young man blinked.

'Well, did they brainwash you?' repeated the reporter.

'I'll tell you, sir,' said the young man, kneading his hands nervously. 'They have ways of getting you to do just about anything they want you to. You know what I mean?'

The silence was broken by the woman reporter, who asked gently: 'How long did they have you, son?'

'Four weeks,' said the young man.

'What do you mean, four weeks?' barked the network TV man. 'Weren't you captured 2 1/2 years ago?'

The young man looked puzzled. Then his face cleared, and he said: 'Oh, you mean the North Vietnamese, is that it? I thought all the time you were asking about my time in Bethesda Naval Hospital.' "

—Douglas B. Hegdahl, returned POW, Washington Star story of September 4, 1969

Colonel Laird Gutterson stepped off the Air Force transport plane and into the cool Southern California sun, home at last after five years as a POW in North Vietnam. March Air Force Base, just south of Riverside, California, was to be his home for the next few days as he went through a "classified debriefing."

Like Douglas Hegdahl and other U.S. POWs returned before 1973, the newly returned Americans marched right back into tight U.S. military discipline. The entire planeload of former POWs was herded into a high-security area, where each was handed a piece of paper that contained an order: "You will not become involved in the POW/MIA issue." They were commanded to sign the papers, which were then collected.

Then, as the former POWs watched, the signed orders were fed into a shredding machine. "We were not allowed to discuss it out loud in a classified area, which meant that they didn't want any record of any kind including the recordings that are always made of classified briefings.... We were given a direct order, we would not speak about this in any way, shape or form, merely look at it, nod your head if you understood it, and give back the piece of paper."

Why would the United States government give such an order? Because a historical myth was being created: no returning American knew of any American who was left behind in North Vietnam; they had all been tracked and accounted for by the POW intelligence system.

A Lonely Soul

Gutterson, as well as other returning POWs, knew that was not true. Less than a week before leaving Hanoi, Gutterson had accidently happened upon the cell of Bobby Keesee, a civilian who had been captured by the North Vietnamese September 18, 1970 and held in isolation since that time. The vaunted POW tracking system had not uncovered his 2 1/2-year sojourn in their midst.

Keesee's name was not on the North Vietnamese list of POWs captured between 1964 and November 15, 1970 nor was he on the DRV list handed over to the American side on January 27, 1973, in Paris. He was an MIA not targeted for return by the DRV, and yet he was held in the same prison camp system with the acknowledged POWs and not detected by POW intelligence—only by accident did he come home.

Nor was the tracking system able to discern the presence of Air Force pilots Robert Sponeyberger and William Wilson, who had been shot down together on December 22, 1972, during the Christmas bombing of North Vietnam. Sponeyberger was held at Hoa Lo for ten days, December 25 through January 3, 1973. Wilson was held there for six days, December 29 through January 3, 1973.

So, there were 16 days in which the other American POWs held at Hoa Lo could have detected new American POWs in Hoa Lo prison. But their presence went undetected—demonstrating conclusively that the North Vietnamese could use the known prison camp system to sift through new arrivals and determine who was to go into the POW population that was targeted to be exchanged, and those who would be withheld, for whatever reason.

The Sifting Program

At least one returnee went through that sifting program before entering the main POW camp system. John R. Alpers, Jr., a USAF pilot flying an F-4D, was shot down over North Vietnam on October 5, 1972. In a letter to Senator John F. Kerry, Chairman of the Senate Committee on Veterans' Affairs, Alpers described how he and his backseater were captured immediately, blindfolded "and taken toward Hanoi. Sometime in the middle of the night we disembarked the truck we had been riding in and were handcuffed to a tree."

Alpers was later taken inside a nearby building, where his blindfold was finally removed.

> I found myself in front of a table behind which were sitting four oriental men in civilian clothes. The one who conducted my interrogation was tall, slim, and used impeccable English. A prolonged effort was made to get me to discuss certain elements of my mission, aircraft, base, and combat leadership chain of command. I also remember numerous questions directed at my own general level of military knowledge, as well as other questions which tried to elicit comment from me about specific technical knowledge of equipment and tactics which I might possess.

When Alpers tried to stay with name, rank and serial number, an AK-47 rifle, its safety off, was aimed at his head. He believes the interrogation was designed for two purposes:

> . . . to ascertain my general level of physical well-being (people with major and/or disfiguring wounds almost never turned up in the Hanoi prison system), and second, whether I might have certain information that could be of immediate use to the Hanoi war effort.
>
> I managed to convince my interrogators that I was just a dumb line navigator [weapons systems officer/F/4] who had only gotten to Southeast Asia several weeks before I was shot down. I obviously made no mention of the fact that I was on my second F4 combat tour, was one of two navigators at Ubon RTAFB doing all the route planning for

all daily wing combat strikes going into North Vietnam, and had previously been a select radar-bombardier in B-52s with specific knowledge of the USAF SIOP [single integrated operations plan for nuclear retaliation against the Soviet Union].[1]

Alpers and his "pilot managed to get through that 'screening' process and were subsequently taken on to the Hanoi Hilton. I now believe that other captives either 'failed the physical' and were disposed of, or were diverted from Hanoi and taken north through Red China to Russia so that the communists could try to exploit certain 'special talents.' "

He also believes that the chief interrogator was Chinese, not North Vietnamese. Alpers closed his letter to Senator Kerry by suggesting that the senator go through the debriefings to see how many returnees had this type of interrogation. Good suggestion—but DoD refused to allow Senate staffers, even those with high security clearances, to review the debriefs. Only two top senators, the Committee's chairman, John Kerry (D-Mass.), and vice chairman, Bob Smith (R-N.H.), had access to the hundreds of files—thus ensuring that most of the records would never be independently reviewed.

Lost in the System?

However, some evidence from returning POWs indicating that Americans in the system did not return has escaped the Pentagon. For example:

- The name "Begley" was seen scratched on the floor of a Hoa Lo prison quiz room in mid 1967. Air Force pilot Burris Begley was shot down December 5, 1966, six months or less before his name was seen scratched on the floor of an interrogation room.[2]

- John Ellison was seen in a photo by a friend of his, retired Navy Commander Robert J. Flynn.[3]

- USN personnel Reuben Harris, William A. Glasson and Larry M. Jordan. "Returnee Phillip Smith claimed to have heard on Peking radio, and read in a Peking bulletin, that an A-3B had been shot down between Hainan and China. The crew was reportedly captured." China returned one crew member's body but claimed no knowledge of the others despite their public acknowledgment that they shot the plane down and captured the crew.[4]

- A releasee saw the name "James P. Williamson" signed on an anti-war letter. . . . Other releasees reported having seen the name "Williamson" on a statement, each in the same circumstances (shown by interrogator during interrogation). . . . Army Corporal James D. Williamson was lost in Laos, January 5, 1968, and is a category 4.[5]

- Returnee James Mulligan memorized the names of six Americans who may have been inside the POW camp system but did not return: James A. Beene, Richard F. Collins, Joseph E. Davies, Bruce E. Lawrence, Paul D. Raymond, and W.C. Pierson, III.[6]

- Larry W. Biediger, an F-105 pilot shot down over North Vietnam on January 29, 1967. Returnee Brunstrom listed him as "returned to Laos."

- Roosevelt Hestle, a USAF, F-105F pilot shot down over North Vietnam on July 6, 1966. Returnee Bolstad's debriefing indicated "Seen at Heartbreak [POW camp], not in system."

- Larry G. Kier, an Army PFC, category 2, loss date May 6, 1970, is a particularly interesting case because of what DoD has *not* revealed. They admit that three returnees communicated with an American POW held in isolation at Hoa Lo prison, Hanoi. DoD has not released the names of these three former POWs; how three POWs determined it was Kier has not been established, nor have the number of locations from which Kier communicated and over what period of time.

Many of the younger POWs in the Hanoi prison system were shipped north to the "Dogpatch" POW camp in 1972. When the POWs arrived at Dogpatch, near the Chinese border, they found "names scribbled on the walls [and in one case etched into a tree] which led them to believe it had held Americans before, but none of them were names anybody had ever seen in our [North Vietnam POW] system. So we felt it was probably the camp for those people who never got into our system. . . . I'm sure they [the names on the walls] were duly reported. . . . " during the POW debriefings, Gutterson believes.[7]

One of the names written on a wall was "Lieutenant Lee Meeks." Not only did he not return; he is not on the DIA list of all POW/MIAs. He is but one of a number of unlisted POW names that appear on several declassified Pentagon records. "LTC Comb, G1/Corps/Pine G-4 fwd/cp arr from Danang Apr 23, 1975" was found on the wall at "Briarpatch" during the summer of 1975 by Arlo Gay, an American imprisoned by the North Vietnamese after the fall of Saigon. A prison guard told him that LTC Comb had been there for one month before being transferred to an unknown location. The United States government says it cannot correlate LTC Comb to any known American.

Joan Ryan, allegedly the wife of an Army helicopter pilot shot down in Southeast Asia who never returned, told DoD in 1984 that she had received six letters from him over a 14-year period. The letters said that eight other Americans were held with him. Mrs. Ryan's husband, assuming he actually existed, is not on the DIA list of POWs and MIAs.

But the returning POWs did not just bring out names. At least one, a Colonel, whose name has been blacked out in the declassified records, also carried a message from the North Vietnamese. "The North Vietnamese were concerned with what the returnees would say to the American public about camp conditions. It appeared they were now trying to make amends," according to a DoD document.

A North Vietnamese official "was sent" to the Colonel "with a special message: 'Don't rock the boat' because the North Vietnamese want economic aid from the U.S."

The returning POWs probably wondered why they should do any PR favors for Hanoi. But Washington knew—if word of the POWs' torture kept Hanoi from getting its money, Vietnam was warning, then the U.S. wouldn't get the rest of its prisoners.

The Halachis File

Each of the returning POWs was assigned a full-time "debriefer" upon his arrival in the United States. John Halachis, a career military intelligence officer, was assigned to one of the POW "memory banks," Robert Craner.[8]

Craner, an Air Force pilot, was shot down over North Vietnam on December 20, 1967, while flying an F-100F. During his more than five years of captivity he was transferred through the North Vietnam POW prison system. Assigned the "job" of becoming a memory bank, he memorized names and vital information for all POWs within each prison he entered.[9]

The men attached to between 50 and 60 of Craner's memorized names did not return and were not accounted for by the DRV. "Some were just taken, some were taken off away for disciplinary reasons, for a variety of reasons. Some were considered by the camp guards [to be] high risk for escape," he says.[10]

For each of the 50-60 named POWs, Halachis filed a report that contained all information stored in Craner's memory. But none of Craner's names were released by the Senate Select Committee on POW/MIAs.[11] Presumably, they remain in classified Senate or Pentagon files.

Halachis told the Select Committee that as he followed the Paris Peace Talks, "it just made sense to any geopolitical analyst that the North Vietnamese would have kept back some prisoners because the reparations question was a major consideration in those talks." He remembers that the intelligence community generally expected another major release because a large number of known POWs did not return.[12]

One thing was certain: it was just not reasonable to conclude that all the POWs had been returned during Homecoming in 1973. But that's exactly what Deputy Secretary of Defense William Clements did on July 11, 1973, when he wrote a "memorandum for the President: . . . . Although our returned prisoners could confirm the deaths of less than 100 men, they are of the firm opinion that none of the other missing men entered the captivity system."[13] Clements had to know that what he was writing was historical fiction only, and the President, if he bothered reading the memorandum, certainly knew the document for what it was: a historical alibi intended to buttress the Administration's policy that all known POWs had returned, at least from North Vietnam.

A few senior ranking bureaucrats, however, attempted to ascertain the truth, which was that the Vietnamese had a separate POW camp system from which many Americans never returned. Secretary of Defense Elliott Richardson, for instance, questioned some of the senior ranking POWs "about a second prison, a secret enclave,"[14] shortly after their return from captivity. No one within the POW camp system had first-hand information of such a secret system, as was to be expected. Some, however, were told they would be sent to " 'survival camps' if they did not cooperate."[15]

Survival of the Fittest

Once the U.S. government had declared that all American POWs were home, it set about ignoring evidence of the U.S. prisoners still alive in Southeast Asia. During the Vietnam War, pilots were instructed in the use of evader symbols and codes to identify the presence and name of a downed pilot to reconnaissance planes overflying the area. After Homecoming, however, the intelligence community stopped taking action when possible signals were located.[16]

Recon planes kept flying and taking photos, but no one was looking for evader symbols, which was unfortunate indeed because on May 10, 1973, a recon plane photographed an evader symbol in Northern Laos, "1973 TH."[17] On July 10th another recon plane photographed the same area and the symbols were still there. "Someone had to maintain the 'TH' symbol by continuously keeping the elephant grass stomped down, until at least 10 July when it was still clearly visible, nearly two months later,"[18] one analyst concluded. Some experts believe the signal was a call for help from U.S. POW/MIA Thomas Hart (TH). The Pentagon denies that, and has ensured the truth will probably never be known.

According to the Senate, the symbols in the recon photographs were not passed up the intelligence chain of until 1976, three years after they were made. The American, or Americans, who maintained that symbol in the elephant grass for 60 days or more, never came home.

Imagery wasn't the only source of intelligence on American POWs in Laos. Throughout the war live sighting reports of American POWs held in Laos poured into intelligence files; by 1970 more than 300 such reports had been received. As will be discussed in greater detail later, the reports continued to arrive in 1973 and after. In March 1973, North Vietnam released two Thais, Sergeants Praphan Xirion and Chem Bamrung Uom. According to the Pentagon, the Thai soldiers "identified photographs" of many U.S. POWs they had seen in captivity. Twelve of those men never returned home from Vietnam and Laos, according to previously secret U.S. military records.

Guilty Consciences?

About two months after returning to the United States, the POWs were wined and dined at the White House before network television cameras. Gutterson, who was sitting two tables away from Kissinger, walked over to him and quietly asked, "Can you tell me if we're doing anything about the men who were left behind?" "I thought [Kissinger] would come unglued," he remembers. Kissinger called one of his aides over and ordered: "Get this man away from me."[19]

A few days later, at Maxwell Air Force Base, Gutterson participated in a "classified" meeting with former American Ambassador to Laos William Sullivan. Gutterson thought this might be the time to clear up some nagging doubts he was beginning to have about his government's handling of the POW problem. So he asked Sullivan why returned POWs had been ordered not to become involved in the MIA/POW issue "in any way." Sullivan was surprised to hear that Gutterson had been commanded to sign an order to that effect. Most of the other POWs at the meeting indicated that they had been commanded to sign the same order.

Sullivan reportedly "blew his stack," saying, "For God's sake, the only pressure we've got on those people is the public pressure put on by the POW organizations." Sullivan then turned to his aide and told him "I want to know what's at the bottom of this and I want to know right now." Presumably, the facts of life were explained to Sullivan shortly thereafter, because nothing further was heard from him.

A few months later, Gutterson was advised that his potential for further upward mobility within the Air Force was nonexistent, and he was strongly encouraged to retire. So, after a career that spanned three decades, one of the few returnees to question the government's actions from within, was quietly shoved out the door.

The Intelligence Community Gets the Message

In the early summer of 1974, Army Morse Code operator Steve Lippert was stationed at Vint Hill Station, Virginia. Working for the Army Security Agency, he monitored communist Lao Morse Code traffic out of Laos.[20]

Shortly after he went on duty one day a lengthy message began to come in. As it was translated it began to draw the interest of several Morse Code operators. The North Vietnamese were holding 250 American POWs in Luang Prabang Province, Laos. The message concerned the reordering of supplies for the POWs—pigs, rice and eggs.

Everyone in the room was excited, wanting to "do something about it," Lippert told the Senate investigators under oath. "Let's go get them. We know exactly where they're at," said one operator. The bay sergeant left the room to find out

> what we were going to do about it. . . . I don't know how long he was gone for sure. But he came back into the room. We were all very anxious to find out what we were going to do about it. I do remember I asked him the question when he opened up the door. He had his head down, and when I asked him, he told me to shut up and sit down. . . . And he said: It doesn't go any further than this room. And he looked, he looked as dejected as I felt after he told me that.[21]

While Lippert did not pass a Senate polygraph on this account, he is sticking with his story, saying he was intimidated by his examiner. That may well be true, because at least one DIA study and other former intelligence officers say it is quite possible that over 200 American POWs could have remained alive in Laos by 1974.

For example, former Army intelligence sergeant Barry Toll has stated under oath that he saw highly classified Pentagon cables around that time reporting over 290-340 POWs alive in Laos. And during the mid-1970s, according to Southeast Asia refugees, including some who later passed polygraph tests, a number of U.S. prisoners were alive in Laotian camps.

While the numbers are still debatable, there is compelling evidence that at least some American POWs were alive in Southeast Asia during 1974, at the same time that the U.S. government had adopted a policy of denying that any U.S. prisoners had been kept behind by the communists.

Government policy clearly stated that there was no evidence that American POWs continued to be held in Southeast Asia. Intelligence confirming the existence of 250 or even two American POWs in one location in Southeast Asia simply could not be allowed to exist side by side with such a policy. So the intelligence had to be destroyed—otherwise the Nixon/Kissinger team, then overwhelmed by Watergate, would be back in the business of hostage politics.

Despite the fact that the United States government knew it had walked away from large numbers of POWs in April 1973, and in spite of the continuing flow of information that they were still alive under Vietnamese and Laotian control, the CIA was only capable of mustering up a November 1975 study that said: "There is also *some possibility* that American military prisoners are still being detained by the DRV. This latter premise is based on information from one source and the fact that French prisoners captured during the 1945-54 period are still held in the DRV." [authors' emphasis][22]

Such "studies" intended for circulation within the intelligence community demonstrate the extreme politization of intelligence analysis. The CIA acted as if pre-April 1973 POW intelligence simply did not exist. Post-April 1973 POW intelligence was ignored or destroyed lest it be at at odds with official policy. Instead of fact creating policy, policy was circulated as fact.

1975: Ford Gets Misled

The official policy stating that all POWs had been accounted for permeated the bureaucracy. The House Select Committee on Missing Persons in Southeast Asia, also known as the Montgomery Committee, met with Kissinger and his staff in the Madison Room of the State Department on November 14, 1975, just before leaving for Hanoi.

Kissinger, by this time Secretary of State, told the Select Committee that "in his opinion, there were no prisoners alive in Vietnam; and only the barest possibility that POWs were in Laos or Cambodia." But even there, he doubted any prisoners remained from the earlier conflict, with the possible exception of "a deserter or two."[23] The only basis for such a statement was official government policy; Kissinger's statement is contradicted by the vast body of intelligence collected between 1965-75—and of course, Kissinger's personal knowledge of the hostage negotiations in which he personally participated.

When the Montgomery Committee returned from Hanoi in January 1976 they requested a meeting with President Gerald Ford in order to brief him on their meetings with the Vietnamese government. The majority of the Committee favored providing aid to Vietnam in return for information on POWs and MIAs.[24]

Kissinger sent a "no distribution" action memorandum to the White House, outlining talking points for President Ford's meeting with the Select Committee:

> We see no change in previous Vietnamese positions linking significant progress on American MIA's to the United States granting aid and other economic concessions to the Vietnamese.
> The Vietnamese gave the delegation a set of documents listing the aid proposals discussed by the U.S.-North Vietnamese Joint Economic Commission in 1973 (one document discusses a 5-year, 3.25 billion dollar program). . . .
> Talks were broken off in mid-1973 when we reached the point where our only alternative was to sign the document produced by the Joint Economic Commission while North Vietnam continued to violate substantially the provisions of the Paris Agreement and continued to pursue the war in Cambodia.[25]

The quality of this briefing paper for President Ford varies from merely heavily distorted to totally misleading and false. The President was not informed that the 5-year 3.25 billion dollar rebuilding program was actually Nixon's offer of aid "without any condition." And the talks had actually been broken off because the Nixon Administration could not produce the money if an agreement had been reached, and because *both* sides, maneuvering for position, were violating the Paris Agreement.[26]

Kissinger's continuous complaining about Vietnamese violations as the exclusive reason for the difficulties between the two governments was misleading in a paper going to the President. Press releases are expected to convey government propaganda to the masses. Presidential briefing papers should be expected to be reasonable, balanced and factual. President Ford was fed "the truth" as Kissinger wanted him to see it, and not as it was.

In fact, the U.S. had instituted the Christmas bombing, not because of actions taken by the North Vietnamese, but because Kissinger had promised one more bombing of North Vietnam if an agreement was not signed before the election, and South Vietnam's president made sure the pledge was kept.

And it can be argued that the U.S. government violated the intent of the Agreement by front-loading the supply pipeline just as the Paris Agreement went into effect—because U.S. airlift capability and superior technology made it possible to deliver vast amounts of material quickly. North Vietnam, in turn, loaded the Ho Chi Minh Trail with comparable war materials, violating both the intent and legal wording of the Agreement.

While the Montgomery Committee was in Hanoi, the Vietnamese government definitely linked the POW/MIA issue to the Nixon offer of $3.25 billion in aid. Interestingly, Deputy Foreign Minister Phan Hien was the Vietnamese official who made the linkage. He was the same Vietnamese official who, one year later, would make an offer through a third country that would provide an opportunity for the United States to buy back its POWs.

During these meetings in Hanoi, the Vietnamese presented a shopping list of desirable aid.[27] The Vietnamese then made public their demand that the United States pay reparations in exchange for "Americans living in Vietnam." On March 29, 1976, the DRV issued a press statement out of its Paris embassy, demanding "that the United States fulfill its obligations under the Paris Agreement to 'contribute to healing the wounds of war' and declares itself ready for its part to undertake the necessary measures to *look for Americans living in Vietnam. . . .* We have expressed our goodwill on several occasions. We demand that the U.S. also have a correct attitude and show goodwill in normalizing relations between Vietnam and the United States."[28] Translation: several times in the past we have attempted to return the POWs ("expressed our goodwill"), in exchange for the $3.25 billion you promised to pay us ("contribute to healing the wounds of war"), and we expressly mean live POWs ("Americans living in Vietnam").

A few months later the Montgomery Committee asked the White House for a copy of the February 1, 1973 letter from Nixon offering aid to North Vietnam "in order to determine whether or not the allegation by North Vietnam that it contained a commitment of U.S. aid to North Vietnam was correct."

The request was refused. Instead, Philip Habib, Under Secretary of State for Political Affairs, responded by summarizing Kissinger's version of what the letter said:

> The President's message did not contain any pledges or promises of aid; it was merely a restatement of our agreement, as set out in Article 21 of the Paris Agreement, to

participate in the postwar reconstruction of North Vietnam. The purpose of the letter was to advise the North Vietnamese of our preliminary financial estimates . . . of our reconstruction program. . . . This letter referred, of course, to the fact that the Executive Branch could not unilaterally make any offer of assistance to North Vietnam, but that such aid would first have to have Congressional authorization and appropriation. The letter did not specifically pledge to seek any particular sum of money for this purpose. . . . [29]

Habib's "summary" was patently fraudulent. The Nixon letter *did* specify a "particular sum"—$3.25 billion plus another $1-1.5 billion in aid. It was *not* a "preliminary financial estimate," but contained a firm figure. The only preliminary estimate was the $1-1.5 billion in additional aid. And, absolutely nothing in the letter speaks to the question of Congressional "authorization and appropriation." [30]

Vietnam's Deputy Foreign Minister, Phan Hien, at a press conference in Manila Airport in July 1976, continued to hammer on the theme of money for MIAs, again stating for the public record that as far as the Vietnamese were concerned, the deal they made with Nixon and Kissinger in 1973, was still "valid":

The position taken by the Americans is [that] the Paris Agreement no longer exists. That is why they refuse to implement Article 21 concerning the contribution to the healing of the wounds of war though the fact is that . . . it was President Nixon himself (who) sent a . . . letter to our prime minister. . . . In this letter he *committed* that the U.S. would contribute . . . $3,250,000 within the period of five years. . . . But they are insisting in asking us to implement Article 8B [on POWs] . . . while they are refusing to implement Article 21 [money] of the same agreement. I have never seen anything like this in international law and international practice. [31]

He seemed to have overlooked the fact that holding hostages for ransom was also outside of international law and practice—as is the deliberate abandonment of a nation's citizens in the furtherance of foreign policy.

Two months later the American Embassy in Paris received a phone call from the Vietnamese. An "urgent meeting" was requested. DRV First Secretary Do Than delivered an oral message from Hanoi, saying they hoped that the upcoming talks between the two governments, in Paris, "will achieve positive results in answering the interests of the two parties." As a gesture of good faith, the Vietnamese were going to turn over the bodies of 12 American MIAs that they had "just discovered." Do Than hoped "that the American party will respond in a positive manner to problems interesting the Vietnamese party"—i.e., reparations and recognition, in that order.[32]

One for the History Books

When Jimmy Carter defeated Gerald Ford in the 1976 Presidential election, it was time for Kissinger to put a legal, ethical and humanitarian face on the U.S. POW policy before leaving office in January 1977. The Carter Administration would inherit this new look—the POW issue would be transformed from a diplomatic poker game to a "basic humanitarian obligation."

On November 12, 1976, the Vietnamese and Americans met once again in Paris. The Vietnamese stayed with their line that the United States had incurred obligations under the Paris Agreement and had a continuing obligation to fulfill that commitment. The United States countered with its new look—the basic humanitarian obligation.

The United States opened the meeting with a statement defining the "new look." The Vietnamese countered, with Counsellor Tran Hoan saying that he followed with interest the U.S. statement, but wished to ask a few questions. First, Did the American side consider the problem of the MIA and the repatriation of remains connected to the Paris Agreement, and if so how? Was the agreement, in U.S. minds, reduced to Article 8B (POW/MIAs)? Second, Hoan asked for U.S. views of Article 21 (money), which called for the binding up the wounds of war and the reconstruction of Vietnam. Third, Hoan asked whether the implementation of Article 8B was a precondition for the normalization of relations between the two countries.

The U.S. countered again with the new look:

> We look to the future and not to the past in our relations with Vietnam. Selective interpretation of the Paris Agree-

ment is not a suitable basis for normalization of relations. We base our requirement for information on the MIA and return of remains on a basic humanitarian obligation established not only in international agreements such as the Geneva Convention of 1949, but also by all accepted standards of international and humanitarian behavior. The resolution of this problem is indeed a prerequisite for the normalization of relations between our two countries. When the fate of our men is known, we shall take concrete steps toward normalization of relations. As for whether Article 21 of the Paris Agreement is in effect, we do not consider that we have any obligation to provide aid.[33]

The two sides then sparred over the issue of whether the Paris Agreement was actually the basis for the U.S. demand that there be a full accounting for its POWs. The U.S. side then clearly told the Vietnamese that what the U.S. had once agreed to pay billions of dollars for was now being demanded free of charge:

. . . we consider that there are humanitarian grounds for requiring information on the MIA even without the provision of the Paris Agreement. All nations recognize an obligation to provide such information. We are sure you do have such information. . . . [34]

When the U.S. side then ticked off a list of the information the Vietnamese could provide, the Vietnamese countered by asking what the U.S. was prepared to do if the information was provided. The U.S. responded: "When our missing men have been satisfactorily accounted for, then we shall be prepared to take concrete steps toward normalization."

The Vietnamese wanted to know "what the 'concrete measures' might be." The U.S. came back with something less than a concrete answer: "the solution of the MIA problem would permit movement toward normalization in a spirit of mutual benefit." The Vietnamese, less than satisfied with this answer, wanted to know if they had to do everything before the U.S. did anything. The U.S. didn't answer the question, instead referring them back to the opening statement by the U.S. side.

After a short break, Hoan said he wished to make a few comments: as he understood it, the U.S. "denies the validity of the Paris Agreement." He agreed that "we should look to the future. Nevertheless, one must resolve the problems left by the past in order to turn to the future."

Then Hoan gave the Vietnamese version of who had violated the Paris Agreement:

> The United States wanted to hide behind the Agreement to withdraw from the war while pouring money and arms into South Vietnam in order to continue the war, not to bring peace. Therefore the DRV had no choice but to respond by sending men and arms to the South in order to counter American actions, in order to preserve the "independence, unity and territorial integrity of Vietnam." Under these circumstances it is clear who violated the Paris Agreement and who implemented it.

Hoan concluded: "as we see it, the fundamental principles of the Paris Agreement remain valid."

Hoan thought Nixon's February 1, 1973 letter was a "specific obligation. It is also a question of honor, responsibility and conscience for the US."

Then Hoan delivered the real message Hanoi wanted Washington to hear:

> ... you may raise the questions which concern you and we shall raise the problems which concern us. On this basis the two parties will exchange views to find a solution which suits both sides .... *We are prepared to fulfill fully, and I repeat fully, our obligation under Article 8B* .... But we consider that the US side should fulfill its obligation to contribute to binding up the wounds of war and the reconstruction of Viet-nam .... [authors' emphasis][35]

A clearer message could not have been sent: Vietnam will return the POWs if the United States pays the reparations it promised in writing. Kissinger certainly understood the message, but for him this was just old news. No deal was struck.

By this time, Kissinger's revisionist version of history had permeated the United States government's thinking. It simply was no longer possible for the bureaucracy to approach the POW issue from a factual viewpoint.

The standard bureaucratic lie became: "Although we have no indication that Americans are still held in Vietnam, we continue to do all we can to check and verify all such reports."[36]

In the court of world opinion this "new look" was a real public relations victory. It demanded that Hanoi unilaterally act in a "humanitarian manner" against its own interests and previous agreements with the U.S. Kissinger had finally succeeded in disengaging from his negotiating failures of 1972-73. And the best part was that no future Administration could reveal that failure unless it wanted to pick up the burden of defending a policy of trading hostages for money. To acknowledge Kissinger's failings as a diplomat publicly is to acknowledge a responsibility to successfully resolve America's darkest political secret: that the U.S. government had always known that POWs were being held hostage to political and monetary demands.

Chapter 15

1977: Carter Cares Less

"And the most unbelievable thing is this phony Woodcock Commission, that came on the heels of your early rush to judgment, presented one damned [POW] folder to the North Vietnamese in Hanoi in March of '77. I consider that a disgrace. The Communists told that to me across a negotiating desk in Hanoi. I couldn't believe it 'til I asked a State Department man to come over and tell me if that outrage was true. It was true."
—Congressman Robert K. Dornan, The McLaughlin Show, April 4, 1981

The newly empowered Carter Administration, from its earliest days, was determined to normalize relations with Vietnam. So on February 8, 1977, Under Secretary of State Philip Habib (a Kissinger associate) called in a high-rating Soviet diplomat and told him the U.S. was going to propose "a special mission to Hanoi... which would be a prestigious one," that would discuss MIAs, the return of remains "as well as other questions between us including how to move toward normalization of relations."[1]

Habib asked the Soviets to give the Vietnamese a message: "We would like to get the mission underway as soon as mutually convenient. Meanwhile we would hope the Vietnamese would be patient on other matters such as UN membership. Movement on the MIA's would of course be helpful on the UN matter, *although we do not intend this as a precondition.*" [author's emphasis][2]

The next day Secretary of State Cyrus Vance sent a message to the Vietnamese proposing a visit to Hanoi by the Woodcock Commission, an ad-hoc group of U.S. dignitaries led by former union boss Leonard Woodcock. The Vietnamese were told that Carter wanted "to move promptly toward normalization of relations with SRV, which is in the interests of both countries."[3]

Vietnamese Deputy Foreign Minister Phan Hien, Hanoi's point man on MIAs and money, said his government would be willing to receive the American representatives in Hanoi—but insisted that the Paris Agreement articles pertaining to reconstruction aid and MIAs "were both unimplemented articles and represented separate and equal obligations. It was not permissible therefore to make the fulfillment of Article 8B a precondition for the fulfillment of Article 21. Neither could US obligations under Article 21 be treated as 'humanitarian assistance.' "[4]

Hanoi had sent a clear, concise message: You can talk about MIAs and we will talk about money—the two are connected, but don't bother showing up with the Kissinger line about "humanitarian assistance."

Phan Hien then sent two messages to the United States government, using third nation diplomats as a conduit: In January the message was "there were American prisoners of war (POWs) still remaining in Vietnam and that these POWs posed a problem to the opening of diplomatic relations between the SRV and the United States. These POWs included some who did not want to return to the U.S."[5] In February, during a private conversation with an Indonesian diplomat, Phan Hien commented on the upcoming visit of a U.S. delegation to Hanoi in mid-March 1977, saying that there were American prisoners of war, some of whom came from wealthy families,[6] still in the SRV and they would not be released until U.S. financial aid for the SRV was forthcoming. The diplomat reported that Phan Hien implied that the information on MIA's was one trump card the SRV held in the forthcoming negotiations with the U.S. and explained that the SRV, having been the victor in the Vietnam War, would take advantage of this situation in negotiating with the U.S. for aid in economic reconstruction.[7]

On March 8, 1977, at a "preliminary meeting," the Vietnamese wanted to know if the Woodcock Commission was going to be empowered to discuss the question of U.S. aid to Vietnam, negotiate and sign agreements. They were told the Commission's "primary purpose was to obtain MIA information and return of remains [and] to listen to what [the] Vietnamese had to say on any issues they wished to raise, and to report Vietnamese views back to the President for his consideration."[8] And, the Vietnamese yet again said the U.S. "should be prepared to examine and solve with good will their primary concern re aid."[9]

So the Vietnamese had sent at least two messages to the Carter Administration that they held POWs and were willing to place them on the negotiating table—as long as the U.S. was also willing to fulfill its February 1, 1973, commitment to provide the Vietnamese with "reconstruction" aid. But the Carter Administration's humanitarian concerns, great though they were, simply did not extend to hostage POWs held for ransom. They were not about to be sucked into that political black hole.

The Woodcock Commission arrived in Hanoi and met with Phan Hien and North Vietnamese Prime Minister Pham Van Dong, who promptly told the Commission that "the issue of POW/MIAs is 'inter-related' with the U.S. obligation to provide reconstruction aid to North Vietnam."[10]

Congressman Sonny Montgomery gave Phan Hien the message that the U.S. was not going to buy back any POWs—telling him that he did not "expect Congress to appropriate any reconstruction aid to Vietnam."[11] So the Vietnamese had no reason to seriously address the issue of POWs under their control.

The Vietnamese got the message—the visit of the Woodcock Commission was not a serious U.S. attempt to resolve the issue. When questioned about POWs, the Vietnamese avoided an unequivocal answer, instead resorting to saying all POWs in areas under its control were returned; and all who "registered themselves" with Vietnam's Foreign Ministry had returned. When asked if any Americans did not register, the reply was: "We only know of those who have registered." But they never said they held no American POWs, but rather emphasized that they understood the sensitivity the U.S. had toward the mention of Article 21 and promised not to mention it again. Instead, they were willing to work with the U.S. and come up with new and creative ways for the United States to provide the promised ransom reconstruction aid while calling it something else.

The Woodcock Commission then took possession of the remains of 12 Americans, returned home and declared there was no evidence American POWs continued to be held by North Vietnam. Upon their return Carter either naively or falsely stated: "The Vietnamese have not tied together economic allocations of American funds with the MIA question."[12]

Then Leonard Woodcock did what the Carter Administration expected of him—he declared the POWs dead. After two days of talks with the Vietnamese government official who had been dropping hints around the world that they wanted to sell back some of America's sons, after two days of the Vietnamese refusing to unequivocally deny the existence of American POWs, and with absolutely no other proof of the deaths of all missing Americans, Woodcock tried to literally and figuratively bury the abandoned Americans for all time.

Just for good measure, Woodcock, obviously far over his head in the snakepit of POW politics, told Congress: "They [the Vietnamese] say no Americans are held alive against their will. I add to that just good common sense, and the passage of time. Why would they be holding Americans against their will? . . . . I add to their assurances just good common sense, that says, they [the MIAs] are not alive."[13]

Vietnam Rejects Full Normalization

Richard Holbrooke, Assistant Secretary of State for East Asia and Pacific Affairs, met Phan Hien in Paris in May of 1977, continuing the discussion started by the Woodcock Commission. Holbrooke's instructions were "to propose to the Vietnamese mutual recognition without preconditions. . . . "[14] No emphasis was placed on POWs by the United States during the talks.

"At one point during the talks, Holbrooke leaned across the table and said," to Phan Hien, "Mr. Minister, let's leave aside the issues that divide us. Let us go outside and jointly declare to the press that we have decided to normalize relations. Hien said no, there must be a U.S. contribution for healing the wounds of war."[15] Another American participant, Ken Quinn, remembers that Vietnam "was offered full normalization of relations and lifting of the trade embargo . . . I was in the room when it happened. They turned it down. They demanded money from us."[16]

So the talks ended without an agreement. The Vietnamese had clearly signaled that they intended to use the POWs they had kept as hostages in order to force the United States to fulfill its pledge to pay reparations. The Carter Administration countered by attempting to remove the POWs from the table with the Woodcock Commission findings.

But the Vietnamese had hostages to sell, and they wanted the money they felt they were owed. So another negotiating session was set for June. On June 2 Hien immediately went on the offensive, castigating the American side for making statements over the last month that would "harden opposition to aid within the Congress."[17] He then went on to make the case that the Nixon letter offering $3.25 billion [plus another $1-1.5 billion] was "a legal commitment which cannot be ignored."[18]

Hien then revealed more of the Kissinger-Le Duc Tho secret negotiations to support the Vietnamese position:

- The Vietnamese had objected to inclusion of the para-graph on adherence to constitutional processes [in Nixon's promise of aid during the Paris negotiations]. The US [therefore] transmitted it to the Vietnamese as a unilateral understanding.
- Kissinger had told Le Duc Tho that he would seek [the] opinion of Chairman and members of [the] House Appropriations Committee regarding the 'commitments' in the Nixon letter.[19]

The Vietnamese concluded that the "question of Congressional/Executive relations is essentially [an] internal matter of concern only to the US."[20] The U.S. must honor its "commitment" and "make a contribution. As to the forms and measures, Hanoi is prepared to be flexible."[21]

Kissinger has always maintained the Nixon letter was not a commitment because the reference to "Constitutional processes" meant the offer of aid was conditional to Congress willingness to provide the money. Hanoi's refusal to accept this qualification clearly indicates that, as far as the Vietnamese were concerned, it was an unconditional offer of aid. And the U.S. government just as clearly knew why the offer of "reconstruction" aid was placed on the table—to ransom the POWs the Vietnamese would otherwise not return.

Hien then "reiterated Vietnamese readiness to have a new long-term relationship with [the] US but restated their position that outstanding problems must be resolved first."[22] Holbrooke responded by saying that the Vietnamese demand for almost $5 billion was unrealistic "since neither [the] American people not the new president nor Congress are willing to accept such a request as [the] basis for [a] new relationship with your country."[23]

During the tea break, Hien and Holbrooke discussed the possibility of providing the aid through "indirect ways," such as international organizations, and food aid on an emergency basis.

But Holbrooke was not able to hold out hope of using this channel and the formal talks never resumed.

Over the remainder of the Carter Administration a few bodies were returned, as well as a live POW, Robert Garwood, in 1979—but both the U.S. and Vietnam worked to maintain the fiction that all POWs had returned during Operation Homecoming. And Garwood, who said he knew other Americans were still being held in Vietnam, was court-martialed and discredited—by the United States government.[24]

The POW Shell Game: Storing the Hostages

By October 1978, efforts to improve relations between America and Vietnam had stalled, and they soon crashed amid Hanoi's invasion of Cambodia and Chinese attacks on Vietnam.

As a result, Vietnam and its Laotian allies were forced to put their American captives into long-term storage. The agreement they forged on the American captives was made public years later. In February 1984, the foreign ministers of Laos, Vietnam and Cambodia issued a joint statement on the POW issue. "The three Indochinese peoples will show themselves to be unified on this question vis-a-vis the American people. If the American government wants to deal with 'us,' then it should cease its hostile acts toward 'us.' The U.S. must show an attitude of cooperation and must cease its policy of hostility carried out either directly or through third countries," the ministers announced.[25]

The united front of the Indochinese nations, dominated by Vietnam, was not merely directed at ending U.S. "hostility." Rather, the joint POW policy was also designed to win war reparations for all of Indochina and diplomatic recognition for the Hanoi's client state in Cambodia, according to a 1988 Pentagon report.

The information come from a Laotian officer via a U.S. "controlled asset of proven reliability with excellent access." According to the "asset": "[T]he Lao government accepted the principle agreed to by the other Indochinese governments of Vietnam and Kampuchea [Cambodia] to retain prisoners for political reasons .... [T]he three Indochinese governments also agreed to move the remaining U.S. PW 'around' to serve their needs."[26]

In effect, the communist Indochinese were simply continuing the POW "shell game" Hanoi used during the Paris Peace talks. American POWs could be moved across the ill-defined borders of the three nations as circumstances dictated. For example, in early 1973, U.S. POWs had been reported being moved from Vietnam—where they should have been released, according to the Paris Peace Accords—to Cambodia, where no POW deal had been struck. And then in September, 1973 the various factions in Laos signed an agreement requiring them to release POWs. That same month, a Laotian villager reported seeing nine U.S. POWs, all wearing flight suits, being transported from Laos to Vietnam.[27]

In other words, if Vietnamese troops guarded U.S. POWs in Laos, Hanoi could claim it did not hold Americans "on its territory," while Laos could assert there were no POWs "under its control." The same game was used by Vietnam and Cambodia during and immediately after the Vietnam War, and may have been resumed in 1978 after Vietnam overthrew the hostile Pol Pot regime and installed its own government in Cambodia.

The implications of the shell game are critical to understanding the POW scandal. In Vietnam, U.S. investigators are theoretically allowed to inspect prisons. Of course, the Pentagon must alert Hanoi to the exact location of the search far in advance, giving the Vietnamese plenty of time to move any U.S. prisoners. And the DIA hasn't made a practice of obtaining aerial pictures of the camps to determine whether prisoners are being moved. In Vietnam, at least, Americans can get into prisons, but in Laos, the Pentagon has admitted, the government has allowed no access at all inside prisons. Even the most incompetent communist bureaucracy could keep U.S. POWs hidden with that kind of advantage.

For many years, the U.S. government has assisted Hanoi's deception by ignoring the POW connection among the three Indochinese nations, dealing instead with each separately on the issue.

Of course, Washington has always known that Laos and Cambodia (except during the Pol Pot interlude) were "client states" of Hanoi, as the U.S. government's official *Vietnam: A Country Study* describes them. In 1981, the State Department even conceded in a classified telegram that: "For better or worse, we cannot separate the Lao MIA problem from that with the Vietnamese."

But because the POW issue was never really "the highest national priority," it was subordinated or linked to other specific concerns in the various Indochinese nations, such as Vietnamese military aggression and Laotian drug trafficking.

For instance, a top official from America's embassy in Vientiane raised both the POW/MIA issue and the Laotian drug market during a January 1991 meeting with Laos' Vice Foreign Minister. The Laotian perceived the U.S. comments as "threatening and linking narcotics and POW/MIA issues." The State Department concluded: "Our pressure on narcotics may well be spilling over into POW/MIA issues. This might be a factor in the languid pace of POW/MIA progress. . . ."[28]

The real message America was sending to Indochina was that the POW issue was just one of many American concerns, not the "highest national priority" it was called back in the U.S. Only in 1992 was Hanoi pressured to promise help in accounting for POW/MIAs in Laos. And as of this writing, that promise has joined the pile of unmet Vietnamese pledges offered over the years. And the POWs remain in storage across Indochina, where they have languished for more than two decades.

1. An American pilot being captured in Vietnam in January 1966.

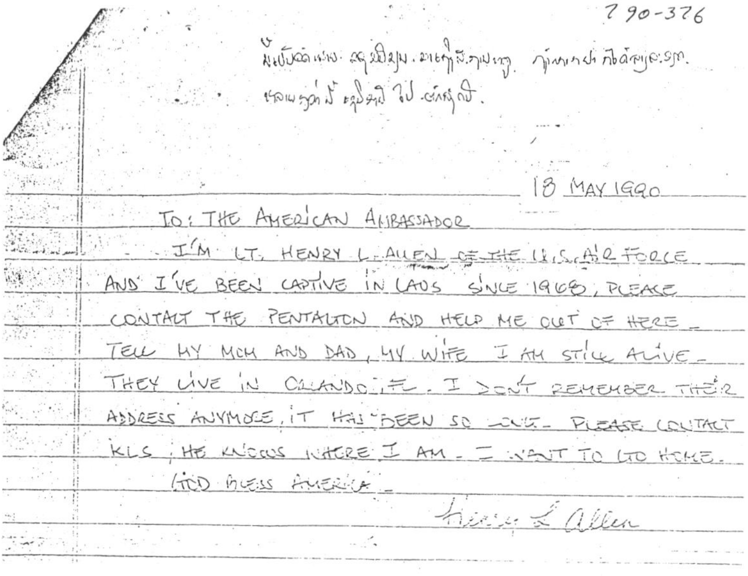

790-376

ນຂໍ້ມາປາກຄ... ... (handwritten Lao script)

18 MAY 1990

TO: THE AMERICAN AMBASSADOR

I'M LT. HENRY L ALLEN OF THE U.S. AIR FORCE AND I'VE BEEN CAPTIVE IN LAOS SINCE 1968, PLEASE CONTACT THE PENTAGON AND HELP ME OUT OF HERE TELL MY MOM AND DAD, MY WIFE I AM STILL ALIVE THEY LIVE IN ORLANDO, FL. I DON'T REMEMBER THEIR ADDRESS ANYMORE, IT HAS BEEN SO LONG. PLEASE CONTACT KLS; HE KNOWS WHERE I AM. I WANT TO GO HOME. GOD BLESS AMERICA.

Henry L Allen

2. Letter dated May 18, 1990, allegedly written by Maj. Henry L. Allen, U.S.A.F., a U.S. POW captured in Laos in 1968, to the U.S. Ambassador. Documentation of this nature was routinely ignored by the U.S. government.

3. Col. Burris N. Begley, U.S.A.F. a pilot downed on December 5, 1966. His name was scratched into the floor of the Hao Lo prison in North Vietnam.

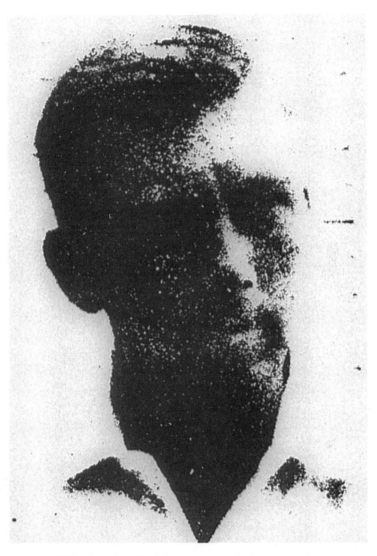

4. SFC Dallas Pridemore, U.S.A., the American soldier who was kidnapped by the Viet Cong from his Vietnamese girlfriend's home. Pridemore was reportedly alive after the war.

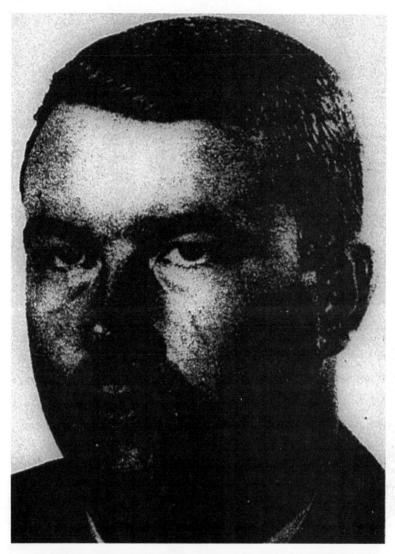

5. HMC Michael LaPorte, U.S.N., a sailor lost in South Vietnam on September 9, 1967. LaPorte was reportedly seen by Robert Garwood in captivity in North Vietnam after Homecoming. It is possible that LaPorte is a secret returnee, last reported in the Los Angeles area.

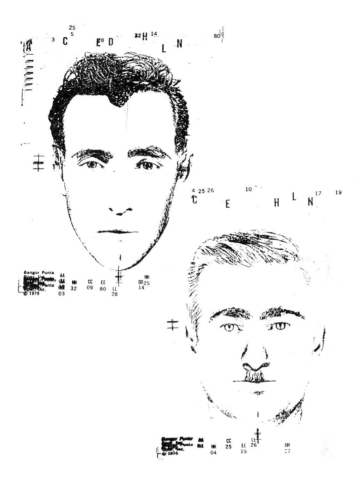

6. In December 1979 Pentagon experts, based on eyewitness descriptions, prepared these sketches of Caucasian men seen in captivity in Hanoi during that year. Pentagon POW expert Bill Bell believes that the man on the left is Charles Duke (civilian), son of Jane Gaylor, and the man on the right Kit Mark (rank unknown) or SSGT Jimmy Malone, U.S.A.

7. President George Bush carries on a heated discussion with Jeff Donahue and Diana Van Renselaar of the National League of Families during a disruption of his speech to a group of POW/MIA families in Arlington, VA on July 24, 1992.

8. Senator Bob Smith (R., N.H.) (left) with Senator John Kerry (D., Mass.) (right) during hearings of the Senate Select Committee on POW/MIA Affairs.

PART V

Hostages

Chapter 16

Americans Alive in Laos

"I wish to assure you that there are no Americans who have been captured and are alive in Laos." —Nouphan Sithpasay, Lao Vice Minister of Foreign Affairs, March 1977

"Refer to the Politbureau, Ministry of Defense, that because U.S. and Thai POWs have been identified by [CENSORED] they be removed from Attopeu Province. Aircraft will pick up POWs at the airfield on 28 DEC at 12:30 hours."
—Intercepted communist radio transmission, Dec. 27, 1980 (censored by U.S. government)

By late 1979, the evidence was clear that American POWs remained alive in Laos. Recently intercepted communist transmissions concerning their U.S. captives had electrified the Pentagon. "Col. Picinich [of the DIA] was visibly excited about recent events. It is the opinion of that office that U.S. POWs are in fact still alive in SEA [Southeast Asia]," wrote a Pentagon official following a December 12, 1979, briefing on the intercepted messages.[1]

The signals' intelligence was backed up by strong evidence from human sources. The Pentagon had begun receiving several reports of U.S. POWs in a specific area of Laos. One of the U.S. sources was described as "a sensitive source with unusually good access." This "sensitive source," reportedly a Laotian woman with access to top government officials, provided a series of reports detailing the presence of up to 30 Americans POWs at the camp.

In November 1979, a second source confirmed there were American POWs in the camp. The source, who passed a polygraph exam, reportedly got the information from a guard at the camp, who said one of the POWs was Lt. Col. Paul W. Mercland. There is no POW/MIA with that name, but experts thought the name might really be a garbled version of Air Force

POW/MIA Paul W. Bannon, American. (It was later learned that the CIA also had a report of a Caucasian prisoner at the camp, but apparently did not share its intelligence with the Pentagon.)

Following the lead of their human sources, the Pentagon soon trained its satellites on the region. There was an immediate hit. The imagery confirmed the location of a mysteriously isolated prison in the region. Based on the photography, CIA analysts determined the camp had been built between April 1978 and September 1979, and was occupied by December 1980.

The camp, whose rustic features soon earned it the Pentagon nickname "Fort Apache," was located in a clearing off Route 12. It was divided into inner and outer areas, both protected by stockade-type fences. The outer fence was about six to ten feet high. Behind this outer wall were fields of crops, guard barracks, a trench, a machine-gun nest, and two observation towers. The towers, with platforms 10 to 12 feet above the ground, were positioned so guards could look into the camp. The inner compound, also surrounded by a tall fence, contained five buildings, including two large barracks.

The CIA analysts confirmed that the camp was designed to keep people in, rather than keeping guerillas or animals out. But there were two other striking things about the camp. First, according to some reports, the photos indicated that some of the prisoners were much taller than others in the camp and rested by sitting with their ankles crossed rather than squatting Asian-style. They also used tools that were too big for the average Laotian. The second remarkable thing about the camp could be seen in the vegetable plots between the inner and outer fences. It was what appeared to be a big "52." "Each number is 1-2 meters wide and 3 meters high. The two numerals appear to be shallow depressions. . . . The location of the numerals is such that they most likely cannot be seen from either of the two observation towers because of trees located in the line of sight," the CIA reported. In addition, it appeared possible that the letter "K" followed the "52."

In other words, it looked as if someone had hacked a signal into the ground that could be seen from the air but not from the camp's guard towers. Said the CIA: "It is thus conceivable that this represents an attempt by a prisoner to signal to any aircraft that might pass overhead."

The significance of the "K" was clear—it was a sign used by downed American pilots to signal distress. The "52", although a much clearer signal, had a more elusive meaning. Some experts thought it represented the number of POWs in the camp. Others believed it was intended to show B-52 bomber crewmen were being held. Years later, one source claimed that "52" was a symbol used by U.S. briefers on maps of Vietnam during the war to denote U.S. POW camps, so they wouldn't be bombed by B-52 crews.

Whatever it meant, the "52" was clearly a man-made signal in a camp reported by other sources to hold U.S. POWs. (Note: The DIA agreed the "52" was man-made when it was first detected, but now claims it was really just a coincidental feature of the landscape.) The satellite photos set the Pentagon scrambling— But it was already too late.

The POWs Are Moved

Perhaps the communists learned of America's interest in "Fort Apache." Or maybe they were just practicing good security. But the "sensitive source" reported that because of security concerns, the POWs were moved from Laos to Vietnam by the end of January 1981.

The NSA had already reported an intercepted communist radio transmission, which, if not referring to the Nhom Marrot prisoners, reflected concerns about other U.S. POWs. The transmission went out on December 27, 1980: "Refer to the Politburo, Ministry of Defense, that because U.S. and Thai POWs have been identified by [CENSORED] they be removed from Attopeu Province. Aircraft will pick up POWs at the airfield on 28 DEC at 12:30 hours."

By February 1981, the "52" had begun to fade away at "Fort Apache."

The Mission Continues

But by this time, in early 1981, the Nhom Marrot sightings had acquired a life of their own within the U.S. bureaucracy. One factor may have been the alleged Vietnamese offer to sell back U.S. POWs, which had recently been turned down by Ronald Reagan's new team. According to some accounts, the Reagan White House, fearing a new hostage crisis just days after the

Iranian hostages had come home, was not about to pay "blackmail" for POWs.

But learning the exact location of U.S. POWs offered the opportunity for a rescue operation, and not a bungled one like "Desert One" in Iran. Reagan was "flabbergasted . . . enthused and excited" after his briefing on "Fort Apache," according to Reagan's National Security Advisor Richard Allen.[2]

The Cavalry Fails to Arrive at Fort Apache

Planning began for a covert operation aimed at Nhom Marrot. Everybody agreed that a reconnaissance team needed to infiltrate Laos and verify that the camp held Americans. Delta Force, the Army's elite hostage-rescue team, would then swoop down for the rescue.

While Delta started planning for its part of the operation, the CIA and Pentagon began putting together the reconnaissance operation. But as so often, the planning turned into a turf-battle. The Army, which would take the credit or blame for the rescue, reportedly wanted a part of the reconnaissance. At a minimum, the military demanded one of its people at least participate in the operation, providing what special operations troops call "eyes on the ground," or reliable intelligence.

But the CIA had other ideas. It wanted to use mercenaries to allow the U.S. government "plausible deniability" if the operation were compromised. And, according to one source, the CIA also refused to place an American on the team.

All the bickering caused what Allen called "an unbelievably long time" to go by before the team actually launched its mission during May 1981, almost half a year after the camp was identified. The tardy operation immediately stalled when the mercenaries tangled with Vietnamese troops and had to withdraw with their wounded. The team regrouped and headed back into Laos, only to discover that it couldn't get a picture of the camp's inner compound—which didn't matter anyway, because there were no longer any Americans in the facility.

Then, on May 21, 1981, *The Washington Post* ran a story on the operation, killing the chance of any further U.S. efforts on the ground. Soon after, President Reagan made a speech on the POW issue: "Recently there have been reports that Americans are still being held captive in Indochina. None of these reports, I'm sorry to say, have been verified. But the world should know that this administration continues to attach the highest priority to the problem of those missing in action."[3]

Representative Sonny Montgomery, Congress' POW "expert," was quoted as saying: "The mission into Laos showed that there are no Americans still alive." And before long, the Nhom Marrot mission was being portrayed as an example of aggressive action that proved the devotion of the U.S. government to its missing men while at the some time showing that there was no hard evidence that U.S. POW/MIAs remained alive in Southeast Asia. Of course, the real lesson of "Fort Apache" was just the opposite: the U.S. hunt for POW/MIAs was seriously flawed, and living Americans did remain in Southeast Asia.

As Rear Admiral Jerry Tuttle, the DIA's point man on the operation, put it: "There were live American prisoners in Laos in 1981 . . . I would bet my life on it, I'm so damned sure of it."[4]

The War Years

By one estimate, 519 Americans were missing in Laos during the war. More than 80 were last known alive, according to the Pentagon. And throughout the war live sighting reports of American POWs held in Laos had trickled into intelligence files. By 1970 more than 300 such reports had been received. The wartime intelligence files are especially important in Laos, because, as Senate investigators noted, "unlike Vietnam and Cambodia, the Pathet Lao leaders have not changed since the mid-1950s. This has produced constancy and continuity in Pathet Lao policy toward prisoners . . . in practice Lao policy has been to hold captives in the area in which they were seized."

In 1971 a Pathet Lao who worked for Soth Pethrasy, the Pathet Lao representative in Vientiane, defected, revealing that "after visits of PW families or PW related visits by press or diplomatic missions, Soth would routinely draft [a] message and carry it to [the] radio room." The defector saw "what appeared to be names and bio data which he assumed were related to PWs."

By then the United States only acknowledged three confirmed POWs in Laos, but believed that "substantially more men captured in Laos are held in NVN [North Vietnam] but we have been able to confirm only a few names and have no idea of the total number." Apparently the Pathet Lao were making some attempt to receive mail for the American POWs. More importantly, if POW information was communicated by radio between Pathet

Lao headquarters at Sam Neua and Soth's office in Vientiane, the U.S. National Security Agency was certainly listening in. However, as discussed later in this book, most of the NSA's POW information is still secret and was never even examined by the Senate POW Committee.

But even without the intercepts, it seems clear the Pathet Lao were holding dozens of U.S. captives. At a diplomatic social event in Vientiane on July 22, 1971, an American diplomat was told "that thirty American POWs are still left in Laos [the others were transferred to Hanoi], located in small town of Muong Poun near abandoned airstrip at Muong Soi."

Three months later a Pathet Lao POW, during interrogation revealed that the NHHS (Pathet Lao) "Headquarters published a weekly bulletin which contained photographs and resumés of Americans captured by the Pathet Lao (PL). Such prisoners were allegedly turned over to the North Vietnamese and sent to Hanoi."

The resumé listed "each prisoner's name, rank, date and place of capture as well as photographs of all documentation found on his person." The Pathet Lao POW "saw copies of the bulletins during the course of his daily work. He estimated that between 1966 and late 1969 he saw photographs of some 30 American prisoners in the bulletins." In late 1969 his "section was reorganized and he no longer received copies of the bulletin." He could not recall any "names or details" of the Americans, but had heard that all American POWs were turned over to the North Vietnamese, but had no independent knowledge that they were sent to Hanoi.

An International Control Commission (ICC) official, judged by the CIA to be a reliable source, reported "that although all 'important' American POWs captured in Laos have been sent to North Vietnam for detention, an unspecified number of American POWs is still held in the Pathet Lao Headquarters area of Sam Neua and Phong Saly."

Shortly after Soth Pethrasy returned from Sam Neua, on September 16, he told the ICC source "that the American POWs in Sam Neua are quite safe because they are kept in relatively bomb-proof caves." Lieutenant General Eugene F. Tighe, Director of the DIA after the Vietnam War, testified before Congress that "there were Americans alive and photographed in Laos in the

Sam Neua area up to a period of about 18 months before hostilities ceased."

Virtually at the same time the ICC official was passing information to the United States government, a Laotian Army lieutenant returned to government control and was undergoing debriefing. His debriefing has never been declassified but, on October 20 his report of "Recent identification of US personnel" held captive in Laos was to be the number-one topic of discussion at a State Department meeting of the MIA Task Force.

In November 1972, two trucks carrying eight "negro and Caucasian American POWs" were seen moving north in Sawannakhet Province, Laos, by NVA Sergeant Tran Duc Cuong, who was infiltrating into South Vietnam along a branch of the Ho Chi Minh trail. No men who made such a trip returned to the U.S.

A Pathet Lao POW captured in January 1973 reported that in April or May 1972 he was assigned to repair a telephone line from NLSH Headquarters in Ban Na Khay Neua to a cave several kilometers to the east. "Source states that he entered cave to repair line and observed total of eight male Caucasian whom PL guards referred to as American pilots." "Identical cave facility was reported by another source on November 25, 1972."[5]

For years and years, U.S. POWs have been reported in the Laotian caves. But many of these caves are unlike the dark and muddy image they conjure for many Americans. The Laotian caves, located in limestone hills, were often elaborately designed, with electricity and even medical clinics. A person could, and U.S. POWs apparently have, live for years in such a facility.

The Top Secret Fall of "Site 85"

Melvin Holland may have ended up in one of those caves. Holland was an Air Force technician assigned in 1968 to a mile-high radar base atop a Laotian peak named Phou Pha Ti. The Americans called it Lima Site 85—but not in public. The base and its mission, guiding B-52 bombers into Hanoi, were secret. In fact, an international agreement forbade the stationing of U.S. ground troops in Laos.

So the Pentagon simply turned Holland into a civilian—a process called "sheep dipping" in the intelligence world. On paper, Holland and others on Site 85 worked for Lockheed. Ann Holland, Mel's wife, was worried about that when the Pentagon first offered him the assignment. But Mel, proud to be picked for such an important mission, went along with the program. Besides, the Pentagon said, Site 85 was surrounded on three sides by cliffs and guarded by 300 fierce Asian mercenaries working for the CIA. There was no danger.

In early 1968, North Vietnamese troops began building a road through the thick Laotian jungle. It was pointed right at Site 85. While the Air Force, State Department and CIA bickered over the enemy's intent, the road kept coming. When the Air Force ordered some limited air strikes, the communists removed their dead and kept on building. U.S. Ambassador to Laos William Sullivan refused requests to remove the men from the mountain, according to official histories and memoirs of the era.

The enemy struck in March of 1968, supported by small planes whose crews dropped bombs by hand in one of the few North Vietnamese bombing runs of the war. The bombing was unusual, but not the determination of the Vietnamese troops, who scaled the cliffs and overran Site 85. U.S. planes later bombed the facility to keep its gear from falling into enemy hands. Mel Holland and 10 other Americans missing from the site were declared dead.

Even in death the truth about their loss could not be known, the Pentagon decided. Their names did not even appear on the DIA's list of POW/MIAs until 1982, and Pentagon officials in Southeast Asia confirmed that in the meantime they had not even been looking for the Site 85 POW/MIAs, Ann Holland says.

Infuriated, Mrs. Holland filed suit to open the Pentagon's records on her husband, and what she found made her even angrier. A Pathet Lao platoon leader reported seeing a white male wearing glasses with light-colored frames being brought to a Laotian communist headquarters soon after the battle, U.S. intelligence reported. "The Pathet Lao escorting the individual stated that he was an American whom they had captured . . . after he had come from the site at Phou Pha Ti," the report noted.

Mel Holland was the only man on the mountain who fit that description, Ann Holland learned. The document was also consistent with at least three other reports that Americans had been captured in the battle. And the communist area where the man believed to be Holland was taken included communist POW camps from which no Americans returned at the end of the war.

"They took something from me and I want it back," says Ann Holland.

The Post-War Years

The communists took plenty, according to declassified intelligence reports. From 1972 to at least 1973, the "T1" prison in southern Laos held 26 American prisoners, according to a communist transmission intercepted by the NSA.[6]

From September 1973 to March 1974, a series of unrelated witnesses reported the movement of nine POWs between two Laotian prison camps. The reports started when a local villager reported seeing nine U.S. POWs at a joint Laotian/Vietnamese prison camp at Pha Dakthong, Khammouane Province, during September 1973. The Americans, said to had been captured in Savannakhet Province, were eventually shipped out of town, the villager said.

Another source, a village chief, picked up the story. He said Pathet Lao officials had mentioned during a meeting on March 6, 1974 that nine U.S. POWs had been moved from Pha Dakthong about 13 kilometers northwest to Pha Katao. Yet another Laotian confirmed U.S. POWs were being moved to Pha Katao. This report, from February 1974, concerned a sighting of five Americans in transit. (Of this group, two had reportedly been captured in the Muong Phine area during 1970, and another fell into enemy hands in the vicinity of Ban Nagnon.) All nine POWs apparently made it safely to the prison at Pha Katao. On March 20, 1974, two Laotian travelers saw six American POWs there. The travelers were told that a total of nine U.S. POWs were in the compound, matching the earlier reports exactly.

U.S. reconnaissance photography confirmed the existence of a well-developed fenced compound in the village. "[T]he facility could easily be used for detention purposes," the DIA reported. The fate of the American POWs taken to Pha Katao has never been made public. Another story hidden from the American public is the full story of a secret Laotian mission codenamed "Baron 52."

A Controversial Message

As discussed earlier, a former soldier has testified under oath that in May or June 1974, U.S. Army intelligence intercepted a communist radio message concerning American POWs in Laos.[7] The communists were ordering supplies, including pigs, for use by U.S. POWs held in Luang Prabang Province, the former soldier testified. That northern area of Laos was easily accessible from

Vietnam via routes 7 and 13, so perhaps these were Americans shifted over from Vietnamese camps.

Interestingly, the number of POWs in the alleged communist intercept corresponds closely to the tally kept by Kahmou Boussarath, who ran the Laotian equivalent of the FBI, CIA and military intelligence from 1965 to 1975. Boussarath, highly regarded by U.S. officials, has said his agents reported that at least 200 Americans were held in Laos when the war ended. He claims to have given many of their names to the U.S. government during the war.

Several other sources indicate that 200 Americans could have been held in Laos after the war, under both North Vietnamese and Laotian control. While the Pentagon says there's "no evidence" any repatriated Americans were held in Laos after the war, declassified intelligence files tell another story.

Americans in Tchepone

Laotian refugee Bounkong Chanthalangsy claims to have seen 12 U.S. POWs imprisoned near the Laotian town of Tchepone, some as late as 1974. The refugee said one of the Americans had a broken leg, which may correlate with the case of aviator Morgan Donahue, who was reported alive on the ground with a broken leg after his plane was shot down near Tchepone in 1968.[8]

Rosemary Conway, a CIA agent held by Laos in 1975, says her guards discussed holding Donahue and other POWs, including aviator John Albright, in Tchepone after the war.

In September 1984, a communist transmission obtained by the National Security Agency mentioned 23 "unidentified prisoners" in Tchepone, a number that just happened to match exactly the number of U.S. POWs a human source had just reported in the area. Then in October 1986, the NSA issued a report about a "probable former American POW Camp" in Tchepone District "where approximately 50 American POW's were detained." The report, still heavily censored, says it was not clear when, or even if, the camp had stopped operations.[9]

The Camps in the North of Laos

In August 1980, a French diplomat passed a report to the U.S. from a Laotian friend "well and favorably known" to the Frenchman, who had just escaped from almost five years in communist prisons. From May 1975 to May 1979, the Laotian had been imprisoned with two American POWs in the prison complex in Phong Saly Province, in the far north of Laos bordering China. According to the Laotian, one of the Americans was known as "Major John." The other, either a lieutenant colonel or colonel, had a name that sounded like Tecker. In May 1979, the men were moved "eastwards," according to the refugee.[10]

Many refugees have reported U.S. POWs in Phong Saly Province. One said he even ran into an American while escaping from Laos in 1979. "After exchanging a few words, we left each other to a different direction," the refugee, a former senior Laotian police official, said.[11]

In 1979, a Laotian prisoner was sweeping the floor in his re-education camp when he overheard the camp director, a police chief, talking to several of his subordinates in the next room. According to the source, the chief bragged loudly that the Laotian government has been successful in keeping secret from the Americans the fact that the Lao government was still holding American prisoners in Phongsaly Province near the Lao/Vietnam border opposite Dien Bien Phu. He also said that the Americans were being held so that Laos could obtain information about modern technology from them.[12]

Around the same time, a Laotian was in a convoy of three trucks delivering supplies to a Pathet Lao unit in Huong Khoua, Phong Saly Province. The source, who passed a polygraph test on his sighting, "observed for approximately 15-20 seconds five or six Caucasian male prisoners accompanied by an armed guard." One of the Pathet Lao guards told the U.S. source that the men he had seen were just some of 50 U.S. POWs detained in the area.[13]

"Baron 52"

Mary and Stephen Matejov emerged from St. Raphael's Catholic Church in East Meadow, New York, on a cool day in March 1973. The funeral Mass for their son, Joe, an electronic warfare specialist shot down over Laos on February 5, 1973 had just concluded. They were ready to get on with their lives. Then someone approached with a shocking message. "We have a message from one of Joe's friends [in Vietnam]," the stranger told the grieving parents. "Don't be surprised if Joe walks in the front door someday."

"What are you talking about?" the Matejovs replied. "We were told in the letter not to write back and ask questions. Not to bring the subject up in writing because the person who sent it could be in trouble for revealing information he shouldn't have revealed," the stranger responded.

"That was the first indication we had that Joe was alive," Mrs. Matejov remembered. Since then, her family and the family of Peter Cressman, another crew member on the eight-man reconnaissance flight, have been trying to find out what happened to their sons. The Defense Intelligence Agency, which has the mission to identify and return any live POWs, claims "there is no evidence that any crew members survived the crash."

Matejov and Cressman worked for the NSA's Central Security Service (CSS), which ran electronic intelligence-gathering flights over Southeast Asia. Their EC-47 lifted out of Ubon Airfield in Thailand about 11 p.m. on February 4, 1973. Two and one half hours later, the pilot radioed a forward air controller and reported receiving 38 mm anti-aircraft fire. After that, the plane dropped off the radar screen and crashed. On February 17, 1973, the entire crew was declared dead, eliminating an embarrassing obstacle to the impending Laotian peace agreement, which was signed the next day.

But in a letter to the Cressmans, the commander of the EC-47's air wing had admitted "a possibility that one or more crew members could have parachuted to safety." And on the day of the shootdown the NSA intercepted communist radio transmissions that stated: "Group is holding four pilots captive and the group is requesting orders concerning what to do with them." One month later a Laotian source provided U.S. intelligence with detailed descriptions of the four captives, identified as Sergeant Peter Cressman, Sergeant Dale Brandenburg, Sergeant Joseph Matejov, and Sergeant Todd Milton."

The first NSA staffer to expose what the government knew was Jerry Mooney. As an Air Force sergeant working for CSS, he tracked more than 300 POWs on the ground in Southeast Asia, of whom only 5% came home. A member of the 6970th Support Group, Mooney's job was to intercept and analyze North Vietnamese communications. Among them were orders to "shoot down the enemy and capture the pilot alive," and "shoot down the enemy and execute the pilot." More importantly, he revealed, in a signed affidavit, "North Vietnamese messages revealed an interest in selecting priority targets to include F-111 aircraft, airborn intelligence collectors, F-4 laser bomb-equipped aircraft and electronic support aircraft." The reason was to repay Vietnam's Soviet benefactors, who wanted access not only to American equipment but also the people who could use it— American POWs. Cressman, Matejov and the other members of the EC-47 crew would be highly prized by Soviet military planners, present both in Laos and North Vietnam.

Despite what the U.S. government told the families, the men had apparently not died but had been captured. "My section received, analyzed, evaluated and formally reported the shoot-down of the EC-47 aircraft in Laos," Mooney says. "Based upon the enemy message which we collected there were survivors who were identified as Americans and transported to North Vietnam . . . . I personally wrote the message that these men had been captured alive. In secure phone conversation with the Defense Intelligence Agency we were in total agreement that these were the crew members of the downed EC-47Q." (By 1993, the DIA had changed its mind and claimed none of the men could have survived. The Pentagon attempted to prove its case by conducting a special operation to search the plane's wreckage. But that operation failed to disprove Mooney's report.)

According to Dr. Roger Shields, a member of the delegation to the Paris Peace negotiations, the names of the four men were on the list of POWs American officials would give the Vietnamese, in expectation of their return. At the last minute, Bill Clements, then Under Secretary of Defense, ordered the names removed from the list.

But the men weren't dead. They were shot down after the United States and Vietnam signed the Paris Peace Accords; flight was illegal under that agreement. The names were scratched from the list because they were an inconvenience that would have complicated Henry Kissinger's life.

A Taxi Driver's Story

In late December 1975, a Laotian refugee was driving his pick-up truck taxi when he was stopped at a communist checkpoint. The soldiers discovered that one of his passengers had a weapon, and when they shook down the driver they discovered a U.S. employee I.D. card he had gotten from a friend. The soldiers tossed him into the back of a covered truck, and he began a 20-day trip.[14]

In early 1976, he reached the outskirts of Viengxay, a communist stronghold where unrepatriated U.S. POWs had been held during the war. Soon he was on the move again, driving over bad roads for three hours east of the village to a prison camp. According to a sworn statement by the refugee, he was imprisoned at the camp, which was surrounded by bamboo trees and centered around a natural cave. To one side of the cave was a stream used for drinking water and bathing. About thirty feet in front of the cave's entrance stood two bamboo shacks for the prison's 12 guards.

The taxi driver spent the month of January at the prison camp, mostly in a bamboo hut. But he was often brought down right next to the cave for interrogation. "I saw five Caucasian prisoners being held in the cave. I was told by my guard that these prisoners were American pilots," he said in a sworn statement. The driver added more detail in a letter, saying that at first, "I wonder[ed] why the communists do not send them back to their country because the war has already ended." In answer to his question, the prison chief said the Americans were being held for their technical skills.

According to the driver, the U.S. prisoners wore light green uniforms and "Ho Chi Minh" sandals made of old tires. They had one pink towel to use during baths in the stream. Skinny but apparently uninjured, the men were under close guard by the Pathet Lao. The Americans also had rashes on their ankles, perhaps from shackles. The guards never allowed the driver to communicate with the Americans, but it appeared the interrogators were trying to determine whether the driver and POWs knew each other.

"During the interrogation the guards would point to the American prisoners and ask me if I had helped Americans. They would also question the American prisoners while they were questioning me and I could see the American prisoners shaking their heads when they [the guards] pointed to me," the driver remembered.

Some DIA reports say the refugee saw the POWs from a Pathet Lao truck. "He saw five American POWs and the Pathet Lao asked him if he knew or recognized the American POWs. He replied no. The Pathet Lao soldier walked to the American POWs and came back after awhile. [The] source guessed that the Pathet Lao asked the American POWS if they knew [the] source," one Pentagon report said.

No matter which version of the story is correct, one thing can be said with certainty about the refugee's report: He passed an extensive Pentagon polygraph test, verified by independent review, showing that he had told the truth about seeing Caucasian prisoners identified by their Pathet Lao guards as American POWs. (Remarkably, after ten years of review, the Pentagon declared the prisoners were really Russian advisors.)

Senate investigators uncovered 35 post-war reports of U.S. POWs in the Viengxay, including 13 alleged first-hand sightings. Many of the accounts came from Laotians who said they'd worked as guards or trustees in the area's prison camps. Most of the reports, like the taxi driver's, concern small groups of Americans. However, one second-hand report from a former prisoner in the area claimed that 43 Americans, captured in Vietnam, were alive there as late as 1983. The State Department cautiously noted: "We cannot rule out the possibility that there were some Caucasians at the site. . . . "[15]

Again, eye-witness accounts of U.S. POWs in this area were supported by a communist radio broadcast, which on November 15, 1979, discussed the movement of three U.S. POWs from Viengxay to elsewhere in Laos for work in the "mines."

Shelton and Hrdlicka

Everybody, even the communists and the DIA, admits pilots Charles Shelton and David Hrdlicka are pilots who never returned from Laos. Shelton was seen alive after his plane was shot down in 1965, and Hrdlicka was photographed and had his voice recorded while in communist captivity following his capture that same year.

In 1982, a Laotian official claimed both men had died in 1968. The Pentagon believes that—but not the men's families. Hrdlicka's wife Carol learned about two 1989 Pentagon reports indicating the aviator was still alive. One report, allegedly from a Frenchman, says Hrdlicka escaped and was recaptured. The other is both far more cryptic and compelling. Written by a U.S. intelligence official in Southeast Asia, it says, "I am talking to General Chang of the 11th Regiment who is suspected of holding D. Hrdlicka and friends—outcome of my conversation to follow."

It hasn't, at least to the Hrdlicka family, which says the Pentagon has promised but then failed to provide them with more details about the two reports.

"If they had proved David is dead, they'd give that to me. They'd have shut me up. There's a reason they [the Pentagon officials who promised details] are lying," Carol Hrdlicka said.

It may be significant that Laos claims it can't return the two pilots' bodies because their graves were destroyed by U.S. bombs. During the Korean War, the communists reportedly used just the same excuse to hide the fate of American POWs they had decided to retain.

Mistaken Identification?

The Senate Select Committee identified 30 reports, six of them first-hand, of American POWs in remote parts of northern Laos after the war. Reports filed during the 1970s concerned groups of fewer than 10 Americans, while reports during the late 1980s recounted sightings of groups of from 16 to 21 U.S. POWs.

The DIA claims the sightings were fakes or reports of sightings of Soviet advisers. What the DIA doesn't want to talk about is an intercepted communist radio message from December 1980 indicating that 20 U.S. POWs were about to be moved from Oudomsai to the Laotian capital of Vientiane. It is unlikely the Laotian government mistook the nationality of the prisoners it had in the north of Laos.[16]

The fate of the Americans once they reached Vientiane has not been made public. However, in May 1986, the NSA collected intercepted radio messages concerning the transfer of "prisoners of war" from the Laotian 586th Battalion to its superiors at the 11th Regiment. As the NSA demurely noted: "The Lao do not normally refer to captured Thai soldiers or Lao expatriates as prisoners of war; it is unclear who they are referring to in this case."[17]

Just A Coincidence?

In late August 1984, Thai intelligence gave the U.S. information on a POW camp in the southern Laotian province of Saravan: "The camp is in the area at the foot of a mountain, surrounded by trench with water from the Nam Phuang [River]. The camp is surrounded by three barbed-wire fences. The innermost barbed-wire fence is connected to the two sleeping quarters of the POW's."[18]

Vietnamese officials trooped across the facilities wooden bridge about once a month to inspect the camp, which was guarded by about 30 Laotian troops of the Kha Lao, or Highland Lao, ethnic group. In the camp were 23 American prisoners of war.

Amazingly, within days of that intelligence report, the NSA received a Laotian radio message concerning the movement of 23 POWs in a nearby area of southern Laos. The September 4 message, "concerning the transfer of 23 unidentified prisoners," ordered a communist center "to respond immediately concerning what arrangements it had made concerning the provision of rations. . . ."

As an NSA analyst dryly noted: "Unidentified prisoner transfers are infrequent but not unusual. Recent collateral [intelligence], however, reported the presence of the same number (23) of American POW's at a camp in southern Laos . . . ."[19]

Had Laos learned the U.S. had identified the U.S. POW camp, and therefore decided to move the American prisoners? There's no way to tell, because other reports on the camp, if they exist, have not been made public.

The Frenchman's Story

In 1988, the Laotian government hired a French building contractor to work on construction projects. The Frenchman, a former Legionnaire, became friendly with his official Laotian guide, who revealed that he'd spent time in a re-education camp, then faked allegiance to communism in order to win his freedom.

The Laotian said 50 to 80 U.S. POWs were held around the old French military prison at Lao Bao, near Tchepone. More Americans were at places called "Nape" and "Vinh."

During the fall of 1988, the Frenchman got a look at the Lao Bao prison while visiting a nearby construction site, he later claimed to U.S. intelligence. "He personally saw a Caucasian ['European-looking'] man through the cell bars. He also stated that he overheard several curse words shouted in 'American English,'" noted an officer at the U.S. Embassy in Paris.

The man, who said he had worked with Americans before during the war in Indochina, wanted no money for his information and offered to attempt to learn more about the POWs.

According to U.S. intelligence, he "probably really believes what he is reporting, but has probably leaped into some rather hasty conclusions from very little, if any, information." But there is no record the man's information was further investigated.[20]

The Price of Information

While the Frenchman didn't want money, it is clear that it will cost the U.S. to get all the information it needs on POW/MIAs in Laos, which, like Vietnam, believes the U.S. owes it money for damage caused in the war. During September 1982, U.S. officials met with Laotian communist officials, who said they wanted to improve relations and turned over some POW/MIA information. "They further indicated a willingness to continue to provide PW/MIA information in return for U.S. economic assistance," reported a top Pentagon official.[21]

And the Laotians hint the cost might be worth it. In August 1991, Laotian Vice Foreign Minister Soubanh Srithirath told the Reuters News Agency: "Maybe there are . . . some Americans alive in the forests, we don't know. That is why we cooperate with the United States in this humanitarian issue."[22]

To those who have followed the tangled dance of diplomacy in Southeast Asia, the fact that the Laotians aren't making an outright denial of the existence of U.S. POWs speaks volumes.

Chapter 17

Cambodia: No Place For A POW

In November 1974, an agent working for U.S. intelligence reported back on a telegram he had seen. The message, from Royalist headquarters to Prince Norodom Sihanouk in Beijing, reported that Americans "Sergeant Glenn Harris" and "Sergeant Michael B. Varnado" were being held by communist forces in Kratie Province as of July 1974. After consulting with his aides, Sihanouk reportedly decided to keep the Americans alive for "political reasons."

Although both Americans were still missing in Cambodia, DIA analysts attempted to debunk the report. They claimed Harris had probably died from throat cuts suffered when his chopper went down, and that Varnado had likely perished from a leg infection. However, it is possible both men may have survived.

According to one report, the Cambodians had imprisoned one U.S. POW with "a scar as wide as the width of a finger on the right side of his neck," a description that might have fit Harris had he survived his helicopter crash. And Varnado was last seen alive, although very ill, on the way to a communist hospital.

The truth about that Cambodian telegram may never be known. The Vietnamese claim Varnado died in 1970, and his remains were returned in 1989. As of this writing Harris is still missing. But what can be said with certainty is that there is evidence that U.S. POWs remained in Cambodia after the Vietnam War.

During the war, Hanoi controlled both large amounts of Cambodian territory and controlled the Khmer Communist Party through the influence of the "five thousand" faction, a group of five thousand native Khmers who had lived in North Vietnam for years and then returned to Cambodia.[1] The Vietnamese and their Khmer allies were detested by Pol Pot and his hard-line faction of the Khmer Rouge, who blamed Hanoi for selling out Cambodian nationalism at the end of the First Indochina War against the French. And local politics were further complicated by the anti-American royalist faction, loyal to Sihanouk.

Dozens of American servicemen became POW/MIAs in Cambodia, and others were shipped there after being captured in Vietnam. But unlike the situation in Vietnam, America never signed a peace treaty with the Cambodian communists. U.S. planes kept bombing the country until August 1973, when Congress shut off all U.S. military aid to Cambodia's anti-communist government.

36 U.S. POWs?

Much of Cambodia was occupied the Vietnamese troops, who, according to official Pentagon history, moved U.S. POWs from Cambodia to South Vietnam and released them in February 1973. And then there were the other American prisoners, discussed earlier in this book, who were secretly removed from Cambodia around the same time. But according to an unconfirmed NSA intercept, some or all of the communist factions in Cambodia never released some of their U.S. captives. In June 1973, "36 American prisoners are located in the area of . . . Sambok Mountain," the NSA reported.

Human intelligence also supported reports of the presence of American prisoners in Cambodia, often under the combined control of Cambodian guerillas and Vietnamese communists. Cambodian communists assumed exclusive control of 15 U.S. POWs during August 1973, one U.S. source reported. As of April 1974, the Vietnamese were operating a POW camp in the Krek region of Cambodia. Under the command of Vietnamese communist Le Van Nhut, the camp contained five U.S. POWs, one of whom was black. Another facility near Mimot held seven Americans. During the day, the Americans built structures and farmed. At night they were shackled. Another source claimed to have seen U.S. POWs at Mimot in 1974, but was run off by Vietnamese guards and told he'd be shot if he came back.[2]

One of those POWs might have been Army Sergeant David Demmon, imprisoned in Cambodia during the 1960s, according to two eyewitnesses, one of whom passed a polygraph test on his sighting. Bunyan Price, a soldier who went down in the same helicopter with Varnado, was reportedly imprisoned in Kratie Province, Cambodia. Air Force officer Samuel L. James, downed in April 1973, well after the official end of the Vietnam War, may also have been captured by the Cambodians. "I heard him on the ground. He was OK," said Rosemary Conway, a flamboyant school teacher and sometime CIA agent who overheard James' radio transmissions while she was flying in a military aircraft.

The Odd Couple

There were also American defectors in Cambodia, such as McKinley Nolan, who switched from a Vietnamese POW camp in Cambodia to one controlled by the Khmer Rouge. One unusual pair of defectors consisted of Larry Humphrey and Clyde McKay. Humphrey was an Army enlisted man who deserted his post in Thailand and snuck into Cambodia during January 1970. He was taken into protective custody and later joined by McKay, a merchant seaman from the munitions ship *Columbia Eagle* who hijacked the vessel to Cambodia in 1970. Humphrey and McKay eventually escaped to join the communists and were last seen in 1971.

Of course, the Cambodian communists—the Khmer Rouge—were not as friendly toward foreign communists as the Vietnamese. After their takeover in 1975, the Khmer Rouge slaughtered huge numbers of their own people, along with most of the "five thousand" faction loyal to Hanoi.[3]

It was unlikely they would have spared foreign prisoners. Sadly, yet more Americans went missing in Khmer Rouge territory during the May 1975 "*Mayaguez* Incident," when U.S. marines were sent in to punish the Cambodians for commandeering a U.S. merchant vessel. In October 1975, Prince Sihanouk declared there were no U.S. POWs in Cambodia.

However, those Americans held under Vietnamese control in Cambodia might well have been taken back to Vietnam with Hanoi troops. And after Vietnam toppled the Khmer Rouge during the Vietnamese invasion of Cambodia in 1978, American POWs could have returned.

In September 1991, a man claiming to be a Cambodian officer reported having seen five U.S. POWs being transferred in a Soviet truck the month before. The man told the DIA that his fiancée worked at the prison that held the Americans, two of whom were pilots. The alleged officer implied that he could get pictures of the POWs in return for a reward. The outcome of the offer is unclear, but the Pentagon has generally refused to pay Southeast Asians for POW information.[4]

However, the complicated politics of Cambodia are still obstructing the search for Americans there. Although the Khmer Rouge signed a 1991 peace treaty with other Cambodian factions, they are still ferocious and have blocked the search efforts of U.S. POW/MIA experts.

Chapter 18

Vietnam: Prison Nation

All Lam Huu Van wanted to do was keep a promise. While he was in a Vietnamese POW camp in the mid-1970s, he saw a number of U.S. prisoners. They passed word that if anyone ever made it out of the camp, they hoped that person would tell the U.S. government that American POWs were still alive in Vietnam. It didn't seem a lot to ask. But it was. If it weren't for Lamn, and another remarkable Vietnamese refugee, Le Thi Anh, the word of those U.S. POWs never would have gotten to the American people.

Lam was a Chinese-ethnic from Vietnam. Educated in the French colonial system, he went to work for France's Securitie Militaire, or military intelligence, in 1947. During 1951, he transferred to the Air Force, where he helped the French in their war against Ho Chi Minh and his guerilla army.

The International Camp at Quyet Tien

Four years after France pulled out of Vietnam in 1954, communist officials arrested Lam on charges of "spying for the French." He would spend the next two decades in communist prisons.

In 1972, Lam arrived at the Quyet Tien prison in North Vietnam's Ha Giang province. There he assumed the duties of teaching Vietnamese to a sad group of men stranded in Vietnam by an historical fluke. They were Taiwanese commandoes. In 1963, Chang Kai Shek's anti-communist government dispatched a hundred-man commando team to infiltrate southern China. Taiwan, with the help of U.S. advisors, had been running such operations into China for years. This time, the mission was sabotage and psychological warfare against the Maoist government.

But the hapless freedom fighters suffered a fatal navigational mistake. Their boat somehow entered Vietnamese waters on the way to a landing site in nearby China. The Vietnamese troops devastated the Taiwanese force, and only about 25 of the team survived. They were soon imprisoned.

The Americans Next Door

Within steps of the Taiwanese troops' building was another cell block, surrounded by barbed wire and low walls. Every morning, gaunt American POWs would come out from the building to spend another day in communist captivity. The Caucasian men, with long hair and beards, wore red and gray striped prison uniforms. They were allegedly aviators, but Lam did not speak English and could not ask them questions.

But three of the Taiwanese did speak English. Sometimes in the morning during toilet time, or at night when the guards were eating dinner, Lam and the Taiwanese would climb on top of their compound's water basin. From there, they could see the Americans and exchange brief conversations.

According to the Taiwanese, the U.S. POWs "repeatedly requested whomever could get out of prison and the country, [to] please report to the U.S. government about them. That hope was almost nonexistent, since every prisoner knew that he was in for life," Le Thi Anh, a Vietnamese journalist to whom Lam told his story, later wrote.

The Americans could not believe that anyone would ever escape to tell the world about their fate. And they certainly would never have believed that someone would escape with the news, but the U.S. government would do nothing about it.

Lam Huu Van's Dangerous Journey

In 1978, Vietnamese persecution began forcing large numbers of ethnic Chinese from their homes in Vietnam. Lam and his Taiwanese friends were by then imprisoned at a camp near the Chinese border, and some of their guards were transferred from prison duties to posts at nearby border checkpoints. Lam and his friends seized the opportunity presented by loosened security to kill their guards and escape across a river to China.

From there, the Vietnamese man made it on to Hong Kong in 1979. There he tried to pass on his information about U.S. POWs. Lam had accepted temporary work at the French Consulate, screening out known communists from among the refugees seeking resettlement in France. He told his boss, a French lieutenant colonel, about his POW knowledge. But the Frenchman replied that U.S. POWs were none of his concern, leaving Lam "with the impression that he was not encouraged to go further," as Le later noted.

Then Lam approached a Protestant minister, who also rebuffed the POW information on the grounds that "he was a religious man" and it was improper for him to get involved in "politics." Finally, Lam made his way to the United Nations Commissioner for Refugees, where American officials were present. Although afraid of working with Vietnamese interpreters who might be agents of Hanoi, Lam was determined to share his information. He waited for hours to see a female interpreter working for the U.S. But as soon as he got even part of his story out, she demanded: "Are you trying to get admitted to the U.S.?"

It was too much for the dignified former intelligence officer, who planned to go to France. "He withdrew without comment," Le said. "He [Lam] expressed surprise, not only at how difficult it was to get some information to the Americans, but also at the underlying assumption by those he has approached that it was he who needed help, while in his opinion, it was the POWs who needed help," Le wrote.

But fate was working for the POWs and their families. Entirely by chance, Lam met a Vietnamese couple in Hong Kong and told them his story. The woman was a friend of Le's, and telephoned the information back to America.

Le Carries the Message

Le Thi Anh is a novelist at heart, but the strange currents of 20th Century Vietnamese history ended up transforming her into an activist of sorts. By the time Lan escaped Vietnam, Le had become a main conduit of POW information from Indochinese refugees to POW/MIA families and the Pentagon.

As a student, she had worked with the Viet Minh resistance against the French occupiers. And during the American war she was no friend of the repressive Thieu regime. But she not a communist, and when the North Vietnamese won the war, she fled to America, where she had studied for many years.

In 1978, she placed an ad requesting POW information in the Vietnamese magazine *Trang Den*. The response surprised her and stunned POW/MIA relatives at the National League of Families, the government-supported organization for the families of Americans missing in Southeast Asia. The outpouring of information in response to the ad proved two things: Vietnamese people were still seeing U.S. POWs after the war, and the U.S. government—despite its promises—was not doing a good job of collecting such information from Indochinese refugees.

The DIA Can't Break the Story

When Le heard about Lam's sighting, she informed the Pentagon and POW/MIA relatives. In 1981, DIA officials interrogated Lam in France. Typically, the DIA's work was less than sound. At one point, the Pentagon's interpreter told U.S. officials that Lam's Taiwanese friends were "Japanese." Luckily, a Catholic priest accompanying Lam pointed out the faulty translatation.

Lam called Le that night, saying: "When I said 'Taiwanese,' he [the DIA interpeter] translated 'Japanese.' The Americans [DIA agents] may think I was talking nonsense [wondering] what the hell were the Japanese doing over there in that prison camp?"

Despite its blundering, the DIA easily determined that Lam's testimony was believable, and he soon passed a lie-detector test (by one account, the DIA kept polygraphing him until he passed out in an unsuccesful attempt to break his story). He was then flown to the Pentagon in October for another round of questioning and a session before a closed Congressional committee.

But he was still interested in helping his former campmates. In April 1982, he wrote to Le about his Taiwanese friends who had escaped. They certainly had far more information than Lam. "Recently," he wrote, "I have received letters from those still in China. I gave their addresses to DIA, I also gave the DIA their photos; I do not know what the DIA plans to do with those. . . ."

The answer—nothing.

Le Ti Anh Takes Things Into Her Own Hands

Ultimately, Le Ti Anh travelled to China on behalf of television producer Ted Landreth, who was then working on the BBC documentary "We Can Keep You Forever." The courtly Vietnamese woman had no trouble tracking down some of Lan's former prisonmates and taking their statements.

Han Van Kiet said he saw about 10 "foreigners" [Caucasians] in the POW camp during May 1975. He asked some of the Vietnamese prisoners about the men and was told they were Americans.

Truong Lam Kim recalled that 10 "American pilots" were kept in the camp. He saw one when he took food to a nearby guard building.

Former First Lieutenant Lam Bang saw the "foreigners" in 1975. He climbed up on a wall and watched them taking a bath.

Le didn't find the English-speaking Chinese POWs in China. The most fluent speaker—who presumably had the most information on the U.S. POWs—had reportedly gone to to live in Taiwan. But although the Taiwanese and U.S. intelligence services have an excellent relationship, the DIA apparently never bothered to track down even this witness.

It has been years since Le found the Chinese witnesses, but there is no indication the DIA ever followed up on the case.

Lam Huu Van has since died. But at least he went to his grave knowing that he tried his best to reveal the truth about American POWs in Vietnam. And Le Thi Anh, saddened by the DIA's poor treatment of Vietnamese refugees and slurred by unsubstantiated charges that she cooperated with Hanoi, has broken her ties with the Pentagon—although she still collects information on U.S. POW/MIAs and is happy to share the reports with concerned Americans.

The DIA Sticks With Its Big Lie

As for the DIA, it not only failed to follow up on the Lam Huu Van case, but now trumpets the case as an example of its success in debunking POW live-sightings. Take the 1972 testimony of the DIA's Major Jeannie Schiff before the Senate POW Committee. "In 1979, we received information from a source who said he saw 50 U.S. prisoners of war between 1973 and [19]78, while he was held in Quyet Tien re-education camp near the Chinese border. We used all-source analysis to investigate this report," remarked Schiff, Deputy Chief of the DIA's POW/MIA office.

Schiff didn't mention that Lam Huu Van passed his polygraph test. Instead, she claimed satellite photos "showed that during the time the source said he saw U.S. POWs in this camp, the gates were wide open . . . . However, to be certain that no POWs had ever been held in this camp, we located some former inmates to ask if they knew of any Americans held there," Schiff reported, obviously missing the irony of her presentation.

If the DIA really found inmates from the Quyet Tien camp with its "open gates," it meant one of two things: either the Vietnamese inmates were held there while the camp gates were "open," meaning there were other security measures to keep them in; or the inmates were not held at the camp while the gates were open, meaning they were not there at the same time the Americans were reportedly there.

No Senators stopped her there, so she continued: "These people all denied that any Americans had ever been held in this camp."

Schiff concluded with a brief lecture for the Senators: "The moral of the story is this. Relying only [on] one source of information would have led us to believe there that there were U.S. prisoners of war in the camp. Taking a multiple-source approach convinced us that this was obviously not the case."

Right.

Jacobs and Johnson

In 1986, a member of the Vietnamese anti-communist "resistance" had a tough break. His leader was in a car wreck, and the police found records showing the man was in charge of hiding U.S. remains. He was soon sent to prison, according to records checked by the U.N. When the man was released in June 1989, members of his group—who knew he was about to leave Vietnam—contacted him for a secret mission. He was ordered to take some sleeping pills, and while he dozed was spirited away to an unknown location.[1]

When the man awoke, he later told U.S. officials, he was at a guerilla camp. And there, with the anti-communist fighters, were two U.S. POWs. They had been imprisoned in a POW camp near the Vietnamese border with China. When Beijing invaded Vietnam, the men were shipped to a camp near Laos (such movements have been reported by several other refugees). On the way, their truck ran off the road, and they escaped. By luck, they ran into a resistance unit, which had sheltered them ever since.

The refugee claimed to have met with the Americans for about an hour and a half. One of the men, a Caucasian, was named Jacobs. A handsome man with brown hair, he said he came from Michigan. Jacobs spoke Vietnamese well and wore a black T-shirt and green military pants. Johnson, a black man, was missing an eye and was not as outgoing as Jacobs. But he also spoke Vietnamese, and wore camouflage-pattern clothing.

Jacobs only had one request for the refugee. If he escaped Vietnam, he should contact U.S. authorities and tell them: "We're still here. Please don't forget us." The refugee did just that, contacting American diplomats as soon as he arrived at his new home in Japan. "His story sounds plausible," cabled the U.S. embassy in Tokyo, which said the man wanted no reward for his information.

In fact, the refugee even offered to take a polygraph test to prove he'd met two American POWs. But that's where the Pentagon paper trail ends. As far as the authors can tell, the DIA has never released records indicating the outcome of the case. And the Pentagon refused to answer questions about it.

What the American Saw

Around June 1977, American marine Robert Garwood's Vietnamese guards told him to prepare for a repair job. He was to go fix a generator. Two guards and an officer drove Garwood to a giant, man-made lake called Thac (sometimes spelled Thach) Ba. There the party got into a motorized dinghy and made for an island about twenty minutes off shore. Once they reached the island, Garwood began climbing a winding path to the generator building. Near it were two other structures built of brick with red tile roofs. The structures had a series of doors, or as Garwood said under oath, "each one was like a motel would be set up."

Garwood went right to the nearby generator building and set to work. After a while, he wandered outside to take a break. "And I looked up at the other buildings and was looking, and Caucasians came out and were standing in the buildings and was kind of milling around there." Garwood saw at least three men, wearing light blue uniforms.

"They were speaking English. I don't recall what the conversation was now," Garwood testified. Suddenly, the officer in charge of Garwood told him to get back inside the generator building, and he soon departed Tach Ba Lake. Back at his prison camp, Garwood—who lived in a mud and thatch "hootch"—took some teasing from one of the Vietnamese prisoners. "One of them said I should demand from the camp commander quarters like the other Americans over in Tach Ba, because they were cement mortar structures with tile roofs," Garwood remembered.

As would be expected, the DIA stated, "as recently as June, 1992, that no such prison as Garwood described at Thach Ba Lake ever existed," Senator Smith said. However, Hanoi later admitted that a prison existed matching the description and location given by Garwood, Smith has said. But the communists say only Vietnamese prisoners were held there.

Bobby Garwood knows better. He survived for years in the huge prison complex called Division 776, a virtual prison nation headquartered at the city of Yen Bai and stretching across a huge expanse of northern Vietnam. Garwood claims to have seen dozens of U.S. POWs in Division 776 prisons. But he also reported Americans elsewhere in Vietnam, which then and even now to a great extent is still a prison nation.

When Garwood saw those Caucasians on the island, he immediately recognized their uniforms from an incident months before. During October 1976, Garwood was dispatched to repair a truck outside the city of Yen Bai. Just a couple miles beyond town on Route 1, right along the Red River, the marine came upon a remarkable sight. A train had stopped at a crossing, blocking the road, and "the whole area was lit up like daylight" by spotlights mounted on open trucks.

The boxcars, surrounded by North Vietnamese guards, were disgorging Vietnamese prisoners. "These people were falling out. They were packed, just literally. . . . There were bodies laid out. There were some people looked like they were dead," Garwood testified.

Then a soldier went to one of the boxcars in the middle of the train and yanked open the door. White men began spilling out. The men, about 30 of them, were dressed in blue uniforms, and one was missing his right leg. "Two of them just lifted him down," Garwood said. He watched in amazement as the other white men jumped from the train. They appeared exhausted and had several days growth of beard.

But the men were not too tired to complain. They were hungry and thirsty. And they didn't know where they were. "Oh, where in the fuck are we, probably in fucking China," someone said, according to Garwood. "That's how I determined that they were Americans, is because they were using—they were using English. They were speaking English, but they were using English four-letter words, which I hadn't heard in a long time," Garwood testified.

By then Garwood had wandered closer to the train to get a better look, and one of the guards noticed him. He was hustled back to his jeep. As they pulled away from the train, the officer in charge of Garwood asked: "What do you think you saw?" Garwood replied: "I don't know." But he did.

About a year later, Garwood was driving in a vehicle that pulled up alongside an American-made truck at a warehouse in the Hanoi suburb of Gia Lan. He looked over and saw five or six Caucasians. And they saw him. "Great. Another fuckin' Cuban," one of them said. Garwood felt insulted. "And I wanted to say: I ain't no goddam Cuban. But I didn't."

The U.S. POWs, most stripped to the waist, soon began loading their truck. Garwood never saw them again.

During his time in Vietnam, Garwood's guards often compared him with other U.S. prisoners, many of whom were apparently a lot less cooperative than he. The guards even mentioned names on occasion. Garwood remembers the following: Jeff, Martin, Lee, Frank, Fred, and Ski. Also: Cartwright, Levin, Al, Bill, and Case.

One time, the guards asked him about a blond, blue-eyed American named Jim, who couldn't speak Vietnamese and couldn't stand the country's trademark pungent fish sauce. "He's from the village of California," the guards explained.

Garwood says he was later given a Pentagon list of POW/MIAs whose remains had been returned to the U.S. since Garwood's release. The former marine said he recognized four of the names as those the guards said were alive during the 1970s.

A Mysterious Letter

In 1987, the National Security Agency reported on indications that a U.S. POW had passed a letter to a Vietnamese man while the two were working together in the U-Minh forest of southern Vietnam. The censored NSA report, which could be the transcript of an intercepted phone call, says the Vietnamese was named Bui Van Phien, sent to work at a reeducation camp. There he met the alleged U.S. POW, whose name has been censored from the NSA report.

The U-Minh Forest, or "Forest of Darkness" in Vietnamese, was reportedly the home of several U.S. POWs kept after the war. Two groups of U.S. POWs were reported in the region during February and March 1973, according to a U.S. intelligence record.[2] Five Americans, four white and one black, were seen on February 15th being moved to the coast. On March 3, a group of ten white U.S. POWs were seen in the same general region. "They (the POWs) seemed happy and said they would be released soon ... in exchange for about 100 communist political prisoners," local villagers reported.

Based upon other corroborating information, the Pentagon considered the information "highly plausible." But no returned U.S. POWs appear to have been held in circumstances matching this report. Perhaps the explanation lies in the fact that the men were being held to trade for communist prisoners. As noted earlier, Saigon retained communist prisoners after the Paris Accord, and the Viet Cong may have held U.S. POWs to trade for them. Just weeks after the report of the two POW groups, communist officials in the area were quoted as saying "unreleased US POWs . . . were being detained as hostages."[3]

More than a year later, in late 1974, the Pentagon received a credible report that U.S. POWs were still alive in the U-Minh Forest, according to a former U.S. intelligence official. The infromation came from an agent who had reported reliably in the past and passed a polygraph test on her information. And in this case, the agent's access to POW information was considered quite good. "The agent was married to the [communist] guy who said he had the POWs," recalled the U.S. official.

Because of the agent's reliability and previous reports from the area, U.S. intelligence placed "high-credibility" on the report. But there was little or no follow-up, because at that time "POW recovery information was not high on the priorities," the source said.

So there was certainly a good chance a U.S. POW was indeed in the U-Minh forest in 1987. And if the NSA intercept was accurate, the American was lucky enough to meet a sympathetic Vietnamese prisoner. "Mr. Bui is a person who is kindhearted and who is sympathetic to American soldiers who came to fight the Viet Cong. He also hated the work detail guards," the report says.

The American gave Bui the letter, hoping it would make it out of Vietnam and to U.S. officials. It may have, but the American people will probably never find out. Many NSA POW files remain classified and are scheduled to stay that way for years.[4]

Hanoi Meets Hackensack

Robert "Bobby" Egan, a 35-year-old New Jersey man with a passing resemblance to John Travolta, typically has a lot on his mind. There's "flipping burgers," which is how he describes running Cubby's Restaurant, his Hackensack Restaurant. And then there's international intrigue.

It all started when Bobby was in high school and became interested in the POW issue. Like many dedicated POW activists across America, he didn't have a missing releative. And he was too young to have served in Vietnam. But he believed American POW/MIAs, "the boys" as he calls them, had been left behind.

Now Egan is not the scholarly type. He's certainly bright, but hard work and big laughs interest him more than book work. So he decided the best way to learn about the POWs was to go ask the people who took them. He started hanging out at Vietnam's Mission to the United Nations in New York.

For reasons that no one but Bobby and a bunch of stiff Vietnamese bureacrats seem to understand, the former roofer and good-time bridge-and-tunnel *paisan* became the toast of the Vietnamese Mission to the United Nations during the 1980s. He went to their diplomatic parties and shared his life with them. Most of all he schmoozed. And listened. And didn't do a lot of judging. And before he knew it, they were telling him about the POWs.

Former Deputy Vietnamese Ambassador to the U.N. Nguyen Can—Bobby swears—revealed that he'd seen several U.S. POWs years after the war. Can wanted to defect too, but Egan says the attempt was bungled by the U.S. government.

Don't believe it? Ask Bobby's good friend Le Quang Khai. When Bobby Egan was learning how to make a buck in the burger business, Khai was working his way up in the Vietnamese Foreign Ministry and becoming a member of Hanoi's intelligentsia. Then he was assigned to get a graduate degree at Columbia University. And before long, he was talking to Bobby.

In 1992, Khai defected. Not only did he confirm that Can knew about POWs. Khai, one of the most senior Vietnamese Foreign Ministry officials ever to defect to the U.S., also said it was "common knowledge" in the Vietnamese government that U.S. POWs had been kept after the war.

Khai was promptly rewarded by the U.S. government with a deportation notice (which, as of this writing, he's fighting). Bobby got visited by the FBI. But he's still talking with his Vietnamese friends. And one of this days, he's going to help bring home the "boys."

Meantime, he's teaching Khai about flipping burgers.

"Stinky" and Clemie McKinney

On August 14, 1985, Vietnam returned the remains of black American aviator Clemie McKinney, according to Pentagon records. There were three odd things about the returned remains. First, U.S. observers did not see McKinney parachute from his plane, but examination of his remains, according to a 1991 Pentagon report, "suggest that death did not occur in the aircraft because L.T. McKinney's showed no sign of high impact." In other words, this appeared to be another case where an aviator successfuly ejected from his airplane without being noticed by other U.S. pilots in the area. The second unusual element was that while McKinney's plane crashed in April 1972, when the Vietnamese returned him they said he had died in November 1972. Since nobody in the normal POW camps reported seeing McKinney in captivity, this suggested he might have been held in the "separate" POW system, possibly just north of the old demilitarized zone separating South from North Vietnam.

But the most odd thing about Clemie McKinney's case was brought up by Bill Bell, the Pentagon POW expert, during his secret Senate testimony. As Bell later reported back to the Pentagon: "A CILHI (U.S. Army Central Identification Laboratory, Hawaii) anthropologist states his opinion as to time of death as not earlier than 1975 and probably several years later."

Bell went on to say there were several reports of a black POW being held in the area near where McKinney was downed. Bell himself had interviewed a Vietnamese refugee who may have seen McKinney killed years after his capture and long after all U.S. POWs were supposed to have been returned.

In one official report to the Pentagon, Bell says the refugee saw the incident in April 1980. There are more details in Bell's Senate deposition. "He [the refugee] observed a black American with armed Vietnamese personnel in pursuit. They [the Vietnamese] shot the American in the leg, killing him. He was hiding under a bridge and he fell into the water. Then they removed his body from the water and carried him away."

When McKinney's remains were returned, according to Bell, "he was missing the lower portion of his right leg, which matches the general description [of the refugee]."

The bottom line: Bell believed McKinney might have been captured and held for years in Vietnam before being killed and then returned to the U.S. Bell testified that three other Americans were seen alive a year after the war in the same area where McKinney was reportedly killed in 1980.

Despite that evidence, Bell said the Pentagon failed to pursue the McKinney case and evidence that other American POWs had been held with him after the war. "I don't think it was ever table with the Vietnamese for investigation because the case was already resolved because the remains came back," Bell said in his sworn Senate statement.

In 1993, the Pentagon, unaware that the authors possessed Bell's testimony and Pentagon reports, denied that any remains returned by Hanoi appeared to have come from men who died after Operation Homecoming in 1973. That was exposed as a lie by yet another series of reports concerning a mysterious corpse. In November 1991, the State Department pressed Hanoi on the case of a deceased American nicknamed "Stinky" by U.S. POW/MIA experts. According to a State Department telegram: "These (still-unidentified) remains, which . . . we assume to be American, were returned in 1989 with tissue suggesting recent death. However the data with the remains indicated the person had died in 1975." As with the previous case, there appears to have been no follow-up investigation.

A Remarkable Coincidence

According to an expert hired by the Senate Select Committee, a June 1992 satellite photo of the Dong Mang (sometimes called Dong Vai) prison depicts the man-made signal: GX 2527. Other experts disagree, saying the signal is probably a fluke of nature.

If so, it's quite a fluke. GX 2527, according to reliable sources, is the authenticator code for MIA Peter Richard Matthes, the co-pilot of a C-130 downed over Laos in November 1969. Each U.S. pilot had an authenticator code, the equivalent of the Personal Identification or PIN Number used by automatic bank machines. The pilot could use the number over the radio so that rescuers would know it was a downed American calling for help and not a clever English-speaking communist calling in rescue aircraft to an ambush.

Perhaps it is just a coincidence that the outside expert says he is "100%" confident the signal was man-made and that it just happens to match the code for a missing American. It must also be a coincidence that the possible signal appeared outside a prison that, according to the CIA, was only rivaled in its elaborate building by another camp known to have held U.S. POWs during the war. And surely it is merely by chance that in July 1975 the CIA observed what appeared to be a "K" written in *morse-code* on the building's roof. Don't mind that "K" is the permanent signal used by American pilots to call for help. It's probably only a coincidence.[5]

Could Peter Matthes have been calling for help in June 1992? We'll probably never find out, because according to a Senate POW staffer, the Pentagon never followed up on the possible signal.

The "Dog Tag" Conspiracy

At the same time Hanoi claims it returned all U.S. POWs, its intelligence agents are faking POW/MIA reports to be smuggled out of Indochina. That remarkable conclusion came from Pentagon studies of so-called "dog tag" reports, which usually involve a refugee reporting information from a serviceman's dog tags and saying he knows the location of that GI—or, more commonly—his remains. The Pentagon says it has received more than 7,000 such reports since 1982, most involving men who returned alive from Vietnam.

The refugee bringing out the information often got it from another person, and U.S. intelligence officials believe the Vietnamese government is actually spreading the reports to "exploit" the POW issue. There are also accusations that Laotian agents have also spread fake POW information.

It is not clear how Hanoi benefits from the disinformation efforts. Some experts say the fake reports are meant to tie up DIA resources, preventing them from being directed at real POW reports. Others suggest hardliners or even Chinese agents are faking information to damage U.S.-Vietnamese relations.

But there are also indications that Vietnamese intelligence has arranged for people leaving Vietnam to see actual POWs, apparently hoping the refugees would report their sightings to the U.S. That supports another theory: that Hanoi is trying to keep the POW issue alive, to prevent the U.S. government from writing off all the POWs—and destroying their value as bargaining chips.

Chapter 19

The Mysterious Fate of Dallas Pridemore

In a country filled with hate, Dallas Reese Pridemore became a victim of love. It happened the night of September 8, 1968, as the blond military policeman lounged in yellow silk pajamas at the home of his Vietnamese fiancée, Huyen Thit Hue. Pridemore had recently divorced his American wife and extended his tour in Vietnam, all to be with a woman he knew he loved. What Pridemore apparently didn't know was that his fiancée was a "secret follower of the revolution"—a communist agent.

Just 12 days before, his commander at the 95th MP Battalion had disciplined Pridemore for staying with his girlfriend. Hue's house, at 665 Xa Cu Kien Thiet, was in the middle of a risky area outside Saigon. But by 7 p.m. Pridemore was back again, his uniform off and his pajamas on, officially absent-without-leave but feeling at home.

Several hours later, around 10 p.m., a force of some 60 Viet Cong guerillas led by Ngo Tung Lo infiltrated the village. Two of the troops entered Hue's home and began searching it. Pridemore immediately tossed his uniform out the back window and into the yard. The 27-year-old had told friends that if he were ever captured in the village, he'd claim to be a civilian. But Pridemore hadn't counted on being betrayed by his woman (who according to one report actually cared for Pridemore and believed she would be able to join him later in a communist sanctuary).

The guerillas marched upstairs and found the tall soldier hiding under his girlfriend's double bed. As they led Pridemore away, the V.C. publicly warned Hue that "nice girls didn't hang out with Americans." Then they promised to release Pridemore in three days.

He never returned.

In November 1991, the Pentagon's top expert on Vietnam POW/MIAs gave secret testimony to the U.S. Senate that Dallas

Pridemore and a number of other U.S. POWs had survived for years after their capture and were still alive when all U.S. POWs were supposed to have been returned in early 1973. Garnett "Bill" Bell's testimony to the Senate Select Committee on POW/MIA Affairs was kept secret, because both the Senate and Pentagon claim there's no proof any Americans were kept behind by the communists.

Bell's testimony also disputed Pentagon claims about Vietnam's cooperation on the POW issue. Pridemore's case showed that Hanoi has attempted to deceive U.S. investigators about the fate of missing Americans. Vietnamese Senior Colonel Tu Tang claimed Pridemore was blown to pieces by a U.S. bomb shortly after his capture. When U.S. investigators proved that wasn't true, a top Vietnamese POW official claimed Pridemore died later in Cambodia of malaria. But that too was a lie.

The truth about Dallas Pridemore's case is embarassing to both U.S. and Vietnamese officials, and both nations have sought to hide the evidence on his fate. But here, based upon Bell's testimony and other records now forced from secret Pentagon files, is what the U.S. government knows about the fate of Dallas Pridemore:

Months before his kidnapping, Pridemore had been introducted to a Mr. Dat, an undercover Viet Cong political agent working for a special communist unit that apparently had the cooperation of Pridemore's fiancée. Through the summer of 1968, even as Pridemore continued his romance, the Viet Cong were plotting his capture.

Immediately after snatching Pridemore, the Viet Cong troops headed to a nearby pagoda. There the guerillas handed their catch over to members of the Saigon-Gia Dinh Special Action Unit, a communist group responsible for a number of terrorist bombings in the Saigon area. At the time, communist officials were planning the fourth stage of their "general offensive" which had rocked Saigon earlier that year during the Tet Offensive. The terrorists hoped "to exploit his [Pridemore's] knowledge of the physical security system deployed throughout the Saigon area."

The communists reportedly first moved Pridemore to a local base in the wilds of Ong Thang Swamp. From there, the unlucky soldier continued his journey deep into the densely jungled hideouts of the most hardcore communist insurgents. He would later be reported to have been spotted in a series of secret POW camps attached to COSVN (the Central Office for South Vietnam, a major communist command in the South) security forces, who apparently first wanted his information on security in Saigon and then hoped to exchange him and other Americans for top Viet Cong cadre in Saigon's hands.

On the 25th of September, 1968, Pridemore arrived at a special POW camp in the Svay Rieng Province of Cambodia, a communist stronghold just across the border from South Vietnam. Commanded by Ngo Van Sung, a guerilla of mixed Vietnamese-Chinese background, the camp staff by one account also included three American civilians from the Communist Party of the United States. The American communists helped in the interrogations, while Viet Cong Rangers, along with an array of spikes and hand-grenade booby traps, protected the camp from U.S. or South Vietnamese attack.

U.S. intelligence officers dispatched one of their Asian agents, code-named C-11426-T, to gather more information about the prison. The agent soon reported the POWs were being held in a major base camp area for the communist Viet Cong and North Vietnamese Army. Two long tunnels, reinforced by concrete beams, ran from the main compound. One of the tunnels, a little less that five feet high by five feet wide, was sometimes used to house the American prisoners. The POWs, their ankles shackled, emerged from the tunnel about 9:30 each morning for indoctrination. After a lunch break for some rice, the prisoners went back to class until about 5, when they had another meal and went back into the tunnel. By mid-January 1969, more than 150 Americans were at the camp, including Pridemore, whose name, rank and date of capture were entered in the camp roster.

Pridemore's journey for the next several years is unclear. Only one thing is known with certainty: he was not returned with other U.S. POWs during 1973's Operation Homecoming. The next reliable sighting of Pridemore, Bell testified, was in May 1974, and what happened to him after that after that only the Vietnamese government can—but won't—say for sure.

By then, Pridemore was being held by Cambodian communists at a coffee plantation near the village of Memot in Kompong Chan Province. Also in the camp was Army deserter McKinley Nolan, who lived there with his Asian wife and son. Nolan was allowed to farm a field behind his house.

As for Pridemore, he worked under communist guard as a mechanic and slept in a shed near the garage. And he slept alone, with no silk pajamas and no woman, a victim of love in a terrible war.

Chapter 20

The Viet Cong's Mata Haris

In early 1989, communist officials led U.S. POW investigators deep into a leech-infested swamp in Vietnam. They were searching for the grave of American POW Bennie Dexter, an airman abducted by the Viet Cong while driving a jeep on May 9, 1966.

But the investigators found no sign of Dexter. "The marshy area was excavated, but nothing was found and there were no indications that anyone was ever detained or buried in the area pointed out by the [Vietnamese] witnesses," reported Bill Bell, the Pentagon's leading expert on Vietnam POWs.

Bell had learned that Hanoi sometimes provided coached witnesses to fool the Pentagon into writing off sensitive U.S. POWs. And the case of Bennie Dexter appeared to be just such a case.

Further investigation revealed that Dexter may have been lured to his fate by a female Vietnamese agent, and had probably been moved into the camp system of the Central Office For South Vietnam [COSVN], the headquarters of the communist Viet Cong. The search led to the Vietnamese border district of Tay Ninh. During the war years, as U.S. and South Vietnamese forces sought to root out communist infrastructure and leadership, the Viet Cong had shifted their camps back and forth from northwest Tay Ninh Province to sanctuary areas across the Cambodia border.

In that area, local villagers reported the remains of six Americans. However, Vietnamese officials forbade American investigators from searching the area because it was allegedly "flooded." But Bill Bell knew that under those "flood" waters was a secret Hanoi wanted to keep—the secret of a mysterious POW camp called "C-53."

The story of camp C-53 began with a pleasure boat trip on February 14, 1965. William Henry Wallis, a 56-year-old Englishman, was cruising the Saigon River with two Vietnamese sisters, Tran Bao Linh, 15, and Tran Le Linh, 20.

The sisters lived with their aunt, a successful Saigon businesswomen. Le Linh reportedly worked with Wallis at the RMK company, where the Englishman handled security issues and may also have worked with the CIA.

When Wallis turned around to head home at the Binh Loi bridge, communist guerillas opened fired on the vessel, exploding its gas tank. What started as an excursion was turning into a one-way trip for William Wallis.

The Viet Cong took the group to what would later be called the C-53 camp, where they were put in three separate bamboo cages. Unlike normal South Vietnamese prisoner camps operated by the COSVN Enemy Proselytizing Office, Camp C-53 fell under the COSVN security forces. It was their facility for special prisoners ranging from anti-communist spies to specially selected Western POWs.

Viet Cong intelligence agents, using Le Linh as an interpreter, called Wallis a "colonel," apparently believing he possessed special information. It is still not clear what Wallis really knew, if anything. But after months of interrogation and re-education classes, the Englishman had still not given the communists what they wanted. He was sentenced to death by the camp communist party committee, executed and buried nearby.

On September 21, 1965, young Bao Linh returned to Saigon without her older sister. U.S. intelligence later received a report that: "After the Englishman was executed, Le Linh agreed to work for the V.C. She was assigned to work on the interrogations of foreign prisoners at the camp as a typist and interpreter."

In 1967, the Pentagon received chilling evidence of Le Linh's work. The military captured the interrogation papers of Philadelphia native Edward Daniel Reilly, Jr., a soldier captured in April 1966. The documents revealed the Vietnamese woman was the interpreter for Reilly's interrogation. The papers also contained the order that the 23-year-old American "must be killed immediately after the interrogation." (His remains were returned from Vietnam in 1989.)

But there is evidence Le Linh may not have liked her work, because in 1968 the camp's communist cadre, apparently fearing she would defect, forced her to marry Hai Minh, an administrator and communist instructor at the facility. Sadly, she still had plenty to do after the executions of Wallis and Reilly. There were more Americans at C-53, and they would not be released at the end of the Vietnam War.

As with many Viet Cong facilities, the C-53 camp was often on the move in the border area between Vietnam and Cambodia. At one point, the camp reportedly held five Americans—three white and two black. "During the day, the U.S. prisoners were allowed to gather and play checkers in a designated house. At night, they were detained separately and schackled," according to a U.S. intelligence report.[1]

In January 1974, almost a year after all U.S. POWs were supposed to be released, a Vietnamese defector identified one of the Americans in the C-53 camp as "Mr. Benny." This American had gotten a letter from home, and he had shown it to his friends in the camp. In the letter was a small photo of an American woman with two kids. Interpreter Le Linh said those were "Mr. Benny's" wife and children.

Bell thinks Mr. Benny was probably Bennie Lee Dexter. He and the other Americans, reportedly held at the C-53 camp for "strategic purposes," were apparently never released.

Remarkably, Le Linh and another Viet Cong female linked to U.S. POWs were allegedly relocated to Australia after the war by U.N. refugee officials.

The men they helped sentence to lifetime communist captivity were not so lucky.

Chapter 21

With The Enemy

"Contribute your effort to the American people's struggle for an end to this dirty aggressive war to avoid useless death which is disasteous [sic] to yourself, your wife and children and your family!"
—*printed statement by Army defector McKinley Nolan to U.S. troops in Vietnam, 1968*

In May of 1968, a communist defector told a curious story to an Air Force intelligence official in South Vietnam. The defector said he had seen an American "negro" working with the communist 303rd Battalion. The American was a big, muscular man who wore black pajamas with a red star. He also sported a nice ring and watch, and around his neck hung a gold chain with an anchor-shaped pendant. He never wore shoes, but always had on a pair of sunglasses. More importantly, the big American packed two handguns: one a 38-caliber revolver and the other a 45-caliber automatic.

The G.I. had been with the Vietnamese for some time and spoke their language fluently, the defector reported. He used his linguistic skills well, rising before 6:00 a.m. every morning to train the communists in marksmanship and tactics, along with helping battalion leaders plan their attacks.

Apparently the black man, who said he came from the middle of America, was considered too important to risk in actual combat. During missions he stayed at the base camp, protected by five bodyguards. For his efforts, the American got Viet Cong rations, two bottles of beer a day, and "Ruby Queen" cigarettes. Sometimes he went swimming. And he became part of a G.I. legend concerning the war.[1]

If you want to learn about this legend, go to any reunion of Vietnam vets and ask them about the mysterious men known as "Salt and Pepper," an integrated pair of turncoats who worked with communist forces in the Quang Ngai and Quang Nam Provinces, also called the MR-1 zone, of South Vietnam.

According to G.I. legend, Salt and Pepper, along with another traitor nicknamed "Porkchop," led Viet Cong raids and lured American units into communist ambushes. Porkchop was also rumored to flag down South Vietnamese trucks and then hijack them. According to one account, he also talked his way into a U.S. motorpool, stole an armored personnel carrier, and then drove it to Viet Cong territory.

Even V.C. grunts spread the legend. One captured communist said American traitors were sent into contested areas to turn the people against the U.S. by killing and raping civilians.

The truth, as contained in previously secret Pentagon files, is not quite so dramatic but just as strange. "Salt and Pepper" did exist, and they were not the only turncoats in the Vietnam War. In all, DIA received some 150 reports on such men. But instead of leading combat raids, the turncoats mostly engaged in propaganda for the enemy. And rather than being renegade Rambos, most of the defectors were men of low skills, deprived backgrounds and limited intelligence.

There were basically two types of collaborators: those who willingly went over to the enemy side, and those who were captured and then cooperated with the communists. Some of the latter group returned to heroes' welcomes during "Operation Homecoming" during the early part of 1973.

One American POW who returned home to a warm welcome had fallen—or deserted—into enemy hands after going AWOL to avoid court-martial for repeated use of marijuana. During part of his captivity, according to a CIA report, the man prepared communist propaganda and gave military advice to the enemy. And a number of officers had collaborated, and returned U.S. POW camp commanders had urged that some of them be prosecuted.

The Nixon Administration, eager to get beyond Vietnam, was well aware of the problems posed by prosecuting Americans returned from a hostile land to a divided nation. After the Korean War, 21 U.S. POWs publicly chose to stay with the communists; other collaborators who returned faced controversial trials that raised complicated questions about personal accountability and communist brainwashing, including the often thin line between collaboration and survival in a communist prison.

In 1973, the Pentagon was well aware that punishing returned POWs had the potential of producing strong negative publicity. So the besieged Nixon Administration decided not to make a major issue out of the returned Vietnam collaborators, who mostly got off with little or no punishment.

The story was different for those U.S. collaborators who remained in Vietnam. The Pentagon now calls them "stay-behinds," even though some may have been *kept* behind by the communists, and others—no more guilty than some returned POWs—may have been frightened into "willingly" staying behind.

Of course, some of the "stay-behinds" probably did remain in Southeast Asia because they had become communists and committed serious acts of betrayal against their nation and/or fellow U.S. soldiers.

That may have been the case with Salt and Pepper, although the exact nature of their collaboration remains unclear. However, the Pentagon believes it has learned the identity of Salt. During the course of a DIA investigation, three independent sources identified the white defector as Marine Sergeant Fred Thomas Schreckengost. The 26-year-old Ohio native disappeared with his buddy and fellow marine Robert Lee Greer during a motorbike trip on June 7, 1964. They were last seen several miles south of Danang, where U.S. troops searching for the men had to withdraw after encountering heavy enemy fire. Both men were later declared dead.[2]

The Pentagon now publicly claims that Greer and Schreckengost died soon after their disappearance, and says their remains were discovered and returned to the U.S. But according to some sources, the remains returned may not really belong to the two marines, and a man claiming to be Greer was reported in Thailand and the U.S. during the 1980s.

The Baggage Handler Defects

Files containing the identity of "Pepper," the black traitor, were lost during the fall of Saigon. But the identity of another black defector is known. His name was McKinley Nolan, and until he got to Vietnam there was nothing in his background to even hint that he would become infamous as one of the few identified U.S. defectors in Vietnam.

In 1963, the lean six-footer graduated from high school and married Mary Alice Brown. They had a son named Rodgers Dewayne, and Nolan went to work as a porter at the Houston Airport. The young Texan seemed to know little and care less about world events and politics. But then, in December 1965, McKinley Nolan was drafted for the war in Vietnam.

Life had not been especially easy on Nolan. He was a black man from the south, and he told the Army that his father was dead and he didn't know his mother. For men like him, there were no draft deferments or trips to Canada. And he wasn't the kind of draftee with the skills or connections to get a safe technical job. So the Army sent him off to infantry school at Fort Gordon, Georgia. In June 1966, he joined the 1st Infantry Division in Vietnam.

Nolan did see combat, suffering a shrapnel wound in December and attaining the rank of Specialist 4th Class. But he never really adjusted to military life, his Army record shows. He was repeatedly fined, busted in rank, and tossed into the stockade for being AWOL and insubordinate.

Things got even worse in May 1967, when he received letters from friends at home claiming his wife was cheating on him. Nolan went to his platoon sergeant, platoon leader and brigade chaplain asking for compassionate leave to go home and repair his marriage. His requests were denied.

On November 9, 1967, McKinley Nolan went AWOL for the last time. He was dropped from the rolls of the Army on the last day of 1967. But unlike other American deserters, Nolan did not hide himself in the bar district of Saigon or smuggle himself out of Vietnam and back to America or Europe. Instead, Nolan went over to the enemy, or, as the Viet Cong described it: "received permission to live in liberated areas according to his wishes."

Statements by Nolan soon began appearing in communist propaganda pamphlets and on Hanoi Radio. The V.C. even released pictures of Nolan meeting with communist officials, enjoying a hearty meal with guerillas and being examined by a female medic.

The communists seized upon Nolan's value in advancing one of Hanoi's favorite propaganda themes: the mistreatment of blacks in America. In one propaganda letter to "his dear colored friends" Nolan allegedly wrote:

> It is not us colored people that the freedom fighters [V.C.]
> dislike. It [is] those who push us to the front. We are the
> first on line and the last one to receive the bread. They [the
> communists] are fighting for Liberty. Why not we colored
> race stick together and help them because we want the
> same things ourselves. . . . Refuse to go the field. Refuse to
> fight. Maybe you will be called "chickens." I rather to be
> chicken than dead.

It was clear from the fractured English and communist jargon
in his statements that Nolan was being coached. Indeed, one
report indicated that the Viet Cong had grown frustrated with
Nolan because of his weak writing skills. But all the same, Nolan
was collaborating with the enemy. And while other Americans
had written propaganda statements after being captured, Nolan
said he had deserted to the enemy and even taken a family.

One of the communist propaganda pictures shows a smiling
Nolan—still in Army fatigues—with an Asian woman, small boy
and baby. It is not clear when the Texan acquired his Asian family,
although by one report his wife, a Cambodian, helped arrange his
defection. (As for his American wife, she claimed to have last
heard from him months before his defection, and only learned
about his fate when a reporter later called to get her reaction.)

Either way, Nolan showed more loyalty to his new family than
he did to his country or newfound Viet Cong friends. Nolan and
his family were seen over the years in various parts of South
Vietnam's Tay Ninh Province and across the border in
Cambodia's Kampong Cham and Kratie provinces. Returned
U.S. POWs reported seeing them during April 1972 in Kratie
Province. The Nolan family later moved with the POWs to
another camp further north in the Province, where he was seen
occasionally near the prison camp.

Nolan later complained the Vietnamese communists were
making him work too hard. So in November 1973, Nolan and his
family slipped out of the Vietnamese camp. He then either turned
himself in or was captured by Cambodian communists. As of
May 1974, more than a year after all American prisoners were
supposed to have returned to the U.S., Nolan was living under
guard in the village of Sangkum Mean Chey, about three
kilometers from the town of Memot in Kampong Cham Province,
Cambodia.

"Nolan may now be physically prevented from leaving area of KC [Khmer Communist] control," concluded the State Department in November 1974. There was even talk of trying to arrange Nolan's release, but that never happened.[3]

After 1974, Nolan's fate becomes hazy. According to one report, he visited Cuba sometime during 1976 or 78. As to his current status, one Vietnamese official recently told the U.S. that Nolan was dead. But a second official claimed Nolan could be "alive and well and currently residing in Phnom Penh."

Blowing With The Wind

According to Bob Dylan's hit song of the 1960s, you don't have to be a weatherman to know which way the wind is blowing. During the Vietnam War, some Americans believed the winds of change were propelling the U.S. to a communist future, and a leftist terrorist group that wanted to hasten that voyage dubbed itself "The Weathermen." In a remarkable coincidence, a marine who decided to throw in his lot with the communism during the Vietnam War happened to be named "Weatherman."

Private 1st Class Earl Clyde Weatherman was a tall, fit, blue-eyed marine with a wild streak, according to the few declassified records concerning his fate. On November 8, 1967, Weatherman escaped from the marine brig in Danang, where he'd been imprisoned for striking a superior. What happened next is still disputed. According to one military report, he stole a marine vehicle and headed off to the Chu Lai area in search of his Vietnamese wife, Tran Thi Nhien. Another version has him paying a Vietnamese driver to take him to his wife, a communist, and the driver instead delivering him to the V.C. In either case, somewhere along the way, Earl Weatherman came under enemy control.

He later reappeared in V.C. POW camp ST-18, located in South Vietnam's Quang Nam Province. Although he joined an escape attempt during the spring of 1968, several other U.S. prisoners believed he was a committed communist collaborator.

On April 1, 1968, Weatherman made another break for freedom. This time, he was reportedly killed. According to a DIA report, he was buried in a field near his camp. "Subject's name was on the died-in-captivity list provided by the Provisional Revolutionary Government in January 1973," the DIA noted.

But the same report says: "Date of death was given [by the V.C.] as 'January 1969.' " Nowhere in the file does the Pentagon deal with the difference in the date of death between April 1, 1968—as reported by returned American prisoners—and January, 1969—the date given by the communists for the marine's death. And that is not the only odd element in Weatherman's case. For example, despite having officially died in a POW camp, Weatherman is not listed on the Vietnam Memorial Wall.

The reason for the confusion is simple: Earl Clyde Weatherman did not die in 1968. According to DIA files and Senate testimony, after the "escape" attempt, the communist guards loudly ordered U.S. POW Bobby Garwood to dispose of Weatherman's body. But Garwood found there really was no body. Instead, the V.C. had faked Weatherman's death—on April Fool's Day no less—to intimidate other U.S. prisoners and allow Weatherman to fade into history.

"He was brought to the camp for the purpose of infiltrating the POW population and reporting to the camp authorities, the administration, all activities, et cetera, among the POW population. When this failed, they faked an escape attempt for the purpose—basically for the purpose of discrediting, or to show the American prisoners that any escape would be just impossible," Garwood told the Senate.

Weatherman continued to serve the communists after his faked death. Garwood saw Weatherman alive as late as 1977, and he was reported by various sources to be working in Hanoi's Department of Construction and/or as an interpretor. Despite alleged attempts by his mother during the 1980s to ease Weatherman's way back into the U.S., he remained in Vietnam, although it is possible that he also took trips to Russia and Cuba.

According to a DIA document, Weatherman had asked Garwood to make his survival known to the U.S. government. "Garwood was asked if Weatherman was staying behind wittingly or unwittingly [sic: the Pentagon probably meant "willingly or unwillingly"], and he replied that it was probably a little of both, and there was a wife and child involved."

Allied Brothers

Pentagon files contain a good many references to American "collaborators" who apparently never returned from Vietnam. A U.S. helicopter crew captured in 1965 was allegedly forced to promote the communist line in South Vietnam. "They were kept in a cave-tunnel and were reportedly in good health. They have adopted the Vietnamese way of life and can speak the Vietnamese and Montagnard languages. The VC have forced them to expound VC propaganda to the local people," according to an Army intelligence report.[4]

Two U.S. intelligence advisers allegedly captured in January 1973 apparently decided to switch rather than fight. "The PW's are currently undergoing Vietnamese language and indoctrination training. They reportedly speak Vietnamese well and are able to sing some VC revolutionary songs," the Department of Defense reported in December 1974.[5]

In one South Vietnamese V.C. camp during the war, 18 foreign POWs—several Americans along with Koreans and a Filipino—were reportedly being "brainwashed." "They have been given Vietnamese names and are not allowed to use their true names. After peace comes to Vietnam and the nation is unified, the POWs will be allowed to return to their homes where they will become active in the communist party . . . ," the Pentagon reported.[6]

Perhaps those were some of the men seen alive after the war. In June 1974, Vietnamese informants told U.S. intelligence about two white and one black U.S. POWs, in good shape and wearing black pajams, at a Viet Cong camp. "The guards pointed out the US PW's and referred to them as 'ong ba dong minh' [three allied brothers]."

In the Vietnamese hamlet of Vinh Thanh around the spring of 1975, a witness who later passed a polygraph exam on his sighting saw a white man living "without any visable constraints. Reeducation cadre explained that this caucasian was an American who volunteered to remain in Vietnam and had become a model worker whom the Vietnamese reeducatees should strive to emulate."[7]

In 1978 or 1979, a Vietnamese refugee, who also passed a lie-detector test, saw an unguarded Caucasion carrying firewood. A communist official said the man "was a former U.S. military man who chose to remain in Vietnam with his Vietnamese wife and children and to work at Dong Hiep as a peasant farmer."[8]

The Pentagon claims it doesn't know the identities of those men "living freely" in Vietnam, except they aren't the notorious Bobby Garwood.

Bobby Garwood Returns From The Dead

In September 1965, Marine enlisted man Robert Garwood was captured by the enemy while driving his jeep in Quang Nam Province, South Vietnam. He wound up sharing the horrific conditions of a V.C. POW camp with William "Ike" Eisenbraun, a tough Korean War veteran and Green Beret. Ike had fallen into enemy hands while serving as an advisor to a South Vietnamese unit hit by a communist human-wave attack.

The battle-tested officer became Garwood's mentor, teaching him how to endure communist captivity. Ike's basic lesson was that Garwood must make an absolute decision to survive, even though death would often seem preferable to life in the communist prison system. The survival skills began with the Vietnamese language, which Eisenbraun spoke well and Garwood ultimately mastered. The officer also showed the young marine which jungle plants and animals were edible, if not appetizing. Indeed, the two men joked about publishing a cook book to be entitled, *100 Ways to Cook a Rat*.

Then Eisenbraun died following a savage beating by the guards. Garwood, as he saw it, was alone. A stronger man or a better soldier would have stuck with his fellow prisoners and done his best to follow the POW Code of Conduct. Instead, Garwood began cooperating with his captors.

Getting Away With Collaboration

There is no doubt Garwood collaborated after his capture, but the degree and uniqueness of his actions is debatable. A marine court-martial later convicted him of collaboration and striking a fellow prisoner—but not, notably, for desertion. However, the conviction for striking a fellow prisoner involved an ambiguous incident. According to some accounts, Garwood lost his temper upon learning that camp guards had fatally beaten his friend Russ Grissett for killing the camp cat. Garwood reportedly back-handed another prisoner, saying: "How could you let them do this to Russ?"

Garwood's actions, while clearly against regulations, were certainly not the worst acts committed by a U.S. POW during the Vietnam War. Returned civilian POW Mike Benge, decorated for bravery both before and after capture, said several POWs commited offenses as bad or worse than Garwood's. For example, a number of collaborators refused to share their extra food rations with desperately ill Americans. One prisoner created detailed targets depicting U.S. airplanes so the communists could train their anti-aircraft gunners. Another POW struck a superior commissioned officer. Those men and others like them escaped serious punishment when they returned to the U.S. in 1973.

Garwood's Sentence

But Bobby Garwood did not come home in 1973. He says he was never given the option. In late 1969, the V.C. removed Garwood from contact with other Americans. He travelled to North Vietnam's Nin Binh province in 1970 and then on to the Bat Bat POW Camp in Son Tay Province, where he would spend most of the next four years.

When the U.S. withdrawl was announced over the camp radio, Garwood approached a senior Vietnamese official. "Why aren't I being released? Why am I not going home? Everyone else is going home."

The officer responded: "What makes you think everyone else has gone home? Who told you that?"

"It's announced on the radio," the marine retorted.

"We didn't announce it, the United States did," replied the official, adding, "Maybe it's everyone they want. That doesn't mean it's everyone that we have."

Garwood was told he would go home when his guards got orders from Hanoi to let him go home. But after seeing POWs still held from France's Vietnam War, along with the other U.S. prisoners, Garwood began to wonder if he would ever go home.

Garwood had not been forgotten, however. Although Hanoi claimed there were no more Americans in Vietnam, the U.S. continued to ask for an accounting of its POW-MIAs. Garwood's name was among those given to Vietnam, former State Department POW official Frank Sieverts told the Senate in 1992.

When asked if Garwood was in Vietnam: "They [the Vietnamese] didn't respond," Sieverts testified. He added that the Vietnamese also refused to "respond" when asked about "[a] great many" other Americans.[9]

"Shazam, Shazam!"

In early spring 1974, almost five years since last speaking with an American, Garwood was given the assignment of teaching

English slang to Vietnamese linguists. Garwood testified that he not only didn't want to teach the classes, but also found himself unable to provide the instruction.

"[W]hen they started off, they had some idioms, some slang American words, that they wanted me to define and I had no idea [of] the meaning. I'd never heard them before.

"One was 'shazam.' I don't know that. I'd never heard of it. I didn't find that out [until] when I got back and watched Gomer Pyle."

Loneliness ate away at the lost American. In mid-1975 he went to a prison official and asked to be placed in confinement with the other American POWs he had seen.

"I said I just wanted to know why I can't be with those people. They're my people. We understand each other. And I said if I'm going to die here, I wanted to be with my own people. I said at least I could be able to exchange stories or religion together. And I told him I was very lonely. And he just said: 'That's impossible.'"

By 1977, Bobby Garwood had used his survival skills to compromise some of his captors. Assigned work as a mechanic, Garwood was often dispatched to fix vehicles away from the camp. He was able to enter Hanoi's hotels for foreigners and purchase goods, such as liquor and cigarettes, unavailable to many Vietnamese citizens. After the guards shared the take, they were beholden to Garwood, who could at any time turn them in for the worst kind of punishment.

Getting Word Out

Bobby soon attempted to win his freedom during a contact with foreign travellers. He slipped a note to a journalist from New Zealand, asking the man to get it to U.S. authorities. The reporter apparently lost his nerve and destroyed the note before leaving Hanoi. He reportedly later told U.S. authorities about Garwood's existence, but America took no action.

Indeed, the U.S. continued to dismiss the possibility of unrepatriated Americans in Vietnam. But in 1978 France told American officials of reports that U.S. soldiers, perhaps deserters, remained in Vietnam. Instead of aggressively pursuing the report, the U.S. State Department scoffed at it, declaring: "such comments are heard fairly often, but to our knowledge remain unsubstantiated."[10]

Despite their ostrich-like stance on the POW-MIA issue, U.S. bureaucrats were unable to ignore Garwood's next gambit. At a Hanoi hotel on February 1, 1979, Garwood passed another note, this time to Ossi Rakkonen, a World Bank official from Finland. Garwood's message contained his name and serial number. Bobby also told the Finn that he knew of 15 more U.S. prisoners in Vietnam. This time, Garwood's information not only got out of Hanoi, but also appeared in the international media. Both Washington and Hanoi were forced to act.

Vietnam allegedly responded by killing Garwood's guards and forcing him to watch the execution of a female friend. Then, Garwood has sworn, he was pressured into reading propaganda statements for a U.S. film crew. The filmed report later implied that Garwood had been a free citizen in Vietnam.

The Demonization of Bobby Garwood

Hanoi even postponed Garwood's release when a Pentagon official and U.S. news reports referred to him as a POW. The International Red Cross told the State Department that Vietnam was "upset by what they view as the implication that the SRV lied about whether any POWs were still in Vietnam."[11]

But Hanoi had little reason to worry. It was also in the interest of the U.S. government to prevent Garwood from being considered a returning POW. Following intense public interest in the case, the State Department concluded: "Perhaps there will be less interest if it is discovered that Garwood had indeed stayed behind voluntarily."[12] Again and again, with little or no evidence, U.S. spokesmen publicly emphasized that Garwood had volunteered to remain in Vietnam.

By branding him as a traitor, the U.S. government was able to keep Vietnam happy and also to discredit Garwood's information concerning other Americans kept in Vietnam.

As soon as Garwood arrived in Bangkok during early 1979 aboard an Air France jet, he realized he was being treated as a captured criminal, rather than a returned POW. Marine representatives read him his rights before putting him on a plane home

Back in the U.S., Dermot Foley, Garwood's lawyer, inadvertently assisted in the process of discrediting Garwood by directing him to keep quiet about his POW information. Foley hoped to use Garwood's knowledge as a trump card in the court-martial process.

Bobby Gets the Message

Another influential source soon signaled Garwood that revealing his POW information might be a mistake. In his Senate deposition, Garwood recalls that shortly after returning to the U.S., he met a former top Pentagon POW official. Garwood told the man he had seen other U.S. prisoners.

> He [the former official] said: "I didn't hear that and you didn't say that." I said: "Why?" He said there was a very good chance that nothing is going to happen and he said that will open a whole new can of worms. He said: "You don't talk to anybody . . . about any other Americans that you saw. . . . "

His lawyer instructed Garwood that if he were pressed on the POW issue, he should give only vague answers. Garwood did just that, and when he told the whole truth years later, the government pointed to discrepancies with his initial accounts.

Meantime, Garwood was convicted for his actions while in enemy hands, receiving far harsher treatment than the collaborators returned in 1973. "He was a scapegoat because of the information he brought out," former POW Benge claims.

Bobby Garwood finally went public with his POW information in 1984 during an interview with *Wall Street Journal* reporter Bill Paul. The ensuing story that December invigorated the POW issue—and infuriated the Pentagon. Behind closed doors, Pentagon experts were forced to admit Garwood had important evidence, especially about his sightings of U.S. prisoners in Vietnam's Yen Bai camp complex. "There is a lot of information on Yen Bai in the files, much of which tends to substantiate what Garwood says," wrote the DIA's Admiral Thomas Brooks.[13]

In public, the Pentagon claimed it was eager to learn anything it could from Garwood. In private, a top Pentagon official noted: "I don't want to talk to this character anymore than anyone else. But I'm out of alternatives."[14]

Despite intense Congressional and public pressure, it took years before the Pentagon conducted a thorough debriefing of Garwood, who in the meantime had passed a private polygraph exam on his POW sightings. During his contacts with the DIA, Garwood was amazed to learn how closely the DIA had kept track of him in Vietnam, even in the giant prison complex at Yen Bai. "They showed me aerial pictures of the camp and they pinpointed to where my hooch was," Garwood told the Senate. "They claimed that they knew where I was at all times" during over 13 years in Vietnam.

That raises questions about how much the Pentagon really knows about other unrepatriated U.S. servicemen in Southeast Asia. And the Garwood case proves the military failed to follow up for years on one of the best sources of information it ever had on the Vietnamese prison system.

The Pentagon still refuses to admit any guilt for the Garwood fiasco. But Bobby does feel remorse—the guilt of a survivor.

As he told the Senate: "I feel guilty because I think to myself: 'Why in hell didn't you take the time, why didn't you try and probe and find out who those people where? Why didn't you ask more questions?' And yes, I feel I have major guilt about that."

Not about being with the enemy. But about coming home when so many other Americans did not.

Chapter 22

The POW Diaspora

"[T]he Soviet Union has been the central focus of U.S. and Allied intelligence activities for most of this century, and China has been watched for almost 50 years. I believe this scrutiny would have likewise revealed at least a hint of American prisoners held in either country had they been taken there. Again, no such evidence has ever surfaced."
—Rear Admiral Ronald Marryott, Deputy Director of the DIA, testimony to Congress on June 28, 1990

"Sejna several times was present when the vans unloaded the [U.S.] POWs at the military counter-intelligence barracks [in Prague] and personally visited the POWs there. . . . "
—debriefing of General Jan Sejna, top Warsaw Pact defector and long-time DIA employee who says he helped ship U.S. POWs to Russia

For many years, the DIA, the agency charged with tracking down leads on missing POWs, has insisted there is "no evidence" that any U.S. POWs were shipped from Indochina to the Soviet Union. Of course, that isn't true. There is indeed evidence that such shipments did occur. But the DIA's dissembling about the Russian connection differs from its usual official quibbling. That's because the whole time DIA officials have been telling the American public and Congress there is absolutely *no evidence* that any U.S. POW ever went to Russia, the agency has had in its employ a man who claims he helped run a communist program that shipped scores of American prisoners from Vietnam to the Soviet Union.

And that DIA employee isn't some lowly clerk. He is said to be the top communist military officer ever to defect to the United States. In addition, the man has a highly sensitive DIA job as an expert on Warsaw Pact tactics and has passed several polygraph tests proving his honesty and loyalty to the U.S.

The defector is Jan Sejna, a former Major General in the Czech army who defected in February 1968. His information is so shocking that although the Senate Select Committee deposed Sejna and promised to make his testimony public, almost none of it showed up in the Senate POW report and the deposition itself has not been released as of this writing—apparently on the orders of the DIA and CIA. The only reason Sejna's information ever escaped the Pentagon was because civilian defense analyst Dr. Joseph Douglass, Jr. forced it to the Senate's attention. The following information on Sejna comes from information Douglass shared with the authors in the hope it might shame the Pentagon into telling the truth about U.S. POWs in the former Soviet Union.

Sejna's information is not yet confirmed, and the general does have his critics in the U.S. intelligence community. But he claims to have passed a grueling DIA lie-detector test on his POW information. (While the DIA doesn't want to talk about Sejna, the agency still employs him in a sensitive position.) And the general's testimony appears to support other evidence on the shipment of U.S. POWs from Indochina to Russia, China, North Korea and Cuba. Put together, the information leaves little doubt that a POW diaspora occurred during the Vietnam War, leaving scores, and perhaps hundreds, of U.S. prisoners scattered across the communist world, tortured by their enemies and abandoned by their own government.

A Soviet Tradition

The Soviet Union imprisoned U.S. POWs after World War II, the Cold War and the Korean War. Given their actions in every previous conflict since 1945, there seemed little doubt the Soviets would abduct American POWs during Vietnam. By the end of the war, the Soviet Union had invested an estimated $3 billion in weapons and 3,000 troops, of whom 13 died, in the Vietnam War. And they wanted a return on their money.[1]

An Established Connection

No one denies that the Soviets had a system for moving U.S. servicemen from Indochina to the Soviet Union. As many as 25 U.S. deserters went from South Vietnam and/or Japan to the U.S.S.R. and then on to Sweden. "Beheiren," the Japanese-Vietnam Peace Committee backed by KGB agents, helped move deserters to and through Japan. Once in the USSR they were handled by the Soviet Afro-Asian Solidarity Committee, under the Communist Party's International Division.[2]

Both the U.S. and Vietnam deny that any U.S. POWs went from Hanoi to Moscow. And Vietnam even still claims that no deserters ever made the trip. But both the U.S. and Vietnamese denials are contradicted by the case of Jon M. Sweeney, a Marine enlisted man who travelled from North Vietnam to Beijing to Moscow at a time the Pentagon now admits he was a POW.

Sweeney, captured in February 1969, eventually pretended to be a collaborator. During his travels, he escaped an armed Vietnamese guard and turned himself in to U.S. officials at the American Embassy in Stockholm on August 31, 1970.

The marine was later found innocent of charges of treason. Responding to a Freedom of Information request from the authors, the U.S. Marine Corps now confirms that "Mr. Jon M. Sweeney was a prisoner of war" during the time he went from Hanoi to Moscow. The Pentagon has refused to release details about Sweeney's trip and whether he saw other U.S. POWs in China and Russia.

POWs Make the Trip

Many other American POWs—especially those with technical and intelligence backgrounds—were shipped to Russia, according to former National Security Agency staffers Jerry Mooney and Terry Minarcin, a Vietnamese linguist. "The Soviets are willing to spend millions of dollars in bribery; they'll use sex, they'll use drugs, they'll use anything they can to get high-tech information," Mooney says. Over the skies of Vietnam were intelligence assets, "high tech pilots [that] came down in parachutes just like manna from Lenin, and fell into the hands of the allies of the Soviet Union."

To think that the Soviets would "not take advantage of that situation, a freebie, no expenditure of funds, no blackmail, no espionage, is absolutely ludicrous," Mooney believes. The analysts involved in tracking the POWs knew "our men would be taken advantage of, would be interrogated and taken on (to the U.S.S.R.) if proved fruitful."

By 1965, U.S. POWs were being screened at the Lam Thao Superphosphate Plant in North Vietnam, according to a declassified CIA report. As of 1966, several Russians, along with a number of Chinese, were at the center. "Two U.S. pilots were taken to the debriefing point at one occasion in 1965; eight in 1966; and an unknown number in 1967." When pilots arrived, "a Soviet, a Chinese and a Vietnamese greeted the pilots and led them into the building. The pilots usually remained in the building for several hours. When they emerged they had changed from uniforms into civilian clothes." The men were taken away, and the source "did not know the destination of the prisoners."[3]

No U.S. serviceman *returned* from the publicly admitted POW system in Vietnam was questioned by Russians, according to the DIA—but this does not mean that it didn't happen.

POW *Guinea Pigs*

In addition to being sources of intelligence value, Sejna says, the Americans were used as human guinea pigs in communist experiments involving biological, chemical and atomic weapons. The general learned of the operations while secretary of the Czech Military Committee, or Defense Council, which coordinated highly secret intelligence operations with other communist nations. "The Soviets wanted to learn if American GIs were any more, or less, vulnerable than Soviet soldiers to experimental agents they were developing. The Soviets also wanted to know if there were any differences between the races—black, white, and Asian—in their biochemical vulnerability. The captive GIs were also used in testing the effectiveness of military intelligence drugs, including a wide variety of mind-control and behavior-modification drugs," Douglas, Sejan's voluntary debriefer, reports. Communist official Dr. Dang Tan corroborated the use of drugs on U.S. POWs after his defection in 1969, according to CIA documents declassified in June 1993. Tan reported "the use of different drugs to weaken their [the U.S. prisoners'] will. I know of this because of my medical background and contacts in the medical field," Tan said. Another U.S. intelligence report even discussed a special Vietnamese POW camp where Americans were subjected to drug treatments.

The Vietnam POWs became part of a long-term program first begun on U.S. POWs snatched from the battlefields of Korea, Sejna says. The men were studied for as long as they survived, then autopsied. In some cases, they were allowed to have children to test the cross-generation impact of certain weapons, Sejna claims.

The program in Vietnam began in 1960, when Hanoi's military Chief of Staff and other Vietnamese officials visited Prague looking for help in their war. Sejna says he was at a meeting where Soviet General Aleksandr Kuschev asked to continue the Korean tradition of sharing their POWs. Vietnam agreed.

The first step in developing the program, as with any effective intelligence/military operation, was security. The communists developed a sophisticated counter-intelligence plan to hide their mission. The process of secretly obtaining U.S. "specimens" was thought out every step of the way.

Sejna says the first shipments of U.S. POWs to Russia, under Vietnamese guard, occurred in August, 1961. This closely matches a separate report from Pavel Ponomaryev, a retired major in the Soviet Air Force. Ponomaryev, who worked in a squadron reporting to the KGB in Vietnam, said he flew two caucasian prisoners, both appearing to be a little under 30 years old, from Laos to a KGB center in North Vietnam during August 1961. "They were under Vietnamese guard," Ponomaryev had said.

The program accelerated, along with the war, around 1964. In addition to facilities in North Vietnam, the Soviets established two "hospitals" in Laos for preliminary work on the U.S. "specimens." (Years before Sejna's information became public, Minarcin—the former NSA official—told the authors he had listened in on highly classified communist radio messages concerning Soviet biological tests on U.S. POWs in Laos.) Most of the U.S. POWs, however, ended up in Russia. To disguise their ultimate destination, they were often shipped through Prague, where Sejna saw a number of them.

By the time Sejna defected in 1968, the program was winding down. But a separate CIA report indicates U.S. POWs were still arriving in Russia during 1970 for "intensive psychological studies of the individuals and utilization of them as required to serve the needs of the Soviet Union." The men were being held at the infamous prisons near Perm, where a British engineer told the authors an American POW was being held in the 1980s.[4]

High-Tech POWs

Even after the medical program apparently wound down, Soviet interest in high-tech POWs continued at a high level. After the U.S. began flying sorties over North Vietnam in 1965, the

Soviet government had escalated its involvement in the air war, immediately dispatching military personnel and equipment and establishing anti-aircraft weaponry test facilities.

In the 1950s and 1960s, Soviet military equipment had performed poorly against American-made equipment used by the Israeli military. Vietnam provided the Soviets with a perfect opportunity to obtain a constant supply of American high-tech equipment and personnel, as well as a laboratory in the skies over North Vietnam in which to test new ideas.

Khamou Boussarath was the chief of security for the non-communist Laotian government during the war. He received strong information that American airmen were being moved to the U.S.S.R. "The Russians wanted the technology . . . about American airplanes," Boussarath said. They "were having trouble in the Mideast. [Russian] MiGs were all the time getting shot down by American-built planes flown by Israel."[5]

According to Mooney and Minarcin, the Soviet military established a "very secure area" near Ron Ron, North Vietnam. The Vietnamese called it "Ban," which means "friends." It was a heavily guarded complex that included two separate POW camps. According to Mooney, the interrogation center in the panhandle was "a very special prison camp. We knew what types of personnel were being taken there, we knew the prison camp held Vietnamese, Soviet and probably East German interrogators. . . . We knew how they were moved on, over to Laos, which was more secure, up in the Sam Neua area. From there they disappeared into history, just like [in] Korea and World War II." A third American claims to have escaped from the facility, but his veracity cannot be verified.

Through analysis, American intelligence established that the Soviets were looking for computer input, targeting data, and specific information that would make it possible to update radars for SAM missiles—anything that would enable their equipment to perform better against their principal adversary, the United States. The information gleaned from POWs at the Ron Ron facility, the former officials say, was exploitable both immediately and on a long-term basis.

American aviators were also reportedly worked on by Soviets at other Vietnamese facilities. "I do know that some Cubans and Russians interrogated some American prisoners and treated them badly," testified Bui Tin, former senior Colonel in the North

Vietnamese Army. During a Senate hearing, he said Russians had interrogated B-52 crewmen during December 1972.[6]

Since, according to the Pentagon, no returned U.S. serviceman was interrogated by Russians, such men were either killed, kept in Southeast Asia, or sent to Russia.

Le Thom, a Laotian who later settled in London, thinks the men went to the Soviet Union. He says he was detained in Hanoi's Hoa Lo prison, where two American prisoners in the next cell were being interrogated by Russians. When he asked a guard what was happening, he was told that the Americans were being processed for departure to the Soviet Union. The guard said other U.S. POWs had shared the same fate.[7]

That report was supported by a Red Army major, who claims to have been told by a KGB officer that a U.S. POW was smuggled in 1967 through a "window" along the Sino-Soviet border used to move war booty from Indochina to the U.S.S.R. "The American was kept alive to tell what he knew about electronic jamming measures on such U.S. aircraft as the RB-47 bombers and Phantom fighters," the Major told an Australian T.V. reporter. The American, by some accounts missing Naval aviator Lieutenant Commander Kelly Patterson, had been sent to the Red Army air defense complex in Sary Sagan, Kazakhstan.

According to the recently published book *Fulcrum,* a Russian pilot was told by his weapons officer that the arming system for the Soviet's RN-40 nuclear bomb came from the minds of U.S. POWs. "The American methods," according to the weapons officer, "we obtained from several U.S. Air Force 'guests,' nuclear-qualified pilots our fraternal Socialist comrades in Vietnam provided us during that Imperialist war."

An American selected by the Soviets and exploited for intelligence purposes would not be allowed to return home; that had been Soviet policy since 1945. Besides, the information inside those high-tech minds was exploitable over the long-term, and it was hard to predict when the next supply of U.S. brain power would come floating down.

The Soviets also wanted U.S. hardware. In 1992 the Pentagon was forced to admit what it had denied for years—that high-tech U.S. equipment traveled from Vietnam to Russia. DIA officials have now inspected an F-111 escape module found in Russia. The DIA claims it has been unable to determine which crew was on the plane that ejected that module, which is a sort of escape pod for the pilot and co-pilot. Mooney, the former NSA staffer, has said for years that an American high-tech FB-111 downed just north of the Vietnamese DMZ on November 7, 1972, "crashed almost intact," and within 100 hours was in transit to the Soviet Union. According to one report, the Pentagon intercepted a Vietnamese radio transmission ordering that a "special team be sent to transport the hulk of an F-111A aircraft that was shot down." And another intercepted message possibly relating to the incident said Vietnamese troops "captured alive the pilot. Conceal the achievement." According to Mooney, both members of the aircrew, Majors Robert Morrissey and Robert A. Brown, were sent to the U.S.S.R. at that time. For years the Pentagon denied that, claiming the plane and its crew were totally destroyed in their incident. But recently the Vietnamese have turned over the ID card of Major Brown, indicating that he or his body was indeed in enemy hands.

Brown's son Steve has visited Russia in search of American POWs. He believes his father and/or other U.S. prisoners, along with captured American equipment, were used to help design the Soviet SU-24 "Fencer" fighter-bomber, similar in many ways to the F-111. Brown says retired Russian Colonel Alexander Chermansky, a former intelligence officer at the Soviet Embassy in Hanoi, confirmed that a captured F-111 was flown from Vietnam to the U.S.S.R. in November 1972. And Brown claims a Soviet woman told him she used schematic drawings of a captured U.S. plane when she worked at a Russian aircraft factory during the Vietnam War.

By exploiting information inside selected POW brains, along with the information gained by inspecting and analyzing captured equipment, rapid upgrades were possible in the Soviet-Vietnamese defenses. It became a never-ending process: increased Soviet competence mandated new American tactics and improved electronics systems, which in turn required a further improvement in Soviet capabilities, made possible by the seemingly inexhaustible supply of Americans parachuting into communist hands.

Likely Suspects

Mike Bosiljevac was just the kind of high-tech guy for whom the Soviets were looking. An electric countermeasures (ECM) expert, Bosiljevac, according to his family, "had also gone through an Atomic Energy Commission fellowship to get a master's degree in radiation shielding." His F-105 jet was hit by a SAM missile over North Vietnam on September 29, 1972, only three months before official American participation in Vietnam combat ended. Bosiljevac and his partner, Lieutenant Colonel James O'Neill, ejected. Other pilots in the area "watched their parachutes, had radio contact with them, and knew exactly where they were. It was one o'clock in the afternoon and Red Crown [the electronic countermeasures aircraft] had contact with them on the ground." Two days later, CBS news broadcast a picture of O'Neill taken in Hanoi.

O'Neill was released five months later during Operation Homecoming. "The biggest shock of his life," he told Bosiljevac's wife, "worse than being shot down, was to look around the airport in Hanoi . . . to give Mike the 'thumbs up' signal. And Mike wasn't there." A Vietnamese prison guard had told O'Neill that Bosiljevac was "alive and well and uninjured," adding cryptically: "and luckier than you." A few months before Bosiljevac went down he was on leave in Hawaii with his wife, Kay. "The Vietnamese are using Soviet intelligence," he told her. "They know everything about me.

Bosiljevac was one of the pilots Mooney spoke of as being specifically targeted, and as the former intelligence expert prophetically stated, the NSA would "assume they [men like Bosiljevac who went missing] were gone forever." Radio Hanoi had even informed Bosiljevac of his son's birth before the Red Cross did. His wife relates that "this fact becomes important years later, when the packages I continued to send Mike were always precisely returned to me on our son's birthday. And letters would be returned without photos that I had enclosed, on Mike's birthday. The last one I received, in 1981, came back with an East German postmark . . . on my son's birthday."

Six months after the last POW returned, she had gone to Southeast Asia. In Thailand, "an American who was attached to MACTHAI [Military Assistance Command, Thailand] took me aside and said, 'I want to talk to you.' " They walked away from the building and he told her, "I found Mike's name on a list with thirty-six others. It was a 'possibles' list." Mike could have been moved to a third country. It was a list of technicians, she remembered.

In 1976, Kay Bosiljevac flew to Paris and spoke with Mark Pratt, First Secretary for Indochina Affairs at the American Embassy. "He took me upstairs and closed the door." There, she claims, he told her they were "having difficulties making inquiries through the French, because in the past, Henry Kissinger would not allow any activity to go on anywhere without being personally involved." When she told Pratt what the MACTHAI official had said about Mike being in a third country. "His response was, 'It's more likely Russia than China.' " That was a diplomatic understatement. After the fall of 1967, Minarcin says the Soviet Union had the exclusive use of "select" captured Americans, except for a few captured in extreme North Vietnam, near the China border.

Bosiljevac's body was returned from Vietnam in 1987, bearing evidence that he had survived at least several years in captivity and been autopsied in a manner not used by the Vietnamese. According to a Vietnamese who defected in 1992, Hanoi "leased" some U.S. pilots to the Soviets. Perhaps Mike Bosiljevac was such a human encyclopedia. Or maybe he was a human guinea pig who, after his strange autopsy, was of no more value to the communists.

Another unlucky POW was an American of Hungarian ethnicity, according to former Soviet prisoner Igor Privalov, who spoke with one of the authors in Moscow. Privalov said he was told by a Soviet officer that an American aviator born in Hungary had been captured in Vietnam and sent to Russia. The men had fled Hungary during the 1965 uprising, married an American woman, started a family, and joined the U.S. military before being captured in Southeast Asia. But he still maintained a traditional Hungarian hatred for Russians, according to the Soviet officer. The American POW refused to cooperate at all with his Soviet interrogators and was so obstinate the Soviets dispatched him to Hungary, where he was tried and "sentenced" by a "People's Court."

After the War

Mooney claims at least 65, and perhaps more than 200, Americans were in all likelihood sent to Russia. Sejna says the number is even higher. And the shipments continued after the war, according to Minarcin. Twenty-eight Americans, mostly intelligence specialists and special operations troops, were shipped to the Soviet Union between December 1977 and January

1978, Minarcin says. The Vietnamese linguist says he listened to Vietnamese radio signals concerning flights from special POW camps to Hanoi. After that, Soviet IL-62 transports piloted by KGB personnel transported the American POWs from Gai Lam International Airport, Hanoi, on a flight path that took them over the Himalayas and on to the Soviet Union. On the last flight, U.S. intelligence picked up a conversation: "There are no more SIGINT [signals intelligence] specialists in country."

Minarcin heard from another intelligence staffer that, upon landing, the American POWs were hustled onto planes or the Trans-Siberian Railroad for a ride to Sokol on the Poloustrov Tajmir Peninsula. There the high-tech specialists could be put to good use. Heavily guarded by the KGB, Sokol was the forward deployment base for the Soviet strategic bomber force.

Minarcin's story of post-war POW shipments to Russia passed a lie-detector test, according to a Senate staffer. And the account is supported by another intelligence sergeant named Barry Toll, who testified the U.S. had a plan to force down one of the planes carrying U.S. POWs to the Soviet Union.

From June 1973 to July 1975, Toll was assigned to the Airborne Command Post system as an intelligence specialist. He served mostly with the flying command post of the the Commander-in-Chief, Atlantic Command. His job was to help brief top U.S. commanders—including the President—if they were forced to the air during a nuclear crisis or war. Toll's duties, which required him to have a security clearance far above Top Secret, included staying up to date on the most sensitive intelligence available to the White House.

During that time, Toll says he saw several "real time" reports going to the President concerning the shipment of U.S. POWs to the Eastern-bloc. Earlier in the war, U.S. POWs had been shipped to East Germany on military planes returning from Vietnam after dropping off airplane parts, Toll swore in his Senate deposition. There was even an unsuccessful U.S. intelligence effort to photograph U.S. POWs arriving in East Germany, he said.

The shipments took on new importance after the war. "During the period September 1973 through April 1975 I can personally recall on at least three, and as many as five, occasions when CIA/DIA and NSA would track the real-time movements of Soviet or Eastern Bloc aircraft carrying U.S. POWs or (on one occasion) CIA operatives from North Vietnam to either the USSR proper, or to either East Germany of Poland. I believe that on one occasion the destination became Bulgaria."

The flights, often including U.S. technical experts, increased after the Mideast's October War in 1973, when Soviet weapons systems were battered by modern Israeli systems.

"It was determined that the Soviet technicians responsible for evaluating such data had requested that American POWs with background in these technologies be sent out of theater into Soviet environs for real-time interrogation," Toll claimed.

From three to five Americans were on each flight, the former intelligence sergeant told the Senate. In one case, U.S. intelligence believed it had identified the names of the men on the shipment, which included a CIA official and two "back-seaters."

Twice the planes carried a communist diplomat along with the U.S. POWs, making if more risky for the Americans to intercept and force down the flight. Toll says there was one mission to intercept and force down such a flight, but the plane escaped into Soviet territory.

The Senate conceded that Toll did hold the command post job and had "access to sensitive message traffic." But some staffers raised questions about Toll's drug-dealing conviction after the war and said they could not locate other members of his unit who recalled the POW messages (although they did locate a lawyer who confirmed Toll's account of being spied on by the DIA after leaving the military).

Amazingly, the Senate failed to compare Toll's testimony with corroborating information from Minarcin, Sejna and Khai. The Committee also failed to obtain the Presidential briefings described by Toll. Instead, the Senate preferred to trust the CIA and Nixon to reveal the shipments. They didn't.

Covering-Up the Diaspora

Perhaps because of the threat it poses to America's most delicate international relationship, the U.S. executive branch has always gone out of its way to hide information about U.S. POWs in the Soviet Union. Even the advent of the policy of glasnost, or "openness," was not enough to prompt even a limited U.S. attempt to free its fighting men imprisoned in Siberia. Indeed, in April 1990 State Department spokesman Richard Boucher was asked by one of the authors why, given the new Gorbachev era and "glasnost," America was not trying to recover prisoners that declassified U.S. government records indicated were sent to the U.S.S.R.

"I'm not familiar with the previous documents, particularly any classified ones" responded Boucher with Orwellian elan. "We do not believe that there are any U.S. POWs in the Soviet Union, [so] we have not raised it." The only outburst of honesty at Foggy Bottom that spring came from a historian who, for obvious reasons, requested anonymity. American POWs in Siberia, he admitted, "just sort of became a non-issue, I'm afraid."

And the DIA wanted to keep it that way. On June 28th 1990, during hearings before the House Subcommittee on Asian and Pacific Affairs, the DIA's deputy director testified on the POW/MIA issue. While willing to discuss Indochina, Rear Admiral Ronald Marryott, in full uniform, avoided speaking about the Soviet Union either to the Congressional representatives or to a waiting television crew.

Instead, he submitted written testimony stating: "The Soviet Union has been the central focus of U.S. and Allied intelligence activities for most of this century, and China has been watched for almost 50 years. I believe this scrutiny would have likewise revealed at least a hint of American prisoners held in either country had they been taken there." Again, no such evidence has ever surfaced.

Congressional pressure finally forced the Bush Administration to ask Moscow about the POWs. During the July 1991 superpower summit, the U.S. allegedly passed a note to the Soviets mentioning U.S. POWs taken to the Soviet Union. But when the President got home, he downplayed the topic.

"Did you ask the Soviets about any prisoners they might have from past wars?" a reporter asked the President during a Rose Garden press conference.

"Yes," Bush replied, "We raised that with the Soviets. They've maintained before and I would expect maintain again that they know of no American prisoners."

The President then backed earlier statements by "General Scowcroft" dismissing evidence of live U.S. POWs in Indochina.

The remark stunned POW/MIA family members, who took it as a clear signal to the Soviets that the Bush Administration was not eager for the truth. Mysteriously, Mikhail Gorbachev later heatedly denied that Bush had ever asked him about U.S. POWs.

In December 1991, the State Department did ask Moscow to account for a number of U.S. POW/MIAs, a move that was promptly leaked to the beltway media as proof the Pentagon was trying hard to determine if U.S. POWs were shipped from Indochina to the Soviet Union.

The next month, one of the authors of this book got a peak at the diplomatic note during a stop at the U.S. Embassy in Moscow. The message started well enough with a firm but polite request for information, noting: "Below is a list of the individuals about whom we have inquired previously but never received a convincing response." But the message went straight downhill from there. The first name on the list was Wilfred C. Cumish, who had been returned by the Soviets in the 1950s. The second name was Sidney Ray Sparks—a Georgia-born soldier who defected to Russia and spent years in Soviet prisons before coming home in the 1950s. The third name on the list was Major Wirt Thompson, a WWII POW never returned from Siberia. They got that one right.

The fourth and fifth names were Colonel Cerny and 1st Lieutenant Cushman, names the authors had researched but could never link to real U.S. servicemen. It is likely they were Europeans looking for a way out of Siberia. The sixth name on the list was William Baumeister. While the authors believe it possible he was imprisoned in the U.S.S.R., during the late 1950s the Pentagon informed Baumeister's family that his remains had been found in Burma and that it was impossible for him to have been held in the Soviet Union. The remaining names were of missing Cold War aviators.

Contrary to stories then being leaked to the national press by the Bush Administration, there were no POWs from Vietnam on the list. And, of the first six people whose return the United States government was demanding, only one could be said with certainty to be an American imprisoned but never returned by the Soviets. This was the official, U.S. government handling of what President Bush called his "highest national priority."

The diplomat at the American Embassy in Moscow, a cordial but overworked man who apparently had more pressing duties than his part-time POW assignment, appeared sincerely surprised when told of the problems with the official list. He wondered how we knew that Cumish and Sparks had been returned. The reply was that the authors had talked with Sparks and had read the report Cumish dictated upon returning to U.S. custody. In addition, the repatriation of both men had been reported in American newspapers.

Privately, the State Department was deeply embarrassed, blaming the Pentagon for unforgivable sloppiness. Department of Defense spokesperson Captain Susan Strednansky would only say that there were no Vietnam POWs on the list because "we don't have any information on U.S. prisoners from Vietnam going to the Soviet Union." She declined to discuss the other names on the list. It took Sidney Ray Sparks, speaking from his home in Georgia, to sum up the boondoggle. "I'm right here. I wonder why they're looking for me over there? I called the Department of Defense. . . . They said they'd get back to me. They haven't called yet."

Once again, the Bush Administration had sent a clear message. How could the Russians believe the POW issue was the "highest national priority," if the Administration could not even produce an accurate list of missing Americans?

And the Moscow Embassy continued to send distressing signals about the true priority it gave to missing Americans. A Russian journalist had received letters for the authors of this book containing information on U.S. POWs in Russia. The journalist didn't have our address, so he took the letters to the U.S. Embassy. There a functionary promised to send us the information.

After months passed, we asked the State Department what had happened to the letters. A spokesman said they had been mailed to us. Worried that the letters had been lost, we asked what information they contained. The State Department said it didn't know, because the officials in its Moscow Embassy had been "too busy" to check the information for potential leads. As of this writing, more than a year after delivery of the letters to the Embassy, they have still not surfaced. Russians have told the authors that over the years, other letters concerning U.S. POWs have been sent to the U.S. Embassy in Moscow. Those letters disappeared into the bureaucracy.

It took a unilateral Russian move to focus attention on U.S. POWs in the former Soviet Union. On his way to a June 1992 summit with President Bush, Boris Yeltsin confirmed that U.S. POWs from Vietnam had ended up in the Soviet Union. "Our archives have shown this to be true. Some of them were transferred to the territory of the former U.S.S.R. and were kept in labor camps. We don't have complete data and can only surmise that some of them may still be alive," Yeltsin told NBC.

The revelations sent the Bush Administration scrambling. The President's men, no longer able to claim that "no evidence" existed of U.S. POWs in the Soviet Union, were forced to come up with a new line. Within days, two themes emerged from the White House. First, the Administration claimed it had never known about any U.S. prisoners held by the Soviets. And second, President Bush emphasized that he would do everything possible to determine whether living American POWs were in the former Soviet Union.

Since almost all of the information in this chapter came from U.S. files available to the President in 1992, it would have appeared difficult for the Administration to claim it had no idea any Americans were ever held in the Soviet Union. But the Administration, confident of its ability to control the uninterested national media, decided to go with the big lie.

On June 16, 1992, Bush officials held a "background" briefing for the White House press corps by two of the Administration's top Russian experts. One was an Assistant Secretary of State whose office had received, and acknowledged, much of the information in this chapter. The other briefer was a high National Security Council official. Both men blatantly misled the media, and the American people, concerning U.S. knowledge of American POWs in Russia. In the White House transcript of the briefing, the men are identified as Assistant Secretary of State for European and Canadian Affairs Thomas Niles and Ed Hewett, Senior Director for Russian and Eurasian Affairs on the National Security Council. However, as is standard for "background" briefings, later in the transcript their comments are intermingled and attributed only to a "Senior Bush Administration Official."

> **Reporter:** Senator [Robert] Smith . . . said . . . our intelligence agencies have known about this [POWs in the Soviet Union] for years and years and have simply classified this information.
> **Senior Bush Administration Official:** I don't know to what you're referring in terms of U.S. intelligence information on POWs/MIAs in Russia or the countries of the former Soviet Union because I've never seen anything on

the subject. So I'm totally unaware of what he's talking about.

Reporter: So you're basically denying this assertion [by Senator Smith]?

Senior Bush Administration Official: I am. I am.

Once the White House had convinced the media that Yeltsin's revelations had come as a total surprise, it made a conspicuous point of promising an immediate search for U.S. POWs in Russia. President Bush wisely ignored the issue of what the government knew about Americans kept in the U.S.S.R. after WWII, Korea, and the Cold War. Instead, he focused only on living Americans from Vietnam, vowing that: "If anyone's alive, that person—those people—will be found."[8]

Malcolm Toon, co-chairman of the recently formed U.S.-Russian POW commission, was immediately dispatched to Moscow. After just five days of work in Russia, Toon, a former Ambassador to Moscow, repudiated Yeltsin's statement that Vietnam POWs had been sent to Russia and that they or other Americans might still be alive.

"I think we're going to end up with absolutely zero . . . my gut feeling is that there's nobody alive under Russian control," he declared. (When Toon was later told of Sejna's information, he suggested the general should be "dismiss[ed]," according to a Senate memo.)

The major media jumped on Toon's remarks, saying they cast "further doubt" about reports of U.S. POWs in Russia, reports the media called "vague." *The Los Angeles Times* declared that attempts by the joint commission to find an imprisoned Korean War POW were a "wild goose chase." Department of Defense spokesman Pete Williams—who knew about the previously secret U.S. files on POWs in Russia—then declared during a July Pentagon press conference that there was "no evidence" U.S. POWs had been sent from Korea to the Soviet Union. Most Pentagon reporters apparently took his word and the topic faded away, along with hope for recovering any of the American patriots packed like animals on to trains and shipped from Korea to Siberia. (As is so typical in America's capital, Williams did not suffer any career damage for knowingly peddling disinformation. After his Pentagon job, he joined NBC-TV as a Washington-based correspondent.)

Such furious establishment attempts to downplay the topic of U.S. POWs in the Soviet Union came as no surprise to one State Department source, who said the search for lost American servicemen was clouded by a hidden agenda among some Bush officials. "The most explosive issue is not the POWs but the Agency [CIA]," said the source in June 1992. The CIA had not only known about U.S. POWs in the Soviet Union, but had also lost many of its own people there. The Agency had never revealed the truth about those Americans. And the CIA might never allow the whole truth out, because that would mean having "to acknowledge the fact that they and our whole government have been deceiving or lying for a long time," the diplomat concluded.

It's also possible that the intelligence community isn't excited about focusing on an issue that might demonstrate its earlier incompetence or deceit. For example, a November 1972 CIA report carried the claim that "The North Vietnamese, despite repeated requests from the Soviets, never provided access to the [U.S.] prisoners." And even in 1982, years after the CIA had debriefed Sejna, the Agency commented in a classified report that: "We have never before encountered even vague rumors among Soviet dissidents or other informants that any U.S. POWs from Vietnam are incarcerated in the USSR. . . . "

So U.S. intelligence not only missed the Russian POW connection, but then lied about it when other sources began revealing the truth. That may be why the Pentagon avoided the DIA when it finally started making a real attempt to investigate the Russian POW angle. In 1992 the military established "Task Force Russia," an Army-led intelligence organization specifically designed to chase down information on U.S. POWs in Russia. The Task Force, at its own insistence, was clearly separated from the discredited DIA. But while the honest, open and hard-working men and women of Task Force Russia won accolades from POW/MIA family members and activists, their organization drew fire from the DIA and State Department. As of this writing, Task Force Russia appears likely to be eliminated or "consolidated" into oblivion, perhaps even in the black hole at the DIA where Russian POW information is hidden.

China

According to Sejna, China was cut out of the Soviet's Vietnam POW program. But Beijing had learned the benefits of stealing

U.S. POWs during the Korean War and wasn't about to pass up another opportunity. The Chinese government has admitted dispatching over 300,000 combat troops to Vietnam. More than 4,000 reportedly died at the hands of US and Allied forces. But, as in Korea, the Chinese inflicted their own casualties. And they apparently captured their own prisoners—prisoners who have never returned to America.

Perhaps the clearest case from the Vietnam War for which the Chinese owe an accounting involves Lieutenant Commander John Ellison and his bombardier/navigator Lieutenant J.G. James E. Plowman, Navy aviators downed over North Vietnam on March 24, 1967.

The information comes from Commander Robert J. Flynn, captured by Vietnamese peasants after his plane went down about 40 miles south of the Chinese border. The "nearest military barracks to where I was shot down was staffed by Chinese. It was the first day that Hanoi was really hit, and I think somebody made a decision to haul me into China."

While in a Chinese prison, Flynn says, he saw a group photo of American prisoners standing in ranks. He identified two men in the front row: John C. Ellison and James E. Plowman. The DIA claims Flynn really didn't see what he says he saw. But two men fitting the Ellison and Plowman's description had been reported outside the Tran Phu Prison in Hai Phong. And Ellison's name had been carved into a tree at a POW camp near the Chinese border, a U.S. returnee reported. Neither man returned from the war.

The National Security Agency had evidence that Chinese units in Vietnam captured and retained at least seven and perhaps as many as 22 Americans. "We were convinced that Americans were taken" to help with China's aircraft production programs, said former NSA analyst Jerry Mooney. According to Mooney, the following men may have ended up in China: James Barr, Ralph Bisz, Willie Cartwright, James Dooley, Hugh Fanning, Stephen Knott and Charles Lee. Mooney says a source claimed to have seen American POWs in a Shanghai factory in early 1975.

A series of secret Navy documents and a newspaper story report that China "banked" some U.S. POWs for Vietnam. "Evidence that the Chinese have been acting as 'bankers' for one of North Vietnam's major bargaining assets—the 600 U.S. POWs—has been building up strongly in Moscow," read a 1973 article in the 1973 *London Evening News*. Chinese officials alleged-ly housed the Americans in China's Yunnan Province, north of Vietnam. The men were far enough from Vietnam to be safe from rescue operations and bombing raids. But North Vietnamese guards told the U.S. POWs they were still in Vietnam. The author of the article, Victor Louis, has been identified as a "KGB agent of disinformation." Yet Louis was the first to reveal the downfall of Khrushchev.[9] And according to the article, the Pentagon did not flatly deny the story. "A Pentagon spokesman in Washington said there had been a number of reports of American POWs being held in China, but had no evidence to confirm it."[10]

Indeed, the Pentagon had classified documents about three U.S. POW camps in China, right where Louis had reported them. "The North Vietnamese sent the U.S. PWs to the PRC [People's Republic of China] because they felt the US could never send aerial reconnaissance or troops into the PRC to rescue these PWs because of the risk of global war," Navy intelligence reported in September 1972.[11]

A Chinese dissident later reported being imprisoned in Beijing with a U.S. POW who thought he was still in Vietnam. Sadly, the dissident can't remember the American's name.

In the 1980s and 90s, more reports emerged of US POWs in the PRC. One account alleged that anti-Soviet Vietnamese officials had fled to China with American POWs. The Vietnamese used American prisoners, one identified as MIA Charles Alva Dale, as servants. In a separate report, Russian sources told a woman that her relative, POW/MIA Charles Scharf, was alive in China as late as 1991.

Even Some for the Koreans and Cubans

Sejna also alleges that some U.S. POWs were shipped from North Vietnam to North Korea. He claims to have learned this at a 1962 Moscow meeting with the North Korean Chief of Staff and Soviet General A. I. Antonov. The North Koreans always wanted to keep some of the Americans being shipped through their country to Siberia, but the Soviets at first refused the request. But North Korea ultimately got permission to share in the POW diaspora, Sejna says. According to a separate CIA report, a North Korean defector reported seeing U.S. POWs from Vietnam out-side Pyongyang in 1968, and "about 10 military pilots captured in North Korea were brought to North Korea," according to a CIA report.[12]

Sejna suspects, but does not know for sure, that East Germany also received U.S. POWs, a claim that is supported by other reports discussed earlier in this book. And there are reliable reports that Cuba, whose interrogators tortured a number of Americans in Hanoi, received some U.S. POWs for their trouble.

Spending Their Prime Years in Siberia

The fate of many American POWs caught in the diaspora may never be known. But by 1992, live sightings of U.S. POWs had begun to escape from Russia. One prisoner named Joe, from Fort Bragg, N.C., was reportedly placed temporarily in the cell of a Russian dissident, who now cannot recall the U.S. POW's last name. Another U.S. prisoner was reportedly operating turbine equipment along the trans-Siberian gas pipeline during the 1980s. Other Americans have also been reported in Soviet prisons. Privalov, the former political prisoner, says a Russian officer he met revealed the fate of two U.S. POWs. They had been shipped from Vietnam to somewhere in the Novosibirsk region of Siberia. By the early 1980s the Americans had been forced to marry and "were constantly guarded [by the KGB] to prevent them from leaving."

PART VI

Paying for Hostages?

Chapter 23

The Reagan Era: Offering to Pay For POWs

The U.S. will "work sensitively and quietly to repatriate any personnel alive, regardless of status, that the Vietnamese authorities find in their search efforts." [authors' emphasis]
—Secretary of State George Shultz, message to Hanoi, February 12, 1984

In January 1981, it was morning in America. Ronald Reagan was President, and he wasn't the kind of man to leave American POWs in Southeast Asia. The Vietnamese may have sensed this, because, once again they sent a new President a discrete offer to permit the U.S. to buy back POWs.

Secret Service agent John F. Syphrit has said he heard the Reagan team discuss the purported offer. George Bush, then Vice President, CIA Director William Casey and National Security Adviser Richard V. Allen took part in the discussion. The offer, reported via China or Canada, was for an unknown number of living Americans in exchange for $4 billion, presumably the same "reconstruction aid" Hanoi had been demanding all along.

One account of the meeting was offered in 1992 by *The Washington Times*, which had interviewed Syphrit. According to that story: "Casey wanted to know what to do about this [offer], the agent said. He said it had come through China and Canada from the Vietnamese. Reagan asked what he thought of it, and Casey said there wasn't anything to it. *Bush agreed. He said it was a lost cause.*" [authors' emphasis]

The agent said Mr. Allen thought "they should look into it some more. But Mr. Casey insisted that the offer constituted blackmail, the agent said."

Discussion stopped when then-White House Chief of Staff James Baker and his deputy Michael Deaver came in the room.[1]

The first and more detailed version of the meeting emerged during 1986 in an article alleging that the Vietnamese offer had been verified. "[T]he new administration learned that Vietnam wanted to sell to the U.S. an unspecified number of live POWs still in Southeast Asia for the sum of $4 billion," wrote *Wall Street Journal* reporter Bill Paul.[2]

Paul had an "irrefutable"[3] second source to confirm what Secret Service Agent John Syphrit had overheard—a tape recording of the meeting at which the third country offer was made. Among those in attendance were Reagan, Casey, Bush, Deaver, Meese, R. Allen and Haig, plus eight staff or intelligence personnel,[4] including Agent Syphrit. "The proposal was discussed by Mr. Reagan and his advisers at a general meeting on security matters, according to one person who says he was in the room [Syphrit], and whose story is supported by another attendee [the tape recording]," wrote Paul.[5]

"During the discussion, it was first decided that the offer was indeed genuine. Then, a number of the president's advisers said they opposed paying for POWs on the ground that it would appear as if the U.S. could be blackmailed." Reagan agreed. "At that point, the president's men were prepared to let the matter drop."[6]

"To his credit, however, Mr. Reagan told William Casey,[7] director of the Central Intelligence Agency, and Richard Allen, then the national security adviser, to try to find another way to get the men home."[8]

Unfortunately for history, the Senate POW committee decided to leave the truth about that 1981 offer unresolved, voting seven to four not to subpoena the Secret Service agent.[9]

Apparently Bush and Casey won out, because there is no record the offer was followed up to test its veracity, at least not during Reagan's first term. But history confirms *The Wall Street Journal's* claim that, while the White House may have ignored an offer to buy back POWs, it was certainly willing to take them back by force.

About two weeks after the January offer, Casey allegedly came back to Reagan and said the DIA knew that there were POWs in Southeast Asia and also knew where they were—apparently referencing the POW camp near Nhom Marot, Laos. By January 1981, the Nhom Marot operation was swinging into high gear. But as discussed earlier, attempts to rescue U.S. POWs reported in a Laotian POW camp near Nhom Marot had been completely bungled by May 1981. And according to one account, when the raid became public, Hanoi relayed the message that it would kill its U.S. captives if America attempted a covert operation to rescue them.

In August 1981, the Vietnamese appeared to position themselves for new POW negotiations by issuing a statement referring to Americans "who were 'reportedly captured but not registered,' and who, because of 'war circumstances,' died or became 'missing' on their way to detention centers."[10] The implication appeared to be that Americans had been mysteriously "lost" during the war, but might be "found" if conditions were right. But the Reagan team apparently still had no stomach for paying "blackmail."

Money Goes Back on the Negotiating Table

Ronald Reagan was a President committed to seeing that American POWs in Southeast Asia, if still alive, came home. As Ken de Graffenreid, Reagan's Special Assistant for Intelligence Programs put it, "the White House was always beating up on Casey and Cap [Weinberger] about the lack of good intelligence support, to what was clearly the President's desire."[11] De Graffenreid thought Casey and Weinberger were never "quite able to get full control of their own bureaucracy on this issue, in order to make necessary changes or give it the priority it deserved."[12]

In spite of the bureaucratic inertia on the POW issue, pressure from the top finally resulted in a new approach. Childress has admitted in writing that by 1983 Hanoi and the U.S. had agreed upon "code words" to negotiate the return of some warehoused remains. Then, on February 12, 1984, Secretary of State George Shultz sent a message to Vietnam's Minister of Foreign Affairs. The message signaled the Reagan Administration's willingness to "work sensitively and quietly to repatriate any personnel alive, regardless of status, that the Vietnamese authorities find in their search efforts."[13]

The meaning of "sensitively and quietly" is nowhere defined in any documents yet declassified. But the implication of the document is clear when it is part of a government-to-government communication concerning POWs both governments publicly claim don't exist, but about whom both governments want to barter.

When the U.S. puts such a proposal into diplomatic play, the government always has a detailed plan of action it is prepared to follow if the proposal is accepted—or even discussed. Logic demands that certain conditions must be met. "Sensitively and quietly" must mean absolutely "secretly." A means must be devised whereby both sides share an equal risk of exposure, so that neither side later has the ability to "blackmail" the other after a partial release of POWs. The implications of the United States proposal would slowly come to light over the years as both governments maneuvered, attempting to put a "sensitive and quiet" program into place that met each side's requirements while simultaneously limiting their exposure.

There was apparently no direct response to the initial Shultz "sensitively and quietly" overture so, a few months later, Dick Childress, the National Security Council (NSC) staffer tasked with the POW issue, recruited an American citizen who was a friend of Achmad Wiranatakusumah, a retired Indonesian general and member of that nation's National Security Council.

The American, I. Irving Davidson, while on business in Indonesia, met with Achmad and asked if he would be willing to be a conduit to the Vietnamese government. He agreed to the concept and Childress flew to Indonesia in June or July of 1984 and met with Achmad.[14]

On August 1, 1984, Davidson followed up with a letter to Achmad's brother:

> Dear Rachmat, I can't impress upon you enough the importance of having brother Achmad follow through in the request for cooperation Dick Childress made of him during our recent meeting in his office in Indonesia.
>
> Please follow through with your brother as soon as you receive this letter as it is most timely now in all our national interest.
>
> Indonesia should be the factor and the influence that causes the Vietnamese to release 300 to 400 bodies, and possibly some live Americans. The attached note from Dick Childress speaks for itself, as will President Reagan's speech.

A note from Dick Childress on NSC stationary, addressed to "Irv," was attached:

Anything our friends can do to help us to quietly solve this problem would be greatly appreciated at the highest levels of our government. We are interested in a solution, not vengeance or propaganda.

As a result of these meetings, according to Davidson's deposition, agents of Achmad met with Deputy Foreign Minister Pho Fan Sung in Hanoi, in early October, 1984. The agents reported back to Achmad, who then told Davidson: "be prepared to handle a shipment of bodies home and possible breathers. . . . He [Achmad] says they are confident there are some breathers—that's live people."[15]

Less than two weeks after these meetings in Hanoi, Childress sent a letter to General Achmad, again on NSC stationary:

I wanted to thank you privately and personally for your efforts with the Vietnamese, to everyone's greater cooperation on the POW/MIA issue. In my discussions with the foreign minister of Vietnam this week, he mentioned Indonesia's approach in September.

We had some confusion resulting from an intervention between two individuals who were supposed to be your intermediaries. Since the issue is so sensitive, I'm sure you agree that we must keep knowledge of the initiative limited to the fewest number of people possible.

Based on a recent call from IID [Davidson], I have informed the other parties that I prefer to work through the originally set-up channels [Achmad, Vietnam, Laos].

I look forward to hearing of any progress and greatly appreciate your efforts on this humanitarian cause.

By now Hanoi had realized its old demand that Congress appropriate the $3.25 billion (plus $1-1.5 billion in other aid) in reconstruction aid was not realistic. So Vietnam began to suggest alternate funding sources that would settle the Paris Peace Accord debt. In 1984, they sent a message to the United States through Achmad's agents suggesting two approaches to meeting their financial requirements:

We would commit the intentions of the U.S. to try and put their rice fields and other agricultural areas back in shape so they can use the land soil to grow food again. . . . What technology has the US learned of to date to help them rehabilitate their land, agricultural rehabilitation?[16]

Also, they wanted U.S. oil companies, if they did all that they were [required] to do, give back all the bodies, to enter Vietnam to look for oil under coproduction, production sharing agreements, contracts, as they do in other countries of Asia. They preferred U.S. companies to anybody else. . . to help build their petrochemical industry. They want to join the rest of the world again and forget the past.[17]

Davidson reiterated that "the report [Achmad] got back from Supeno [Achmad's agent in Hanoi] was that there were breathers."[18] The Vietnamese "said there were live prisoners. Some had converted to communism for various reasons," Davidson testified.

The living Americans were "part of the deal."[19] But Hanoi "needed financial assistance if it were to find missing Americans or their remains."[20] Vietnam's opening monetary demand was for "several hundred million dollars."[21] So Hanoi was prepared to negotiate the return of remains, as well as Americans who were not in a captive environment.[22]

Larry Ward, an associate of Ann M. Griffiths at the League of Families, a quasi-governmental POW/MIA support and advocacy group, was selected to be a non-government representative for the next meeting in Hanoi. Davidson's notes suggest that Ward was to meet with Reagan prior to leaving for Indonesia and Hanoi. After Ward went to Hanoi, he reported "the SRV is prepared to negotiate and even to discuss the question of live servicemen possibly still in Vietnam."[23]

Childress Forced Into Damage Control

The negotiations wobbled on December 4, 1984, when *The Wall Street Journal's* irrepressible Bill Paul revealed that Bobby Garwood had seen many other U.S. POWs in Vietnam. Garwood was summoned from his job at a Virginia gas station to meet with Dick Childress at a local bar. According to Garwood's deposition, the White House official said he was "upset" with the article and wanted to know exactly what Bobby had told Bill Paul and whether Paul had recorded the interview.

Garwood, according to his sworn Senate testimony, asked Childress why he was asking such questions. "He said that his concern was that there were delicate negotiations going on between Vietnam and the United States about the remaining possibility of live Americans still in Southeast Asia and that *The Wall Street Journal* article had seriously harmed and possibly broken down these negotiations. I said: 'Well, what's done is done. There is nothing we can do about that.' "

Childress then reminded Garwood that he was still under the jurisdiction of military law and could face charges for withholding evidence on the POWs:

> He told me my life would be turned upside down, that I should consider cooperating with him and recanting the story in *The Wall Street Journal*.
>
> He says: "I have a direct line to the White House." He says: "Whatever you need, whatever you want, I can get for you if only you just work with us."
>
> I was telling him: "No." I said: "There is nothing you really have that I want (or) need." I said: "The only thing I want that you can do is get those people home." He said: "We are trying to do that, but you are interfering with that."[24]

Garwood responded that he only escaped Vietnam because the American people had found out he was still there, and telling the truth about the remaining prisoners was the only way to get them out too.

But Childress disagreed, saying the Vietnamese had tightened their security after Garwood's departure. "You shut the door on the possibility that anyone else may ever have the opportunity that you did," Childress reportedly said.

Trying to Keep the Deal On Track

In January 1985, Assistant Secretary of State Paul Wolfowitz sent his boss George Shultz a memo marked "super-sensitive." The memo, from the same Administration soon to experience the Iranian arms-for-hostages scandal, outlined a plan to pay Vietnam for remains and "possible live POWs."

Childress and Ann M. Griffiths soon began preparing to "go to Hanoi the week of February 25. . . . With Bud McFarlane's agreement NSC staffer Dick Childress's plans to go to Hanoi to negotiate for the return of MIA remains [sic] held by the SRV in return for a sum of money to be provided secretly [CENSORED] wealthy individuals."[25]

So Childress and Griffiths went to Hanoi and placed money on the table. For twelve years the Vietnamese had demanded compensation in return for their cooperation. Now an offer was on the table.

Childress now claims that when he got to Hanoi, the deal turned out to be for remains only—about 400 remains warehoused in Hanoi.[26] And Davidson has said Hanoi's offer to sell "breathers" was ruined by some sort of leak. But that is not what his notes, written at the time, said. Other players have also changed their stories, which is not surprising, since both Vietnam and Indonesia were promised the deal would be handled in a discrete fashion.

The Senate, in its less-than-thorough investigation, never got to the bottom of the 1984 offer. According to its final report, "the committee could not conclusively determine whether individuals in the government of North Vietnam discussed the possibility of there being live POWs in 1984; the Select Committee does find that the sale of remains was discussed."

That admission is remarkable in itself, since both Hanoi and Washington have repeatedly claimed that Vietnam never tried to sell remains. But the real story, never really pursued by the Senate, is that the sale of living U.S. POWs continued to be on the table, at least implicitly.

After all the talk about "breathers," is it reasonable to believe that live Americans were suddenly totally off the bargaining table when Childress arrived in Hanoi? Or is it more reasonable to believe that live Americans were at least implicitly part of the negotiations? All that is known for sure is that Childress and Griffiths went to Hanoi in response to a Vietnamese offer to begin solving the issue of remains and "breathers" for "several hundred million dollars."

The United States government knows what Childress's counter-offer was, but no one is talking. What we do know is that both sides came away from the table with a very positive attitude. Over the next six months the Vietnamese government would dramatically improve its promises of cooperation on the

POW/MIA dispute, proposing a joint effort to resolve the issue within two years.

Childress came away from the table equally impressed. A few months after returning to Washington, D.C., he telephoned Captain Eugene "Red" McDaniel, USN (Ret.). Since both were active in the League of Families, they had an established working relationship. Over the course of a one-hour conversation, McDaniel "specifically asked Mr. Childress if he thought we had Americans still being held in captivity in Southeast Asia. He responded by saying, 'You're damn right I do.' . . . Mr. Childress told me that he specifically briefed the President on the POW/MIA issue. . . . I asked Mr. Childress when we would expect to get some of the POWs back and he said in two or three years," McDaniel later testified before Congress.[27]

In late August 1985, Childress and Griffiths returned to Hanoi, where they met with Acting Foreign Minister Vo Dong Giang, who began to tell them of an abrupt change in Vietnam's policy toward the POW issue. Giang attributed this to an improvement in Vietnam's economic, social and security conditions. He then cryptically warned that "setbacks in the economy or security could still occur, and would affect SRV ability to carry out the plan, leaving the door open for retreat from these commitments."[28] In other words, Vietnam's cooperation was still contingent on money and security (i.e., no leaks) issues.

In response, Childress "raised the live POW issue at length . . . noting that this is an issue of high emotional content but expressing the desire to *sensitively* resolve it."[29] The White House official then referred to Secretary of State Shultz's February 12, 1984, "sensitively and quietly" letter to Vietnam's Foreign Minister, "and pointed out various circumstances where Americans could be in Indochina without knowledge of the central authorities. He also indicated that should there be ralliers in Vietnam who have changed their minds and wished to return home that we would accept them."[30]

But the U.S.-Vietnam negotiating history was such that Hanoi absolutely would not initiate a dramatic policy change just because the U.S. dangled something of interest, such as money. Their experience with Kissinger and Nixon precluded accepting American promises until substantial earnest money had been placed on the table.

Hanoi's cryptic warning in August 1985 indicates that Vietnam and the U.S. did come to a financial understanding. At a minimum, Vietnam and the United States have agreed on a sum of money for the repatriation, over a period of time, of the 400 remains warehoused in Hanoi—which had been reported to the U.S. by the defector whose codename was the "Mortician."

The Childress-Giang August 28th dialogue exchange suggests that money may have been paid to start the flow of remains out of the Hanoi warehouse, and that Childress was trying to keep the "sensitively and quietly" concept alive with further negotiations to pay for the return of defectors, ralliers and deserters. If this was in fact the case, it was the first-ever sign of a brilliant negotiating tactic by the American side: Get the process started and Hanoi comfortable with the concept and hooked on the flow of dollars. Then it might be possible to slowly expand the category of American they would be willing to "sensitively and quietly" sell to the U.S.

The authors believe that at some point secret negotiations resulted in a testing of the "sensitively and quietly" concept, with the secret repatriation of Americans. The process would probably have started with deserters, defectors or "ralliers," especially those not on the official U.S. POW/MIA lists. There are five reasons for this belief:

- This category—deserters, defectors and ralliers—was placed on the table by the Vietnamese earlier in 1984 when the Indonesians were the go-betweens.

- Childress focused on this category during the August 1985 meeting in Hanoi.

- By 1986, the U.S. had begun focusing on the POW category, not just defectors, ralliers and deserters. An interim period of minimal-risk program testing would be required before such a secret returnee program could have been considered viable by Hanoi or Washington, D.C.

- The "secret returnee" phenomenon began to appear in earnest within the borders of the U.S. in 1986.[31]

- No later than November 1990, an agreement was in place between the U.S. and Vietnam whereby any U.S.

POW/MIA other than those in close confinement, if located by American teams in the field, would be allowed
to leave Vietnam via American military aircraft, without
prior approval of the Vietnamese government.[32]

In June 1986 the United States increased its pressure on Vietnam to include all categories of Americans still in Southeast Asia,
telling Hanoi:

> In the United States' view, the highest priority should be
> given to resolving the question of Americans still alive in
> Vietnam. In this regard, the United States has noted Viet-
> namese public and private statements on this question and
> appreciates Vietnam's stated willingness to investigate
> reports of such Americans. The United States is prepared
> to participate in and support such investigations.
>
> If such investigations, or exchanges of information
> among the three Indo-China countries under the February
> 1984 Communique, reveal the presence of Americans in
> any condition, the United States position continues to be
> the one outlined in the February 12, 1984, letter from
> Secretary of State George Shultz to you.[33]

What program could the U.S. possibly put in place that would
reasonably assure the bureaucracies of both countries that the
secret repatriation would not be revealed? Although we can only
speculate, we do know that a program was agreed upon between
the two countries.

On November 6, 1990, an American team was in the field in
Vietnam looking for an alleged American by the name of Walter
T. Robinson. The Pentagon learned Robinson was not really an
American, and that's probably why documents regarding his
case have been released. But the records show something far more
important than the fact that a dark-skinned Vietnamese was
trying to escape Southeast Asia by pretending to be a U.S. POW.

The records show that by 1990 the U.S. had a firm standard
operating procedure for handling any Americans they might
find. The Pentagon SOP was: "If the team meets with someone
who clearly was in the U.S. military or is an American linked to
DoD, the team would fly him out of Vietnam aboard their C-12

aircraft with him transmitting Don Muang airport and moving immediately to Clark Airbase for additional processing."[34]

There was no requirement that the team sit on any American military personnel located, contact the Bangkok Embassy and pray the power of the U.S. government was brought to bear in time for Uncle Sam to bail the team out of a very precarious position—and at long last bring home a POW. There was no worry that Vietnam would swoop down and arrest the team or shoot down a U.S. airplane extracting an American POW/MIA. There was no worry because it was obvious Washington and Hanoi had finally reached an "ironclad" agreement.

The routing was automatic, with a "sensitive and quiet" processing center already in place at Clark Air Base. There was no requirement to obtain any type of permission from the Vietnamese before exiting the country with what normally would be considered an extraordinarily explosive political problem in tow.

Only if an agreement was in place to "sensitively and quietly" repatriate any American military/DoD person located by U.S. teams, "regardless of status," could such routing be used. And, since the U.S. and Vietnamese could not know in advance what category the person would come under—POW, defector, rallier, deserter, stay-behind, spook, etc.—an agreement was in place for the U.S. to take possession of any American in these categories.

But this protocol, at least the parts now declassified, appears to address only scattered Americans "living freely." It does not address the sudden release and shipment home of, for instance, an entire POW camp of Americans.

Intelligence strongly suggests that some Americans are still kept under tight guard. Presumably these are the "first heroes" described by Solzhenitsyn. They are the men who wouldn't crack, who kept the faith, who are still waiting to come home.

Despite all the evidence, it is also possible that all the negotiations and SOPs came to naught, and no Americans, except Bobby Garwood, have returned from Southeast Asia since 1976. Perhaps—but as the next chapter shows, not likely.

Chapter 24

The Secret Return of U.S. Servicemen from Southeast Asia

"Fantasies."
—Senate Select Committee on POW/MIA Affairs

"You can't believe everything you read and hear."
—MIA Glen Lane, as quoted by a close friend who said he met Lane in the U.S. during 1982

By 1982, the war was all just a memory. The loyal "little people," hill tribesmen who fought like devils and somehow humped their rucks on tiny shoulders across denied borders right alongside their U.S. special forces brothers, were now suffering under communism or living in the stink of Thai refugee camps. The highland camps that once seemed important enough to kill and even die for—camps that held the bones of many a brave defender and attacker—now were battered only by the monsoon, infiltrated only by the stealthy crawl of jungle vegetation. And the men who had gone down swinging, who had disappeared into the boondocks and never come back, now lived on only in the minds of those who knew and loved them at home and in Southeast Asia.

Or that's what "the major" thought in 1982. He was a veteran hero of the secret Indochina wars, a well-known career officer who had worn the Green Beret with distinction, then moved on and up to quieter, peacetime duty in the States with his family. He had no idea that a memory from Vietnam was about to become rock-solid real. And as of this writing, more than a decade later, what started in 1982 is still enough to worry him, a man who so many times risked his life, but would only tell the following story on the condition that his name not be used.

"I don't want to be regarded as yet another whacko," said the major, whose story came to the authors' attention by accident. But he stands by the following account absolutely, if reluctantly, knowing that it could hurt both the family of a friend and the government he served for more than 20 years.

The anonymous telephone call came unannounced and unexpected to the major's home. "He said: 'It's an old friend.' He wouldn't tell me his name. He said: 'Just come on out an meet me at this country and western bar.' "

The major was curious but also a little suspicious. "I packed a little .380 [pistol] in my boot just in case." But the gun wasn't necessary. The man in the bar really was a friend, in some ways more than friend. It's hard to describe your relationship to somebody with whom you shared two tours in Vietnam, somebody you trusted your life to on many a combat patrol. There he was at the bar—tall, lean and mean with an unforgettable gap-toothed grin. Even though they'd been out of touch for many years, the man at the bar, the major realized right away, was Glen Oliver Lane, United States Army Special Forces.

"We hugged right there in the middle of the bar," the major remembered. And suddenly he remembered. After their last tour together, when the major was back for a short stay in America, Glen Lane had gone missing. And last he'd heard, Lane was still an MIA.

"I thought you were dead," the major admitted. "Well, no, I ain't. You can see that," Lane retorted with typical attitude. And then Glen Lane set one other thing straight. "You've got to realize, things have changed," Lane explained. He was now going by a new name: Gary Brubaker. But his friends could call him "Doc," since he was a qualified medic.

The major didn't think much of the name change. During the 1960s, both men had been assigned to SOG, the Studies and Observation Group that ran top-level covert operations across Southeast Asia. SOG troopers often wore enemy uniforms and adopted false names, just as Special Forces soldiers in other units routinely used false identities on other sensitive operations they usually had going around the world. Perhaps "Doc" was on a classified mission. Or he had left his family, with whom he'd had problems. Maybe he was even running from the law. After all, he had a mean streak. "He had a big grin," the major says. "But there was never any humor in his grin."

There were a number of reasons Lane could be using a new name. "I didn't really want to know," he says. So they sat and drank a few beers and talked about men they had known and battles they had fought. And then the major got up to return to his quiet, new life. He asked "Doc" for his phone number. But the tall Green Beret said he didn't really have one he wanted to give, but he'd be back in touch.

The Long Nights of Glen Lane

About two years later, "Doc" got back in touch with the major. But now, the calls weren't social. The war was catching up with Glen Lane, who often called late at night for rambling, drunken conversations with the major. The calls would come, sometimes several times a day, stop for months, then suddenly start again. Lane had an incredible sense of guilt. "He would just talk about how he should have died when he had the chance," the major remembers.

Maybe it was a hunch, or perhaps curiosity just got the better of him. Either way, the major decided to check a list of POW/MIAs. Sure enough, Lane was there. But he wasn't on the list of U.S. returnees. He was on the list of men who died while missing.

Lane had been lost when his "spike," or reconnaissance, team, code-named "Idaho," disappeared in Laos on May 20, 1968. Also missing in the mission was fellow Green Beret Robert Owen. A U.S. team looking for the men had found nothing but heavy enemy fire, some of it from captured U.S. weapons. The official Pentagon conclusion: Lane and Owen were dead or captured.

"I asked him flat out," the veteran recalls. "I asked him why the hell he was listed as dead." With typical sarcasm, "Doc" replied: "You can't believe everything you read and hear."

The major kept pushing, though, and finally Lane opened up "No, of course he didn't come out in 1973 . . . . he said he had been left behind" the major explained. "He had been switched back and forth [from Laos to Vietnam] several times. All of a sudden [in 1977] they [his Vietnamese guards] had given him a new set of clothes, cleaned him up, given him a shave, and they were out of there."

Lane went from a Vietnamese prison to Hanoi, then on to Bangkok, where he was met by U.S. officials. "He indicated that he wasn't the only one. A couple others came out when he came out," the major says.

When pressed for more details, Lane said: "I can't tell you that. It's all classified." Besides, Lane said, "I'm still working for the government." According to the major: "He admitted he had been down 'South,' " where he was wounded in the leg. To the special operations community, that meant Central America, perhaps Nicaragua, or "over the fence," as Special Forces troops called covert missions in support of the Contras.

But there was one more question the major had to ask. "I knew that he had people. And I asked: 'What about your family?' He said he had never told them."

The major last heard from Glen Lane in 1991, and he never would have told his story except for a strange series of coincidences that brought him to the attention of the authors of this book. He realizes his story seems almost unbelievable. But he also knows that he's not the only American who swears that U.S. POW/MIAs have secretly returned from Indochina.

"Sensitively and Quietly?"

The secret, or "sensitive and quiet," return of American POWs from Southeast Asia appears to be one of the most closely held intelligence operations in the history of the United States. Don't look for much information on this issue in the Senate POW report. While that committee was probably the only organization powerful enough to resolve the debate over secret returnees, it conducted only a perfunctory "investigation." The findings—all of two paragraphs—were that there is "no factual support" for the proposition that U.S. POW/MIAs returned secretly to the U.S.

In reality, there is evidence—but as yet no conclusive proof—that Americans returned during two main periods: the late 1970s and then again in the mid-to-late 1980s.

The evidence of secret returnees in the 1980s correlates with the Reagan-era negotiations discussed in the previous chapter. Less is known about the alleged 1970s returns. One source suggests the return of Glen Lane's group was linked to Jimmy Carter's Amnesty Program. Perhaps some sort of deal was struck with Hanoi around the time of Carter's sudden offer of full normalization of diplomatic relations in 1977. When the Vietnamese balked, demanding all their "reconstruction" money, the process was dragged out until U.S.-Vietnamese relations were shattered soon after by America's tilt toward China and the Vietnamese invasion of Cambodia. Even if some POWs got out around 1977, the rest would likely have been stuck (unless they had already been shipped to the East-bloc) until the 1980s, when serious U.S.-Vietnamese talks began anew. For now, that is just a theory, buttressed by the evidence that follows.

Confusing Pentagon Reports

As did the communists during the Korean War, the communists in Southeast Asia attempted to indoctrinate U.S. prisoners for subversive activities in the U.S. In some cases, the Americans were reportedly scheduled to return home long after the end of American involvement in the war.

The military received information on one training camp, under command of a North Vietnamese named Le Van Nhut, which indoctrinated foreign POWs in South Vietnam during the war. Eighteen foreign POWs, including several Americans along with Koreans and a Filipino, were being trained. "They have been given Vietnamese names and are not allowed to use their true names. *After peace comes to Vietnam and the nation is unified,* the POWs will be allowed to return to their homes where they will become active in the communist party in the US and will participate in communist political activities," according to U.S. intelligence (authors' emphasis).[1]

Even Pentagon statistics suggest some Americans might have "trickled" out of Southeast Asia after Homecoming. The JCRC "monthly statistical summary" for December 1976, says that four Americans were "rescued" in Southeast Asia. But the Pentagon now claims no American POWs were rescued *during* the war.

JCRC also says that, through December 1976, 724 Americans had been "released." Yet the DIA 1980 roster of all American military and civilian returnees, wartime and postwar, totals 689. So, at the end of 1976, there were thirty-five additional "returnees" not fully explained by the Pentagon. Could one of these men be the Colonel described in an NSA intercept from Southeast Asia? "Intelligence sources indicate that on 13 May 1975 an American Colonel disappeared in the British Embassy and escaped," the NSA reported.[2]

British author Nigel Cawthorne researched the message, learning that on May 13, 1975, England did not have an embassy in South Vietnam or Cambodia. Both Britain and the U.S. had embassies in Laos, so presumably the escaping U.S. colonel would have gone to his own embassy rather than the English one. And besides, there appear to be no declassified records of a U.S. colonel "escaping" to the American Embassy in Laos. As Cawthorne concluded: "That leaves Hanoi, where the British had an embassy, but the Americans did not. Who was he [the colonel]? How did he get there? And how did he 'escape?' The British Foreign Office won't say."[3]

At one IAG meeting, the members were briefed on the report of an Indochinese refugee. Because the Pentagon refused to cooperate with final fact-checking of this book, it is difficult to tell exactly what the refugee said. Here is the pertinent note from the previously classified meetings of the 1981 meeting. "[CENSORED]—30 Americans for 3 years, last seen in Aug. 1978. He gave names of 3 U.S. PWs, also other names and descriptions. The three were returned to the U.S."

So here is a refugee who said he knew about U.S. POWs in Vietnam from 1975 to 1978. He gave three names, and the Pentagon commented: "The three were returned to the U.S." Were these secret returnees, or did the source give the names of three men who returned in 1973 or before? It's impossible to tell from the Pentagon record.[4]

A State Department record reports the claims of a Vietnamese refugee "concerning five alleged former American prisoners repatriated to the United States from Vietnam." From "hearsay" information provided by the source, the State Department relayed to Washington the names of two Americans allegedly returned after the war. According to the story, Vietnamese citizen Nguyen Van Phuc had hidden one of the POWs in his home for ten years, and received a giant reward from the U.S. government for helping free the Americans.

Of course, the State Department has refused to release the names of the two alleged returnees. The report notes: "Neither of the American names mentioned . . . is associated with an *active* case." [authors' emphasis][5]

The Soviet Connection

In an elegant Moscow hotel dining room filled with gilded mirrors, retired KGB General Oleg Kalugin described to one of the authors of this book how at least two U.S. POWs quietly returned to the U.S. Kalugin, a top KGB expert on the United

States, later repeated his evidence under oath before the Senate Select Committee.

After the end of the Vietnam War, during a period of increased Soviet-Vietnamese cooperation, Kalugin decided to attempt an intelligence operation based on the successful recruitment of a British official in a Korean War POW camp. The Soviets wanted to recruit U.S. POWs to return home and spy for the Kremlin. Sometime between 1976 and 1978, Kalugin has said, Hanoi presented files on a "handful"—of U.S. POWs—perhaps five to 12—still in Vietnam and available for Soviet interrogation. Kalugin dispatched his aide Nechiperenko to Vietnam, where the KGB man questioned a Navy pilot and a CIA pilot.

According to a State Department account of Kalugin's story: "The Vietnamese informed the KGB when the recruited American prisoners returned to the U.S. [in the late-1970s]. The KGB tried to follow up a few months later, he said, but either the phone numbers given by the prisoners were false or they had been changed, and no contact was made."[6]

Later, following alleged KGB pressure when the story went public, Nechiperenko claimed he had questioned U.S. captives before 1975 but never after. (The debate opened by Kalugin forced the CIA to reverse years of flat Pentagon denials and admit that at least one of its agents was indeed interrogated by the Russians before the fall of Saigon. No returned Navy pilot, or any other serviceman, was questioned by Russians, the Pentagon still claims.) But Kalugin, a KGB maverick, has always stuck with his account. Kalugin insists there were Americans in Vietnam after 1975, the KGB interrogated them, and they later returned to the U.S.

Kalugin's account, which itself is not even mentioned in the senate's brief conclusions on alleged secret returnees, appears to be corroborated by other Russian and Vietnamese sources never contacted by the senate staffer who "investigated" the issue.

The exact extent of Russian contact in Vietnam is still obscured by continued official denials by Washington, Hanoi and Moscow that any U.S. servicemen faced Soviet questioning in Southeast Asia during or after the war. But the truth cannot be kept hidden forever. Senior Vietnamese official Bui Tin swore under oath during a senate hearing that Soviets questioned U.S. POWs during the war. Other evidence comes straight from Russia. In March 1992, a U.S. businessman and his Russian colleague, a fluent English speaker, entered a bar in St. Petersburg. The Russian had mentioned he was a former KGB agent and he carried some sort of I.D. card that allowed him to go right to the front of lines at Russia's chaotic airports. The Russian didn't look all that impressive, with his slight build, balding grey hair and thick glasses. But the American businessman was still impressed that night at the bar.

As U.S. intelligence described the incident: "A patron of the bar noticed the source was American, and started to loudly proclaim how he did not like the way Americans mistreated black people. At this point Mr. [CENSORED. Authors' note: apparently the KGB man's name] flashed some sort of credentials from his wallet. Upon seeing his credentials the whole room cleared and a bartender came to stand nearby to protect the source [the U.S. businessman]."

As the evening wore on, the American complimented his Russian friend's English. "Mr. [CENSORED] responded he had learned English in Vietnam by interrogating American prisoners of war . . . [he]made some comment about it be easier to kill Americans than to learn English."[7]

In 1974, when all U.S. POWs were supposed to be home, a Vietnamese soldier on leave in Hanoi watched a strange volleyball game at the State Science Committee Building. A Russian team was playing a group of American POW/MIAs.[8]

At about the same time, a young Russian physicist assigned to a KGB unit was working in Haiphong, according to report relayed to the authors by a Senate source. The Russian reportedly saw a number of Americans kept after the war, and even became friends with some of them. He later refused to share his story with a representative of the Senate committee. "He's a prime example of the folks who know [something] but won't talk," the Senate staffer said.

A senior Russian military officer and POW expert, in a Moscow conversation with an author of this book, admitted he had personal knowledge of almost 100 U.S. POWs alive in Vietnam as of 1988. He said he was familiar with their "psychology," and that some had made an "accommodation" with their captors.

Returnees in the 1970s?

Clearly, there is credible evidence that Soviet officials had contact with U.S. POWs held in Vietnam after the war. As for the eventual return of those men to American, that is at least partially confirmed by Vietnamese Foreign Ministry defector Le Quang Khai. The former Vietnamese official says a number of U.S. POW/MIAs were "released" after 1975. Khai says the men known to him went to such Eastern-bloc countries as East Germany and Yugoslavia. POW/MIA shipments to Eastern Europe after 1973 have been confirmed in sworn testimony by two former U.S. intelligence officials, one of whom took and passed a polygraph test on the shipments, according to a Senate staffer. Khai believes "released" POW/MIAs certainly could have gone on from Eastern Europe to the United States. (According to declassified Pentagon records,one U.S. POW, marine Jon Sweeny, and several deserters made the same trip during the Vietnam War.)

Could the U.S. have quietly repatriated U.S. POW/MIAs during the 1970s, either through the Eastern-bloc or directly from Indochina? Former NSA staffer Jerry Mooney said America had the ability, and other intelligence officials discussed such transfers. "There was a persistent rumor [in the NSA] that we had bought people out. This was in 1976," said Mooney. "I've always had the feeling that we did do it."

Indeed, even *official* Pentagon lists indicate that American POW/MIAs may have returned after the war. Texan Lawrence Lee Aldrich, a member of the U.S. Army, was lost without a trace on May 6, 1968 and declared dead. The Pentagon thought he might have been blown to pieces by an errant bomb. But according to the DIA's own list of POW/MIAs: Aldrich was "poss[ibly] seen 94Y79[?] USA." Harry E. Mitchell, a sailor, apparently fell or jumped from the USS *Long Beach* as it steamed off the coast of North Vietnam during May 1968. The DIA says Mitchell was "09/79 possibly seen in USA." Then there's sailor Michael Louis LaPorte, a medic who disappeared and was declared dead after jumping into enemy territory in 1967. According to one account, he was later seen back in his hometown of Los Angeles. While that is not reflected on the DIA's list, the Pentagon does have a report that LaPorte actually survived his incident and was seen alive in Ba Vi and Hanoi during the mid-1970s. He may have been one of the POWs released to Eastern Europe and then on to the U.S.

The Legend of Greer and Schreckengost

A controversial former Special Forces officer named William "Liam" Atkins claims that in 1979 he saw a remarkable file in a marine personnel office in Arlington, Virginia. According to his account, Atkins was doing research on marine Bobby Garwood, who had just returned from Vietnam years after the end of the war.

The paper trail took Atkins to the office of a friend, a marine casualty officer. The officer showed Atkins that Bobby Garwood wasn't the only marine POW/MIAs still alive. Two other men were still on the Pentagon payroll. In fact, the officer said, they were back in the U.S. Their names were Robert Lee Greer and Fred Schreckengost, who disappeared together while riding motor-bikes in Vietnam on June 7, 1964.

Apparently unbeknownst to Atkins, Greer and Schreckengost were one of the most mysterious couples in the history of the Vietnam War. As detailed earlier in this book, Schreckengost had been identified by multiple sources as the "Salt," or white man, in the bi-racial pair of Vietnam turncoats dubbed "Salt and Pepper."

Later, Greer—or a man impersonating him—showed up in Thailand. According to former CIA contract employee and Laotian POW Rosemary Conway, the incident occurred in 1987. Conway was teaching English in Bangkok when another English-language instructor offered help getting her a job at the Satri Voranart School.

The other teacher said he'd been offered the job, but didn't need it any more since he'd gotten a grant from a American foundation. When Conway met the man, the conversation drifted into her 1975 experience in a Vientiane jail, where she'd been imprisoned as a CIA agent for persuading anti-communist Laotian pilots to fly their planes out of the country before the communists could seize them.

The man said he could identify with her story, since he had been a U.S. POW. He went on to explain how he'd been sent to the Eastern-bloc, then secretly returned to the U.S. via a Scandinavian country in 1979. The man said he'd been given a new identity by the U.S. government, went to school in Florida and worked in the Middle East before marrying a Thai woman. His name, said the man, was Robert Greer.

On another occasion, a man claiming to be Greer reportedly asked a park ranger to identify his name on the Vietnam Wall in Washington, D.C. And California journalist Dave Hendrix, an editor with the *Riverside Press-Enterprise* and expert on the lore concerning Greer and Schreckengost, reported that two men claiming to be the mysterious pair even attempted to turn themselves in to the Pentagon during 1987. The attempt fell through, and the DIA claims the men were "imposters," Hendrix has reported.

The mystery of Greer and Schreckengost is compounded by the Pentagon's claim that both men died soon after their disappearance. That, of course, contradicts the reports of Schreckengost as "Salt" and the near-legendary travels of the man or men claiming to be Greer. But Hendrix has pointed out that the remains the Pentagon claims to be Greer's can only be identified by the Pentagon's own records—in this case, an easily modified dental chart. No independent records maintained by Greer's family or civilian doctors can be used to verify the Pentagon's identification.

"That's why there's going to be a tiny little doubt," Greer's brother Ronald was quoted as saying.

"Stay Behinds" Come Forward in the 1980s?

As revealed in previous chapters, there is now no doubt American offered Hanoi money for the return of U.S. POW/MIAs and developed a plan for secretly—or "sensitively and quietly"—returning such men. One category of Americans on which a secret returnee program could be tested were the AWOLs, deserters, defectors, "ralliers" and stay-behinds. These were people who might not be on any official government list and had an incentive not to expose their past, fearing they could be punished or at least humiliated for breaking military regulations in Vietnam or cooperating with the enemy.

In the unlikely event that such a man came forward with a story about being secretly returned to the U.S. by the Pentagon, his claims would be hard to verify, especially if he were not on the official POW/MIA list. Even if it were proved the man had been missing in Southeast Asia, his story about being returned with other Americans might well be met with derision by the DIA, which would almost certainly reveal sordid details about the man's previous behavior.

Many beltway journalists, who faithfully tell the government's side of the POW/MIA story, would be primed with a steady stream of documents and sources for a blizzard of articles discrediting the returnee. And, as in the case of Bobby Garwood, the more important elements of the returnees' account might well be contained.

Even if a "secret returnee" program were exposed, the story would be relatively easy to handle if only "defectors" were in the pipeline. The Pentagon could describe it as a humanitarian effort totally separate from the "real" POW issue.

Such an operation might even provide a test for the more risky return of "real" POWs. The "test" could either have been a trial of the actual mechanics of secret repatriation, or a test of public reaction to the concept of secret repatriations, showing whether repatriations conducted earlier could now be made known without damaging U.S. credibility.

Could there have been a test in the summer of 1988? That's when John Dikkenberg, a reporter with the *South China Morning Post*, believed he uncovered a series of flights into rural Cambodia to extract Americans. The Department of Defense received an advanced copy of Dikkenberg's story and paraphrased its contents in a classified cable:

> A reporter . . . has written an article regarding American POWs in which a Hong Kong pilot claims to have flown POWs, deserters and their families from Kampuchea to a secret base in the Philippines.

"Thirty 'US soldiers and some of their wives and children, were released because Hanoi wants to normalize relations with America and the West and because it wants to get rid of the 'embarrassing MIA myth,' " according to Denny Murphy, the American pilot who claimed to have flown them out.

The flights were made in January, February and March, 1988. "There were at least as many American deserters, defectors and stay-behinds still in Indochina as I have picked up," Murphy said. He also claimed that the operations were done with the blessing of the US, Vietnamese, Kampuchean and Philippine governments. "I was given pre-arranged flight plans to out-of-the-way airstrips, and when I landed, they would be waiting there. I returned them to a location in the Philippines, where, presumably, they entered some 'halfway' program."

The groups Murphy says he flew out "were all blacks and Hispanics." He was not aware of any "officially listed MIA's among the group." A second source of Dikkenberg's provided a roster of the 30 secret returnees (the middle initials of all but two were provided to the authors by a source in Washington, D.C.):

Henry S. Amos	Paul R. Author	Jerry D. Brahns
Lyle E. Buehl	Bruce D. Campbell	Peter K. Cates
Henry F. Chase	Gene Davis	Bruce Davis
Leon Evans	Ray C. Fairchild	William M. Glenne
Ronald E. Hacker	Washington Hogge	Jerry O. Taft
Thomas Lukeman, Jr.	Theodore Roosevelt Kelly	Richard K. Martin, Jr.
Donald Mercer	Robert N. Monohan	Royal E. Moses
Daniel G. Moses	Jesus Narva	William Oliver
Richard L. Pappas	William J. Posner	Edward D. Shaw
Everrette K. Smith	John L. Smith	Theodore Wilson

Dikkenberg's second source said Donald U. Mercer was a Navy pilot from Jacksonville, Florida—Donald U. Mercer is not on the DIA list of POW/MIA. But there are eight exact or close matches, either to names on the Vietnam Memorial wall or the DIA list.

Murphy also said that "all other American blacks and Hispanics living in Indochina had been given the chance to 'come home' or stay behind. A number had jumped at the chance, some had reneged and a few had changed their minds after initially volunteering to go back to the US or a Western country."

"Breathers" in the 1980s?

There are even reports that "real" POWs came home in the 1980s. Hendrix, the California editor, located a fascinating and reclusive man named George Russell Leard, a former Air Force computer expert with a very high security clearance. Leard, who had worked on secret personnel records related to flight testing, claimed he had also participated in a classified POW repatriation progam between 1984 and 1986. The program, which fit many details of the then- publicly unknown U.S.-Vietnamese negotiations for "breathers" outlined earlier in this book, was allegedly shut down when the Iran-Contra scandal unfolded. By then, a number of American POWs were supposed to have been returned.

Leard's alleged information was leaked to the POW activist community by his former wife. Another source who knew Leard confirmed his repeated comments about being involved with such a program. Finally, an author of this book, having been rebuffed by Leard, met with the airman's parents, who independently confirmed that during the late 1980s he had discussed details of the alleged POW repatriation program and even gotten them access to highly secure Air Force facilities. Leard, his parents said, had been sworn to secrecy by the Pentagon and was upset that his information might be revealed in public.

Hendrix even managed to snag an interview with Leard, who reportedly admitted his involvement in the program. Hendrix's article embarrassed the Senate Select Committee into action. Leard was subpoenaed to appear before Senate investigators in mid-December, 1992, days before the investigation shut down.

Less than one week before he was to fly to Washington, D.C. and be deposed, according to one source, he was visited by "government agents." His mood changed and he became morose. He then flew to Washington, D.C. and declared he had no knowledge of any POW repatriation program.

The Senate, with literally days left in its investigation, had a problem. There was simply not enough time to square Leard's denials with other information indicating the airman might really know something about secret returnees. So the Senate decreed that Leard was the "victim of his ex-wife's fantasies." The Senate appeared equally uninterested in following up the many other leads concerning U.S. servicemen allegedly returned from Indochina and the Eastern-bloc. With little or no investigation, they declared there was "no factual support" for claims that U.S. servicemen returned from Indochina and the Eastern-bloc after 1975. But the Senate apparently barely—or perhaps never—checked many of the following accounts:

- A Denver store owner has claimed to be a secret returnee who "escaped" from Indochina during the mid-1970s. A computerized records expert working for the authors discovered the man had a highly unusual credit history. "I can find nothing on him" for the period he alleges to have spent in communist captivity, the expert said. The businessman reportedly agreed to reveal his story to the Senate if they dispatched an investigator for a face-to-face interview. The Senate apparently declined the offer.

- A stranger called Pennsylvania resident Linda Pepper, asking if she were the same "Linda Pepper" once married to a Vietnam vet. It was the wrong Linda Pepper, who learned the man was searching America for his former wife, who believed he had died while a POW/MIA. Obviously, the caller said, he had come home alive.

- A POW wife began to receive telephone calls from a man who identified himself as a Navy medic. Since she was unlisted, the woman asked the medic how he got the number. He replied that several secretly returned POWs were being kept in the Seattle area and he was assigned to care for them. They were in bad shape and appeared continually drugged. But one of these men had written her name and telephone number on a piece of paper. The alleged medic had copied it and called her. He talked to her over a period of 2-3 months. One day he called and said he had contacted the League of Families. The phone calls stopped after that. The president of the League, Ann Mills Griffiths, had been with Childress during the negotiations that placed money on the table to start the "sensitively and quietly" program—and the League was the wrong place to call if you wanted to expose the program.

- In 1986, Reverend Charles F. Shelton, a chaplain at Keesler Air Force Base, was talking to Sergeant Michael J. McFall. When McFall saw photos on Shelton's office walls of his unrepatriated POW father, he began to tell Shelton of a secret operation to which he had been assigned as a medic. USAF C-130's had flown to an air base near Hanoi to pick up American POWs who were secretly being repatriated. They were flown to Clark Air Base in the Philippines.

- Another POW wife was approached by a military officer in 1986 and told that her husband was alive and would eventually come back to the United States. He was in U.S. custody but had significant medical problems that were being dealt with. For a time she received updates on his condition and location but, after losing her patience and attempting to contact him after he arrived stateside, her military contact was terminated. She has learned what she believes to be her husband's new identity and has tracked him across the U.S.

- A number of other men have told the authors they secretly returned to the U.S. from communist captivity during and after the Vietnam War. Those who claim to have returned secretly during the war say other Americans, known by name, were left behind. Because these men are not listed on official POW/MIA lists, and the authors do not have access to classified Pentagon records, these claims were impossible to check.

The authors did use the Freedom Of Information Act to ask the federal Witness Protection Program whether it was used to hide returned U.S. POWs. The government responded: "We are unable to confirm or deny the existence of records or information responsive to your request . . . [D]isclosure could identify confidential sources. . . . "

Former DIA director Eugene Tighe said while he did not know about a secret returnee program, it could have existed, since some classified DIA programs are known only to a handful of people. Americans could have returned from Indochina without the knowledge of even most people working on the POW issue for the U.S. government, Tighe said. The retired Air Force Lieutenant General said a secret program to repatriate U.S. POW/MIAs would not surprise him at all. Said Tighe: "The idea that things like this could happen is very real."

Indeed, sources inside DoD and one other government agency have allegedly told several POW/MIA relatives that a program does exist to "sensitively and quietly" remove Americans from Southeast Asia and even Russia. But the truth about his project will probably never be known, since the only organization with the capability to investigate it did not have the will to do so. (Perhaps the Senate POW Committee believed there was no reason to launch a serious investigation of the secret returnee program. In an ambiguous comment during Senate hearings on November 7, 1991, POW Chairman John Kerry said he had asked a senior Hanoi official about returning U.S. POWs. According to Kerry, the official said: "I'd like to [bargain]. But there ain't nobody. I can't negotiate with you and have a *secret return* of somebody who doesn't exist." [authors' emphasis] Of course, perhaps the official meant that Vietnam had *already* secretly returned its American captives. All that can be said for sure is that the Senate failed to attempt a true investigation of the issue.)

Good Motives/Bad Policy

When the U.S. proposed "sensitively and quietly" repatriating U.S. POWs during 1984 and 1985, it was certainly done with the best of intentions by the few people on the inside who actually gave a damn about the POWs.

Those few deserve the thanks and gratitude of all Americans for what they attempted—because, for the first time since the Cold War started, it perhaps became possible to begin the process of bringing home Americans held in communist captivity. Indeed, if some people within the system actually rescued POWs, it would explain their bitterness towards critics who have questioned their efforts. Dick Childress, for example, refused to answer our questions on this and other topics.

If some American POW/MIAs were brought home, has the job been "sensitively and quietly" finished? We doubt it. Satellite imagery and human intelligence continues to this day to identify American POWs, sometimes even by name, still held in captivity in Vietnam and Laos. But the bureaucracy is determined to bury these last troublesome individuals who don't have the decency to just quietly die, so the U.S. can recognize Vietnam, lift the embargo and get on with drilling oil wells and building hotels.

But there is another important concern beyond the recovery of missing Americans. The major who says he met Glen Lane after the war told the authors he asked himself "half a million times" whether it was right to reveal the secret returnee program. At first, he said, "I thought if we're bringing these guys out and nobody knows about it, that's cool. At least they're bringing them out."

After all, the major said, war is a rough business, and sometimes there's nothing to do but accept that somebody—even a good friend—has been lost in the line of duty. But then he began to consider the full implications of Glen Lane's return. It proved America had left POWs in Southeast Asia. But, more importantly, it showed the government has lied about it for all these years.

"The crime all along is not necessarily that we left people behind. But at least tell the damned truth [about it]."

PART VII

Accessories After the Fact

Chapter 25

A Mindset To Debunk

"It's an area where intelligence has succumbed to policy."
—*Current DIA Staffer*

"People working that issue could not find a POW if a POW dropped on their head."
—*Ken de Graffenreid, former NSC Intelligence Chief, on his Reagan-era investigation of the DIA*

In 1979, a Laotian refugee revealed that he had seen five U.S. POWs in a communist prison camp. The DIA started an investigation. The former taxi driver told U.S. officials he knew they were American prisoners because their guard told him. The refugee explained the details of his 1976 sighting passed a polygraph exam on his statements.

But there was one problem. There was no category on the DIA's reports for a confirmed sighting of unrepatriated U.S. POWs. All post-war sightings had to fall into one of two categories: "resolved," meaning they were fake or concerned someone who wasn't a prisoner; or "unresolved," meaning the Pentagon hadn't yet figured out whom the refugee had seen.

Unresolved sightings caused problems. Pesky Congressmen and POW activists said they represented proof of U.S. POWs in Southeast Asia. So such sightings had to be "resolved," which almost always meant finding some way to discredit the source.

So the DIA set to work on the taxi driver. For years the Pentagon kept asking him questions. So many demands were placed on him by Pentagon officials and other people, the refugee said, that he lost his job. Finally, the taxi driver refused to have anything more to do with the U.S. government. "He is afraid he will lose his job [again]. He says he has given all the information to the American authorities already. . . . Lastly, he says there is one thing he can certify, that he saw five American POWs by his own eye," a Pentagon translator wrote after a conversation with the refugee.

But the DIA still hadn't solved its problem. The case was still unresolved. Years went by. Finally, in 1990—ten years after the refugee went public with his report and almost 15 years after he had seen U.S. POWs—the DIA "resolved" the sighting. Officials declared the refugee had really seen Soviet advisors, not U.S. POWs.

No matter that the men's guards said they were American prisoners, or that they were under guard and appeared skinny. The DIA said that since some other Laotians from that area had not seen U.S. POWs, but had seen Russian advisors, that the men under guard in 1976 had to be Soviets. (The experience of Bobby Garwood, the only acknowledged U.S. POW/MIA to have lived in Southeast Asia after the war, suggests that reports of Russians might sometimes actually refer to U.S. POWs. "When we went through checkpoints, people would come up to the vehicle and they would ask who I was. And the guard or the driver would respond that I was either Cuban or Russian," Garwood swore in his Senate deposition.)

Of course, the Pentagon didn't give the third-degree, or polygraph exams, to the people who said they had *not* seen POWs. Those witnesses were assumed to be reliable because they were reporting the official U.S. line. And just in case the "resolution" of this case ever went public, the Pentagon "forgot" to put some other facts in the file. For instance, the DIA failed to mention the existence of 35 other reports concerning U.S. POWs in the same area, including 12 other alleged first-hand sightings in addition to the taxi driver's. Most importantly, the DIA forgot to mention that on November 15, 1979, a communist radio transmission was intercepted that discussed moving "three U.S. POWs" from the area of the refugee's report to another location where they could be put to work in the "mines."

The Debunking Mindset

Outside experts called in to examine the DIA's POW operation dubbed the attitude in cases like the one above "the mindset to debunk." Pentagon analysts have traditionally attempted to discredit POW witnesses, and failing that, to explain away their sightings. The reason is simple, according to famed investigative reporter Jack Anderson: A U.S. government bureaucracy will never willingly acknowledge a problem it can't solve.

Interrogating POWs in the Garden

The failure of American intelligence gathering on POW/MIAs began during the war. In January 1972, a special Army intelligence unit in Laos dispatched a secret cable to the Pacific Command concerning efforts "to develop critical and sensitive information relating for example to the downing of US aircraft and the disposition of US prisoners of war."

The intelligence officials were begging for money, because they had more North Vietnamese prisoners than they could handle, and information was going to waste. "One of the problem areas most seriously affecting adequate intelligence exploitation of NVA [North Vietnamese], [CENSORED] ralliers and prisoners of war is the lack of facilities for interrogation. . . . There is only one interrogation room and interrogations are conducted in the cells, in offices, in hallways, and sometimes in the garden when the hallways are full.

"It is imperative that an adequate facility be constructed to properly house, segregate and interrogate knowledge sources," the officials pleaded to their eminently well-housed superiors in Hawaii. The outcome of their request is unclear. All that can be said for sure is that gathering intelligence on POWs in Laos certainly didn't have the priority of many other activities in Southeast Asia.[1]

Shutting Down

Once President Nixon declared in March 1973 that all the POWs were home, the Pentagon began shutting down its POW operation. Even when good intelligence reports fell into the DIA's lap, they were ignored, according to a senior military intelligence officer assigned to Southeast Asia during the mid-1970s. The officer recalled an excellent report, backed by a polygraphed source, that placed U.S. POWs in South Vietnam during 1974. In effect, the report was never followed up because it contradicted official U.S. policy, the officer said.

The lights remained out at the DIA through the Carter years, when only a token crew of POW experts was on duty in the Pentagon. President Reagan dramatically increased the priority of the POW issue. But even Reagan was unable to get the national security apparatus solidly behind the search for U.S. POW/MIAs.

The NSC Investigation

In 1983, National Security Adviser Robert "Bud" McFarlane assigned one of his top deputies to investigate how well the intelligence community was doing in its search for U.S. POW/MIAs, according to a Senate file.[2] The man assigned to the job was Ken de Graffenreid, the NSC staffer responsible for "oversight of all intelligence programs and policy in the U.S.G. [United States government]."

The intelligence expert was horrified at what he found. Since U.S. POW experts did not believe Hanoi had a motive to hold American prisoners, they were discounting reports concerning the existence of the POWs. "This did not lead to an intellectually honest judgment [about the POW/MIA] issue," de Graffenreid concluded.

The Pentagon mentality, apparently shared by the CIA, was worse than a cover-up, because a cover-up could be solved by firing the involved parties, the intelligence expert later told a Senate investigator. But the debunking mentality produced a "systematic bias in the process."

Unlike more diplomatic evaluators of the DIA, de Graffenreid made clear what the central problem was in the POW/MIA hunt: "People working that issue could not find a POW if a POW dropped on their head."

Independent Studies in the 1980s

Over the years, several probes have revealed serious and recurring problems in the DIA's POW operation. As summarized during one Senate hearing:

- September, 1985: Admiral Thomas Brooks, a former DIA official states: 1. Follow-up actions have not been pursued. 2. A mindset to debunk has resulted in sloppy analysis. 3. The analysts do not have an open mind.
- March, 1986: Colonel Kimball Gaines, a former DIA official, states: 1. The database is a wasteland. 2. There are unhealthy attitudes. 3. There is no coherent or disciplined collection effort. 4. There is not enough analysis. 5. there is almost a total lack of management.

6. There is intense effort initially focused on veracity of sources with a view toward discrediting them. . . . 9. The bias toward discrediting sources has resulted in reduced objectivity in the analysis.

- September, 1986: General Eugene Tighe, former Director of DIA in his report states: 1. There is evidence that Americans remain alive in Vietnamese custody against their will, even in the limited sample of reports we reviewed. 2. An unresolved case, according to DIA, means we 'haven't yet proved these reports are false.' 3. The greatest problem associated with the POW/MIA issue is the lack of professional analysis of the available intelligence. 4. There is little evidence that any significant analysis of the intelligence received has been accomplished in recent years. 5. The routine approach to each source has been 'he's probably wrong.' . . . 7. There is a dominant emphasis on the negative. 8. National technical means have never been levied proactively in an attempt to locate POWs. 9. The POW office only pursues leads that will help discredit the source. 10. The credibility of the DIA's judgment that a refugee account is a fabrication must be considered low. 11. DIA's use of the polygraph is wrong; it is not a substitute for analysis, and DIA does not seem to understand the frailties of the test. 12. We doubt every resolution of a case labeled as fabrication—we find most of these judgment without meaning, and untrustworthy. 13. There is an enormous volume of unanalyzed hearsay reports. Hearsay reports are impeached by DIA from the start—this is an irresponsible distortion of the intelligence process. . . .

The "Mindset" Alive and Well

In March 1986, the Pentagon received a report concerning 50 U.S. POWs allegedly seen in central Laos late the previous year. Here was the reporting officer's immediate reaction: "It is difficult to believe that the Vietnamese and/or their Laotian allies could actually still be holding US POW's captive—particularly such a large group—undetected, till now, or that Americans could have survived under such conditions for so long. It is equally difficult to identify a possible motive for such an action on the part of Vietnam."[3]

Ross Perot's "Special Research Project"

That sort of attitude, coupled with allegations of incompetence in the Pentagon's POW intelligence effort in Southeast Asia, prompted Ross Perot to demand a special investigation. In late 1986, the government dispatched DEA man Bob Hearn to Southeast Asia.

He soon reported back. The Pentagon's Indochina POW operation was "stodgy, plodding and not very up to date." The DIA POW office consisted of "a lot of guys working over their heads poring over reports that they don't know what to make of." Over all, "the effort being expended on POW/MIAs does not look like the USG [United States government] gives it a high priority."[4]

Debunking Dooley

Navy aviator Lieutenant Commander James E. Dooley was flying an A-4E "Skyhawk" jet when he was downed near Do Son, Haiphong Province, on October 22, 1967. A man resembling Dooley was depicted in a communist propaganda photo during the war. And when U.S. POWs returned in 1973, one of them reported hearing that Dooley's name had been written on a prison wall. More importantly, two Thai Special Forces soldiers released by North Vietnam identified Dooley's photo as showing an American with whom they'd been imprisoned.

Then, in 1987, a North Vietnamese refugee told U.S. officials that he'd seen an American jet downed in the area where Dooley went missing. The refugee said the incident occurred during 1968. The pilot bailed out floated down in a tri-colored parachute, then swam out to sea in an attempt to escape communist troops. The North Vietnamese chased him in a boat, which the pilot fired upon before being captured. Once the enemy captured the pilot, they stripped him of his one-piece flight suit, put him in the sidecar of a motorcycle and drove him away to North Vietnamese officials waiting in a Chinese-made car.

The DIA concluded the refugee's report correlated to the downing of naval aviator J.M. Hickerson, downed in the same area about two months after Dooley and repatriated at the end of the war. But Senate investigator Tracy Usry, working on a 1991 probe that preceded the Senate Select Committee, was not convinced.

Usry learned from Hickerson that he had been downed inland, not near the beach. His parachute was white, not tri-colored. He had never entered the water or fired his pistol trying to escape. He was wearing a two-piece rather than a one-piece flight suit, and he went to prison on the back of a bicycle, not in a motorcycle and car. In short, his capture was nothing like the one described by the refugee.

So could the refugee have really reported the capture of James Dooley? Not according to the Pentagon, which claims there's no evidence Dooley was captured. And that it's "improbable" he survived his shoot-down. Therefore, he wasn't captured, and that means the two men who saw him in prison must have been mistaken. As of this writing, the Pentagon lists James Dooley in "Category 5," meaning his "remains have been declared non-recoverable." In other words, according to the Pentagon, there's no reason to even look for James Dooley.

A History of Cover-Up

Anyone who trusts the DIA to do an adequate job of investigating the fate of U.S. POW/MIAs from Indochina must be ignorant of the Agency's work on those missing from earlier conflicts. For example, the DIA's repeated denials that any Americans were imprisoned by the Soviets after World War II and Korea could only be attributed to incompetence, dishonesty or a combination of the two. Moscow has now admitted holding Americans after both wars. And clear evidence has emerged that DIA had enough intelligence to know the truth, but never acted on it. Yet remarkably, the very men who dissembled about the World War II and Korea POWs are in charge of locating Vietnam POWs.

For example, Colonel Joseph A. Schlatter, then head of the Defense Intelligence Agency's Special Office for POW/MIA Affairs, declared in the late 1980s that no U.S. POWs had been held in the Soviet Union after World War II. "I'm standing also on the fact that the Soviet Union has been the central focus of all U.S. intelligence operations for at least 50 years of this century . . . and I find not a single shred of evidence showing American soldiers after World War II in that prison system."

Yet the authors of this book later used the Freedom of Information Act to force out of the Pentagon literally hundreds of records concerning American POWs imprisoned in the U.S.S.R. after World War II. Once we located the records, the military even refused to release many of the files—some dating back to 1946— on the grounds that U.S. "national security" would be damaged by telling the whole truth about the fate of missing GIs from World War II.

The Pentagon employed a similar cover-up on the fate of U.S. POWs shipped from Korea to Russia. Lieutenant General Allen K. Ono, then U.S. Army Deputy Chief of Staff for Personnel, personally signed a letter denying a story by co-author Sauter, then at TV station KIRO, reporting that the Pentagon had evidence of such shipments:

> Unfortunately, considerable misinformation periodically surfaces concerning Americans from the Korean War and World War II. . . . The latest media coverage was an investigative report by KIRO/CBS News of Seattle, Washington . . . . The Special Office for Prisoners of War and Missing in Action, the Defense Intelligence Agency, and the U.S. Army Center for Military History have looked into the many allegations that continue to arise. Please allow me to share some of the information these agencies have presented to help clarify the issue.[5]

The DIA's research, Ono declared, showed: "The Soviet Union has been the central focus of U.S. and allied intelligence for almost 50 years. Similarly, one must conclude that this scrutiny would have revealed at least a hint of American POWs in the Soviet Union . . . no such evidence has ever surfaced."

As had happened in the case of POWs from World War II, the authors soon found official records showing the Pentagon was lying and that there certainly were far more than "a hint" of Korean War POW shipments to Russia. But rather than tell the truth, the U.S. government—up to the White House level—ordered the facts hidden from the American people. In early 1991, White House National Security Adviser Scowcroft personally blocked the release of a classified 36-year-old White House document requested over a year before by the authors. Entitled "US POWs in USSR," the report detailed evidence that U.S. POWs were shipped from Korea to Siberia.

On White House stationary, Scowcroft, who has denied there is any substance to the POW issue, ordered the National Archives not to release the document, declaring the report was still "SECRET and should be properly secured."

But the Pentagon and White House failed to count on one factor in their effort to suppress the truth about U.S. POWs in the Soviet Union—the collapse of communism in the U.S.S.R. In 1992 and 1993, Russian officials confirmed that American POWs from both World War II and the Korean War had ended up in Soviet prisons. Sadly for them, the U.S. government had managed to hide their existence so long that the chances of recovering any of them alive is slight.

And what are the consequences for a man like Colonel Schlatter, whose "investigation" of U.S. POWs in the U.S.S.R. was either deceitful or incompetent? As of this writing, a Pentagon insider says, he is slated to be promoted to the position of deputy-chief for all Pentagon POW operations.

Mike Peck Falls on his Sword

Such policies, along with gross errors in the handling of the Indochina POW issue, wore away at Colonel Mike Peck, the highly decorated Green Beret veteran of Vietnam assigned as chief of the DIA's POW/MIA office. In March, 1991 word leaked that the Peck had resigned his job. In a five-page resignation letter, Peck revealed that the office was devoted to busy-work, rather than a resolution of the POW scandal. "The sad fact, however, is that this is being controlled and a cover-up may be in progress. The entire charade does not appear to be an honest effort, and may never have been. . . . That national leaders continue to address the prisoner of war and missing in action issue as the 'highest national priority' is a travesty."

The Pentagon had assigned the aggressive Vietnam War hero to square away DIA's POW/MIA office. But Colonel Millard "Mike" Peck, a highly decorated Green Beret veteran of Vietnam, didn't have the stomach for the job. When he left, Peck outlined a litany of problems with the Pentagon's hunt for POW/MIAs, many of them similar to the flaws raised during the independent studies of the 1980s. But instead of trying to fix the problems Peck had outlined, the Pentagon, acting in the best DIA tradition, attacked the messenger, saying Peck had only quit to avoid being fired.

Peck's departure caused a brief flap. But the Pentagon's POW operation seems to be immune to real change. While the Senate POW investigation embarrassed the Pentagon into dramatically increasing the size of its POW staff, many of the key players are the very same people whose work drew all the criticism during the 1980s. They were debunkers then and they are debunkers now. As the Senate's POW investigation discovered, the hunt for U.S. POW/MIAs is still being bungled.

Distressing Signals

On January 22, 1988, a U.S. spy satellite photographed a rice paddy near the Laotian town of Sam Neua, an area holding prisons from which U.S. POWs never returned at the end of the war. Years later, the picture would spark a major flap, but for months, it simply sat in a secret vault.

Then, almost a year later in December 1988, a CIA analyst realized there was something special about the rice paddy in the picture. Across the paddy was emblazoned a giant "USA," along with a smaller image that appeared something like a "K" to photo analysts. The CIA immediately passed the photo to the DIA, which according to the Senate POW committee, "sat on" the picture for four years.

Then, in 1992, word of the "USA" symbol leaked out during the Senate investigation. Pentagon escape and evasion experts—from the Air Force's Joint Services Survival, Evasion, Resistance, and Escape Agency (JSSA)—said the "USA" could have been a distress signal from a downed POW, and the "K" possibly a classified symbol used by pilots in need of rescue. In other works, a U.S. POW could have been desperately signalling for help in January 1988. But his silent plea was totally ignored by the U.S. government.

Eventually, years after first finding out about the symbol, the Pentagon was finally embarrassed into checking out the "USA." U.S. investigators ultimately declared it had been produced for fun by a Laotian boy. But by then the "symbols scandal" had exploded.

Air Force escape and evasion experts brought in by the Senate told of special symbols and numbers that pilots were trained to use if shot down. Some of the symbols were letters and shapes with special, classified features. The experts also discussed the issue of so-called "authenticator numbers" given to pilots. These four-digit numbers, like the PIN or personal identification numbers used by bank machines, were unique personal identifiers. A pilot could use the numbers over his radio, or in a symbol, to identify himself and signal possible rescuers that it was really a U.S. pilot on the ground, not a crafty Vietnamese unit trying to draw rescue crews in for an ambush.

So the Senate dispatched two investigators over to the DIA office handling satellite photos to see if they had detected any of the symbols. One investigator described the visit in a memo:

> I got only a blank stare when I asked them if they were familiar and had a list of DoD escape and evasion symbols, so they could be identified if they ever showed up on imagery. They did not know what I was talking about. This is a disgrace. This may be one of the only ways live POWs can possibly communicate to the outside world, and DIA photo-interpreters are not even aware of the program. The point is, they should be. Almost all pilots were schooled in using distress signals, and it boggles the imagination to think DIA has possibly been seeing symbols for 20 years without knowing what they were."[8]

The Senate also determined that CIA analysts did not know about distress symbols. The POW committee concluded: "This lack of knowledge about pilot distress signals is but another example of bureaucratic jealousies or incompetent coordination in critically important analyses."

Worse was yet to come. When debate erupted over alleged "authenticator codes" on old pictures of Southeast Asia, the Pentagon was forced to reveal it had lost many of the codes. In other words, America had given pilots a code to signal their presence on the ground, then thrown out the code lists.

In the end, the Senate Committee discussed several possible distress signals spotted on the ground in Southeast Asia. One of them, identified with "100%" confidence by a Senate consultant, was the symbol "GX 2527." Although the consultant had no idea of this when he found the alleged symbol, it corresponded to the authenticator code of a missing American aviator, and was located near a suspicious prison where another possible symbol had been spotted years earlier.

Predictably, the "GX 2527," seen on a June 1992 photo, has become the subject of bitter debate between the Pentagon and its critics. Only one thing can be said for sure about that symbol and others seen over the years—if U.S. POWs made them with the hope of being rescued by the Pentagon, they were sadly disappointed.

See No Evil

One grotesque failure by the Pentagon involves its failure to use satellites in support of live-sighting investigations. Let's say a refugee claims he saw American POWs in a specific place in Vietnam. The Pentagon's first step, as we have seen, would be to discredit that source. Failing that, especially in cases where there's outside pressure from someplace like a Senator's office to pursue the sighting, the military might launch a live-sighting investigation. Since the Pentagon gives Hanoi plenty of advance warning on where it wants to go, there's almost no chance a U.S. POW would still be around when American officials arrived for their inspection. And because Vietnamese officials go on the inspections, no sane guard or villager at the site would tell the truth about U.S. POWs who might have been there before.

But the live-sighting inspections could still produce important evidence, based upon a long-standing and well-practiced intelligence technique used in international inspections. The technique has recently been employed during inspections of Iraq for weapons of mass destruction. When U.N. inspectors showed up at an Iraqi facility, it was often obvious that suspicious equipment had been moved out before they arrived. But the U.N. inspectors had thought ahead. They had the U.S. take satellite photos of the Iraqi facilities before and after announcing an upcoming inspection. Then, if right after the announcement of an inspection, Iraqi trucks starting taking gear from a facility, the U.N. would know something important was held there and be able to track it to its next hiding place. A Senate POW investigator described the process as "catching them loading trucks with nuclear equipment and driving them out the back gate, as our UN inspectors are knocking on the front gate."

Amazingly, when that same Senate investigator visited the DIA POW section, he found: "They do not, surprisingly, ensure photo collection or issue an intelligence emphasis on specific facilities when we know our Hanoi JCRC office is conducting a short notice inspection, i.e. looking for a sudden increase of buses or trucks at the installation before the visit." In other words, the Pentagon has wasted a critical opportunity to determine whether the Vietnamese held U.S. POWs after the war at specific locations mentioned by refugees. More importantly, the Pentagon had botched chances to trace the movement of possible U.S. prisoners in Vietnam. As the Senator investigator, perhaps mildly, noted: "This is unacceptable."[7]

The Fox Guarding the Henhouse

In early January 1989, White House official Dick Childress met in Vientiane with the Laotian Vice-Foreign Minister. Childress had information that Eugene Debruin, a known Laotian POW never returned at the end of the war, was living "of his own free will" with his Asian family in Khammouane Province.

"The Lao government was requested to contact provincial and local officials to determine if Mr. Debruin is living in this area or if another Caucasian might be living there."[8]

P.R. Agents for Hanoi

One of the most remarkable features of the Pentagon's debunking efforts is that while DIA officials are quick to revile and question the motives of their U.S. critics, the same officials kow tow to Hanoi. A review of recent public testimony by Pentagon officials indicates that they routinely praise the cooperation of the Vietnamese. Occasionally, more outspoken government workers will note that Hanoi "could do more. " But the general tone of the remarks is similar to those pronounced by a senior U.S. POW official, who in early 1993 said: "They [the Vietnamese] are bending over backward to help us."

In reality, U.S. officials know the Vietnamese have been holding back POW information, warehousing the remains of hundreds of U.S. servicemen, lying to investigators, and even coordinating disinformation campaigns. In the mid-1980s, Hanoi said it would open its files and solve the POW problem within two years. That, of course, never happened. When U.S. officials asked for access to important POW documents, the Vietnamese said they been "eaten by insects." But then, when confronted in late 1992 with proof positive that they actually had extensive POW files and photos, Hanoi agreed to allow U.S. investigators to see them—for a price. Finally, said everyone from the President of the U.S. on down, the Vietnamese are really cooperating. But many of the "new" records and photos turned out to be worthless. Then, when the famous December 1, 1972 Soviet document appeared implying Hanoi had withheld hundreds of U.S. POWs, the North Vietnamese suddenly "found" yet more documents to refute the Soviet report.

And even when Hanoi allows the U.S. to examine the books, it's often clear that they've been cooked. Of course, you won't hear that in public Pentagon testimony. But if you can get access to the U.S. government's internal files, you'll find examples such as an account of a July 1991 visit by U.S. POW investigators to the Vietnam's Military Region 4 military museum in Vinh City, Nghe Tinh province.

When the investigators asked to photocopy some documents, the request was denied. What's more, it appeared someone had gone through the museum and removed incriminating evidence. For example, there were obvious gaps in the museum's exhibit register. One U.S. POW investigator noted: "This suggests that the register viewed by the team by the team was not original, as claimed by the museum staff, but had in fact been selectively recopied from an original at some time in the past. The Team also noted that certain items of high interest that appeared in the register were not available for examination."[9] The Pentagon report is unclear about exactly how many "high interest" items of POW evidence were being hidden by Hanoi.

Even the quasi-governmental National League of Families has been forced to challenge the Pentagon's rosy depiction of Vietnamese cooperation. As the League noted in a February 1993 memo called "Insurance Against a [U.S.] Write-Off," Hanoi only "accounted" for two Americans in 1992, the least productive year since 1982.

The Media Mindset

Sadly, the media show relatively little skepticism about official U.S. declarations concerning Hanoi's "cooperation." The POW/MIA issue has drawn remarkably little serious attention from the major media. Indeed, one of the few previous books on this issue, *Kiss the Boys Goodbye*, was co-authored by a former "60 Minutes" producer frustrated by her inability to pursue a serious probe of the issue at the CBS TV show. Another former CBS employee, Ted Landreth, had similar problems in distributing his

1987 BBC documentary "We Can Keep You Forever." Landreth's Harvard education and years at CBS gave him impeccable media credentials. But his documentary, the most definitive yet on the POW issue, still ran into problems. "Stations which had agreed to buy the documentary were suddenly not talking to the distributor," Landreth recalled. He soon learned why.

The management of one station reported getting a call from the White House. "If you put that British program on the air, you can forget about coming around the White House for the rest of the Reagan Administration," the management was told.

That station and many others declined to air the documentary. "This was pretty stunning, as you can imagine," Landreth said.

Landreth got that feeling again years later, when he and former *Time* writer Ed Tivnan gathered strong evidence on the shipment of Vietnam POWs to the Soviet Union. The PBS show "Frontline" and *The New York Times* had originally supported their research. But "Frontline" soon dropped out, and when the story was ready in the late summer of 1991, *The New York Times* killed it.

The newspaper's top executives, according to Landreth, said they believed the story but felt it should be covered by a staff writer. But the former CBS staffer felt there were other factors at play.

"The *New York Times* had never, never done any original reporting on the POW issue. In effect, it was a matter of the *Times* having to say: 'Whoops, here's a story that we completely and totally missed.' "

The *Times* preferred to lose the story—even have it never appear in print and allow the official cover-up to continue—rather than have its own staff shown up by two free-lancers, Landreth concluded.

The Los Angeles Times proved more daring, and published an article in October 1991. But U.S. TV networks still refused to touch the topic. Landreth was only able to get the story aired in Australia, on Channel 9's "60 Minutes."

"At [most] fault [in the POW scandal] is the media, not the government," Landreth concluded. "The media simply let us down on this one."

A Citadel of Deceit

Several separate sources alleged as recently as 1988 that American prisoners of war were being held in an underground prison next to the Hanoi tomb of Vietnamese leader Ho Chi Minh, a member of a Senate investigating committee said Tuesday.

But Defense Intelligence Agency officials said there is no credible evidence such a prison ever existed. They said the water table in the Vietnamese capital is too high to permit such a facility to be built." —Associated Press, August 4, 1992

The September 10, 1992, Defense Intelligence Agency report began: "Since the U.S. withdrawal from Vietnam in 1975, at least 18 sources, firsthand and hearsay, have provided DIA with details about an underground POW detention facility or facilities in Hanoi."

So began the first-ever recommendation from inside DIA to look seriously at the possibility that an underground facility could be built. And if it could, had an underground structure actually been built that could correlate to the information 18 sources had provided?

The DIA was not making the recommendation because it wanted to—Senator Bob Smith's (R-NH) line of questioning during the Senate Select Committee on POW/MIA hearing on August 4th had backed the DIA into a corner.

When the hearings opened, Smith immediately went on the offensive:

> . . . Sources reporting over a 15-year period have filled in details concerning the construction and operation of this underground U.S. POW detention facility at the Citadel next to Ho Chi Minh's Tomb. . . . I will now summarize what the sources of these reports stated. . . . And I ask my colleagues and the American people to listen for the common denominators—that is: locations, descriptions, and the type of people involved—listen for the patterns, and then you decide at the end, if you accept the official U.S. government position . . . I quote—"There is no evidence to sustain a belief that U.S. POWs were detained after Operation Homecoming in this area." You decide if you believe that statement. . . .

Senator Smith then proceeded to present a summary of 14 of the 18 DIA reports:

Source #1054

... a Vietnamese source who left Vietnam with his wife and settled in England in late 1979. In July, 1981, he sent a letter to the American Embassy in London and passed on the following information: In June 1974, the source was assigned to a work detail ... trimming trees under guard inside the Citadel, on the west side of Ly Nam De Street. While perched in a tree one afternoon, he saw 4-5 Caucasians standing next to the ground floor of a building, where he estimated there were about another 70 inside. The PAVN [People's Army Vietnam] security officer on his work detail told him that they were American pilots and mechanics.

In the Fall of 1978 ... he again saw Caucasians inside the Citadel on a second floor balcony. He could overhear them, and he knew they were not speaking Russian, because he had studied Russian in school.

DIA states that the source's information is unsubstantiated at best, and most of it is probably a fabrication.

Source #01162

Source ... was told by a subsource, who was the son of a PAVN major, that not all American POWs had been released, and that Vietnam had kept a number of important prisoners of war to use as hostages to acquire war reparations. The subsource lived with his father, the major, on Ly Nam De Street.

In 1978 ... the [subsource said] that American POWs were being held inside the Citadel. ...

DIA states that the source was evasive during his interview, and they recommend no further contact be made with the source.

Robert Garwood

In 1978, former American prisoner of war Robert Garwood, while still in Vietnam, stated he saw several Americans at a compound on Ly Nam De Street near a cistern. He drew a sketch of the exact location.

DIA labels Garwood as a convicted collaborator, and does not place credence in his reporting. [Authors' note: although he gave a deposition on his sightings and passed a polygraph test.]

Source #1542

In 1978, source . . . states he saw a group of American POWs bathing at a cistern inside a compound on Ly Nam De Street. The source drew sketches pinpointing exactly where he saw the POWs.

In 1982, . . . source said he again saw a group of American POWs at the compound on Ly Nam De Street, and, that this time they were not bathing, but were just sitting around, and some of them were talking.

There is, in fact, a cistern at this compound, because I personally visited it unannounced in 1986.

DIA states that the source could not have seen what he said he saw from his vantage point. The source did pass two polygraphs. [Authors' note: DIA also said source's story could not be true because there was no cistern there— When Smith proved them wrong, DIA changed its story.]

Source, # Not Known

In late 1979, this source, who was a Vietnamese truck driver, was assigned to deliver a truck load of paper to the military publishing house at the Citadel, on the west side of Ly Nam De Street. While assisting with unloading the paper from the back of the truck, he glanced over the storage building into the next compound. He saw 14-18 male Caucasians wearing faded blue laborer uniforms standing in a courtyard.

We have not been sent a DIA evaluation on this file, nor have we been sent the entire file.

Source #5633

Source . . . was an acquaintance of a PAVN captain who told him that a small number of American pilots had been moved to Hanoi after the war where they were being held in a secret underground prison.

The captain said the entrance to the prison was inside a residential dwelling next to Ho Chi Minh's mausoleum.....
DIA and JCRC state that because of the hearsay nature of this report and the lack of detail, nothing can be done with the report.

Source #1101

Source . . . was a former ARVN warrant officer who served with airborne units during the war. In June, 1980 he came to Hanoi where he lived. . . . In July or August, 1980, he had a conversation with one of his neighbors, who was the son of a PAVN colonel and lived on Ly Nam De Street. This appears to be the same son who talked to source #00162 in 1978 about POWs in the Citadel.

. . . The son told source . . . that on the previous evening he had overheard a conversation between his father, the PAVN officer, and his mother . . . over 50 American POWs at the Citadel were being moved that evening into an underground facility there, because a U.S. delegation in Hanoi at the time was scheduled to visit the Citadel area the following day.

Source . . . adamantly stated that the time frame was July/August 1980, and the record does show that there was a U.S. delegation visit to this area in August, 1980.

DIA states that this is limited hearsay information, and that there is no substantive reporting in this area. [DIA said no U.S. delegation was in that area during source's time frame. When that was exposed as a lie, they switched to the above line.]

Source #5862

In 1981, source . . . stated that he was told by a North Vietnamese lieutenant colonel that a number of Americans were being held inside the Citadel in the Ly Nam De area of Hanoi. . . . DIA states the source indicated deception on a polygraph, though we are not sure what the control questions were that he failed on.

Source #8682

In 1984, source . . . a former Cambodian Communist official, attended a study course in Hanoi along with 17 other Lao and Vietnamese officials. The source states that Vietnamese leader Pham Van Dong wanted to demonstrate the bravery of Vietnamese troops and the power of communism by showing how the Vietnamese were able to humble the Americans.

On the morning of September 12, 1984, Pham Van Dong, the source and the other Lao and Vietnamese officials left the Hanoi Central Party Committee office. They drove for about fifteen minutes (with their eyes covered) and then entered an underground prison where their blindfolds were removed. The source estimated that the prison size was about 100 meters by 100 meters.

He was shown three large cells, and states he saw about 100 Americans in each cell. The American prisoners were dressed in blue civilian clothes. They were slender and pale, some with long beards. Some were bald, and some had canes. The source estimated their age to be in the late 30's.

DIA states that an unnamed polygrapher concluded the source was a fabricator during a polygraph session that was labeled as unproductive.

Source #7591

. . . source . . . states that he was told by a Vietnamese army officer that as late as 1985, there was an underground detention facility adjacent to Ho Chi Minh's tomb which was holding American prisoners of war. The facility, according to the army officer, was constructed in 1970, as the Ho Chi Minh mausoleum was being constructed. . . . The civilian construction workers who built the facility had to undergo extensive background checks covering three generations of their families. He describes the security at the tomb as being very tight. He states the underground detention facility was constructed underneath Be Dinh Park, right next to Ho Chi Minh's tomb.

Source . . . states he first heard about the underground facility from friends at the Vietnam National School in 1980. And when he again visited Hanoi in 1985, the army officer provided the same information. The source also talked about the transfer of American prisoners there taking place at night.

There is no DIA assessment of this report in the file we received.

Source #10675

Source . . . was a former public security first lieutenant assigned to the criminal investigative office at Quang Ninh Provincial Public Security Office. Between 1977 and 1983, he was directly involved with operations to recapture 2 escaped American POWs—one was in February, 1977, and the other was in April, 1983. He believes one of these POWs was recaptured, and the other one was not. [One was a Navy pilot.]

. . . both of these POWs had escaped from camps . . . administered by the Ministry of National Defense. And, because of this, a decision was made in early 1985, to transfer responsibility for the detention of American POWs to the Ministry of Interior. The source learned of this decision from a friend, a lieutenant colonel in Hanoi who worked at the Ministry of Interior in the General Department of Security. This friend had been at a meeting with the director and deputy director of the Ministry of Interior in 1985 when the files of U.S. POWs still held were transferred by the Ministry of National Defense. The friend stated to the source that when the meeting concluded, the director, deputy director, and he went to inspect two sites in Hanoi that had been chosen to hold the Americans that the Ministry of National Defense had previously been holding.

One of these sites was a facility beneath Ho Chi Minh's mausoleum on Hung Vuong Street. In late 1986, the friend confirmed to the source that American POWs were now held there.

There is no assessment of this report by DIA in the file we received.

Source #8621

In December 1986, source . . . a Vietnamese herbal doctor in Hanoi at the time, was called upon to go to the Citadel, on the west side of Ly Nam De Street, to treat a PAVN general for kidney stones. While there . . . he observed 4 to 5 tall, thin Caucasians with brown hair, wearing striped prisoner uniforms.

The source asked the general's 30 year old son about the prisoners.

The son stated they were American pilots who were kept confined in an underground prison in the compound, and that over 30 prisoners were being held there. The source... sought no favors for his information. In a follow-up interview . . . he stated . . . that he had done some electrical work in 1970 when Ho Chi Minh's mausoleum was being constructed, and that the security measures had seemed very excessive at the time for a monument. Roads had been blocked off, and all workers had to be escorted.

DIA states that if the herbal doctor's account is true about seeing Caucasian prisoners, then the chance viewing could have been a set up. . . .

Source 4989

In 1988, according to a CIA report, there was information provided to the U.S. Government about 200 American prisoners in an under-ground prison in Hanoi. We are waiting to see the whole file on this matter.

Source #10919

. . . source . . . was told in November 1980 by a PAVN captain that there were two American pilots in the Ministry of National Defense residential area in the vicinity of the Ho Chi Minh monument in Ba Dinh ward. On one occasion, both the source and the PAVN captain went into the Citadel area to talk to a guard they knew. While there, the source reports he actually saw one of the American prisoners through the gate. The American pilot was wearing a striped prisoner uniform and was sitting on the ground.

DIA states that the story appears to be a fabrication.

Smith declared that "the presence of a secret underground facility for American POWs in Hanoi at the Citadel is the only rational explanation for all of these sightings and reports over the years. The majority of the ultimate sources of information on the underground prison are construction workers who worked on the prison, or people associated with senior PAVN [Vietnamese] officers who knew about the prison."

The Senator went on to review all the harshly critical studies showing that the DIA had incorrectly dismissed POW evidence in the past—strongly implying that even the POW sightings totally rejected by the DIA might be true. He concluded his prepared comments by stating that "our staff investigators have informed me, after spending hundreds of hours reviewing the files, that nothing has changed in the last five years since these secret critical reports were written."

The DIA Responds

A panel of DIA officials then testified. And every word from them seemed to reconfirm what Admiral Thomas Brooks, Colonel Kimball Gaines and General Eugene Tighe had written.

Robert DeStatte, Senior Analyst, DIA Analysis Branch, directed his comments to the "Hanoi cluster" of 18 reports related to underground prisons in the Hanoi area:

> I spent approximately 10 of the last 18 months in Hanoi. . .
> . I had freedom of movement throughout Hanoi and the surrounding area. . . .
>   I traveled around the city every spare moment I had. One of the things that I have looked into is the possibility of an underground facility of some sort. *I can't find any evidence that there is even a basement in any building anywhere in the country.* [authors' emphasis]

So the DIA's senior POW/MIA analyst could not find evidence that Vietnamese could build basements, much less underground prisons. So how did he arrive at such a conclusion?

He walked and peddled a bicycle on the surface of Hanoi's streets and not once did he see an underground prison. In broad daylight he stopped and questioned Vietnamese citizens on the streets about their nation's greatest state secret. None of them admitted seeing an underground prison. None admitted seeing an American POW held by their government after Homecoming. DIA's conclusion: there were no American prisoners held after Homecoming—at least not in Hanoi.

Following Up

Even the DIA leadership must have realized what an embarrassing performance the agency had mounted for the Senate Committee. So someone inside the government made the decision to actually initiate a professional look at the possibility of an underground prison facility in Hanoi.

The DIA asked the Defense Nuclear Agency to perform the following tasks:

- a. Make a preliminary determination of the possibility of constructing underground facilities in the Hanoi environs.
- b. Perform a quick look at available intelligence reports and historical and current [blanked out] for the purpose of identifying underground facilities signatures.

After researching the issue, the Defense Nuclear Agency (DNA) concluded that the Vietnamese could easily have used Soviet technology to build underground structures in the Hanoi: "These techniques have been routinely employed since the 1960s. The . . . Soviet Union expertise in soft ground tunneling is well known; there is no reason to believe that this expertise is not available to the North Vietnamese. . . . In terms of technical feasibility, the North Vietnamese could have constructed either underground cut-and-cover facilities or a tunnel system in the environs of Hanoi during the time period of interest."

That proved the Vietnamese probably could build basements. So did Hanoi build an underground facility under Ho Chi Minh's Tomb? The DNA went to work. Eight reconnaissance photos of the area, taken between December 1972 and December 1975, while the tomb was under construction, were used for the study.

DNA concluded:

Analysis of available [CENSORED] indicated a below grade infrastructure far more elaborate than what one would expect from simply a mausoleum. This infrastructure includes the approximately 30 ft and 20 ft wide inter-connecting buried passageways between structures. . . . It is interesting to note that the public is not allowed on the backside of the tomb area where the majority of these ancillary features are located, and the latest [CENSORED] indicates that this area is still secured by fences, walls and foliage and controlled by guard houses.

. . . it was entirely feasible for the North Vietnamese to have constructed underground facilities in the environs of Hanoi, (2) portions of the Tomb's ancillary structures are buried, and (3) the function of certain features at the Tomb are unknown and warrant further investigation.

In other words, there was a highly guarded underground system right where the refugees had claimed to have seen U.S. POWs in an underground prison. Senior DIA analysts had once again been proven wrong.

On September 10, 1992, DIA felt compelled to prepare a "Collection Support Requirement" for the "Ho Chi Minh mausoleum and Ministry of National Defense area." The memo defensively complained that "Until recently DIA was limited in its ability to categorically confirm or deny these reports." Now, however, new and wondrous "advances in technology and analysis," apparently not available a few weeks before, "have greatly enhanced DoD's ability to determine the presence or possibility of underground facilities. In particular, analysts at the Defense Nuclear Agency (DNA) have a unique capability in the area of underground construction analysis."

The report revealed that DNA and DIA analysts had identified "a below grade infrastructure [Pentagonese for underground] that is far more elaborate than what one would expect from simply a mausoleum." The report concluded that "it is entirely feasible, from an engineering standpoint, for the Vietnamese to have constructed an underground detention facility in Hanoi."

Time to Investigate

The DIA believed that "The urgency attached to this issue will not allow the U.S. to wait for further analytical efforts to be employed to confirm or deny the presence of an underground facility in Hanoi. The only expedient solution to this question is for the Vietnamese to allow a U.S. team to conduct a live sighting investigation of the Ho Chi Minh mausoleum and the Ministry of National Defense [the Citadel]." In other words, after years and years of delay, the Pentagon should finally send someone to check out Ho Chi Minh's Tomb and see whether there was a prison underneath it.

U.S. inspectors would need the help of special equipment designed to locate underground facilities. "It is essential that *detection and analytic equipment* be allowed into the country and into the facilities for use by the DNA team members," in order for a true investigation to be performed, the DIA report said. "Because of the detailed technical data needed to satisfy this tasking, it is imperative that team members, particularly DNA members, be allowed to conduct all testing and analysis required," the DIA report emphasized. "The successful conclusion of this investigation can only be achieved through physical and scientific examination/inspection of the facilities in question," it concluded.

The Vietnamese were approached and told that "with approval we [U.S.] wish to invite a small team of DoD experts to Vietnam who will accompany the LSI on an investigation of the Ho Chi Minh mausoleum and the Ministry of National Defense complex to investigate the possibility of underground facilities used to hold American prisoners. The experts will also need your approval to bring in some detection and analytic equipment to effectively conduct this investigation. We cannot impress upon you enough the high level U.S. interest with regard to this matter, including the Senate Select Committee. Appreciate your assistance."

By October 22, "a team of four people (two DIA and two DNA) [was] on standby to journey to Hanoi and finish out the investigation into this issue . . . . If complete access is not allowed, DNA has equipment that could be used to conduct a non-intrusive inspection."

But according to a Senate source and a DIA staffer who wrote the report recommending "detection and analytic equipment," the team never went to Hanoi. "Larger issues" got in the way of the DIA's investigation, according to the Senate source.

But it doesn't matter. After sitting on the refugee reports for years, then delaying any scientific investigation for months, the DIA ensured that any U.S. POWs held under Ho Chi Minh's tomb are certainly long gone. Eventually, Hanoi admitted there were bomb shelters under the Tomb, and even let Senator John Kerry look at them. Of course, it wouldn't be very hard to hold POWs in a big bomb shelter. And the existence of shelters says nothing about what else could be there—or rather could have been there. One returned visitor from Hanoi reports rumors that the Vietnamese have been filling in some sort of underground structure near Ho Chi Minh's tomb. And Pentagon POW expert Bill Bell noted in sworn Senate testimony that a communist technical expert who knew the truth about what was under the tomb "was soaked with gasoline on the streets of Hanoi and was burned to death" after the U.S. began getting reports of an underground camp there.

The POW "October Surprise" of 1992

On October 17th, 1992, Presidential POW emissary John Vessey Jr. and Senator John McCain (R-Arizona) jetted off to Hanoi for the "POW October Surprise" of the 1992 Presidential campaign. The men returned to Washington with promises that Vietnam had finally decided to release the mother-lode of POW/MIA information, including a huge storehouse of photos showing POWs and crash sites. Both men downplayed the fact that Vietnam had for years been denying having such files, and even claimed their records had been "eaten by termites." The Bush loyalists also brushed past reports that the Vietnamese admitted possessing the files only after threats of Defense Secretary Dick Cheney that if Hanoi didn't admit having the files, the U.S. would break the news.

Instead, President Bush—no doubt still smarting from his shouting match with POW families just months before—called a press conference to proclaim the information represented "a significant breakthrough" in accounting for U.S. POW/MIAs. Administration sources were also quite quick to claim there were "no quid pro quos" for the photos. The implication was clear: Hanoi was finally producing important POW evidence, and voluntarily, at that.

Months later, after the election, the Pentagon quietly announced that most of the "new" pictures were really duplicates. Hanoi had really turned over not 4,785 photos, as had been anticipated, but 1,750 pictures and a bunch of copies. Of the "new" pictures, hundreds were already in the Pentagon's files. As for the rest, not one picture showed a living American still missing from the war. At most, 17 photos showed the bodies of missing Americans, all of whom had long been declared dead anyway. One family member was told only three cases would be resolved by the photos.[10]

Not that resolving 17 or even three cases was unimportant; for the families involved, receiving photographic evidence confirming the death of their loved ones was life changing. However, there was no escaping the fact that America had allowed itself to be duped again. The photographs were no "breakthrough," they were just another small step in a process Hanoi had dragged out for 20 years.

And as it turned out, that small step turned out to be expensive. As *The Washington Post* later reported, the Pentagon's middleman paid up to $20 a piece for the pictures—many of which had been publicly available in Hanoi for as little as 30 cents.[11]

It was just another rip-off, similar to Hanoi charging France twenty times the real cost of returning French war dead. But in the scheme of things, those expensive pictures were just a drop in the bucket. Laos once charged the U.S. $190,547 to rent a helicopter for a mission to just one crash site, part of a "fortune" the U.S. has paid for limited Laotian cooperation on the POW/MIA issue, Jack Anderson reported in 1991.[12]

Over all, the U.S. has been spending an estimated $100 million a year trying to account for American POW/MIAs in Southeast Asia. Officially, those efforts have not brought a single living American POW home.

An Unacceptable Message

In early 1992, Dr. Steve Morris, a visiting professor at Harvard University, found a document in a Moscow archive that would stretch DIA's debunking skills to the maximum. It was a six page "Report of the Deputy Chief of the General Staff of the Vietnamese Peoples Army," presented by Vietnamese Lieutenant General Tran Van Quang "at a meeting of the Politburo of the Central Committee of the TV [Central Committee of the Workers Party of Vietnam]" on September 15, 1972.

According to the general, "The total number of American POWs captured to date on the fronts of Indochina, in other words in North Vietnam, South Vietnam, Laos and Cambodia totals 1205 people. Of this number, 671 people were captured in North Vietnam and 143 pilots [were captured] in South Vietnam." Sixty-five Americans had been captured in Cambodia, 43 in Laos, and 283 non-pilots in South Vietnam, for a total of 1205.

When the Defense Intelligence Agency learned of these documents, the response was predictable—there was no rejoicing or positive anticipation that, at long last, there might be definitive information from within the communist system that gave substance to the proposition that American POWs were kept after the war. The DIA, after all, had received thousands of reports over the years from refugees and defectors that Americans were still being held. And now, documentation was being dropped in their lap by a Harvard professor—documentation that might make it possible to force the communist Vietnamese government to admit they held live POWs.

Analysts realized at once that the purported Vietnamese source for the report, Tran Van Quang, was an important figure who had, at least during the French War, run Hanoi's Enemy Proselytizing Division, which is in charge of foreign POWs. And DIA employee Jan Sejna, the Czech defector, said he had worked with Quang on projects involving U.S. POWs during the 1960s.

In an internal report, the DIA conceded: "It is . . . completely plausible that a person of his distinguished command background, and eminent political standing, would be the person who could offer a political thesis to the politburo which involved . . . political arguments advocated for the toughest deal to be made with the American negotiators."

No matter. The report could not be allowed to stand. If it were accurate it meant the Pentagon had failed to detect hundreds of U.S. POWs in Southeast Asia. So the DIA set to work debunking. Robert R. Sheetz, Director of the DIA Special Office for Prisoners of War and Missing in Action, on April 12, 1993 wrote that the Russian report "implies that North Vietnam was holding 1,205 American prisoners of war at a time when the North Vietnamese officials were saying that the number was only 368." In fact, the report does not "imply" any such thing. It clearly states that 1,205 is the number of American POWs held as of September 15, 1972. That number is then broken down by pilot vs. non-pilot, and further, by country of capture: North Vietnam, South Vietnam, Cambodia or Laos.

Sheetz said the "Numbers in this document cannot be accurate if discussing only U.S. POWs." For instance:

- The number 1,205 grossly overstates the number of Americans who survived their incidents, let alone were captured by the North Vietnamese and survived captivity until late 1972.
- A complete scrub of all unaccounted-for cases, which includes results of the most recent joint investigations on the ground, only leaves 92 individuals for which the USG has any reason to suspect they could have survived.

The facts are considerably different. 1,274 U.S. POWs lost in Southeast Asia before September 15, 1972 were classified Category 1 or 2, meaning they could have been captured. Hundreds more were lost under completely unknown conditions. Certainly some of those could have fallen into enemy hands. Even men listed as killed in action by the DIA came home at the end of the war, so it is certainly possible that others listed as KIA were actually captured as well, then not returned.

Sheetz's claim that there were only 92 Americans "for which the USG has *any* reason to suspect they could have survived" is DIA disinformation at its worst. The government has been caught in its web of lies and simply has no choice but to issue such statements and hope the mainstream press remains as ignorant of the truth as it has in the past.

The DIA knew a large number of POWs were held hostage. It also knew the Nixon/Kissinger team walked away from the hostage POWs rather than continue to be manipulated by the North Vietnamese. But for the DIA to admit that hundreds of Americans continued to be held after Homecoming would be to admit their own incompetence, or worse, raise the specter of criminal wrongdoing within the bowels of the bureaucracy.

So DIA sent its allies out among the mainstream press to push the Company line: "DIA believes that this document is referring both to U.S. POWs and to allied POWs, particularly ARVN commandos. The confusion probably lies in an inaccurate translation from Vietnamese to Russian." This line was presented to *The Washington Post*, which ran a story on April 15, 1993, entitled "Asians Classified as American, POW Expert Says."

If Asians were really "classified as American," the North Vietnamese POW lists turned over to the U.S. government in Paris on January 27, 1973, would have reflected this inability of the communists to tell the difference between Americans and South Vietnamese. That did not occur. Only one ARVN serviceman was on the lists presented.

And, if Asians—South Vietnamese commandos—were classified as Americans, it would have shown up in the lists of POWs the North Vietnamese released during the war. That didn't happen, either. Besides, an internal DIA record says there were no more than 400 Asian commandos, still leaving a discrepancy of several hundred U.S. POWs reported in the Soviet document but never repatriated.

Of course, the DIA failed to tell the press about other POW/MIA reports it had supporting the Soviet document. Vietnamese defector Dr. Dang Tan told the U.S. in 1971 that Hanoi's statements that it then held fewer than 400 U.S. POWs were "untrue." According to declassified CIA records, Tan reported "that already by mid-1967, when I departed NVN, over 800 American POWs were then in captivity in NVN.

"Those unnamed American POWs will continue to be exploited by NVN and will serve as the tool for NVN in blackmailing the USA," said Tan, who also reported that U.S. prisoners were separated into categories such as "progressives," and reactionaries called "wayward" or "stubborn" in Vietnamese.

A CIA report partially based on Tan's information conluded: "Names of American POWs, and the number in captivity, are considered to be a state secret and will not be released for political reasons."

In 1978 a communist North Vietnamese intelligence analyst by the name of Le Dinh defected to the West. "Le Dinh heard at staff meetings that about 700 Americans still remained in Vietnam [after Homecoming]. The information was attributed to remarks by senior officers to the effect that the SRV retained a 'strategic asset' of over 700 American prisoners that could be used to force the U.S. to pay reparations," says the DIA's February 28, 1980 final debriefing report.

Le Dinh was a lieutenant in the North Vietnamese Army, and from 1971 through 1975, worked in the Ministry of Defense, having "direct and indirect access to information related to American prisoners, both before and after January 1973." He had "direct responsibilities for planning and coordinating interrogation efforts against U.S. PWs . . . [and] had access to dossiers maintained on the POWs," for two years after Homecoming.

And Le Dinh had told the DIA in early 1980 that about 700 Americans continued to be held hostage after Homecoming. DIA admitted Le Dinh had "access to PW/MIA information within this ministry [North Vietnam's Ministry of Defense]." DIA also knew the report out of the Soviet archive closely correlated to Le Dinh's debriefing.

The Le Dinh and Russian reports agree on the number and location of Americans not repatriated. The Russian report indicates more than 600 extra POWs were being held on September 15, 1972. Counting those Americans lost after that date, the number matches the Le Dinh figure of 'about 700' U.S. prisoners captured but not repatriated at the end of the war. In addition, both Le Dinh and the Russian document indicate there are more Vietnamese POW camps than known by the U.S. Le Dinh said there were 12 Vietnamese POW camps by the end of the war, with the Russian document putting the number at 11.

Most importantly, Le Dinh and the Russian document agreed on the motives behind Hanoi's POW policy. One Pentagon POW expert told the authors that the Soviet report alone cannot prove the number of Americans retained by Hanoi. But it does appear to be conclusive evidence of Hanoi's policy of secretly retaining U.S. POWs. This is the critical message of the Soviet document.

Le Dinh and the Russian report agree on the following policy issues:

- The categorization of American POWs. Both the Russian and Le Dinh reports say Americans were placed into various categories, with one of them being "progressives," or those who accepted communism and/or Vietnam's views on the war. Both sources imply the Vietnamese had a plan to withhold POWs from wealthy families. Le Dinh called them "the sons of rich families," and the Russian document referred to them as the "products of rich families."

- Both reports agree on the Vietnamese motive for retaining American POWs. The Russian document quotes the Vietnamese as saying they would hold U.S. POWs for political "concessions" and to obtain U.S. war reparations. According to the Russian report, the Vietnamese general wrote:

"Nixon must compensate North Vietnam for the great damage inflicted on it by this destructive war."

- According to the Le Dinh report, he said "the SRV (Vietnam) retained a 'strategic asset' of over 700 American prisoners that could be used to force the U.S. to pay reparations."

A close reading of the general's documents indicates that two North Vietnamese Politburo decisions made in March and April 1972 caused dissention within the Communist Party. "Both of these [Politburo] decisions touch on the questions of exploiting these American POWs captured in time of war. This disturbs the public opinion of the whole world and the USA. There are various thoughts on the question of American POWs . . . but even among us there is a group of comrades whose opinions differ from the opinion of the Politburo."

The Politburo had decided to use American POWs as a counterbalance to the vastly superior U.S. military and industrial power—in other words, as hostages to manipulate the Nixon Administration. This decision was apparently questioned or actively opposed by elements within Hanoi's ruling elite who were strong enough to make the Politburo defend its decision.

The general's report was a clear message to the dissenters to get in line with the Politburo decision:

> . . . The question of American POWs has great significance for the resolution of the South Vietnamese problem. . . . We intend to resolve the question of American POWs in the following manner: 1. The government of the USA must demonstrate concessions, in other words, a cease fire and the removal [of] Nguyen Van Thieu, and then both sides can begin discussing the question of repatriating POWs to the Nixon government. 2. . . . we can free some more pilots from the number who are progressively inclined. Nixon should not hinder the return of these pilots to their homeland and not undertake any disciplinary measures toward them. 3. Nixon must compensate North Vietnam for the great damage inflicted on it by this destructive war. . . . If we take a path of concession toward Americans and liberate POWs we would be at a great loss.

Lieutenant General Tran Van Quang in this report accurately outlined the strategy that was followed by the North Vietnamese. Within a week of the report's appearance, three American pilots were released, and the North Vietnamese did warn the U.S. not to take "any disciplinary measures toward them." And they did demand reparations—as we have shown, it had in fact been an essential part of their negotiating posture since 1968.

But North Vietnam would concede their number one point at the bargaining table that same month—the removal of South Vietnam's President Thieu. This made even more important the use of American POW hostages as leverage in the final negotiating stages and the implementation of the Paris Agreement.

The United States was forced to place $3.25 billion on the table in advance of any POW release just to get the repatriations started—but the North Vietnamese held back the majority of the POWs to ensure the actual delivery of promised "reconstruction" aid. As we have seen, however, the money wasn't delivered and the hostages were not returned.

As of this writing, there is still not enough evidence in to make a final determination about the accuracy of the Soviet document. But one thing can be said for sure: the DIA is not telling the truth when it says the report's numbers are totally inconsistent with the facts.

In reality, the reports give numbers that closely match the number of POW/MIAs that many Pentagon experts believed Hanoi possessed during the war.

A former Director of the DIA, retired Lieutenant General Eugene F. Tighe, recently said what the DIA already knew: "We had a list [of POWs in 1973] that was really significantly larger than those who came back . . . we had been expecting a lot more people. It was terribly shocking. Finally, we are getting proof of what we said—the numbers [in the Soviet report] don't surprise me at all."

The Shredding Party

Perhaps it was just a coincidence. But soon after the DIA found out about the Soviet POW report, Pentagon POW/MIA officials quietly ran thousands of POW files though a refrigerator-sized shredder at the U.S. Embassy in Bangkok, the military later admitted. By the time the U.S. Ambassador to Thailand learned of the shredding, which took place during March 25 through 27,

1993, it was too late. The original files of the Joint Casualty Resolution Center, the agency which looked for U.S. POWs during the war, were gone.

Major General Thomas Needham, Commander of Hawaii's Joint Task Force Full Accounting, reportedly claimed the shredding was simply a "consolidation" of records. But POW experts said otherwise.

While copies of the shredded reports themselves existed elsewhere, the hand-written notes and additions to the files in Thailand were irreplaceable. "They were basically informational notes and memoranda—the meat of actual investigations," retired Major George Petrie was quoted as saying. The major, a former POW investigator, said the DoD may have destroyed the original files to "simplify case files as much as possible, declare them [the POWs] dead and move on."[13]

Senator Bob Smith complained about the shredding, which apparently involved files the Senate POW committee had requested but never received. So the Pentagon was forced to initiate an "investigation," conducted by none other than the office of the Commander-in-Chief, Pacific Command, an office closely tied to the fortunes of Joint Task Force Full Accounting.

While POW activists hoped for a fair investigation, it didn't really matter. Documents requested by the Senate, and by the authors of this book, and by many POW family members—documents that hundreds of American citizens would gladly have removed from the government's hands if there had been a need to "consolidate" them for reasons of saving space—had been shredded. And there was really nothing anyone could do about it.

Chapter 26

Dirty Tricks

"It is clear that Congressman Hendon will be using our files to discredit us (and he will have lots of ammunition there). We need to ensure . . . we receive support in our efforts to damage-limit Congressman Hendon."
—*classified memo by Commodore Thomas Brooks of the DIA, September 1985*

"I think they're about seven felons in DIA right now."
—*Former Senate POW Investigator, 1993*

By September 1985, even the Pentagon had to admit its POW operation was in sad shape. As detailed in the previous chapter, senior DIA official Adm. Thomas Brooks had concluded, they had "never employed some of the most basic analytic tools" to look for POWs.

Brooks was so alarmed that on September 25, 1985, he dispatched an urgent memo to DIA's Vice Director for Operations, Brig. Gen. Jim Shufelt. For years, that memo was kept classified by the Pentagon. Now it's clear why.

The problem, as Brooks saw it, was clear. The DIA was failing in its job of mounting a top-notch search for U.S. POWs—a search President Reagan had publicly declared was one of America's "highest priorities."

The solution to this potentially embarassing problem? Hide DIA's flaws.

The first recommendation in Brooks' memo—given higher priority than fixing the failures in the POW hunt—was to avoid criticism from Congress. "I see the most important thing we must do right now is to be cementing relationships on the Hill," Brooks urged. "We have not done our job as well as we should have in days passed and we will not withstand scrutiny very well. Yet we will receive plenty of scrutiny in days to come. We must make all preparations to minimize the criticism this scrutiny will bring."

Being a good military intelligence officer, Brooks was quick to identify the main enemy: Rep. William "Billy" Hendon, Republican from Asheville, N.C. Hendon, a dedicated POW activist, had worked for a short time in the Pentagon after his first term in Congress from 1980-2. Now he was back in the House, and because of his Pentagon stint Hendon knew where the bodies were buried in the POW-MIA swamp at the Pentagon.

"Billy" was a wiley foe who combined the back-slapping manner of a Carolina good ol' boy with the political instincts of a machine politician. And he was also an expert on the POW issue.

Warned the admiral: "It is clear that Congressman Hendon will be using our files on discredit us (and he will have lots of ammunition there)."

Worst of all, Hendon was as dedicated as a kamikaze pilot about the POW issue and didn't care who got hurt if it meant bringing "the boys" home. That made him a rarity in Congress, where most Congressmen were trying to bring military projects home to their districts and prided themselves on good relations with the Pentagon.

"Damage-Limiting" the Truth

Lacking the leverage of district defense projects, Brooks recommended a more aggressive approach: "damage-limit Congressman Hendon."

The admiral went on to describe a strategy of forming "necessary alliances" with key congressional representatives and staffers from the House Intelligence committee and Asian and Pacific Affairs subcommittee. He singled out several leading congressmen as possible allies in the effort to "damage-limit" Hendon's attempt to expose the truth about DIA's blundering.

In short, Brooks ordered members of the U.S. intelligence community to blunt an investigation by a U.S. Congressman. And the DIA plan was classified for no other apparent reason than to keep it from becoming public knowledge. Indeed, the paragraph of Brooks' report containing the phrase "damage-limit" includes absolutely no intelligence information. While solely concerning Congressional political strategy, those sentences are specifically classified "C," for confidential.

Later Pentagon records show a continuing interest in Hendon. A March 14, 1986, DIA memo mentions that "Billy Hendon, R-NC, is now moving to disassociate himself" from a certain person who claimed knowledge of U.S. POWs. The memo goes on to repeat purported comments from a Hendon staffer. An April 25, 1986, report concerns Hendon's meeting with former Congressman and POW activist John LeBoutillier. The men discussed a controversial piece of POW evidence, and the DIA's informant reported: "[H]e [Hendon] is charging ahead with the information. . . . "

The specific outcome of DIA's "damage-limit" strategy remains shrouded by official silence. The key congressional players mentioned in the Brooks memo have been quiet about details of their relationship with the DIA. Perhaps all that can be said with certainty is that Billy Hendon was never able to expose the full truth about the POWs, and the Brooks memorandum remained classified long after Hendon had left Congress.

Sadly, such plotting by the executive branch against POW activists was not an isolated event. U.S. government agencies, up to and including the White House, have engaged in what can only be described as "dirty tricks" against POW family members and activists. There is evidence that both the DIA and White House engaged in illegal domestic intelligence gathering on the activities of American citizens. It is an area of the POW scandal that has drawn scant attention. When exposed, it has prompted little or no action from organizations with mandates to protect the rights of U.S. citizens to express their views without being subjected to government surveillance or intimidation.

Phone Taps, False Arrest, and Psychological Abuse

In late 1985, retired Air Force Lt. Gen. Eugene Tighe, former head of the DIA, was asked to review the agency's POW operation. "Man, did we ever go into a hostile environment," Tighe later said about the commission he assembled to examine the DIA. Indeed, Tighe became convinced that someone was bugging his commission's offices in the Pentagon. Another member of the commission says Tighe was correct—"We were eavesdropped."

Other members of the commission, all experts on intelligence, were also convinced that someone had them under surveillance. "It was the conclusion—I believe unanimous conclusion—of each of our members that our room was bugged through the telephone system," Tighe told the Senate under oath.

At the time, Tighe called in two Air Force security specialists. "They found an electronic device on the phone," one commission member said. The DIA reportedly later insisted the device had nothing to do with surveillance.

"Who was doing it? I don't know," the retired general said. All that can be said with certainty is that the 1986 findings of Tighe's commission—that American POW/MIAs likely remained in Southeast Asia—was extremely damaging to the DIA.

Tighe also learned some disturbing details about DIA's treatment of Asian refugees with POW information. "I was very concerned with the way DIA polygraphic teams were acting, scaring the hell out of Southeast Asian refugees," Tighe said. In one case, according to a Senate POW investigator, the DIA polygraphed a refugee until he passed out. Despite his treatment, he never wavered from his story of seeing unrepatriated U.S. POWs and was determined to have passed his lie-detector test.

On other occasions, refugees were placed under virtual house arrest and threatened by DIA officials, according to a number of long-time POW activists. Then, in several cases, their names were publicly released—despite pledges of confidentiality by the Pentagon.

Vietnamese Foreign Ministry defector Le Quang Khai, who asked for political asylum in the U.S. during 1992, was badgered by various federal agents, including some who implied he'd only be allowed to stay in America if he agreed to return first to Vietnam as a spy. One day, DIA officials showed up at his apartment in New York and began asking him questions about Hanoi's retention of U.S. POWs— ignoring the fact that Khai still shared his apartment, which was probably bugged by Hanoi, with a security agent from the Vietnamese Mission to the U.N.

Treatment of Refugees

Even the State Department grew upset at the DIA's tactics. In 1983, a Laotian refugee escaped into Thailand. He soon told U.S. officials that he had seen live Americans in 1978. The DIA, no doubt trying to debunk the source, wanted to question the refugee about exactly how he had escaped the communist secret police of Laos. That upset the U.S. Embassy in Vientiane, which was apparently providing sensitive assistance on the case. If pressed for details totally unrrelated to his POW sighting, the source "will cease cooperating with U.S. authorities. More importantly, the life of our source may be put in jeopardy," the embassy wrote in a telegram.

"We do not see how this line of question contributes to the resolution of our POW/MIA accountability program," the diplomats said.[1]

It is no wonder that some refugees fear volunteering POW information to the U.S. government.

The White House's Boys?

In March 1983, retired Army officer Chuck Allen approached Ted Sampley with a business proposition, according to Sampley's sworn testimony to the Senate POW committee. Allen explained to the former Green Beret and Vietnam vet that he represented the Center for POW/MIA Accountability, a non-profit organization in Washington, D.C.

The center wanted to hire Sampley for an intelligence operation. But the target wasn't in Southeast Asia. It was at the Vietnam Veterans Memorial, the Wall, in the capitol of the United States. Sampley testified that his mission was to infiltrate a group called the Veterans Vigil Society, which had pledged to maintain a 24-hour-per-day vigil at the Wall until there was a full accounting for U.S. POW-MIAs. "My assignment was to determine how much money the Vigil was taking in, where and how it was being spent, the names of its members, if they were 'doing drugs,' and if they had any connections to [POW activist and retired] Lt. Col. Bo Gritz [a leader of private POW rescue missions to Indochina] . . . ," Sampley swore under oath.

Sampley was also asked to collect information on a POW rescue operation to Laos supported by the Vigil. "He [Allen] said that the United States government 'disapproved of private forays' and if I could identify the people who were planning such a mission, their passports would be seized by the government."

Allen then showed Sampley an address book allegedly listing the names of FBI and National Park Police investigators who were also investigating the Vigil. If Sampley would infiltrate the Vigil for a week, he'd be paid $500 in expenses and another $500 in fees, Allen allegedly said.

In April 1983, Sampley reported to Allen at his Fayatteville, N.C. office. The retired Lt. Col. picked up the phone and relayed Sampley's information to someone named "Dick." Ultimately, according to Sampley's deposition, Allen revealed that "Dick" was Richard Childress, director of Asian Affairs in the Reagan Administration's National Security Council. Sampley has testified under oath that he was with Allen on a number of occasions when he reported to Childress.

Unfortunately for the project, according to Sampley, he found no evidence of illegality at the Vigil. He was paid $500, half of what he was promised, and sent on his way. Allen admits Sampley was paid money, but says it was for a magazine article—not surveillance. "We never passed any information at all to Childress," said Allen.

Childress—whose White House tenure sparked at least one other complaint concerning domestic surveillance of POW activists and a separate allegation of improper fund-raising for anti-communist Laotian guerillas—he refused to answer questions about Sampley's allegations. Instead, Childress urged the authors to examine Sampley's criminal record, which does include arrests and convictions for activities releated to his POW activism. Childress's only comments on Sampley's specific allegations were: "I can't answer questions. . . . I can't play the stupid domestic games."

Barring an independent investigation, the veracity of Sampley's claims cannot be determined. But, sooner or later, Dick Childress and the White House did get to know the name Ted Sampley. His interest in the POW issue awakened by his dealings with the Center for POW/MIA Accountability, Sampley went on to become one of the most vocal critics of the U.S. government's POW policy.

A League Of Their Own

In the 1980s, Sampley and many other POW activists and family members did much of their fighting against the National League of Families, which had been organized during the war as the "official" POW/MIA family group. The "League" hadn't always been a U.S. front, however. For years, especially during the Ford and Carter Administrations, the organization served as the main obstacle to a total write-off of the POWs. Indeed, the League's oversight proved essential in prompting the Pentagon to continue to gather POW-related intelligence from Indochinese refugees. And when the Reagan Administration assumed office, it was the League that helped bring the prisoner of war issue back to a central position in U.S. foreign policy toward Southeast Asia.

But along the way, the League once again became institutionalized. Its long-time executive director, Ann Mills Griffiths, was even given a secret security clearance and a key position on the Interagency Group (IAG), the group that coordinates POW/MIA policies of such key executive branch agencies as the Pentagon and State Department.

Eventually, Griffiths used her access to obtain secrets and wield bureaucratic power far exceeding her official role, according to Pentagon records, and the League, with funding through a government charity and its unique role in POW/MIA decision making, became a quasi-official arm of the government. Where once the organization had fought the Pentagon bureaucracy, it now became the chief defender of the status quo. The League attempted to block increased declassification of POW/MIA documents, the formation of the Senate Select Committee, and the emergence of public controversy over the role of the Soviet Union in the POW scandal.

A May 1986 State Department memo indicated the remarkably close relationship between the ruling faction of an ostensibly private organization and the U.S. government. The memo reported that activists in the League had sued to obtain the organization's membership list, hoping to send independent information to the members. The State Department noted with alarm that "Rambos" (activist POW relatives) might "take advantage of the frustration many members feel over what they perceive as a paucity of results after years of effort."

Should free-thinking family members win control of the League, the State Department concluded, "Mrs. Griffiths would obviously be replaced," leaving more activist League officials and their Congressional allies such as Billy Hendon in the forefront of the POW movement. That would mean Congress "might support the more radical and unhelpful resolutions which up to now we (and Ann) have headed off."

Luckily for the status-quo, the "Rambos" were unsuccessful.[2]

The League also became embroiled in scandals during the 1980s concerning attempted gun-running to Southeast Asia, alleged illegal funding of anti-communist guerillas in Laos, and manipulation of Pentagon data concerning POW/MIAs. Former DIA POW/MIA chief Colonel Mike Peck even blasted the League in his 1991 farewell letter upon leaving the position.

The highly decorated Green Beret Vietnam Vietnam veteran claimed: "From what I have witnessed, it appears that any soldier left in Vietnam, even inadvertently, was, in fact, abandoned years ago, and that the farce that is being played is no more than political legerdemain done with 'smoke and mirrors', to stall the issue until it dies a natural death."

Peck reserved special scorn for the League:

> I am convinced that the Director of this organization is much more than meets the eye. As the principal player in the grand show, she is in the perfect position to clamor for "progress," while really intentionally impeding the effort. And, there are numerous examples of this. Otherwise, it is inconceivable that so many bureaucrats in the "system" would instantaneously do her bidding and humor her every whim."

As for Griffiths, she claims that the League opposed the government during the Carter Administration because the U.S. was doing little to account for lost Americans, but began supporting the government when the Reagan Administration truly made the POWs an issue of the highest national priority. But many POW/MIA family members and activists remained unconvinced.

The Lawyers Crush Rambo

Perhaps it was only a coincidence, but the outspoken Sampley eventually became the target of lawyers from another private organization closed linked to the government—the Vietnam Veterans Memorial Fund. The lawyers sued Sampley because as part of fund-raising for his non-profit POW/MIA activities, he sold T-shirts emblazoned with the image of the Vietnam Memorial's Three Man Statue. According to the lawyers, the man who designed the statue—a person who happens to be a self-proclaimed draft dodger—owns the copyright to the depiction of three Vietnam grunts. Therefore, according to legal logic, Sampley—a Vietnam veteran—has no right to use a picture of the public monument without paying the designer. As of this writing, the lawsuit threatens to render Sampley penniless— along with his wife and son, respectively the daughter and grandson of a Vietnam POW/MIA.

The Pentagon has apparently also maintained a program of surveilling potential POW whistle-blowers.

Watching The Whistle-blowers

It began as early as July 1975, when Army lawyer J. Lawrence Wright got the job of representing an angry young staff sergeant. The sergeant's name was Barry Toll, a highly decorated Vietnam infantryman who had recently quit a sensitive intelligence position. Toll wanted a lawyer who'd seen combat in Vietnam, and Wright fit the bill.

Wright soon learned that Toll had been assigned to an Airborne Command Post, part of the command and control apparatus connecting the U.S. military with the President of the United States. Toll's job on the airplane required him to see some of the most secret information known to the White House.

"SSG Toll said he could no longer serve in the military. More precisely, he could not continue as part of the direct Chain of Command," Wright stated in a 1992 affidavit to the Senate POW committee.

Toll expressed the fear that he was under surveillance by the DIA, and asked Wright to take a walk with him on the grounds of Fort Monroe, Virginia. During the walk, the sergeant explained that he was upset about the fall of Saigon and the killing in Cambodia, and about the fact that so many Americans had died in Southeast Asia only for the communists to win the final battle. But Toll also had a much more specific complaint relating to secrets he had learned on the job. "He believed that the Administration knew one set of facts but those were contrary to what the American public was being told," the lawyer testified.

During the summer of 1975, Toll never revealed those secrets to his lawyer. And the DIA refused to allow Wright to sit in on its debriefings of Toll. "I was told by Defense Intelligence Agency representatives that my security clearance was not high enough to even know what type of security clearance SSG Toll had," Wright said.

The lawyer would not learn for years that Toll's burden, his secret knowledge, was the fact that top U.S. officials knew Americans were kept behind in Southeast Asia and the East-bloc after Vietnam.

But even back in 1975, it was clear the DIA was very worried about what Barry Toll had seen. On one occasion, the sergeant called Wright from an airport, saying DIA agents were following him.

Then, about six months after Toll left the Army, Wright testified, he received a phone call from a man identifying himself as a DIA colonel based in Washington, D.C. "The gentleman told me that they had been following SSG Toll for six months and that they had 'lost him.' He wanted to know if I had any idea where SSG Toll would be."

Wright responded that the DIA probably knew more about that than he did, adding: "Everything I had seen from SSG Toll pointed to a highly dedicated professional soldier disillusioned with out government. I told him that I did not think that made [Toll] a subversive."

DIA Collects Intelligence on Garwood

Of course, if the DIA would follow a disgruntled intelligence sergeant, it would certainly be interested in the actions of a returned POW who claimed other Americans were left behind in Southeast Asia.

While the DIA has been accused of showing little interest in Bobby Garwood's information on POWs, previously hidden records show the agency was keenly interested in Garwood's private life.

A March 14, 1986, DIA memo reported that: "Bobby Garwood is moving to Los Angeles to take up permanent residence. . . . Several factors in the Washington-area have contributed to the move. The service station where Garwood is working will be closing. Because of a domestic spat with his girl friend, his landlord has asked him to move. . . . " The memo goes on to describe a potentially embarassing personal problem between Garwood and his woman friend.

Keeping An Eye on the Media

The DIA also kept a close eye on attempts to tell Garwood's story, and other POW information, to the American people. (The following information about possibly illegal Pentagon intelligence gathering comes from a handful of 1985-6 DIA records released under the Freedom of Information Act. Some of the files have been censored, and there is no way to tell what other records containing domestic intelligence on American citizens may still be locked up in the DIA.)

"A film is being prepared about Garwood's life. Ralph Macchio (the Karate Kid) will star. Garwood has coached Macchio in

Vietnamese. Reportedly the movie will portray Garwood as an innocent PW who came home only to be court-martialled by the Marines," a DIA memo reports. (The film was made but never shown in the U.S.)

DIA files also contain information on news organizations including CBS, NBC, and *The Washington Times*. "An NBC Task Force is also planning a film regarding the POW issue, and will be in contact with Garwood after his move to California," reports one memo. A January 17, 1986, document refers to DIA's attempts to get videotape from a CBS producer.

Some records contain information on upcoming news stories concerning POWs, along with information concerning reporters. For example, another January 17, 1986, memo discusses Dave Hendrix, a reporter and editor at the Riverside (Calif.) *Press Enterprise* (and contributer to this book). One version of the memo released under the Freedom of Information Act, with parts censored by the Pentagon, indicates the DIA was tracking Hendrix's investigation into the fate of unrepatriated U.S. POW Charles Shelton. According to the memo: "Hendrix, the reporter in Riverside, California, is pursuing his story on Shelton. [Censored] has been called several times by Hendrix—[Censored] says that Hendrix is missing several screws—and learned the following....." The memo goes on to describe Hendrix's investigation.

Snooping on Activists

The DIA also keeps files concerning POW activists. A November 9, 1985, report details a Virginia meeting of the Vietnam Veterans Coalition. About 35 activists attended the meeting, and "everyone was well dressed and 'not shabby,' " the DIA's source reported.

The Pentagon informant passed on comments made by people at the meeting, which ironically included admissions by two Green Berets that they'd taken part in an earlier plan "to monitor" POW activists.

In some cases, the Pentagon censor has made it impossible to determine the subject about whom the DIA was collecting information. A January 17, 1986, memo says: "[Censored] have come to a parting of the ways after working together for quite awhile. [Censored] now believes that [Censored] actions are self-serving and that [Censored] is only interested in publicity for himself."

The same memo goes on to dish up information on an apparently different separate group of Americans. "I asked [Censored] if [Censored] had mentioned seeing personnel from DIA in [Censored] office recently. He says that [Censored] mentioned having seen the 'big guys from DIA' come out of [Censored] office [Censored] says that he has standing directions from [Censored] to leave the area immediately should DIA personnel come into the area."

Those named in the DIA reports were not happy to find their views had been written down without their knowledge and filed away by a U.S. intelligence agency. Well-known POW activist Mike Van Atta, who publishes a newsletter often critical of the Pentagon, is mentioned in one of the reports. "I've been a thorn in their side," Van Atta said when he learned the DIA had collected information on him. The decorated Vietnam vet had long suspected he was being targeted by the government. "I don't know whether it [the DIA surveillance] is legal or illegal, [but] for many years I've been very angry about it."

Dave Hendrix, the California reporter, put it this way: "The collection of such information strikes at the heart of people being able to live securely under the protection of basic civil rights. The retention of such information, even if not actively sought by the DIA, raises fears about its possible misuse and the paranoia that would require knowledge of such details."

Illegal Domestic Spying?

According to experts from the American Civil Liberties Union, the DIA may have violated the law both by collecting information on U.S. civilians and then by maintaining it in official files (aside from wasting resources it should have used looking for POWs in Southeast Asia).

But when news of the DIA's files broke during late 1992 in newspaper stories by one of the authors of this book, the Pentagon denied it had violated the law. "The Defense Intelligence Agency is not engaging in any illegal activities," said Major Bryan Whitman, a Pentagon spokesman.

Whitman said the Pentagon was not "collecting" information on American citizens. "These were memos of incoming phone calls. They were unsolicited. It's legal," Whitman claimed in December 1992. In other words, the Pentagon claimed, while it might be illegal for the DIA to "collect" domestic intelligence, it is legal for the agency to "accept" unsolicited information about American citizens.

The Mysterious Informant

At the time the Pentagon was explaining away its records in late 1992, the source of the DIA files was unknown, having been censored from the documents before their release to the public. Since then, uncensored copies of the DIA reports have escaped the Pentagon. The full records reveal that a prime source of DIA's information on the political activities and business interests of U.S. citizens was none other than a Navy officer assigned to the service's Bureau of Personnel.

And contrary to the Pentagon's claims, phone calls from the officer, then-Lieutenant Commander Frank Brown, did not come out of the blue. For instance, Brown kept the DIA well informed of his ongoing attempts to obtain a videotape of Bobby Garwood from a CBS producer. "Brown expects to have access to the first cassette this Thursday or Friday (27/28 Feb) and will give it to us to have the thing copied. He expects to have access to the second cassette within the next several weeks and will also make it available," the DIA noted in a 1986 record.

DIA records show a long-term relationship between Brown and the DIA, which at least once asked Brown to obtain specific information. There is no doubt the Defense Intelligence Agency used Brown as an informant to gather information on the legal domestic activities of U.S. citizens.

And while that information "gathering" or "collection" may or may not be a violation of the law, maintaining files on the information provided by Brown and other sources is clearly illegal, the ACLU claims.

"What's illegal is when they write it down in a permanent government file," said Kate Martin, director of the ACLU's Center for National Security Studies. Federal statutes specifically prohibit U.S. intelligencies agencies from maintaining files on the legal political activities of U.S. citizens.

That raises serious questions about information in Pentagon records such as a March 14, 1986, memo mentioning U.S. citizen Joel Cook and his relationships with the government-sponsored National League of Families (NLF) and the "Rambos," the Pentagon's name for independent activists critical of the NLF and the U.S. government.

"Previously thought to have been close to the NLF, Cook has reportedly aligned himself with the Rambos and is supporting several proclamations that originated in the [Rambos'] Unity Summit," the DIA reported. The only possible interest DIA could have in this information lies in its significance for the domestic political debate on U.S. government POW policies.

Despite the concerns of the ACLU about such snooping, the Pentagon says it sees no reason to stop maintaining information on American POW activists and journalists. "I have no reason to suspect we're doing business any differently [now]," Whitman, the Pentagon spokesman, said.

Dirty Tricks Finally Trip Up Billy

Perhaps the greatest irony of the "dirty tricks" campaign came in June 1992, when Billy Hendon finally read the 1985 Brooks memorandum urging that he be "damage-limited." "That's a felony right there," concluded Hendon. And by then Billy was once again in a position to do something about it. He was back on Capitol Hill, this time working as a staffer for Senator Bob Smith (R-N.H.), vice-chairman of the Senate Select Committee on POW/MIA Affairs. Smith, an POW advocate beloved by many POW-MIA relatives, had assigned Hendon to work on the committee's staff.

Once Hendon saw the Brooks memo, he was convinced all 12 Senators on the committee should see it. Almost seven years after being written, the memo was still classified, obviously to prevent embarrassment to the Pentagon. The memo contained only a few sections that could be possibly be related to national security, and those items—such as the name of a Vietnamese refugee source which had already been censored from the document—could easily be removed.

Since the memo was only classified "confidential," the lowest standard classification, Hendon arranged to have it delivered in a sealed envelope to each of the Senators. But instead of sparking a Senate investigation into POW dirty tricks, the memo got Hendon fired for failing to use proper security measures in distributing the memo to the Senators.

"I uncovered the cover-up and got fired for sending it to U.S. Senators," Hendon said at the time. It was as if some of the Senators and their staffers didn't want to know the whole truth, Hendon thought at the time. And it turned out that he was right.

Chapter 27

The Senate Sell Out

"My agenda as chairman of the [POW] Committee was to get as close to the truth about the fate of the POWs and MIAs as was humanly possible. . . . "
—*Senator John F. Kerry (D-Mass.), Chairman of the Senate Select Committee on POW/MIA Affairs, 1993*

"If I ever see the United States Senate again, I hope it will be in hell. Because I found nothing but dishonesty up there."
—*An investigator for the Senate Select Committee on POW/MIA Affairs, 1993*

If Senator Bob Smith had more hair, the truth about America's POW scandal might have been exposed long ago. The rapidly balding Smith—6'6" and well over 200 pounds—has never been accused of being a blow-dried, Kennedyesque politician. Instead, he's a plain-spoken, rock-ribbed conservative from New Hampshire, a Vietnam vet nationally known for his efforts on two main issues: cutting government pork and fighting for the truth about U.S. POW/MIAs.

The POW issue has always seemed personal for Smith, perhaps in part because his father went missing after a civilian airplane crash in the U.S. Whatever the reason, Smith—a former teacher and real estate broker with a fondness for country music—has pursued the POW issue for years, first in the House and then in the Senate, usually working alone or with the handful of other legislators who share his passion. It is not the kind of issue that wins many votes or positive attention from the media, which has failed miserably in its coverage of the POW issue. Indeed, his pursuit of the issue has even posed political problems for Smith, since those responsible for bungling the recovery of Vietnam POWs are from the highest ranks of his own political party. About the only rewards Smith received for his crusade came from the gratitude of POW/MIA relatives and their activist supporters, along with the knowledge that he was doing the right thing.

A New Proposal

In March 1991, Smith began pushing a new proposal for the Senate to establish a Select Committee to investigate the POW issue. Such a committee would respect no political sacred cows, employing a large staff and subpoena power to answer the most sensitive questions about the history of U.S. POWs from World War II to Vietnam.

Senate Resolution 82 was a good idea, but despite Smith's fierce dedication, the proposal was going nowhere fast. Then, with the terrible irony characteristic of the POW scandal, a hoax set the issue afire. It was the public release of a picture purporting to show three U.S. POWs alive in captivity years after the Vietnam War. The snapshot, dubbed the "Three Amigos" picture by the DIA, produced a media feeding frenzy on the POW issue. Numerous family members identified the men as their husbands and fathers, even though the photo later turned out to be bogus.

But at the time, it reminded the American people of their missing prisoners of war. And the picture came out on the heels of other developments in the issue, most notably the bitter departure of the DIA's top POW/MIA expert Colonel Millard "Mike" Peck, a Vietnam War hero who made public allegations of incompetence and possible cover-up in the Pentagon's POW effort.

For the first time in years, it seemed possible that an unbiased and extensive investigation might actually probe the depths of the POW scandal. But the very publicity that appeared ready to move the issue forward brought forth a new set of Capitol Hill players with motivations far different from those of Smith.

Kerry Sees the Light

Into the sudden media spotlight butted the immaculately coiffed head of Senator John Forbes Kerry (D-Mass), a man whose visage and ambitions bore no small resemblance to President John Kennedy. But Kerry's profile was not associated with courage by POW family members and activists. While he was a Vietnam vet, people active in the POW issue were deeply suspicious of Kerry, who had been a leader of the anti-war movement. During the spring of 1991, Kerry had pronounced that: "It [the POW issue] has got to be put to bed—for the sake of those families, for the sake of this country and our politics, and in order to move on." He had then come out against the formation of a select committee.[1]

When the issue began heating up that summer, Kerry suggested having POW hearings in one of his standing Senate committees, deflecting attention from Smith's goal of forming a powerful new select committee. But faced with the reaction of outraged POW activists, and seeing the momentum of the select committee, Kerry got the message. He switched positions and suddenly began pushing for a POW select committee—to be chaired by none other than himself.

Of course, everyone knew that Kerry was no POW expert. But that didn't matter, because the big-haired Senator was from the majority Democratic Party and had the main attribute needed to seize control of the Senate's POW probe—he looked good on TV. Indeed, as the Senate moved to a vote on the Select Committee, one author of this book was contacted by a network television show in search of an expert Senator to interview. The author suggested Smith, but the network ultimately selected Kerry, admitting he knew less about the issue but looked better on TV than the sometimes stiff New Hampshire Yankee. On several other occasions, sources say, TV network talent bookers chose Kerry over Smith for exactly the same reason. As one Senate investigator described Kerry: "He is slick. He is the slickest guy I've ever seen."

Energized by his new role, Kerry joined Smith in helping push the bill establishing a POW committee. By early August 1991, the Senate had voted to form the Select Committee on POW/MIA Affairs, and Kerry had been designated its chairman.

Kerry Urges a Soft Line

One of John Kerry's first moves was to visit Vietnam, taking along his daughters for an eight-day trip in August which also included stops in Thailand and Cambodia. It is not known exactly what Kerry told Hanoi about his Senate committee. But after the trip, Kerry had dinner with Assistant Secretary of State Richard Solomon. According to a previously classified State Department report, Kerry told the State Department that: "relaxing the [trade] embargo would increase U.S. leverage on the SRV [Vietnam] and improve cooperation on POW/MIA matters."[2]

Of course, at the time of Kerry's trip, POW family groups and experts were all convinced that Vietnam should be forced to start telling the truth about U.S. POWs before being rewarded by a relaxation of the then-tight American trade embargo on Hanoi. But here was Kerry urging that the embargo be loosened before Hanoi began real cooperation. More importantly, Kerry was pushing a soft line on Vietnam even before his committee's hearings began, sending clear signals about his views on where the POW issue should be heading—toward normalized relations with Hanoi.

Kerry Looks For a Weak Partner

Smith, on the other hand, was not about to support Vietnam until it began real cooperation in accounting for live American POW/MIAs. And by the end of August, 1991, it looked as if Smith was about to become Kerry's co-chairman on the POW committee.

So on August 29, 1991, Kerry had his long-time aide Frances Zwenig contact the Bush Administration State Department. Instead of putting the bureaucracy on notice that it was about to come under intense scrutiny, Zwenig asked for a favor. She explained that Kerry wanted to ensure that Bob Smith did not become co-chairman of the committee.

Kerry's choice was Sen. John McCain (R-Ariz.), who, despite his experience as a Vietnam POW often served as an apologist for Republican inaction on the prisoner issue. McCain too had proposed softening the U.S. line on Hanoi, and he had also passed legislation, dubbed "the McCain Amendment," that appeared to open POW/MIA records but actually made it virtually impossible for the public to receive information on the fate of specific POW/MIAs. And in May 1991, "McCain . . . referred repeatedly to the need to find ways to defuse the POW/MIA issue with the American public," the State Department reported.[3]

Perhaps most importantly, McCain was not regarded as the smartest member of the Senate, and had limited credibility on Capitol Hill because of his major involvement in the "Keating Five" scandal, in which he received perks linked to his support of corrupt savings and loan executives. In short, McCain was controllable and could be trusted to avoid raking up any serious POW muck.

It was a remarkable event: a liberal democratic Senator approaching the conservative Bush Administration bureaucracy for help in controlling a Senate select committee—the same committee expected to investigate the Bush Administration.

It would be hard to believe if the approach had not been recorded in a classified State Department telegram describing the talk with Zwenig: "The Senator [Kerry] would prefer to see McCain get the [co-chairman] job (and McCain is reluctantly willing to do it), but Senator Smith is campaigning actively for it. Zwenig thinks a call from Assistant Secretary [of State Richard] Solomon to [Republican leader] Senator [Bob] Dole would help get the right decision made. And quickly."[4]

Leaving nothing to chance, Zwenig then gave Dole's travel plans and phone numbers to State Department officials, the telegram reported. But Kerry had apparently miscalculated either the scruples of the Bush Administration or the power of Bob Smith among POW activists. The State Department and Dole's office later said they had not responded to Kerry's request. And Dole was soon forced by public pressure to make Smith, not McCain, co-chairman of the Senate committee.

The Committee Is Formed

Despite her failure at back-room political fixing, Zwenig was rewarded with a job as staff director of the Senate POW Committee, a role for which she had few qualifications other than loyalty to Kerry. A lawyer and former Peace Corps volunteer, Zwenig was unfamiliar with many military and intelligence topics vital to an understanding of the POW issue and the ability to penetrate stonewalling by the Pentagon and intelligence agencies. Her role in the investigation would later spark bitter resentment among military and intelligence professionals assigned to the committee staff.

Zwenig's lack of experience on the issue should have been balanced by Dino Carluccio, one of Smith's appointees to the committee who soon became deputy staff director. The New Hampshire native had spent years as Smith's expert on the prisoner issue, and was excited to be in a position to force the truth out of the executive branch through depositions and subpoenas. But Carluccio's role reflected a critical weakness in the select committee. Smith's man had one main agenda—to force out the truth at whatever cost. And his single-minded pursuit of the issue was accompanied by an intense and sometimes brusque personal style exacerbated by youth. Then only 24 years old, and with little tolerance for fools, Carluccio was taking on the protocol-bound Senate and national security establishment. Worse yet, Smith had designated former Congressman and POW fire-eater Billy Hendon as his personal representative to the committee. The Carluccio and Hendon team, while a font of POW expertise, would prove a major irritant to many others on Capitol Hill.

And then there were the rank-and-file Senators on the committee, in some ways the least important players on the issue. Most of the 12 appointees knew little about the issue and often failed to attend meetings of the committee, especially those with little media coverage. As one investigator described it: "Some of them were just going through the motions. It was really a disgrace in some cases."

The significant exceptions were McCain and Charles Grassley, an Iowa Republican who had long been interested in the POW issue. The two men would become fierce adversaries, with McCain defending the status quo at every turn—and using his staff membership to alert the Pentagon to committee plans—and the taciturn Grassley, a farmer back home, pushing for a real investigation and full disclosure at any cost.

The Committee Leaks To Its Targets

But there would be no chance of the Senate committee achieving anything near full disclosure. From the very beginning, Senate aides began leaking the committee's plans to the targets of its investigation. The leaks began at the top with Frances Zwenig and started, according to Senate records and staffers, even before the first major committee hearings. (Zwenig did not return phone calls requesting her comments on this book, but did deny any wrongdoing through a spokeswoman during the Senate investigation. She was rewarded for her work on the Senate committee by the Clinton Administration, which made her chief-of-staff for the U.S. Ambassador to the United Nations.)

The first hearings, set for early November 1991, were designed to place the Pentagon's POW officials under oath. These men were key to the entire POW issue, especially because of the Pentagon's long-standing contention that there was no proof—or even evidence—that Americans POWs had been held in

Southeast Asia after the Vietnam War. Either these Pentagon officials had honorably searched for evidence of POWs who in truth did not exist, or they were incompetent and/or possibly dishonest members of a bureaucracy unable or unwilling to locate U.S. prisoners in Southeast Asia. For the first time, a committee existed with both the expertise and legal power to answer that question.

Smith and his allies planned tough questions for several of the officials, especially the DIA's Charles "Chuck" Trowbridge, who had spent years denying that any firm evidence existed of U.S. prisoners in Indochina. But before Smith could get Trowbridge under oath, the Senator's plans were revealed to the Pentagon.

According to a Department of Defense document dated October 25, 1991, Zwenig had informed the Pentagon that "Senator Smith insists on Mr. Trowbridge's participating as a witness. . . ."

"We need to block this," an official had handwritten on the document. The reason: Zwenig had told the Pentagon that "Sen. Smith wants to call Chuck T. a liar in public."

When Trowbridge was later called to testify, he proved able to dodge many of Smith's questions.

The McCain Agenda

The November hearings also featured public displays of John McCain's seemingly inexplicable behavior concerning the POW issue. During one hearing, the Senator castigated former Senate investigator and Vietnam veteran Tracy Usry for contradicting various DIA claims, including the Pentagon line that no U.S. prisoners were shipped from Vietnam to the Soviet Union. But later that day McCain showed a far different reaction to the testimony of former North Vietnamese Colonel Bui Tin, who had accepted the South Vietnamese surrender in 1975.

Tin, a leading communist during the war who later defected to France, had interrogated Americans during the war. During the Senate hearing he lied under oath, saying: "I state categorically that there is not any American prisoner alive in Vietnam." McCain reacted to the testimony by moving to the witness table and warmly embracing the Vietnamese official.

In coming months, the short but intense McCain would again and again surprise observers with his emotional outbursts. Unlike skeptics on the committee, McCain appeared incapable of accepting—or even listening to—any serious criticism of the U.S.

government. When Philip Corso, an intelligence officer in the Eisenhower White House, confirmed numerous reports that U.S. POWs had been shipped from Korea to Siberia and their fates kept secret, McCain sputtered that the testimony "strains my imagination" and stormed from the hearing room.

During other Senate hearings, McCain called one author of this book an "asshole" and browbeat POW activists and family members, even reducing the sister of one missing serviceman to tears during her testimony. McCain's chief aide on the POW/MIA issue, Mark Salter, also verbally attacked activists, and even had a fist-fight with the son-in-law of a POW/MIA in a Senate building. The son-in-law, POW activist Ted Sampley, was convicted of assault, but claims Salter provoked the incident.

Sampley, with support from some former prisoners of war, claims that McCain's behavior may be due to guilt over his conduct in Vietnamese POW camps. Sampley has even suggested that McCain may be some sort of "Manchurian Candidate" compromised by the Vietnamese into serving their interests. While at least two Vietnamese defectors say some U.S. POWs were compromised, and Sampley has pointed out discrepancies concerning McCain's captivity, there is no hard evidence to substantiate the allegations.

There have also been claims that McCain felt compelled to support the Bush Administration's POW record in return for political support the Senator received in the wake of the "Keating Five" scandal. Other observers believe McCain, the son of an admiral, is suffering from survivor's guilt or lacks the psychological and intellectual capacity to accept that any U.S. official would write off a POW.

While McCain's motives remain unclear, his support of the Pentagon's record was almost absolute during the Senate's investigation. It therefore came as no surprise when Salter, McCain's POW committee staffer, emerged as one of the Pentagon's leading informants on the plans of the Senate committee. He would play a key role in perhaps the most appalling episode of the entire Senate investigation.

The Senate Sabotages Its Own Briefing

One of the most charismatic investigators on the POW committee's staff was John McCreary, a white-bearded lawyer and long-time DIA employee. McCreary had served in intelligence posts far removed from the POW issue, and left a prestigious job as head of the U.S. National Strategic Warning Staff to work on the committee. McCreary was widely regarded as an exceptional intelligence officer, and he was reportedly one of the few U.S. intelligence experts to predict Iraq's invasion of Kuwait. In addition, he had served during the 1980s on the Tighe Commission, a panel of experts which evaluated the POW issue for the Reagan Administration. Not only was McCreary a pro, but he was also willing to buck the conventional wisdom on important intelligence questions.

Once on the committee staff, McCreary began analyzing the human intelligence reports on U.S. POWs in Southeast Asia. Working with former Congressman Billy Hendon and Bob Taylor, another experienced investigator, McCreary sorted the POW reports and assigned, or "clustered," them into the geographic areas where the POWs had allegedly been seen.

The idea was to focus on the information content of all the reports, as opposed to the DIA's process of examining each report in minute detail with an eye to debunking it. According to the Senate investigators, by analyzing the trends in almost 1,000 separate reports, the truth would emerge about whether U.S. POWs remained in Southeast Asia after the war.

As the investigators told their bosses in a special briefing: "This is a long-standing and proven method of analysis used by the US Intelligence Community. I want to stress that this is the same method of analysis used by the US Intelligence Community to track SCUD Missile firings by Iraq during the war. . . . A similar process also is used in tracking SS-25 mobile missile units in the Commonwealth of Independent States."

By the end of March, 1992, the investigators were preparing to brief the committee's Senators on the findings of their study. But McCain had determined that an independent briefing of the Senators must be avoided at all costs. So in late March, McCain staffer Mark Salter quitely contacted the Department of Defense, according to a Pentagon memo.[5]

"According to Salter, the conclusion of the 'intelligence' briefing was that Americans were still being held prisoner in Laos and Vietnam as late as 1989. Senator McCain felt it was critical that DIA be present at this briefing to rebut the assertions. . . , " reported the Pentagon memo.

At first, the Pentagon refused to intrude on the private workings of a Senate investigation. But just hours before the briefing, on the morning of the April 9th, Salter leaked a summary of McCreary's findings to the Pentagon. Pentagon briefers rushed to the Senate, prepared to attack the Senate investigators' findings before they could be fully presented to the committee.

But deputy staff director Dino Carluccio, Smith's man, had a plan. He ordered Senate security policemen to bar the Pentagon team from Senate Room 407, the location for the classified briefing. That tactic failed when a majority of the committee voted to allow DIA staffers into the briefing.

What followed was probably one of the most chaotic briefings in the history of U.S. intelligence. McCreary explained that his team had plotted the location of POW reports across Indochina. While "clearly outrageous, inflated, exaggerated or impossible reports" had been excluded from the analysis, some reports rejected by the DIA as "fabrications' had been included on the map. The reasoning was simple: since the Pentagon stood accused of falsely rejecting many reports, some of those rejected could really be true, and they should be compared with other reports to see if a pattern emerged.

Although this technique had been used with success in other areas of intelligence, it angered McCain, who contested the use of any reports dubbed as "fabrications" by the DIA. Smith countered with support of McCreary's analysis while Kerry tried to get the briefing back on track. But by then Salter's work had succeeded: the Senate's own investigators had been deprived of a chance to present their case without interruption.

Eventually, according to the Pentagon memo, all the Senators but Smith left the briefing while it was still in progress. "After being challenged by the DIA team. . . , Hendon and Smith began criticizing DIA. As it became more difficult for DIA to respond, Smith blamed his fellow Senators for DIA having to defend itself. Smith said DOD [Department of Defense] should never have been allowed in a closed briefing and that his fellow Senators brought this folly about by voting to allow DOD to participate," the Pentagon memo reported.

As the Defense Intelligence Agency experts began faltering in the face of Smith's and Hendon's evidence, staff director Zwenig told the Pentagon officials they should not respond to any more questions, and the meeting broke up, according to the memo.

A Report Too Hot to Handle

Had the Senators on that April day cared to hear the report of their own investigators, here's what they would have learned: *"The intelligence indicates that American prisoners or war have been held continuously after Operation Homecoming [in early 1973] and remain[ed] in captivity in Vietnam and Laos as late as 1989.* The intelligence indicates that no American prisoners of war have survived in Cambodia," reported the investigators in their briefing. [authors' emphasis][6]

The Senate staffers went on the say the American POWs were presumably still alive in Southeast Asia, but definitive findings could not be made because of the lag-time between when a refugee saw a POW and the time his report made it to the U.S. In other words, many sightings of U.S. POWs in Indochina after 1989 had theoretically not yet been received by the Pentagon.

These shocking conclusions contradicted years of official denials by both Democratic and Republican administrations. The briefing was simply too politically hot for the Senate to handle.

One investigator said: "Kerry got scared when he found out what the hell was going on. Because this was not his agenda. His agenda was to open ties with Vietnam. I think he was stunned shitless on the 9th of April when we briefed that the intelligence indicated that there were guys alive through 1989. I think that just stunned him."

Destroying the Briefing

The finding of the Senate's professional investigators could not be allowed to stand. "On 9 April 1992, the Chairman of the Senate Select Committee, Senator John Kerry of Massachusetts, in response to a protest by other members of the Select Committee, told the Select Committee members that 'all copies' [of the POW briefing] would be destroyed," along with computer files of the briefing, McCreary wrote in April 27 and May 3, 1992, Senate memos. The original briefing and 14 copies were reportedly shredded on April 10th.

When staffers later questioned the legality of destroying the records, according to McCreary, the committee's chief counsel, William Codinha, made light of the issue. "Mr. Codinha replied 'Who's the injured party?' He was told, "The 2,494 families of the unaccounted for US Servicemen, among others.' Mr. Codinha then said, "Who's gonna tell them? It's classified,' " recounted one of McCreary's memos.

(Kerry and Codinha have since claimed there was never any order, or intent, to destroy "all" copies of the briefing. Both men say their actions on the committee were guided by an intense desire to reveal the full truth about the fate of U.S. POW/MIAs.)

An Independent Counsel?

But the next day, April 16th, all six intelligence investigators on the Senate staff requested an independent counsel to protect them against charges of criminal wrongdoing in connection with the destruction of the briefing files, which may have been illegal under public records laws such as Title 18, United States Code, Section 20171. Their action apparently got Kerry's attention, because he allegedly called the investigators together at 9:30 p.m. He told the men that the issue was "moot," because a copy of the briefing had been in the Office of Senate Security "all along."

McCreary, in his memos, claimed that one copy of the briefing was indeed in the Office of Senate Security by that time, but it had been placed there at 1:07 p.m. on April 16th. In other words, all the original copies had been destroyed. But when that sparked a controversy, someone produced an extra, presumably "bootlegged" version of the briefing. (McCreary claimed the extra, possibly illegally copied briefing came from the office of John McCain.) According to McCreary, a lawyer with extensive experience handling classified records, the destruction of the original briefing papers was similar to acts in the Iran-Contra Scandal and may well have involved criminal conduct.

However, the committee's leaders saved their outrage for another security-related flap in June, when two staffers broke technical regulations governing the distribution of a low-level classified document to various Senate offices. The document, the controversial "Brooks Memorandum," was stamped "confidential," the lowest common level of classification. Some staffers even felt it was illegally classified to hide its explosive political statements.

Indeed, the 1985 memo outlined a plan to "damage-limit" POW investigations by Billy Hendon, then a Congressman. By now Hendon was a Senate staffer working for Smith, and not pleased to learn what the Pentagon had been doing to him years before.

In their haste to show the newly discovered "Brooks Memorandum" to Senators on the POW committee, Hendon and deputy staff director Dino Carluccio failed to follow all applicable regulations. Both men were quickly forced out of their jobs for "security" reasons, although Carluccio was later allowed to work with the committee in his status as an aide to Smith.

The Numbers Game

By June 1992, the select committee had turned to the critical question of POW/MIA "accounting"—in other words, the debate over how many Americans there were for whom the Indochinese communists could really be expected to account. The issue boiled down to the number of servicemen who were last known alive in communist hands, or whose losses indicated they could have been captured by the communists. These were the cases Hanoi would be pressured to resolve.

According to retired Army General John Vessey, the President's Special Emissary to Hanoi, about 135 Americans were "last known alive" or fell into the category of those for whom Vietnam should be able to account.

But Kerry rejected even the "Vessey List" of 135, eventually declaring that "valid questions" existed about the fate of only 43 Americans, far below the hundreds of Americans carried in that category by Smith, independent POW/MIA experts, and previously classified U.S. intelligence records. A Senate investigator remarked: "He [Kerry] simply didn't want to find out the truth [about the number of POWs]."

In July, a possible motive for Kerry's lowballing emerged.

No Live POWs Are Required

On July 14-15, 1992, Kerry's staff director travelled to Vietnam with Pentagon officials, who later reported on her meetings with Vietnamese officials. It was during a talk with Le Bang, Hanoi's top expert on the U.S., that Zwenig made a stunning statement concerning Kerry's expectations. "She said Senator Kerry believes the Vessey cases can be resolved by the recovery and identification of remains, through records, from witnesses of deaths, or some combination of these. She said that Senator Kerry believes SRV [Vietnamese] explanations of deaths could be based upon past policies and inadequate records in the South," the Pentagon reported in a cable to the U.S.

In other words, Zwenig gave Hanoi a road map on how to settle the POW issue without providing all evidence in its possession. More importantly, she never mentioned the return of living Americans as a requirement for resolving the issue.

If the Vietnamese had any doubt about Zwenig's point, she soon settled it. "Senator Kerry sees the SSC [Senate Select Committee] as a way to bring this issue to a close," Zwenig was quoted as saying.

Punish the Loud Mouths

Before ending his meeting with Zwenig, Le Bang took the opportunity to attack Americans who raised "unfounded issues" regarding the POWs. He mentioned the faked pictures of U.S. POWs (without, of course, mentioning the role of Vietnamese intelligence agencies in spreading fake POW information). In this area, the Vietnamese had a point, because the faked photos had taken a toll among POW/MIA family members in both heartache and money. Just as importantly, the hoaxers had wasted the time of official investigators and the credibility of the entire POW issue.

But it was not just criminal hoaxers that Le Bang was discussing. He also raised the issue of men "falsely accusing the SRV of trading prisoners for money." "He referred to [recently fired Senate staffer and former Congressman Billy] Hendon, [former Congressman and POW activist John] LeBoutillier, and others saying that they hurt the families of the missing, the USG [U.S. government], and the interests of the SRV."

Hendon and LeBoutillier had certainly hurt the reputation of both the U.S. government and Hanoi, but mostly by accurately pointing out their deception on the POW issue. Indeed, on the specific issue raised by Le Bang, both former Congressmen frequently stated the real link between POWs and U.S. aid. Apparently, Hanoi was upset that the men kept telling the truth about the existence of U.S. POWs in Southeast Asia after 1973 and their connection to financial considerations.

Hendon and LeBoutillier would pay for their outspokenness. Both men later came under investigation by the POW committee for their fund-raising on the POW issue.

A Strategic Error

In August 1992, the committee took more testimony on refugee reports of Americans in Southeast Asia. Then in September, the committee began grappling with one of the most bitter elements of the POW issue: what the Nixon Administration knew about the POWs in 1973 and whether Henry Kissinger and other top officials had done everything possible to win their release.

By the end of September's hearings on the Paris Peace Accord, Kissinger's role was still hotly debated. But a new consensus had developed that top U.S. officials at least suspected that U.S. POWs were being retained by the communists in 1973. Former CIA chief and Secretary of Defense James Schlesinger, supported by other Nixon-era officials, told the committee: "I think that, as of now, that I can come to no other conclusion, Senator. That does not say that there are any alive today, mind you. But in 1973, some were left behind."

The admissions did more than make newspaper headlines across America. They also highlighted a tremendous strategic error by the Senate committee. Instead of first determining whether POWs might have been left behind (the hearings on 1973) and then examining the evidence that they might still be alive in Indochina (the live-sighting issue), the committee had reversed the process.

Indeed, the DIA—with the concurrence of some committee Senators—had earlier downgraded and even rejected some postwar live-sightings on the very basis that there was no evidence Americans were left behind in 1973. But, as four Senate investigators pointed out to committee leadership in a September 28 memo: "They [the Paris Peace Accord hearings] established and documented a simple truth—the government left men behind and key officials knew it."

That raised serious questions on the DIA's earlier debunking of live-sightings. "[Before the recent hearings] DIA's analysis and testimony deserved the benefit of the doubt, based on the accepted belief that no one was left behind. Refugees couldn't possibly see what was not there. [But] the revelations produced by the hearings on the Paris Peace Accords, however, provide a new context to the intelligence—prison guards and service personnel could and would see men left behind," the investigators wrote.

That meant the April intelligence briefing that POWs survived until at least 1989 was now even more plausible. The Senate investigators asked their bosses to reexamine the issue of live-sightings. Predictably, their request was not acted upon.

Perjury?

The new testimony that top U.S. officials believed men were left behind in 1973 raised another issue: perjury. The four investigators wrote, "In testimony before this committee [months ago] on 5 November 1991 . . . Deputy Assistant Secretary of State [Ken] Quinn stated he was not aware of any judgment at any time in the Executive Branch that there were Americans left behind in Laos or Cambodia. Deputy Assistant Secretary of Defense Carl Ford and DIA's Mr. Trowbridge made similar assertions as to Southeast Asia in general. This testimony is misleading at best."

The investigators recommended that Kerry "direct investigative counsels to review all prior sworn testimony for serious misrepresentation."

In other words, the investigators wanted the Senate to determine whether U.S. officials had perjured themselves. This recommendation, too, was apparently ignored. As one investigator told the authors, by this point in their investigation, the attitude of many Senators was: "Get this rattlesnake off my back."

Sticking With The Script

The rattlesnake threatened to strike again in October, as the committee prepared hearings on purported POW distress signals seen on the ground in Southeast Asia years after the war.

On October 6, Zwenig wrote Kerry: "I am working on the script w/ DIA." The next day, according to a Department of Defense memo, Kerry called the Pentagon "very upset" about leaks concerning the alleged distress signals.

Apparently the Pentagon did not want to use the "script" suggested by Zwenig, because Kerry conceded to Pentagon official Ronald Knecht "that a script would be unwise," according to a military record.

Instead, Kerry suggested to the Pentagon—a supposed target of his investigation—how to get rid of annoying questions concerning the signals. "He [Kerry] urges the Department to come on very strong. 'We are appalled. These leaks jeopardize any American in captivity. . . . ,'" the Pentagon reported.

Here again was the Senate giving advice to the very people it was supposed to be investigating.

Mixed Signals

The Pentagon went on to debunk the distress signals and other satellite intelligence during hearings in October. Once again it fell to McCreary, the intelligence expert who had used satellite intelligence to predict the invasion of Kuwait, to set the record straight. His comments came in an October 16, 1992, memo to the committee. "The Department of Defense presentation . . . was amateurish and deceptive," he wrote. As for the DIA's testimony on the photos: "I concluded that DIA has done an unforgivably incompetent analysis of the material. It has once again misled the committee. . . . "

The NSA and CIA Stonewall

While the DIA misled the Senate, other executive branch agencies effectively ignored the POW inquiry. For example, the Senate had information that the CIA was far more involved in the POW issue than admitted previously. There is even a report that CIA agents nearly rescued a U.S. captain who escaped from his Vietnamese POW camp and made it to Haiphong before being recaptured in 1976. But the CIA refused to provide many of its files to the Senate.

An even more important source of information was lost because of a combination of Senate incompetence and executive branch stonewalling. For years, former National Security Agency employee Jerry Mooney had been saying that the agency possessed voluminous files proving that large numbers of Americans had been captured but never returned by the communists. He also claimed the NSA had intercepted communist radio messages proving that U.S. POWs were held after the war in Cambodia, Laos and Vietnam.

At first the NSA denied holding such messages, but finally the agency admitted it couldn't find the records Mooney was talking about, in large part because technology and filing systems had changed dramatically since the 1970s. In March 1992, the NSA accepted a remarkable compromise, Mooney claims. The agency cut a secret deal with Mooney and the Select Committee. Mooney would be allowed to help locate the lost POW files, which would then be turned over to the Senate. In return, Mooney agreed never again to discuss his classified POW information.

"It was beautiful the way it was set up," Mooney said. But the former Air Force intelligence expert soon realized that the Senate did not understand, or did not really care about, the treasure chest to which it now had the keys. "Here's the first time a Congressional committee had the right to get into SIGINT [signal intelligence], and they didn't give a damn," he recalled.

Only one Senate investigator had the clearance to work with Mooney to excavate the files. He soon quit the committee and was never replaced. As a result, the most important POW files—which could not leave NSA facilities—were never checked, Mooney recalled. "It still pisses me off when I think of it. Because it [the Senate access] will never happen again."

One Senate investigator said the committee was able to verify some of Mooney's memories concerning specific intercepted messages. "As an intelligence guy, once I saw that a significant part of what he said was accurate, there's no reason to disbelieve the rest of it," the investigator said.

But after the Senate allowed the special agreement to collapse, so did cooperation from the National Security Agency, which reports to the Pentagon. "NSA gave us a first-class runaround," said the investigator. Finally, the NSA agreed to deliver a large quantity of records. Although Mooney knew they were not the best records, they still might have contained important information. But they were not turned over to the Senate until the last moment, and the committee refused to fight for an extension of its deadline. "They had 150 boxes of which we looked in 29 with any degree of thoroughness," the investigator said.

"It was so bad, that if it wasn't malicious, it was an incompetence or a failure to cooperate on a scale that is staggering. But that was characteristic, by the way, of the executive branch. They were not interested in finding out the truth. Nor in honestly representing what the information says," the investigator added.

Those unexamined NSA files, along with the CIA reports and many other POW records, remain secret and will likely never be declassified fully in the lifetime of anyone reading this book.

The NSA records were not the only ones delayed by the Pentagon until it was too late for investigators to analyze them. One investigator recalls trying to get the personal files of a senior Pentagon official known to have critical POW information. "I asked and asked and asked," recalled the investigator, who never received the files.

Pentagon officials sent other crucial reports straight to the Library of Congress, hidden away in microfilm reels of unimportant records. While the records were ultimately to be placed in the library, they should have gone to the Senate first. "We had no idea what boxes to look through. It's ridiculous. It's another little trick they played," the investigator said.

The Pentagon played the same trick with reporters when it "released" thousands of POW documents with no index, even though the documents had been carefully screened before their release. The Pentagon also refused to allow journalists to make photocopies of the records.

On one occasion, Senate staffers learned the location of an important document only after being contacted by one author of this book, who had accidentally found the memo at the Library of Congress and called the Senate to obtain comments for a newspaper article. Investigators rushed over to the library just in time to find the record and use it during a hearing. Many other important documents were never located, and are presumably buried in the Library of Congress to this day.

Why did the Pentagon and CIA stonewall the committee? And why did the committee fail to insist on full cooperation? Mooney thinks he knows the answer. "I think they [the Senate committee] got too close. There were too many people on the top deck who were going to get burned."

Certainly the Senate did not always appear eager to pursue controversial leads. The evidence of secret returnees mentioned in an earlier chapter is one example. Civilian defense analyst Dr. Joseph Douglass, Jr., who tried to push the committee to look more closely at the shipment of POWs to Russia, speaks for others when he says: "It became clear to me that the select committee, certainly the key staff who guarded the gates, did not want to know or learn."

Getting To The Witnesses

By the end of October, McCreary concluded, constant leaks to the Pentagon had destroyed the committee's ability to conduct a true investigation. Worse yet, the leaking—much of it allegedly from Zwenig—was discrediting and perhaps even endangering witnesses. "She told them [the DIA] every move we were going to make before we made it, basically, cooperating with the people we were supposed to be investigating," said another investigator.

McCreary discussed this in an October 30 memo entitled simply "Obstruction of the Investigation." In the memo, he recounted the cases of two witnesses: Vietnamese defector Le Quang Khai and DIA employee Jan Sejna, himself a defector from the Czech military.

Sejna—by some accounts the highest-ranking East-bloc officer ever to defect to the U.S.—had served as a general in top Czech defense posts, including positions with access to highly classified Soviet operations. After his defection in 1968, Sejna had been recruited by the DIA, which verified his truthfulness with a series of polygraph examinations and set him to work in a highly sensitive job analyzing the Warsaw Pact.

There he had toiled as a highly regarded employee until he made a terrible mistake: telling his bosses that he knew about American POWs shipped from Korea and Vietnam to the Soviet Union. He had apparently mentioned at least part of his knowledge soon after his defection, but the true extent of his information only became apparent in 1992.

This caused a serious problem for the DIA, which for years had told the American people and Congress that there was "no evidence" any U.S. prisoners had gone from Korea and/or Vietnam to Russia. Yet here was a long-time DIA employee who claimed to have seen communist documents on the Korean shipments and even personally witnessed U.S. POWs being shipped from Vietnam to the Soviet Union via Prague.

According to McCreary, the Pentagon was immediately informed when select committee investigators decided to talk with Sejna. The executive branch's reaction was swift. One important U.S. official "called for his [Sejna's] dismissal." The CIA sent the Senate a letter purporting to debunk Sejna's claims. And all this happened before the hapless general had even been deposed by the Senate. "This anticipatory discrediting of a Select Committee potential witness is tantamount to tampering with evidence," McCreary wrote.

The tampering with Le Quang Khai was even more serious. Le, a Vietnamese Foreign Ministry official studying at Columbia University, had publicly stated in September 1992 that U.S. POWs were held in Vietnam after the war. McCreary deposed Le the next month, and two days after the investigator submitted his report to the committee, someone calling himself an FBI agent contacted Le.

"The contact with Le two days after preparations of my MFR [memorandum for record], despite the passage of a month since his public declarations, is highly suspicious and more than coincidental," McCreary wrote.

The investigator concluded that all sensitive Senate files were being leaked to the Pentagon, a process which was "jeopardizing the livelihood, if not the safety, of Senate witnesses. In addition, the Department of Defense's continuing access to sensitive Committee Staff papers is resulting in obstructions of the investigations by the Senate Select Committee by various agencies of the executive branch."

One of McCreary's fellow investigators agreed, blaming Kerry for the obstruction: "He [Kerry] was basically all along in collusion with the executive branch on this issue."

Kerry Sets Clinton Straight on the POWs

Kerry even ran an errand for President Bush in November, taking to Hanoi the first direct communication from a U.S. President to a Vietnamese dictator since the Nixon Administration.

The Senator refused to reveal the contents of the letter, but did wax philosophic in an interview with *The Washington Post*, known for its dismissive tone on the POW issue. " 'I'm not here to close the book' if it turns out that it should be kept open, Kerry said, but he made clear that he thought that was unlikely," reported the *Post* on November 16, 1992.

Kerry also took time to correct a statement by President-elect Clinton, who had repeated his campaign promise to demand a real accounting for U.S. POW/MIAs across the world.

"As for Clinton, Kerry said the president-elect misspoke at a news conference last week when he said that his administration would not extend diplomatic recognition to any nation 'suspected' of withholding information about U.S. prisoners or missing servicemen. Kerry said he and Clinton had discussed those comments and Clinton recognized he had 'set up a test no one could meet. That wasn't what he intended.' "[7]

The Senate Caves In

The Senate Select Committee was certainly not going to make the Bush Administration meet any tough tests of cooperation on the POW investigation. The Senate committee knew, for instance, that a former Secret Service agent had reported hearing several Reagan Administration officials discussing a 1981 Vietnamese officer to sell back U.S. POWs.

The former agent, John Syphrit, had since moved to another part of the Treasury Department, the parent agency of the Secret Service. When contacted by Senate investigators, Syphrit said he was willing to testify, but only under subpoena. His reasoning was simple—he feared retaliation from his superiors in the Bush Administration, probably because Bush had allegedly been part of the 1981 discussion. If Syphrit was telling the truth, it meant Bush had helped make the decision to turn down an offer to buy back U.S. POWs—and then taken part in a cover-up, since the Reagan Administration had repeatedly denied any such discussion ever occured.

Not surprisingly, the Bush Administration put pressure on the Senate not to subpoena Syphrit, claiming it would set a bad precedent and break down the trust between the Secret Service and those they guarded. On the other hand, the former agent claimed to know about perhaps the most critical and politically explosive allegation ever about the POW issue. It was also likely that a White House tape still existed verifying the agent's claim. And, most importantly, the Senate had promised to get to the bottom of the POW scandal without fear or favor.

Despite all that, the select committee voted 7-4 not to subpoena the agent, leaving the question of a possible presidential-level POW cover-up unresolved forever. "As far as I am concerned, this is one more instance in which this committee caved in to the desires of the executive branch it was established to investigate," proclaimed Senator Grassley.[8]

As one disgusted Senate staffer said: "Can you imagine if that kind of stuff happened during Watergate?"

Speaking of Watergate

Indeed, the ghost of Watergate did appear in the POW investigation. The Senate wanted a copy of the April 11, 1973 Watergate tapes, which may include critical information on Nixon Administration POW policy.

"Lawyers for President Nixon informed the Committee that access to the recording would be given only if this Committee agreed not to seek any other White House records from this time period," the Senate report noted.

So here was a disgraced former President and proven prevaricator imposing conditions on a Senate committee seeking the truth about Americans lost servicemen. The Senate's reaction was to roll over. The committee simply accepted Nixon's refusal, rather than seeking judiciary help.

At least Nixon agreed to answer some of the committee's questions. President Ronald Reagan, who allegedly turned down that offer to buy back U.S. POWs, refused to answer any questions from the Senate.

As for then-President George Bush—whose fingerprints were all over the POW issue from his time as Director of the CIA in the 1970s to his tenure in the Oval Office—the Senate decided not even to attempt questioning him. After all, in the chummy bi-partisan spirit of Washington, D.C., the Senators decided it would be inappropriate to challenge "the unique concerns about Executive Privilege."

What this meant was that the POW/MIAs, their families and the American people, they would never get the privilege of learning the truth about their Presidents' role in the POW issue.

The End Game

As the Senate's POW investigation staggered toward its conclusion in late 1992, it was clear to most observers and the Senate's own investigators that the committee had only just begun its job. Family members and advocacy groups began requesting that the committee be extended. They were joined by Bob Smith, who also said the Senate should consider extending its investigation. But the idea was blocked by Kerry, McCain and other Senators.

During hearings on November 11, 1992, Dolores Alfond, sister of a Vietnam POW/MIA and leader of "The National Alliance of Families," a POW family group, begged the committee to extend its work. Alfond, whose organization is the main POW group representing POWs from all U.S. wars, began reciting a list of unresolved issues and unanswered questions still before the committee.

Suddenly, John McCain marched into the hearing room, telling Alfond there was no way the committee would be extended and that he was "sick and tired" of her criticism of the U.S. government.

The exchange reduced Alfond to tears. "The family members have waited years and years and now you're shutting down," she choked out.

The message was clear: a final POW report would be written, even if the investigation was grossly incomplete. One committee investigator said he was astonished to see the no-show Senators starting to draft the report: "They did not look at the data. They did not show up for the hearings. They did not show up for the briefings. And yet they all made findings as if they were well informed."

Rewriting History

But the committee's final report would not merely be incomplete. It would also be tainted by last-minute historical revisionism. Although the final report was marred by incorrect statements of fact and sneering innuendo about a number of Americans, these people were never given a chance to correct the record. As ordinary U.S. citizens, they had no option but to accept the garbled text of the final report.

Henry Kissinger was better connected. He received a leaked version of the final report, apparently from the office of Senator Hank Brown (R-Col.). His lawyer, Washington insider Lloyd Cutler, set to lobbying immediately, and Kissinger's men were soon invited by Kerry to peruse those parts of the report concerning their boss.

Several sections of the report were changed, all of them improving the depiction of Kissinger and other Nixon-era officials.

It is still not clear exactly how much of the report was changed at Kissinger's insistence, especially because he had apparently had allies on the committee staff all long. However, the following passage had been part of the original report, but the highlighted portion was apparently dropped after Kissinger's complaints:

> But there remains the troubling question of whether the Americans who were expected to return [in 1973] but did not were, as a group, shunted aside and discounted by government and population alike. The answer to that question is essentially yes *and it is in this sense that a form of abandonment did take place.* [authors' emphasis]

As Kissinger noted in a letter to the Senate committee: "A key element of legislative or diplomatic statesmanship is to win the other side's approval of language which comes closer to the draftsman intention than to the other side's. . . . " Sadly, in this case the "other side" up against Kissinger consisted of the POW/MIAs and their relatives, who had no expensive lawyers to lobby the Senate committee or friendly Senators to leak them the report. Unlike Kissinger and Nixon and Reagan and Bush, the POWs and their relatives would be forced to rely on the integrity of Kerry and company.

Dolores Alfond was shocked and saddened by the incident. "As a family member," she said, "I cannot understand why these people are being allowed to negotiate the truth."

The Final Report

By now many POW/MIA relatives and activists had given up all hope that the Senate Select Committee on POW/MIA Affairs would issue a full or fair report. They bombarded Smith and Grassley, the two Senators viewed as advocates for the POWs, with messages urging the legislators to denounce the final report and issue their own statement backing the findings of the professional Senate investigators (who had concluded that POWs were kept in Southeast Asia after the war and could still be alive).

But the men elected to stay in the game rather than storming off the field. The pro-POW Senators, especially committee co-chairman Smith, fought an exhausting line-by-line battle over the final report, even adding footnotes expressing the belief that hundreds of live sightings did indeed constitute "evidence" that American prisoners had been kept in Indochina.

Meanwhile, committee member Brown and his establishment allies had more important concerns—last minute political logrolling. They demanded that the Pentagon produce a list of POW "heroes" for inclusion in the final report. The list, it was made clear, had to include Senator McCain, whose apologies for the DIA had by then drawn criticism from the media, POW/MIA relatives and even former POWs. Not surprisingly, Brown's list of "heroes" made no mention of the men Pentagon expert Bill Bell had secretly told the Senate were left behind in Southeast Asia. For many on the Senate POW committee, men like Dallas Pridemore and Clemie McKinney were apparently just embarrassing loose ends to be swept under the rug, and certainly not "heroes" to be praised in public. But McCain was quick to crow in triumph. As *The New York Times* reported: "Senator John Mc-Cain . . . said he hoped that the report would show that there is no proof that Americans are alive there. . . . "

In the final rush to judgment by Kerry and the committee's majority, entire sections of the final POW report were accidently left out. Weeks after the report was finally "released" in January 1993, the missing sections had to be slipped back into the official record, which still contained typos, duplications and references to accidently omitted material.

And so the most intense investigation ever into the POW issue whimpered to a halt in early 1993. The 15-month effort, backed by $1.9 million and subpoena power, certainly could have answered many questions surrounding the POW scandal.

But instead of making clear findings, the Senate succumbed to mealy-mouthed "bipartisanship." As George Orwell wrote: "The great enemy of clear language is insincerity." And perhaps no one should have been surprised that so little clear language appeared in the committee's 1,223 page final report.

The insincerity of the Senate's effort is clearest in its answers to the central questions at hand. Were Americans still in communist prisons after early 1973? Concluded the Senate: "We acknowledge that there is no proof that U.S. POWs survived, but neither is there proof that all those who did not return had died. There is evidence that indicates . . . the possibility of survival, at least for a small number, after Operation Homecoming."

On the other critical question—are Americans alive today in Southeast Asia?—the Senate again abdicated responsibility: "[T]he Senate cannot provide compelling evidence to support that possibility today," their report states, again avoiding any real conclusions.

Even committee staffers were surprised, and disgusted, at the final report. Said one, "That's where we were when we started the committee. Wow! That's progress." A second staffer commented, "People look at this and say: 'What did these guys do? They've been at it for a year and a half and they can't agree."

A third staffer was bitter about the report: "It's such an act of national betrayal. They made a promise they were going to try to get to the bottom of this and they didn't even try.

"Kerry and McCain clearly had their own agendas and misrepresented what the data showed. . . . Did they accurately quote from the documents they had in front of them? No. When they talked about issues did they follow them through to completion to the extent that they brought out in the public all the things that we knew about issues? Absolutely not, in no case, unless it served their own agenda, which was, I suppose, to kill this issue."

A fourth Senate staffer, a highly experienced investigator, said: "It [the committee] had a shot at really doing something. And the chairman [Kerry] prevented it from happening. He blocked it every step of the way. It was the most frustrating and unbeliev-able thing I ever saw in my life."

"We left people on every battlefield in every war we've ever fought," summed up an investigator, who described what he believed the Senate committee had really proven.

"The United States is callous about it. It doesn't give a shit. If you're caught, you're a loser. That's the way we think. And that's the way the government acts."

Chapter 28

Survivors' Rights

"The motivating factor over the years became protecting the President from another hostage crisis."
—Lieutenant General Eugene Tighe, USAF (Ret.), former Director of the Defense Intelligence Agency

"The genius of you Americans is that you never make clear-cut stupid moves, only complicated stupid moves which make us wonder at the possibility that there may be something to them which we are missing."
—Gamal Abdel Nasser

The whole POW scandal—the attitude and inaction that has left Americans to rot in Southeast Asia—was summed up in a single paragraph of one March, 1987 White House memo.

It was a report on a conversation between then-Vice President Bush's Chief of Staff Craig Fuller and Colin Powell, then Deputy National Security Adviser and as of this writing Chairman of the Joint Chiefs of Staff. The men were discussing how to keep Ross Perot from going to Hanoi for POW negotiations.

It's not clear in the memo who said what, although it appears Powell was being paraphrased. But it really doesn't matter. Because Bush's man and Powell agreed on the basic point: "We still believe that it is not wise for Ross to go ... after 14 years they have denied live Americans ... if they were to produce live people, can you imagine what will be asked for?" [ellipses in original]

The memo summed up: "Our policy interests not served by Mr. Perot's interests at the moment."[1]

That's because Ross Perot's interests have been getting American POW/MIAs out of Southeast Asia, even if it means paying Hanoi the money promised to them. And even if it means embarrassing just about all the people who have run American foreign policy for the last two decades.

As Perot said when he first saw the memo: "Our core problem is summed up right here in this little three-line statement. See, this town focuses on how things look, not how things are. Everybody has been worried to death, since this whole issue keeps coming up [and] how will it look if they ever come home?"[2]

Justifiable Concerns

Think of it this way. What do George Bush, *The New York Times*, Warren Christopher, CBS, Brent Scowcroft, *The Washington Post*, Senator John Kerry (D-Mass.) and top Pentagon and State Department bureaucrats in the Clinton Administration all have in common?

Their reputations will be damaged, and in some cases devastated, if living U.S. POWs return from communist control.

Imagine a returned U.S. POW asking Bush whether he did enough while Director of the CIA and then President to recover U.S. POWs. What would the POW say when he saw editorials and stories in the major media urging America to get past the POW/MIA issue and mocking POW activists? How would Christopher explain his top State Department job in the Carter Administration, when the U.S. government offered Hanoi recognition with no strings attached and no POWs required? What would a returned American prisoner want to tell Scowcroft, who helped negotiate the Paris Peace Accord, then years later sneered at the possibility that any prisoners remained in Southeast Asia while at the same time ordering that key POW records be kept secret from the American people?

Finally, how would a U.S. POW react if he met the Pentagon and State Department officials, many in POW-related positions for the last 20 years, who since 1973 have said there was "no evidence" that any U.S. POWs were retained by the communists after Vietnam?

For the last two decades, the same faces have turned up again and again in the POW issue—the same signatures over and over on the secret telegrams, the same bylines on the news stories. Not that this is something uniquely sinister about the POW issue. Rather, it is the way of Washington, D.C.

Yet there is one unusual thing about the POW issue. On most other topics, the political power elite is divided. Republicans want less government, Democrats more. The hawks push increased defense spending, the doves decreased military funding.

Human rights activists say sanctions will goad foreign nations toward democracy, big business claim capitalism will coax the countries into providing greater rights.

But not on the POW issue. No national leader is stupid and/or gutsy enough to declare there are no POWs. And only one—Ross Perot—is bold enough to maintain without qualification that living Americans were left in Indochina. Just about everyone else in both the government and the beltway media takes the safe, ambiguous approach—admitting it's possible, while sticking tight to the herd as it declares that hope is fading and the time is coming to "get beyond" Vietnam.

Unlike most other issues, there is really only one acceptable position on the POW issue in Washington, D.C.—paying lip service to the notion that America should recover its fighting men, while simultaneously relegating the issue to a secondary position.

This leads to some ludicrous positions that must be tough to squeeze into even for the notoriously flexible beltway crowd. For instance, in 1992 the Bush Administration declared that recovering U.S. POWs was "the highest national priority" at the same time its State Department was trying to stop POW meetings in Russia because they "got in the way" of "important" bilateral issues, according to a leaked State Department memo.

In early 1993, President Clinton declared his devotion to the relatives of POW/MIAs at the same time his top deputies were refusing to meet with them.

And when a Russian document emerged indicating that hundreds of U.S. POWs were never returned by Hanoi, the major media rushed to ask top Nixon, Carter and Bush officials about its veracity and implications—without ever explaining that if the document is indeed true, those same officials will be exposed as incompetents or liars. Perhaps their reticence arises from the fact that if the document is true, the American people will ask what the media was doing to uncover the POW scandal all these years.

None of this means there was a POW conspiracy, although in some ways that would be easier to accept than the truth. In reality, resolving the POW issue is simply not of central import to those who set the real agenda of America. If it were, the brightest men and women in U.S. intelligence, along with the best technology, would be assigned to POW duties. They're not. If it were, the U.S. would make real progress on the POW issue a top priority in relations with countries like Russia and China. It doesn't. If it were, the President would assign a top-level negotiator with real power to talk with the Vietnamese, Laotians, Chinese and Russians. He hasn't. If it were, the media would dog the POW story. They don't.

The depressing truth is that the POW issue is viewed as an inconvenience by many people in Washington, D.C. POW/MIA relatives don't have a lot of votes, and they certainly don't have the kind of campaign money or skilled lobbyists it takes to sway most politicians.

There is no permanent Congressional POW committee with leadership posts and power to attack aggressive legislators. The Pentagon and State Department have no top-level posts solely devoted to POW/MIA issues. Nobody expects to win a Pulitzer Prize for reporting on missing American servicemen.

So the issue just staggers along, driven by the visceral feelings of the American people and the efforts of a relative handful of POW relatives and activists. And barring a miracle, the issue will plod on until it dies a sad and natural death.

Some things in the POW issue never change. One is the DIA's debunking mentality and general incompetence, reported for years. In 1983, a White House study concluded: "People working that issue could not find a POW if a POW dropped on their head." In 1985, Admiral Thomas Brooks, a former DIA official, stated that that "mindset to debunk has resulted in sloppy analysis" and "the analysts do not have an open mind." The next year, Colonel Kimball Gaines, also a former DIA official, declared: "the database is a wasteland; there is almost a total lack of management;" and "the bias toward discrediting sources has resulted in reduced objectivity in the analysis."

Later in 1986, retired Lieutenant General Eugene Tighe, former Director of DIA, concluded: "an unresolved case, according to DIA, means we 'haven't yet proved these reports are false;' the greatest problem associated with the POW/MIA issue is the lack of professional analysis of the available intelligence; there is little evidence that any significant analysis of the intelligence received has been accomplished in recent years; and the routine approach to each source has been 'he's probably wrong.' "

In 1991, outgoing DIA POW/MIA chief Colonel Millard "Mike" Peck declared: "a cover-up may be in progress. The entire charade does not appear to be an honest effort, and may never have been. . . . That national leaders continue to address the prisoner of war and missing in action issue as the 'highest national priority' is a travesty."

Finally, the 1993 Senate POW report noted: "Several Committee Members express concern and disappointment that, on occasion, individuals within DIA have been evasive, unresponsive and disturbingly incorrect and cavalier." A less diplomatic view was provided by the internal files of the POW committee and individual Senators. Those records suggested several senior Pentagon POW officials were suspected of perjury and, in one case, mail fraud.

Guaranteed Employment at the Pentagon

In most other organizations, such scathing criticism would force a change in personnel. But not in the Pentagon's POW/MIA operation. A number of those in senior POW/MIA positions have been working on the issue for years and even decades. Consider:

- William Gadoury, long-time Pentagon POW/MIA investigator in Laos. A 1986 independent study raised serious questions about the effectiveness of Gadoury and his fellow Pentagon investigators in Southeast Asia, whose efforts were called "stodgy, plodding and not very up to date." They're still at it.

- Major Jeannie Schiff, as of this writing Deputy Chief of the DIA's POW/MIA office. Her 1992 Senate testimony on a Vietnam live-sighting was misleading and/or incompetent at best.

- Charles Trowbridge, reportedly the future head of POW/MIA analysis for the Pentagon. He has been working on on the POW issue since 1971 and as as of this writing claims he has yet to find any "evidence" that U.S. POWs remained in Indochina after the war. Senate investigators recommended his testimony be examined for perjury.

- Colonel Joseph Schlatter, slated for position as Deputy Chief of Pentagon POW/MIA Office. As former head of the DIA's POW/MIA office in the late-1980s, he travelled the country saying there was not a "single shred of evidence" that U.S. POWs had been held in the Soviet Union after World War II. His office also said there was "no evidence"

U.S. POWs from Korea were held in Russia. Both statements have now been proven to be outright lies. At least one Senate staffer suggested he be investigated for possible mail fraud for an alleged "dirty trick" targetted at a U.S. Senator.

- Robert Sheetz, former head of the DIA POW/MIA office scheduled at this writing to assume the top Pentagon slot for POW/MIA issues. Senate staffers suggested the possibility he committed perjury during a Congressional hearing.

- Major General Thomas Needham, commander of Joint Task Force-Full Accounting, under investigation as of this writing for shredding thousands of POW/MIA records.

And then there are the POW policy-makers at the State Department, Pentagon and White House. Many of them held their positions throughout the 1980s under the Reagan and Bush Administrations. They're gone now, replaced by the men who went along with the POW/MIA write-off during the Carter years. For example: Winston Lord, aide to Kissinger during the Paris Peace talks and then State Department Policy Planning Director during the Carter POW sell-out, is as of this writing about to assume a top State Department job with influence on the POW issue. Current National Security Adviser Anthony Lake and Secretary of State Warren Christopher also served in the Carter Administration.

Imagine what Hanoi makes of this game of bureacratic musical chairs. Senator John Kerry said the Carter years were still a fresh memory when he met with the General Secretary of Vietnam in 1991.

"He (the Vietnamese official) could not understand in 1991 what this issue meant, why it was real, or if we were serious. And he turned to me and he said: 'Senator, I do not understand this. When I was negotiating with Jimmy Carter in 1978 for normalization, nobody raised this issue with us. It was not on the table.' So he had no sense that this was anything but an American trick in the 1980s and 1990s to sort of find a different way to prosecute the war against Vietnam," Kerry said.

Too Pure to Pay

And just to maintain the status quo, President Clinton is still employing retired Army General John Vessey Jr. as his emmisary to Hanoi. The aging Vessey, said to be an honorable man, is probably not the sort of Machiavellian envoy capable of extricating America POWs from the oily remnants of the Paris Peace Accord's hostage ransom negotiations.

Vessey told the Senate that he has never offered money to the Vietnamese in return for U.S. POWs, saying that would be a "bad idea."According to the straight-arrow general: "There are rules of international warfare. There's the Geneva Accords. And I believe that we should promote civilized behavior among nations and that we all ought to respect the dead, the captured in warfare according to those rules, and that we should expect nations to abide by those rules."

POW/MIA family members see little hope of change, even from the allegedly reformist Clinton Administration. "It's kind of depressing, You keep thinking we've got a new President. You get your hopes up. And [then] they put the same people in charge," said Ann Holland, whose husband Mel disappeared from a classified Laotian radar site in 1968. She added: "Sometimes I think we're fighting a losing battle."

Things could change. The media and government could wake up tomorrow and make the POW issue a true priority. But they won't. They've already decided this isn't really an important issue, taking the line that there probably were no Americans left in Southeast Asia. And when isolated pieces of evidence escapes, it's easier to debunk or ignore them than to pursue them. After all, the best thing that could come from really pursuing the issue would be a public revelation of the truth—that Americans were left in Southeast Asia, and that some are almost certainly alive today in Indochina and Russia.

Then what would the beltway crowd do? They'd have to treat the issue seriously and figure out some way to get U.S. POWs back home. And that would mean, yes, a new hostage crisis.

Clinton's Promise

Perhaps President Clinton could be the man to resolve the POW issue. His fingerprints aren't anywhere on the history of the issue. And bringing the boys home from Vietnam might help him deal with the fact that he never went to war there.

Clinton certainly claims commitment to the issue. In a prepared statement released April 2, 1993 he said:

> I truly believe that the power of the Presidency could resolve this issue. As the Chief Executive Officer of all federal agencies, the President should not just state that the resolution of this issue is a "national priority"; he should make it the national priority, and direct that all agencies to cooperate and resolve it [sic]. Before I would normalize relations or provide assistance to any of the countries [sic] involved, they would be required to open their files and actively assist in solving this issue. I firmly believe that America should never leave its warriors on the battlefield. This is not a political issue; it is a moral test of those values and traits that made America great.

But there are certainly plenty of people in the bureaucracy urging the President to stick with the status quo. There are certainly many reasons to avoid pushing the POW issue. And making the return of America's POWs truly the "highest national priority" wouldn't be easy.

"See, that's not the issue," Perot said. "The issue is they're our men, they went into combat for us, we left them, we owe it to them to bring them home. It won't look pretty back here, but we can build a consensus here that it's the right thing to do."[2]

Perhaps. But many who know the POW issue best have lost faith that the U.S. government will ever willingly do what is needed to bring the prisoners home.

With no faith left in their government, many POW/MIA family members and activists have belief only in a justice far beyond the petty political concerns of Washington, D.C.

They place their faith in a promise much stronger than the long-abandoned pledges of successive Presidents. They rely on the words of *Jeremiah 31: 16-17*:

> Thus saith the Lord: Refrain thy voice from weeping, and thine eyes from tears; for thy work shall be rewarded, saith the Lord: and they shall come again from the land of the enemy; and there is hope in thine end, saith the Lord, that thy children shall come again to their own border.

Endnotes

Chapter 1

1) Nov. 23, 1979, memo for the Chairman, JCS; Library of Congress POW/MIA Microform reel no. 55. Hereafter referred to as "reel."
2) *Ibid.*
3) Garwood deposition to the Senate Select Committee on POW/MIA Affairs. Hereafter referred to as "Garwood deposition." All information concerning Garwood is from the deposition unless otherwise noted.
4) Pentagon's "Uncorrelated Information Relating to Missing Americans in South-east Asia." Volume 15, page 434. Hereafter referred to only by volume, (vol.), and page, (p.), numbers.
5) Vol.15, p. 434.
6) Vol. 7, pp. 311-313.
7) June 30, 1975, speech as quoted in *National Review*, Aug. 21, 1981.
8) Jan. 1969 memo RM-5729-1-ARPA: "Prisoners of War in Indochina."
9) Jan. 9, 1990, DIA Memo: "Possible American Stay-Behinds in Vietnam."
10) *New York Times*, March 25, 1993, p. A-4.
11) Oct. 25, 1988, Pentagon intelligence report IIR 6 024 006 89.

Chapter 2

1) 15 April, 1976 State Department telegram,"Subject: Information on French POWs."
2) See 20 times: 8 April 1976 State telegram "Subject: Repatriation of French Remains from North Vietnam and Information on French POWs." Also: 4 March 1976 State Department telegram "Subject: Repatriation of French Remains from North Vietnam."
3) Jan. 1969 Rand memo RM-5729-1-ARPA "Prisoners of War in Indochina" by Anita Lauve Nutt; and statement of Anita Lauve to House Select Committee on Missing Persons in SEA, 7 April 1976 as reprinted in "Americans in Southeast Asia: The POW/MIA Issue" William Homolka, New World Books, NY, 1986.
4) *Newsweek*, Jan. 4, 1965, p. 24.
5) May 19, 1976 Department of State telegram, "Subject: More Information on French POW/MIA."
6) Vol. 10, p. 250
7) 5 June 1971 State Department telegram, "Subject: Repatriation of French PW in 1954."
8) 24 February 1972 DIA memo, "Subject: Debrief of Moroccan Personnel Recently Returned from North Vietnam."
9) 25 March 1983 State Department telegram, "Subject: POW/MIA Affairs/Former French Servicemen." 8 April 1983 State Department telegram "Subject: POW/MIA Affairs: Former French Servicemen."
10) From files of Tracy Usry.
11) 22 April 1982 State Dept. telegram "Subject: POW/MIA Affairs: Report of Possible Americans in Vietnam."

Chapter 3

1) "Treatment and Indoctrination of U.S. Prisoners Held by the Viet Minh." November 1954. USAF Technical Memorandum OERL-TM-54-1.
2) Undated INSCOM record, from FOIA.
3) June 17 1955 Pentagon record from the Defense Advisory Committee on Prisoners of War: "Recovery of Unrepatriated Prisoners of War."
4) *Ibid.*
5) Gutterson remembers the title "On Limited War." In Kissinger's 1957 book *Nuclear Weapons and Foreign Policy*, Chapter 5 is entitled: "What Price Difference? The Problems of Limited War." This appears to be the declassified version of the paper Gutterson remembers.
6) Henry Kissinger, *Nuclear Weapons and Foreign Policy* (New York, 1957). Southeast Asia, Indochina and South Vietnam were all mentioned as potential points of conflict.

Chapter 4

1) Vol. 7, p. 361.
2) As quoted by Bobby Garwood.
3) As quoted by a Top Secret Soviet document (Dec. 1, 1972, Top Secret Report for the Central Committee of the Communist Party of the Soviet Union. Hereafter the "Dec. 1, 1972, Soviet Report").
4) *Ibid.*
5) *Ibid.*
6) Uncorrelated Info. Vol. 7, page 333.
7) FIR-317/09165-78.

Chapter 5

1) June 24-25 1992 hearings of the Senate Select Committee on POW/MIA Affairs.

2) CINCPAC 25 Jan. 1968: Weekly Bright Light Report for 16-22 Jan. 1968 p. 3.

3) From the files of Tracy Usry, former Senate investigator.

4) 051808Z Feb. 73 Naval Message Reel 58.

5) DIA File Record Summary, Reel 58.

6) File Record Summary, DIA, Reel 28.

7) Uniontown, PA, Herald Standard May 1990; Homecoming Data; March 22, 1990, statements by U.S. Army Personnel Command.

8) From the files of Tracy Usry.

9) *Ibid.*

10) 1: June 1992 Senate hearings; 2: 051808Z Feb. 73 Naval Message Reel 58.

11) JCS Memo of February 3, 1971, "Subject: Meeting of NSC Ad Hoc Group on Vietnam, 2 February 1971."

12) Undated (probably 1986) letter "Ref. Comment of Task Force Examination of DIA's POW/MIA Analysis Center," from Maj. Gen. John Murray to Lt. Gen. Perroots, USAF, Dir. DIA.

13) Full date [CENSORED], FIR-317/09121-74; Vol. 14, pp. 280-285.

14) 27 July 1981 DIA "Congressman Request for Briefing."

15) Uncorrelated Files. Vol. 5, pp. 202-9.

16) Keith William Nolan, *Operation Buffalo: USMY Fight for the DMZ.*

17) Uncorrelated intelligence. Vol. 1, pp. 371-373.

18) Senate POW report, "The Insider."

Chapter 6

1) Department of Defense Intelligence Report, Sept. 6, 1973, "Sub: Intelligence/Information Report-Bright Light" with OACSI Comment.

2) March 10, 1993 FOIA response from Army INSCOM.

3) March 17, 1993 FOIA response from Army INSCOM.

4) March 12, 1993, FOIA response from INSCOM.

5) March 3, 1993, FOIA response from Army INSCOM.

6) Aug. 29, 1977 State Department telegram. "SUBJECT: US/VN Relations: MIA."

7) DIA Debriefing of Le Dinh.

8) Undated DIA analysis from April or May 1993. "TAB 3: Documents Obtained by Gen. Vessey From the Vietnamese, April 1993."

9) Minutes of the Son Tay Raid Panel Discussion, USSOCOM Commanders Conference, MacDill AFB, FLA 29 March 1988 (p.9).

10) Senate report.

11) Uncorrelated Info. Vol.7, pp. 438-9.

12) Dec. 16, 1971 DOD Message. "Subject: [illegible] US PW Camp in VN."

13) June 24-25 1992 Senate hearings.

14) April 13, 1993, DIA Response to FOIA.

15) Transcript of Senate POW hearings June 24-5, 1992.

16) *Ibid.*

Chapter 8

1) Berlintel 790, March 7, 1966, and previous related messages.

2) Department of State outgoing telegram, secret, July 15, 1966 to Amembassy LONDON, with an EXDIS copy to Harriman.

3) Department of State outgoing telegram, May 13, 1966 from Harriman to AMEMBASSY London and Saigon, #6825 to London, #3437 to Saigon.

4) *Ibid.*

5) Department of State outgoing telegram, secret EXDIS, June 26, 1966, 1182 Canberra, 1692 Hong Kong, 7803 London, 4073 Saigon.

6) Incoming State Department telegram, secret July 18, 1966, from AMEMBASSY London-423 to SECSTATE.

7) FPJMT strategy paper, FPJMT-NE, April 11, 1974.

8) The State Department approved at least one $15,000 shipment of drugs to the V.C. through Cambodia, according to documents released to the select committee. This probably happened on multiple occasions.

9) Department of State message from Frank A. Sieverts to Harriman, Sept. 21, 1968.

10) Incoming State Department telegram, Vientiane 2184, Oct. 11, 1966.

11) Department of State message from Frank A. Sieverts to Gov. W. Averell Harriman, Sept. 21, 1966, p. 2.

12) *Ibid.*, p. 3.

13) Library of Congress, reel 21, POW/MIA Document Project.

14) Incoming Department of State telegram, secret EXDIS, Berlin 956, p. 1.

15) *Ibid.*

16) *Ibid.*

17) Department of State outgoing telegram, Berlin 956, Jan. 27, 1967.

18) *Ibid.*

19) Department of State incoming telegram, secret-EXDIS, Berlin 997, Feb. 2, 1967.

20) Department of State incoming telegram, secretary—EXDIS, Berlin 1037, Feb. 9, 1967.

21) *Ibid.*

22) Secret-EXDIS memo from Frank A. Sieverts to the Secretary of State, "Subject: Report of Captured U.S. pilots in East Germany—INFORMATION MEMORANDUM," Feb. 11, 1967.

23) Department of State outgoing telegram, secret-EXDIS, #138146, Feb. 15, 1967.

24) Department of State incoming telegram, secret, London 6625, "Subject: Captured US Fliers in GDR," Feb. 16, 1967.

25) Department of State incoming telegram, secret, Feb. 21, 1967.

26) Department of State outgoing telegram, secret, 154917, March 14, 1967, signed Rusk.

27) Department of State incoming telegram, confidential, Berlin 1631, June 2, 1967.

28) The German Embassy in Washington, D.C. provided this information, stating that it came from GPA (German Press Agency) on December 29, 1992.
The Germans were searching the East German files for information related to the negotiations—but the files were massive and there was no anticipated date that the search would be complete, according to German Press Officer Helga Schmidt.

Chapter 9

1) Office of the Services Attaché, Australian Embassy, Phnom Penh, Cambodia, secret, Jan. 26, 1968.

2) Department of State, top secret/NODIS, "Summary Chronology."

3) *Ibid.*

4) *Ibid.*

5) *Ibid.*, May 27, 1968.

6) *Op. cit.*, July 10, 1968.

7) Statement of Philip C. Habib, before the House Select Committee on Missing Persons in Southeast Asia, August 2, 1976. The U.S. and DRV did not begin negotiations until 1968—unless there were secret sessions in 1967 that have never been revealed.

8) Reel 40, Vietnam era POW/MIA documentation, Library of Congress.

9) Department of State, The Director of Intelligence and Research, secret-NODIS, Jan. 29, 1969.

10) *Ibid.*

11) Foreign Service of the United States, incoming telegram, Paris Embassy, secret, control 1438, April 12, 1969.

12) *Ibid.*

13) *Ibid.*

14) Initially classified secret, RM-5729-1-ARPA, Jan. 1969, Anita Lauve Nutt.

15) *Ibid.* This is precisely what Nixon/Kissinger did on Feb. 1, 1973. Nixon's letter offering the DRV $3.25 billion, without condition, was hidden from Congress and the public for years. This passage in the Rand Report continues to be classified and hidden from the public.

16) *Ibid.*

17) Department of State incoming telegram, from AMEMBASSY Paris to SECSTATE, Paris 10179, July 4, 1969.

18) *Ibid.*, p. 3.

19) Incoming Department of State memorandum, from AMEMBASSY Saigon to SECSTATE, Saigon 13816, July 9, 1969.

Chapter 10

1) Walter Isaacson, *Kissinger*, (New York, 1992), p. 244.

2) *Ibid.*, pp. 243-245.

3) *Ibid.*

4) *Ibid.*, pp. 236-237.

5) *Ibid.*, p. 253.

6) Incoming telegram to AMEMBASSY Paris from SECSTATE, control #2983, June 24, 1970.

7) Department of State confidential telegram, from SECSTATE to USMISSION Geneva, #689, "Repatriation of French POWs in 1954," May 28, 1971.

8) Study entitled "Prisoners of War," secret, X29454, Oct. 27, 1971.

9) Memorandum of conversation with Xuan Thuy, Vo Van Sung, Phan Hien and Henry Kissinger, August 16, 1971, as reported in the Report of the U.S. Senate Select Committee on POW/MIA Affairs, January 25, 1993.

10) *Select Committee Final Report.*

11) August 1973 Kissinger told South Vietnam President Thieu that his strategy was to act as if the POWs were of no importance.

12) Department of State telegram, #015960, Jan. 28, 1972.

13) White House Memorandum of conversation between Le Duc Tho and Kissinger, September 26, 1972. In select committee final report.
14) Cable from General Haig, White House, to Col. Guay, Paris, Oct. 20, 1972. In select committee final report.
15) Cable from Pham Van Dong to President Nixon, Oct. 21, 1972. Cited in Select Committee final report.
16) Cable from Nixon to Pham Van Dong, Oct. 22, 1972.
17) Even though Nixon clearly abandoned the position, he and Kissinger continue to exercise tortured revisionist history by claiming that an ironclad agreement had been reached with the DRV on this issue. That is not true, and they have no reasonable historical basis for continuing to make the assertion. Their only salvation to date has been the USG's unwillingness to expose this lie—for to do so would diplomatically and politically concede that the United States did agree, on Feb. 1, 1973, to pay ransom for POWs—and this is something the USG will never do. It is preferable to continue the fictional version of history.
18) Transcripts released by the Senate Select Committee.
19) See Nguyen Tien Hung and Jerrold L. Schecter, *The Palace File*, (New York, 1986).
20) *Op. cit., The Palace File*, p. 146.
21) *Ibid.*, p. 467.
22) *Ibid.*, p. 480.
23) Kissinger was involved in the decision to bomb and did agree with the decision.
24) From select committee records.
25) To Dick Kennedy, from Henry A. Kissinger, Jan. 11, 1973. The document is blacked out after the statement: "Ironclad guarantees on our prisoners in Laos and Cambodia, but the excised portion is related to "major understandings" or verbal agreements.
26) WSAG meeting on January 29, 1972.

Chapter 11

1) Written statement of Dr. Simstein, verified in all essential parts by a second Navy officer who was attached to the Q.R.R.T.
2) Pat Butler, *The State*, South Carolina, September 24, 1992 article, p. 1.
3) Sanders's April 21, 1993 interview with Joseph Futrell.
4) The Senate Select Committee on POW/MIAs was aware of this incident but did not investigate. To do so would have required a drastic revision in the mindset of the chairman. The focus of the committee would have, of necessity, changed from the question of POWs alive after Homecoming, to an investigation of cover-up and systematic lying before the committee on the part of the DIA and former senior level bureaucrats who worked in the Nixon, Carter, Reagan and Bush Administrations. Inside the beltway, conducting such an investigation is a sure ticket to political oblivion.

Chapter 12

1) WHP435, from General Scowcroft to Minister Heyward Isham, Jan. 31, 1973.
2) Because both Nixon and Kissinger blocked extensive portions of the record from being released, it is not clear whether or not Kissinger's false messages back to the White House claiming he had reached "ironclad" agreements when in fact he had not, were actually believed by the President and his key aides.
3) Before the select committee.
4) Before the select committee.
5) Top secret/sensitive/exclusively/eyes only, from Col. Guay to Gen. Scowcroft.
6) Rand Corporation, Anita Lauve Nutt, "Prisoners of War in Indochina," RM-5729-1-ARPA, still classified report.
7) Select committee documents. Nixon's letter was declassified only after the Vietnamese revealed its contents in 1977. Prior to declassification, State attempted to conceal its true contents by issuing Congress an alleged summary of its contents, which ranged from misleading to false.
8) This issue is addressed later in the text.
9) WHP436, to Col. Guay from Gen. Scowcroft, Feb. 1, 1973.
10) 1969 Rand Report cited earlier.
11) Message from Col. Guay to Gen. Scowcroft, PSN 042227, Feb. 2, 1973.
12) From select committee files, *Prisoners of War/Missing in Action*. Dated Feb. 6, 1973, it appears to be a talking paper. The sensitive source was the Canadian government, unknown at what level, probably ICC.
13) Department of State, EXDIS, confidential, U.S. POWs in Laos, Feb. 21, 1973.
14) Department of State, AMEMBASSY Vientiane to SECSTATE, 11652, March 19, 1973.
15) *Ibid.*

Chapter 13

1) NSC memorandum, top secret/sensitive/codeword, XGDS 2 and 3 by author Henry Kissinger.
2) Select committee report, pp. 107-108.
3) Department of State secret telegram, NODIS, control #4768Q, March 15, 1973.
4) State Department, AMEMBASSY Vientiane to SECSTATE, 01977. The authors believe the Pathet Lao reference to total numbers of U.S. POWs being known, by name, by the USG, possibly references the 60

American POWs the Pathet Lao concentrated in one location in January 1973. The USG had files on most if not all of these POWs, and the QRRT members did no know if the extraction mission would require force. These facts strongly suggest that active negotiations were in progress between the PL and USG, perhaps through a third party such as the USSR, for the return/ransom of these people.

5) Committee final report, p. 108, which cites Walter S. Dillard, *Sixty Days to Peace, Implementing the Paris Peace Accords, Vietnam, 1973*.

6) In documents released by the select committee. No control number.

7) On Feb.12, 1973, Navy Commander Robert H. Shumaker smuggled out of the Hanoi Hilton a "log/journal" and gave it to Dr. Roger Shields. A source, an American at the Hanoi but not identified by name on the Shumaker log, but certainly identified during debriefing, said there were 87 American POWs in Hanoi from South Vietnam and Laos, 35 officers and 52 enlisted. But only 67 were returned.

8) Nixon wrote the select committee saying he could not recall telling Admiral Moorer "to send this cable." Perhaps he does not remember. The Chairman of the Joint Chiefs of Staff could not, and would not, however, send a cable which significantly impacted foreign policy without the approval of Kissinger and Nixon.

9) Select committee report, p. 110.

10) Senator McCain's influence is asserted at this point in the select committee's report. He and a minority of the committee had a footnote inserted stating: "Some members of the Select Committee believe that the U.S. threat to halt troop withdrawals referred only to the prisoners on the DRV/Laos list. . . . " McCain, throughout the hearings, was the vociferous defender of all Republican bureaucrats and military officers. Frequently he resorted to buffoonery when witnesses with views contrary to his were testifying. Grimacing, laughing uproariously, vigorous headshaking, etc., were the order of the day on the rare occasions when the committee was hearing testimony from unscripted witnesses. McCain referred to co-author Sanders as an "asshole," at the end of Sanders's appearance before the committee in 1992, and refused to shake his hand. While some would allege "asshole" to be an accurate statement, McCain had not seen or spoken to Sanders since 1982, when the two of them had a verbal altercation over Charles Keating's questionable fund raising tactics on behalf of McCain's Congressional campaign. Therefore, McCain had no factual basis for making such a derogatory comment—the incident does, however, serve to demonstrate McCain's gross lack of objectivity as a Senator entrusted with the mission of seeking the truth.

11) Select committee report, p. 111; cable from Godley to Secretary of State Rogers, March 22, 1973.

12) Department of State #2176 from Vientiane to SECSTATE.

13) Department of State, AMEMBASSY Vientiane to SECSTATE, March 26, 1973, 02231.

14) *Ibid.*

15) Memorandum from Richard Kennedy and John Holdridge to Kissinger, March 27, 1973; select committee report, pp. 113-114.

16) Select committee report, p. 114.

17) Secretary of Defense to the Assistant to the President for National Security Affairs, Subject: U.S. POW/MIA Personnel in Laos, March 28, 1973. In December 1992 Nixon attempted to defend his actions during the spring of 1973 with the rather disingenuous statement that: "Although everyone was aware of the *possibility* that the release was incomplete, I had no personal knowledge that any U.S. serviceman still alive had been kept behind." The use of "personal knowledge" seems to be an attempt to separate himself from the body of information being uncovered—someone may have known they were left behind, but not Nixon, is the extremely weak inference.

18) Before the select committee.

19) Letter to Senators John Kerry and Robert C. Smith.

20) The McCain faction of the select committee has attempted to place this Nixon speech in a vacuum and disregard the voluminous historical flow. They allege that Nixon was clearly informing the American public that all of our POWs were *not* home.

21) Select committee report.

22) Select committee appendices, p. 5.

23) Select committee final report, p. 100.

24) Select committee testimony.

25) Memorandum of conversation between Le Duc Tho and Kissinger, May 23, 1973. The memorandum is at least 35 pages long, with 2/3 of it blacked out. Kissinger's team of lawyers met with select committee staff and negotiated at length with portions would be blacked out—an outrageous breach of the public faith from a committee sworn to get at the truth.

26) Senate report, p. 1193

Chapter 14

1) Alpers's letter to Senator John Kerry, Senate Committee, Nov. 7, 1991. Alpers was not deposed by the select committee.

2) Senate Select Committee on POW/MIAs, final report, Appendices.

3) The DIA, in typical form, takes a giant leap of faith and says that Flynn , while held captive in China, had actually seen a photo of the infamous Hanoi parade of POWs. Ellison was not in that parade so Flynn could not have seen a photo of his friend, according to DIA logic. The truth is that nothing Robert Flynn describes about that photo would lead any reasonable person to conclude the photo in question was of the Hanoi parade. Flynn identified a second POW in the photo, standing beside Ellison—James Plowman, Ellison's crewmate, who did not return. Flynn did not know Plowman, but recognized his pre-capture photo during debriefing.

4) In another leap of logic, DIA thinks that Ross R. Terry, a returnee who was at Hoa Lo, went around writing only his first name on the walls. DIA did not interview Terry to confirm this suspect analysis.

5) One returnee suggested this was a pen name but DIA did not find a returnee who used such a "pen name."

6) 23 years later Mulligan had a long conversation with Admiral Stockdale, the Senior officer at the Hanoi Hilton and a vociferous advocate of the theory that everyone they knew of came home. Mulligan stated that he had no recollection of the names in his debriefing report. The select committee later contacted Mulligan, who now asserted that "the information listing him as the source is in error." Amazingly, the select committee printed that statement in its final report. They had the ability to access the transcripts of Mulligan's debriefing, through the DIA, and the determine the veracity of that statement. There is nothing in the record indicating that was done. In al probability, this is just another example of a military mind that has pressure brought to bear and gets on board with the prevailing attitude.

7) Laird Gutterson interview, April 11, 1993.

8) Select committee deposition of John Halachis.

9) This information comes from Halachis's memory because DoD refused to give the Senate Select Committee access to the reports. Instead, the Senate was told they would have to trust DoD's interpretation of the documents, without independent verification.

10) Halachis, p. 30.

11) Each MIA name released by DoD to the select committee had an identifying name(s) attached, telling which returnee provided the information. Craner's name is not listed beside any of the released names.

12) He mentions 400-500 at one point in the transcript and later, 500.

13) Memorandum for the President. Subject: "Status Determination," July 11, 1973, signed by Clements.

14) Select committee final report, p. 325.

15) Select committee final report, p. 326.

16) Select committee final report, p. 326.

17) Select committee final report, p. 259. The TH may have been TA. The 1933 may have been 1973 or 1573, but JSSA believes it is 1933 TH.

18) Select committee final report.

19) Gutterson interview.

20) Select committee deposition of Steve Lippert, Jan. 20, 1992.

21) *Ibid.*

22) CIA study CIOL-00167-75 cover letter only released, signed by George T. Kalaris.

23) Memorandum of conversation, Nov. 14, 1975.

24) Department of State briefing memorandum, s/s 7600259, secret—sensitive—no distribution, Jan. 6, 1976.

25) Department of State telegram, 105030, top secret 010062, Jan. 21, 1976.

26) This assumes that there was actually an intent to deliver on Nixon's offer of aid—it is quite possible that the $3.25 billion was just a scam to get the repatriation of POWs started and get back those the DRV was willing to part with—without compensation.

27) "Summary of Select Committee Discussions With Vietnamese and Lao Officials."

28) State Department telegram, Paris 09140, March 29, 1976.

29) Letter from Habib to Montgomery, Aug. 2, 1976.

30) A separate note talked of constitutional requirements of each country, it was not in the letter or attached to the letter.

31) State Department telegram, Manila 10210, July 13, 1976. Authors' emphasis.

32) State Department telegram, Paris 25889, Sept. 6, 1976.

33) State Department secret telegram, Paris 33718. Nov. 12, 1976.

34) *Ibid.*

35) *Ibid.* Author's emphasis.

36) State Department telegram 281646, Nov. 16, 1976.

Chapter 15

1) State Department NODIS telegram, 028457, Feb. 8, 1977.

2) *Ibid.* Authors' emphasis.

3) State Department telegram, Sec State 027695, Feb. 8, 1977.

4) State Department telegram, Islamabad 1807, Feb. 22, 1977.

5) CIA, FIR-317/09160-77.

6) The documents found by Professor Morris in a Russian archive in 1993 also say that sons of wealthy families were going to be held after the war. The Russian document goes on to explain that these wealthy Americans were actually the sons of high ranking American military officers—who they assumed would be the wealthy ruling elite. And, this theme is in the 1980 final debriefing report of defector Le Dinh.

7) CIA, FIR-317/09157-77. Also, see Senator Bob Smith (R-NH) Sept. 21, 1992 publication: "Policy-related events/decisions/comments from 1973 onward concerning unaccounted for American POWs and MIAs in Southeast Asia," p. 40.

8) State Department NODIS telegram, Paris 06795, March 8, 1977.

9) *Ibid.*, p. 2.

10) From Senator Smith's Sept. 21, 1992 report referenced earlier.

11) *Ibid.*

12) State Department telegram 065699, March 24, 1977.

13) Smith 9/21/92 report.
14) Smith 9/12/92 report.
15) Smith report, p. 43.
16) *Ibid.*
17) State Department telegram, Paris 16317, June 3, 1977.
18) *Ibid.*
19) *Ibid.*
20) *Ibid.*
21) *Ibid.*
22) *Ibid.*
23) *Ibid.*
24) Other POWs the Pentagon had written off as traitors, and had removed from the roster of POWs and MIAs, returned during Homecoming and were not prosecuted.
25) Feb. 1, 1984 State Department telegram. "Subject: POW/MIA: Indochinese Foreign Ministers' Communique."
26) DIA Report, May 13, 1988, "Subject: Lao government policy for retaining U.S. PW."
27) *Bamboo*, p. 95.
28) Jan. 15, 1991 State Department telegram.

Chapter 16

1) 12 DEC 1979 memo for NCR (Defense). "Subject: contact report."
2) *L.A. Times*, Aug. 6, 1992, p. 2.
3) June 19, 1981 State Department Telegram. "SUBJECT: POW/MIA Proclamation And Raising Issue With Lao."
4) Quote from p. 117, Colvin, Rod. *First Heroes*. New York: Irvington Publishers, 1987. This excellent book also was first to report other elements of the Nhom Marrot raid and the POW issue.
5) day [illegible], Jan. 1973, State Department Telegram. "Subject: PW/Rallier Interrogations-Reported Sighting of Eight Causcasian[sic] PWs in Laos."
6) April 14, 1984 message. "Daily Asian [CENSORED] Summary 105-84 Five of the prisoners died and were buried near the jail. "The remaining 21 prisoners were moved to Hanoi on an undisclosed date," according to the report.
7) Jan. 20, 1992, deposition of Steve Lippert.
8) (Riverside) *Press Enterprise*, March 13, 1986, p. A-6.
9) Oct. 30, 1986, NSA Report. "SUBJ: [CENSORED] Probable Former American Prisoner Of War Camp Location In Laos."
10) Aug. 7, 1980 State Department telegram. "SUBJ: Reported American POWs in Laos."
11) (Riverside) *Press Enterprise*, March 13, 1986, p. A-6.
12) Dec. 23, 1985 DOD Message. "SUBJ: Hearsay of American Prisoners in Phongsali Province, Laos."
13) Undated DIA report. "Polygraph Record. PW Firsthand. No Deception Indicated."
14) Senate hearing transcripts of June 24-5, 1992.
15) April 29, 1986 State Department telegram. "SUBJ: American, Thai and Filipino POWs Allegedly Held in Viengsay, Northern Laos." At least three accounts say more than 200 U.S. prisoners were held in the area.
16) intercept: Senate Report, p. 225.
17) May 29, 1986, NSA Report. Title [CENSORED].
18) Aug. 29, 1984 NSA document. "Subject: Thai HUMINT Report of American POW Camp in Laos."
19) Sept. 13, 1984 NSA report. "SUBJ: Unidentified Prisoner Transfer In Southern Laos."
20) Date illegible, apparently late 1988. ERR: 6 832 0120 89.
21) Feb.25, 1983 Pentagon Memo. "SUBJECT: U.S. Response to Lao Initiatives."
22) WA Times, Aug. 21, 1991, p.7.

Chapter 17

1) P. 255, *Vietnam: A Country Study*.
2) Vol. 9, p. 224.
3) P. 255, area handbook.
4) Sept. 20, 1991, DIA report. "Sub: Alleged First Hand Live Sighting of Five American Prisoners in Cambodia."

Chapter 18

1) Aug. 2, 1991 State Department telegram. "SUBJECT: Reported Meeting With Two POWs in Vietnam."
2) Vol. 7, pp. 149-151.
3) Vol. 7, p. 167.
4) Feb. 6, 1987, NSA report. "SUBJ: [CENSORED] Probable Vietnamese Refugee Allegedly Holds Letter From American POW."
5) Aug. 10, 1992, CIA paper. "Possible POW/MIA-Associated Markings in Southeast Asia."

Chapter 21

1) From the INSCOM files on McKinley Nolan.

2) 27 July 1981 DIA "Congressman Request For Briefing."
3) 18 NOV 1974 State Department message. "Subject: American Defector in Cambodia."
4) March 17, 1967, Army intelligence report. "SUBJECT: Americans [sic] PWs."
5) Vol. 9, p. 599.
6) Vol. 10, p. 525.
7) undated DIA report. "Polygraph Record. PW Firsthand. No Deception Indicated."
8) Undated DIA report. "Polygraph Record. PW Firsthand. No Deception Indicated."
9) Senate Hearings, 25 June 1992.
10) 4 August 1978 State Dept. Telegram. "Subject: Possibility of Living Americans in Vietnam."
11) Senate testimony of Frank Sieverts, 25 June 1992; 16 March 1979 State Department Telegram "SUBJ: American Citizen in Viet-Nam."
12) 27 Feb. 1979 State Department Telegram. "Subject: Reported American in Vietnam."
13) Sep. 25, 1985 DIA memo for Brig. Gen. Shufelt. "Subject: The POW/MIA Issue."
14) 8 March 1985 Memorandum for the Secretary of Defense. "Subject: PVT Robert R. Garwood—Current Status."

Chapter 22

1) P. 22 *The USSR in 3rd World Conflicts* Bruce D. Porter, Cambridge University Press, Cambridge England, 1984; Soviet Union sent 3,000 troops to Vietnam, 13 were killed, according to Soviet articles reported in the 9 Sept. 1991 *NY Daily News*, p. 13; also Sauter interviews with Soviet Vietnam veterans in Moscow.
2) Sweden: p. 45, *Amnesty: The American Puzzle*, Edward F. Dolan, JR/Franklin Watts, New York, 1976; Beheiren: information from KGB defector Stanislav Levchenko, quoted from *Dezinformatsia — Active Measures in Soviet Strategy* Richard H. Shultz and Roy Godson, Pergamon-Brassey, WA, 1984; trip: JAN 92 *New York Times* p. A6, "Russian Offers Americans Access to K.G.B. Files."
3) 10 June 1971 CIA document "Preliminary debriefing site for captured U.S. pilots in Vinh Phu province and presence of Soviet and communist Chinese personnel at the site."
4) March 12, 1982, CIA Report. "SUBJECT: Alleged Soviet Incarceration of U.S. Vietnam Prisoners of War.
5) David H. Hendrix article in the *Press-Enterprise* (Riverside, CA), 3-13-86, p. 6.
6) "Soviet Officers Said to Have Questioned U.S. Vietnam Prisoners," Reuter 7 NOV 91.
7) P. 147, *The Bamboo Cage*, Nigel Cawthorne, London, Leo Cooper, 1991.
8) L.A. Times News Service, June 25, 1992.
9) P. 239 and 242, *KGB: The Secret Work of Soviet Secret Agents*, John Barron, Bantam Books, 1974, NY.
10) London "Evening News" 1 Feb. 1973.
11) Sep. 19, 1972, Naval Message. "SUBJECT: Communist Attitudes about the War and Disposition of US PWs."
12) 9 March 1988 "Alleged Sightings of American POWs in North Korea from 1975 to 1982." FOIA.

Chapter 23

1) *The Washington Times*, Aug. 11, 1992, p. 3.
2) *The Wall Street Journal*, Aug. 19, 1986: "Pay for U.S. Prisoners in Communist Hands."
3) After checking his notes which contained his agreement with the Secret Service Agent who provided the tape recording, John Syphrit, Bill Paul advised co-author Sanders that he (Paul) could not confirm or deny that the second source for his article was a tape recording. He did say: "I will tell you it was an irrefutable source." A Secret Service agent is never an irrefutable source—trustworthy though they are.
4) Ken de Graffenreid, Special Assistant for Intelligence Programs, vaguely remembered having knowledge of the offer. A second "intelligence official" was interviewed by Mike Ross, a reporter for the *Los Angeles Times*. The unidentified intelligence official had "contemporaneous or direct knowledge of a January, 1981 overture from the Vietnamese to return American POWs." (Quote from Senator Bob Smith's letter to the unnamed official.) The list of attendees came from the authors' 1988 notes when they were following the story—as did the number "15" at the meeting—verified by a source who had direct access to the information.
5) Paul article.
6) Co-author Sanders in 1988 interviewed a senior staffer of one of the Cabinet members in attendance at this meeting, asking that person whether the President was tape recorded. Two days later, after checking with the former Cabinet member, the answer was: the capability was present for the President to be tape recorded.
7) Senator Smith stated for the record that Max Hugel, CIA's Deputy Director for Operations in 1981, "and a close personal friend of then CIA Director William Casey," in 1992 told him "that he was, indeed, aware of the offer—that it was common knowledge at the higher levels in the intelligence community." Hugel, under oath, said "he had no knowledge of an offer, nor remembered telling anyone he had." (Quotes taken from select committee final report, p. 355.)
8) *Op. cit.*, Paul.
9) Senators Smith, Grassley and Daschley voted to subpoena. Reid, Robb, Bob Kerry, Kohl, McCain, Brown, and Kassenbaum voted no. John Kerry waited until the vote was decided and then voted yes. Helms did not vote.
10) Senator Smith Sept. 21, 1992 report; and FBIS analysis group report, Feb., 1992.
11) Senate investigator John Taylor interview with de Graffenreid, Aug. 7, 1992.
12) *Ibid.*, Taylor's assessment of de Graffenreid statement.
13) This 1984 wording was exposed in a June 1986 letter from Assistant Secretary of Defense Richard L. Armitage to Foreign Minister Thach. It is discussed in greater detail later in the chapter.

14) Irving Davidson deposition taken by the Senate Select Committee on POW/MIAs. Davidson produced notes written by him on the day critical events occurred, as well as correspondence between Childress and Achmade, and Davidson to Achmad's brother.
15) Davidson's deposition, pp. 50-51.
16) Davidson, p. 51.
17) Davidson, p. 54.
18) Davidson, p. 53.
19) Davidson, p. 57.
20) In 1992 Supeno was interviewed by an undisclosed American official. Supeno said the Vietnamese did not specifically say there were live POWs, but that the Hanoi government did not control all lower level Vietnamese officials (according to the select committee final report, p. 357). The select committee avoided the real issue being addressed—the return of Americans in a status other than POW. If Supeno was questioned about this, the answer was not provided by the select committee report. From all information available after this date, it is evident that non-POW Americans were placed on the table and the United States decided that its opening tactic would be to buy them back along with the 400 bodies the "Mortician" revealed were stored in Hanoi.
21) Select committee final report.
22) The USG has always differentiated between Americans held in captive environments—locked up and/or heavily guarded, as opposed to other Americans who, in some manner, came to terms with their fate. These people are not considered by the USG to be POWs and do not come under DoD's tightly defined "held against their will." Of course anyone who willingly, or as a scam to get better treatment after being abandoned by the USG, became a communist, would absolutely not be a POW.
23) State Department, memorandum from Paul Wolfowitz to the Secretary of State, Feb. 13, 1985.
24) Select committee, Garwood deposition.
25) *Ibid.* Childress, in 1992, before the select committee rather disingenuously stated: "We traced the offer all the way up to the Vietnamese. . . . It was not for live prisoners." In fact, Childress initiated the contact, he did not trace it to the Vietnamese. The offer was never for "live prisoners," it was for defectors and remains—he also knew that going into the negotiations in Hanoi, Feb. 1985.
26) Davidson deposition. 250-650, and 400 were the numbers discussed being warehoused and for sale.
27) Hearings before the Committee on Veterans' Affairs, United States Senate, Feb. 27, 1986, volume 1, p. 446.
28) State Department telegram, Bangkok 52138, Aug. 29, 1985.
29) State Department telegram, Bangkok 52138, Aug. 29, 1985.
30) *Ibid.*, p. 5.
31) Discussed in a later chapter.
32) Documented later in this chapter.
33) Armitage letter to Thach, June 1986. There was an "attachment" to this letter which "reiterates the list of U.S. supporting actions previously conveyed to the Vietnamese." (O-22983/86, The Assistant Secretary of Defense, June 21, 1986.) Point 4 of the attachment is: "The United States will work sensitively and quietly to repatriate any personnel alive, regardless of status, that the Vietnamese authorities find in their search efforts."
34) State Department telegram, State 375601, Nov. 6, 1990. The military/DoD personnel instruction are quite direct. The directions for any civilian Americans are tentative and complicated, with citizen status and potential problems with the Thai—because, for some reason, civilian American citizens must evacuate through Bangkok, not Hanoi. This is obviously part of the U.S.-Vietnam agreement on "sensitively and quietly" repatriating Americans but it is not known why the routing changes.

Chapter 24

1) Vol. 10, p. 525.
2) Vol. 1, p. 1997. Also listed as: vol. 7, p. 346.
3) *Bamboo Cage*, p. 109.
4) Meeting of the IAG on April 7, 1981. Reel 19.
5) Nov. 19, 1990 State Department Telegram. "SUBJ: Hearsay of the Repatriation of Former Prisoners."
6) Jan. 18, 1992, State Department Telegram. "SUBJECT: [CENSORED] Meets with DOS, DOD Officials."
7) Aug. 5, 1992 Pentagon message. "SUBJ: IIR 1 517 0351 92/Interrogation of American POW's by Russians."
8) *Bamboo Cage*, p. 100; vol. 7, p. 340.

Chapter 25

1) Jan. 25, 1972, cable from JANAF Attaches Vientiane to CINCPAC. "SUBJECT: Intelligence Exploitation of NVA/PL/Deuanist."
2) Aug. 7, 1992, Senate Memo. "Phone Interview With Ken de Graffenreid"
3) March 26, 1986 DOD Message. "SUBJ: Reported Sightings of Americans."
4) Dec. 30, 1986 State Department Telegram. "SUBJECT: Official-Informal."
5) Letter from General Ono to an unknown name blacked out retired general, March 26, 1990.
6) April 27, 1992, untitled note re April 23rd visit of Senate investigators to DIA's photo interpretation center.
7) April 27, 1992, untitled note re April 23rd visit of Senate investigators to DIA's photo interpretation center.
8) March 27, 1989 State Department Telegram. "SUBJ: Lao Livzihighting [sic] Investigation."
9) Aug. 22, 1991, "Translation of Military Region 4 Museum Exhibit Registry" from JCRC Liaison Bangkok to Cdr, JCRC (p. 482-3 gb).
10) Department of Defense POW/MIA Newsletter, January 1993.

11) *Washington Post* Foreign Service, March 14, 1993.
12) *Washington Post*, June 24, 1991, p.B 12.
13) *Washington Times*, April 18, 1993, p.A5.

Chapter 26

1) Dec. 9, 1983 State Department Telegram. "SUBJECT: Reported Sighting of U.S. POWs in 1978-9."
2) May 24, 1986, State Department Memo. "SUBJECT: EAP/VLC Status Report for May 23."

Chapter 27

1) Hearing on prospects of normal relations with Vietnam. April 25, 1991.
2) Aug. 30, 1991 State Department Telegram, "Subject: CODEL Congressional delegation Kerry Visit to Vietnam and Cambodia."
3) May 18, 1991, State Department Telegram. "SUBJECT: Weekly Status Report-Vietnam, Laos and Cambodia, May 17, 1991."
4) Aug. 30, 1991, State Department Telegram. "Subject: Official-Informal."
5) April 13, 1992, Memorandum For The Record. "Subject: 9 April Senate Select Committee on POW/MIA Affairs Briefing."
6) Briefing for the Senate Select Committee on Prisoners of War and the Missing in Action, April 8, 1992.
7) *Washington Post*, Nov. 16, 1992, p. A-14.
8) *Washington Times*, Nov. 25, 1992, p. 4.

Chapter 28

1) March 21, 1987—3:40 p.m. "Telecon With Colin Powell."
2) *New York Newsday*, Aug. 21, 1992. Sidney Schanberg column.

Index